Study Guide

What Is Psychology?

SECOND EDITION

Susan Doyle-Portillo
Gainesville State College

Ellen Pastorino
Valencia Community College

WADSWORTH
CENGAGE Learning

Australia • Brazil • Japan • Korea • Mexico • Singapore • Spain • United Kingdom • United States

For product information and technology assistance, contact us at **Cengage Learning Customer & Sales Support, 1-800-354-9706**

For permission to use material from this text or product, submit all requests online at **www.cengage.com/permissions** Further permissions questions can be emailed to **permissionrequest@cengage.com**

ISBN-13: 978-0-495-50710-9
ISBN-10: 0-495-50710-5

Wadsworth
10 Davis Drive
Belmont, CA 94002-3098
USA

Cengage Learning is a leading provider of customized learning solutions with office locations around the globe, including Singapore, the United Kingdom, Australia, Mexico, Brazil, and Japan. Locate your local office at: **international.cengage.com/region**

Cengage Learning products are represented in Canada by Nelson Education, Ltd.

For your course and learning solutions, visit **academic.cengage.com**

Purchase any of our products at your local college store or at our preferred online store **www.ichapters.com**

Printed in the United States of America
1 2 3 4 5 6 7 11 10 09 08

How to Use This Study Guide

Why spend money on a student study guide when you have already purchased a textbook? Simply put, because it can help you to succeed in your psychology course! This study guide was written by the co-authors of your textbook, Dr. Susann Doyle-Portillo and Dr. Ellen Pastorino, to enhance and extend your comprehension and retention of the material in the text. This study guide summarizes the content of each chapter in the text, provides activities that allow you to apply what you have learned, and enables you to assess your level of learning *before* you find out how much you know (or don't know) on an exam in your course. As such, this study guide is best used *after* you have read and studied the content of the chapter thoroughly. Reading this study guide will not replace the need to read the actual text—no study guide does that! So, before you get started, take a moment to familiarize yourself with some of the unique features of this study guide.

Learning Objectives

Each chapter of the study guide begins with the learning objectives for the corresponding textbook chapter presented by the title of the chapter section, which contains the information needed to accomplish the objective. These objectives represent the tasks that you should be able to accomplish after having read and studied the chapter. You may wish to have these learning objectives handy while you are listening to lectures in class so that you can listen in a guided fashion—looking for the information needed to accomplish these tasks.

The Big Picture

The learning objectives are followed by **The Big Picture** feature of the study guide. This feature provides a narrative summary of the corresponding textbook chapter that condenses the material of the chapter into a concise, typically 2-4 page summary. For your convenience, **The Big Picture** is organized by the major sections and learning objectives of the textbook chapter. Read this summary *after* having read the chapter in the text to help solidify the Big Picture of psychology in your mind.

Outlining the Big Picture

After the narrative Big Picture summary comes a feature called **Outlining the Big Picture**. This feature provides a three-level outline of the corresponding textbook chapter that provides space for you to take notes as you read the text. You may also choose to have this outline handy during lectures to summarize each of the major sections of the material in the text and chart your progress towards mastering the chapter learning objectives.

Seeing the Big Picture: A Mental Map of the Chapter

Some students learn best through verbal means, but others learn best when they can see the material in a visual format. For this reason, we provide a visual depiction of each chapter's material in a feature called, **Seeing the Big Picture: A Mental Map of the Chapter**. This map condenses the material of the chapter in a flowchart-like format on a single page. Use this feature after reading the textbook chapter to ensure that you can truly "see" how all of the concepts fit together in the Big Picture of psychology.

Key Points of the Big Picture

Next is a feature called **Key Points of the Big Picture**. In this section, all the key terms from the corresponding textbook chapter are provided along with their definitions and where possible, pertinent real-world examples of the key terms. Reading these examples will further increase your understanding of these key terms *and* enhance your memory for them. This section can also be used to assess your comprehension and retention of these terms. Use a blank sheet of paper and cover the definition before seeing if you can recall the meaning of the key term. If you can't, you need to go back to the textbook and review these terms.

Fill-in Review of the Chapter

This section also provides you with a means to test your recall of the information by asking you to fill-in some of the chapter concepts into a series of statements. These statements are organized by the major sections of the textbook chapter, allowing you to work your way through the chapter material from beginning to end. As an added study aid, the statements marked with an asterisk (*) are ones that encourage you to continue building the Big Picture of psychology by connecting the material in the current chapter to material from previous chapters in the text.

Use It or Lose It!

In this section, you are asked to further put your knowledge of the chapter to the test by filling in the missing information in a table. This task is an excellent way to see what you really know about the concepts!

Self-Check: Are You Getting the Big Picture

The next section of the study guide is the **Self-Check: Are You Getting the Big Picture** section. In this section, you will answer some true/false, multiple-choice, and short-answer questions that allow you to assess your comprehension and retention of the material from the corresponding textbook chapter. Try to do this section without consulting notes or the chapter, that way you can tell if you need to go back and study more before you take an exam in your course. Strive for perfection here. Don't be satisfied with getting 70% of the questions correct. Try to get 100%! Remember, taking the study guide self-check doesn't count towards your grade, but taking an exam in your course will!

Developing a Bigger Picture: Making Connections Across Chapters

An important aspect of mastering the material of any course is in seeing how all of the material from all of the chapters fits together into a comprehensive whole. In others words, you should strive to see the Big Picture of the material instead of merely learning the content of each chapter as a discrete body of knowledge. To help you develop this Big Picture view of psychology, we have included a **Developing a Bigger Picture: Making Connections Across Chapters** section, in which you will be asked to use knowledge from the current chapter, as well as, previous chapters to complete certain tasks.

Label the Diagram

The label the diagram feature of the study guide is a wonderful study aid for all students, but visual learners will find it especially useful. In this section, you will use your knowledge of psychology to fill in the missing information in one of the figures from the textbook chapter. Again, try to do this without looking at your text or notes. That way, you'll see if you truly know your stuff or if you have more studying to do.

The Big Picture Review

In this section, you'll fill in the missing information in a table or chart that summarizes a body of knowledge from the text. This feature is a great way to see if you have mastered the details of important chapter topics.

Solutions

Unlike many student study guides, we provide answers to <u>all</u> the exercises in the study guide. This is true even for the short-answer questions and fill-in features. We feel very strongly that having access to the solutions is necessary for you to find this study guide useful. After all, what good would it do you to write an essay answer to a question, but not be able to determine if your answer is correct? Use the solutions section responsibly. Consult the solutions section <u>after</u> you have made an honest attempt to answer the questions on your own. Fudging and looking at the answers *before* you work through the exercises will prevent you from getting the full benefits of this study guide.

Study Aids in the Main Textbook

In addition to the numerous study aids in this student study guide, don't forget that you also have some great study aids in the textbook itself. Each textbook chapter includes a chapter outline, learning objectives for each section, margin glossary definitions of key terms, and Let's Review multiple choice questions after each section of the chapter. At the end of each chapter, you will find a Concept Check exercise, Use It or Lose It: Applying Psychology questions,

Critical Thinking for Integration questions, a Visual Summary of the chapter contents, and a Key Term list. To get the full benefit of your textbook, we urge you to use these features as you are reading and studying the chapters.

ThomsonNow

Also consider ThomsonNow, the robust online study and learning tool, available for purchase. This online resource can help you gauge your own unique study needs. A Pre-Test helps you identify what you need to study more--you receive your score automatically. Based on your results, you receive a Personalized Study plan that outlines the concepts you need to review. Then, working from your Personalized Study plan, you are guided to visual images, video exercises with questions, learning modules and animations, and other resources to help you master the material. For more information about ThomsonNow, visit www.thomsonedu.com/thomsonnow .

Study Tips for Successful Students

Becoming a successful student means working with the way your memory works instead of working against it. Keeping this in mind, take a look at the following tips for becoming a better learner.

Don't Cram for Exams!

Cramming for exams is a horrible way to study. When you cram, you do not give yourself enough time to engage in elaborative rehearsal (see Chapter 6 of your text). Information must be processed deeply or elaborated if you are going to have much chance of recalling it on exam day. To do this, you must think about the meaning of the material and how it relates to what you already know about the world. One good way to do this is to create outlines or mental maps of the material. We have provided some examples of outlines and mental maps in each chapter of the study guide. We encourage you to use these as starting points from which you can flesh out your own maps and outlines as you study.

Pay Attention and Don't Skip Class!

Skipping class and not paying attention in class are two of the biggest mistakes that students make. If you do not attend lecture, you will never be exposed to information that may be of vital importance for passing exams. Often professors elaborate and extend the material of a text in their lectures. If you're not there, you will miss all of this information. And, don't be fooled into thinking that you can just get someone else's notes. No other person's notes will ever make as much sense to you as the notes you would have taken yourself! It's also not enough to merely show up to class. You must pay attention as well. If you are too tired or distracted to pay attention, you will not process the information efficiently into your long-term memory. So, get enough sleep and leave your troubles at the door when you go to class.

Take Good Notes

When in class, be sure to take good notes. These days with many professors using overheads or electronic slide shows to present their lectures, many students have decreased the amount of notes that they take in class. They falsely assume that the only important information is that which appears on slides, overheads, or the blackboard. This couldn't be further from the truth. Often professors use these tools to present the *outline* of the material with the real meat of the lecture being presented only in an oral form. When in class, you should try to get down on paper as much of the discussion as possible. This way, you'll have a complete record of the material from which to study, and you won't get home only to find that you don't understand the few concepts that were on the board or the overhead. As an added bonus, the act of writing down the information on paper will also help you remember the information on test day.

Use Overlearning

Don't stop studying until you know the information in the chapter like the back of your hand! Don't settle for familiarity with the material. To be successful, you must *know* the material. One good way to test whether or not you really *know* material is to use recall tests of memory—for example essay questions and fill-in-the-blank type questions. We have provided these types of questions in each study guide chapter. If you cannot answer these questions without consulting your notes or your text, then you know that you have more studying to do!

Stay Calm

Relax! Learning should be fun and enjoyable—not something that you fear and dread. Try to adopt a healthy point of view about learning. Don't see exams and quizzes as chances to fail—see them as challenges that offer the opportunity for success! To help control anxiety, don't procrastinate and wait until the last minute to study. Procrastination only leads to panic. Instead, divide your study time across a series of days and weeks. You may not have to study longer, just in a more distributed fashion. For example, eight hours of study, spaced across eight days, will result in much greater learning than eight hours spent in one day of studying. No kidding!

Psychology in the World of Work

You might be thinking—Why should I take psychology, when I'm not a psychology major? Psychology is one of the best choices you can make when choosing an elective course. This is true because psychology is relevant to almost all majors. People in the world of work from fields as different as farming, engineering, medicine, law, sales/marketing, management, education, social work, and psychology all use psychological knowledge to help them do their jobs better. Because psychology is the scientific study of mental processes and behavior, it is relevant to any profession that involves interaction among humans or between humans and animals—and that covers just about every profession! At the end of each textbook chapter, the section entitled *Are You Getting the Big*

Picture? shows specifically which careers might use the information contained in that chapter. You may also find the following websites useful to you as you think about your own career path:

http://www.apa.org/science/nonacad_careers.html
This website from the American Psychological Association details nonacademic careers in psychology for scientific psychologists. Included on this site are biographies of real people who have degrees in psychology but work in a variety of nonacademic, industry and government positions. Give it a look; you'll be surprised at the diversity of positions that utilize psychological knowledge.

http://www.bls.gov/search/ooh.asp?ct=OOH
The website from the U. S. Department of Labor includes a link to search the *Occupational Outlook Handbook*, which gives the projected outlook for all manner of occupations. Using this link, you can find educational requirements, typical working conditions, salary ranges, and so on for virtually any profession.

Table of Contents

1

What Is Psychology?

Learning Objectives

After studying each of the following sections of the chapter, you should be able to:

Correcting Common Misconceptions About the Field of Psychology

1. Identify common misconceptions about the field.

So, What Is Psychology?

2. Define psychology.

The Origins of Psychology

3. Describe the origins of psychology and understand how historical perspectives paved the way for modern approaches.

Careers in Psychology

4. Describe the training of a psychologist and discriminate among the different subfields of the profession.

Psychological Research: Goals, Hypotheses, and Methods

5. Identify the goals of psychological research.
6. Understand the steps of the scientific method and distinguish between predictive and causal hypotheses.
7. Discuss the advantages and disadvantages of the observational, correlational, and experimental research methods, and the types of conclusions that can be drawn from each strategy.

Ethical Issues in Psychological Research

8. Describe the main ethical principles that guide psychologists as they conduct research.

The Big Picture

The Big Picture: What Do Psychologists Study?

In the aftermath of tragedies, such as Hurricane Katrina, psychologists are left asking many questions. How did people deal with the impending storm? How did people cope with the staggering losses they suffered? What role, if any, did prejudice play in the handling of this tragedy? Are Katrina's victims more likely to suffer from mental illness as a result of the stress they endured? And so on. However, psychologists are not just interested in tragedy and mental illness. We are also interested in questions about the everyday human condition. What makes us fall in love? What affects how well we are able to persuade people to donate time and money to charity? How does memory work? In fact, questions like these predominant the field of psychology.

Correcting Common Misconceptions about the Field of Psychology

This section covers Learning Objective 1. Unfortunately, many people don't understand what psychology is all about—at least until they begin to study psychology as you have. There are many misconceptions about what psychologists do. Psychology is not just giving advice, studying mental illness, or common sense.

So, What Is Psychology?

This section covers Learning Objective 2. Rather, psychology is the scientific study of behavior and mental processes. As scientists, psychologists use the scientific method. We generate theories and then use experimentation to determine whether or not these theories seem to have merit.

The Origins of Psychology

This section covers Learning Objective 3. Psychology has its roots in the ancient fields of philosophy and medicine, but it wasn't until 1879 that psychology became a science. This year marks the date that Wilhelm Wundt opened the first psychological laboratory at the University of Leipzig in Germany. With the opening of this lab, the experimental or scientific study of behavior and mental processes began.

Early psychologists had several approaches to understanding behavior and mental processes, which included structuralism, functionalism, and psychoanalysis. Structuralism was developed by one of Wundt's students, Edward Titchener. Structuralism seeks to understand the mind by breaking it down into its basic elements and examining its structure. To do this, Wundt and his students used a technique called introspection, in which research participants were asked to observe their own mental processes and then describe them to the researcher.

Functionalism soon overtook structuralism as the dominant approach to psychology. Headed by American psychologist William James, functionalists were influenced by Darwin's theory of evolution and the emphasis it placed on the role that characteristics play in helping a species survive in its environment. Similarly, the functionalists attempted to uncover the function or purpose of behavior and mental processes in helping us live our lives.

Also in the late 1800s, Sigmund Freud was changing the face of psychology in Europe. Freud emphasized the influence of the unconscious mind on behavior and mental processes. Taken largely from his work with his medical patients, Freud developed his psychoanalytic theory that highlighted the power of unconscious sexual and aggressive motives to direct conscious thought and behavior.

In the early 1900s, psychology began to take another direction. Behaviorists like J. B. Watson perceived a weakness in the approaches used by Wundt, James, and Freud in that they lacked a precise way of measuring mental processes. Watson and others believed that if psychology were to ever be taken seriously as a science, it would have to focus solely on the study of directly observable behavior.

In the 1950s, American psychologist B. F. Skinner furthered the study of behavior by focusing our attention on the consequences of behavior. Through his work, psychology began to focus on how reinforcement and punishment can shape the behavior of an organism.

From the early 1900s to the 1960s, behaviorism was the dominant force in American psychology. But this began to change in the 1960s with the rise of humanistic psychology and cognitive psychology, which emphasized the notion of free will and the importance of cognitive processes in directing behavior.

Careers in Psychology

This section covers Learning Objective 4. Today, psychology is a field of diverse perspectives. These include the biological, evolutionary, cognitive, psychodynamic, behavioral, sociocultural, and humanistic approaches to understanding behavior.

While it is possible to find employment in the field of psychology with a master's degree or bachelor's degree, today most people in psychology hold doctoral degrees. A doctoral degree usually requires 5-7 years of study beyond the bachelor's degree. In graduate school, psychologists receive training in some subfield of experimental psychology, clinical psychology, or counseling psychology.

All psychologists—regardless of their particular subfields—share the common goals of trying to describe, predict, explain and control or change behavior. To help attain these goals, psychologists use the scientific method: they define an issue to be studied; formulate a hypothesis; choose an appropriate research strategy; conduct the study to test their hypothesis; and analyze their data to support or disconfirm their hypothesis.

Psychological Research: Goals, Hypotheses, and Methods.

This section covers Learning Objectives 5-7. Hypotheses can be causal or predictive in nature. To test a causal hypothesis, you must use an experiment that has controlled or manipulated variables and random assignment of participants to the different groups of the study. Predictive hypotheses can be tested using a variety of research techniques including naturalistic observations, quasi-experiments, case studies, and correlational studies. Regardless of the design being used, psychologists will have to take care to run their studies on samples of participants that are representative of the population of interest.

Ethical Issues in Psychology

This section covers Learning Objective 8. Another concern of all psychological researchers is ethics. Universities and colleges typically require that all psychological studies be reviewed by an institutional review board to ensure that all ethical guidelines are met before the study is conducted. Some of these crucial guidelines include maintaining the dignity and welfare of participants by getting their informed consent, maintaining confidentiality of participant data, and thoroughly debriefing participants after the study. Ethics also extend to animal subjects. Animals must be treated humanely and in accordance with all laws. Any pain or discomfort to the animal must be offset by significant scientific gain. Animals should only be subjected to discomfort when no other viable research alternative exists.

Outlining the Big Picture

Chapter 1: What Is Psychology?

The Big Picture: What Do Psychologists Study?
Hurricane Katrina: Illustrating the diversity and complexity of psychology
Notes:

_____

_____

_____

_____

_____

_____

Correcting Common Misconceptions About the Field of Psychology (Learning Objective 1)
"Psychology Is Just About Giving People Advice"
"Psychology Isn't Really Science, It's Just Common Sense"
"Psychology Is Just the Study of Mental Illness"
Notes:

_____

_____

_____

_____

_____

_____

_____

So, What Is Psychology? (Learning Objective 2)
Psychologists Won't Always Agree on Why People Behave as They Do
Psychology Will Teach You About Critical Thinking
Notes:
_____

_____

_____

_____

_____

The Origins of Psychology (Learning Objective 3)
Early Approaches: Structuralism, Functionalism, and Psychoanalysis
    Wilhelm Wundt and Structuralism
    William James and Functionalism
    Sigmund Freud and Psychoanalytic Theory
Behaviorism: A True Science of Psychology
    John Watson's Behaviorism
    B. F. Skinner and Behavioral Consequences
Beyond Behaviorism: Humanism and Cognitive Psychology
    The Humanists
    Cognitive Psychology
Modern Perspectives and the Eclectic Approach
    Biological and Physiological Views
    Evolutionary Views
    Cognitive Views
    Psychodynamic Views
    Behavioral Views
    Sociocultural Views
    Humanistic Views
    The Eclectic Approach

Notes:

_____

_____

_____

_____

_____

Careers in Psychology (Learning Objective 4)
Training to Be a Psychologist
Major Subfields of Psychology
Doing Therapy: Clinical and Counseling Psychologists
Women and Minorities in the Field of Psychology
    Spotlight on Diversity: Gender, Ethnicity, and the Field of Psychology
Notes:

_____

_____

_____

_____

_____

Psychological Research: Goals, Hypotheses, and Methods (Learning Objectives 5-7)
The Goals of Psychology
The Scientific Method
Hypotheses
    Predictive Hypotheses
    Causal Hypotheses
Research Methods
    Naturalistic Observations
    Case Studies
    Correlational Studies
    Experiments

Notes:

_____

_____

_____

_____

_____

_____

Ethical Issues in Psychological Research (Learning Objective 8)
Ethical Guidelines for Participants
Ethical Guidelines for Animal Research
Notes:

_____

_____

_____

_____

_____

Are You Getting the Big Picture?
Notes:

_____

_____

_____

_____

_____

_____

Seeing the Big Picture: A Mental Map of Chapter 1

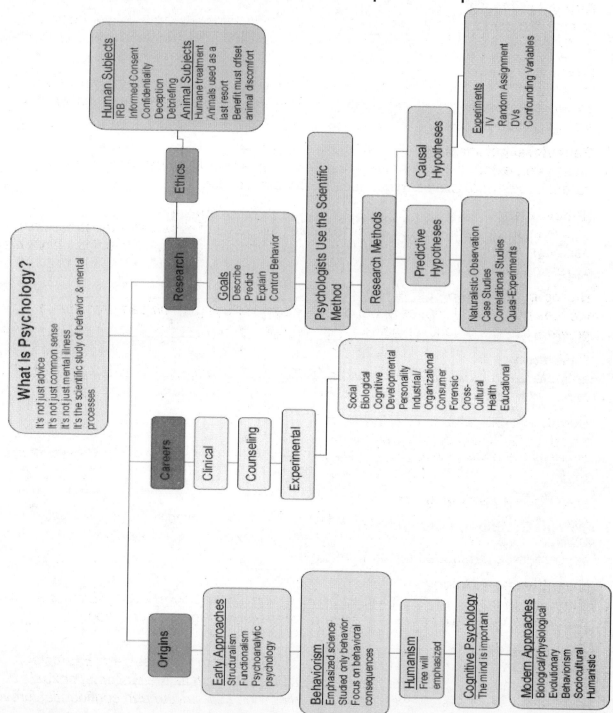

Key Points of the Big Picture

Applied research:
scientific study to solve a problem. *Example: Conducting research on what type of public service messages are most likely to persuade young people to practice safe sex.*

Basic research:
scientific study about the specifics of a behavior without concern for its application. *Example: Conducting research to determine if IQ is correlated with the number of siblings a person has.*

Behavioral perspective:
focuses on external, environmental causes of behavior. *Example: Asking how a parent's style of discipline may affect the behavior of her child.*

Behaviorism:
a psychological perspective that emphasizes the study of observable responses and behavior. *Example: A psychologist studies how rewarding people for losing weight may increase their weight loss.*

Biological/physiological perspective:
focuses on physical causes of behavior. *Example: Asking which part of the brain governs emotional functioning.*

Case study:
an in-depth observation of one person. *Example: The study of Phineas Gage, a 19th century railway worker who survived having a steel rod shot through his brain.*

Causal hypothesis:
an educated guess about how one variable will influence another variable. *Example: Predicting that using this study guide will increase your grade on the next psychology exam.*

Cognitive perspective:
focuses on how mental processes influence behavior. *Example: Looking at how your ability to formulate arguments against the message of a television ad affects how likely you are to be persuaded by that message.*

Cognitive psychology:
the study of mental processes such as reasoning and problem solving. *Example: Studying how people are able to store and retrieve memories of childhood.*

Confidentiality:
researchers do not reveal which data was collected from which subject. *Example: Anything you learn about your research participants such as their income, sexual orientation, level of self-esteem and so on must be kept private and confidential forever.*

Confounding variable:
any factor that affects the dependent measure other than the independent variable. *Example: Sex could be a confounding variable in a study examining the hypothesis that the more one studies, the better one's grades will be.*

Correlation:
the relationship between two or more variables. *Example: The more one exercises, the lower one's resting blood pressure tends to be. Exercise is negatively correlated with blood pressure.*

Debriefing:
after an experiment, subjects are fully informed of the nature of the study. *Example: Explaining to your participants that the purpose of the study they just participated in was to examine whether or not men and women like the same types of movies.*

Dependent variable:
the variable in an experiment that measures any effect of the manipulation. *Example: In a study testing to see if a drug causes depression in those who take it, the dependent variable would be the level of depression in the participants.*

Eclectic approach:
integrates and combines several perspectives when explaining behavior. *Example: A researcher may examine the biological, social, and cognitive factors affecting one's level of self-esteem.*

Evolutionary perspective:
focuses on how evolution and natural selection cause behavior. *Example: Asking whether aggression aids (or hinders) the survival of the human species.*

Experiment:
a research method that is used to test causal hypotheses. *Example: Randomly assigning participants to either take a drug or a placebo to test the hypothesis that taking the drug causes a person to become depressed.*

Functionalism:
an early psychological perspective concerned with how behavior helps people adapt to their environments. *Example: Asking why seeing color helps us survive.*

Generalizability:
how well one's findings apply to other individuals and situations. *Example: A case study of one man is not very generalizable to all people.*

Humanism:
a psychological perspective that emphasizes the personal growth and potential of humans. *Example: Looking at how people are motivated to reach their potential as human beings.*

Humanistic perspective:
focuses on how an individual's view of herself/himself and the world influences behavior. *Example: Asking whether one's feeling of belonging to a family may allow one to seek to help others.*

Independent variable:
the variable in an experiment that is manipulated. *Example: The level of a drug that a person takes in an experiment that tests the hypothesis that taking the drug causes depression.*

Informed consent:
research subjects agree to participate after being told about the aspects of the study. *Example: Participants are told that they will be asked to fill out a questionnaire on memory as part of a study, but their responses will be kept confidential, and they are free to quit the study at any time.*

Institutional Review Board (IRB):
a committee that reviews research proposals to ensure that ethical standards have been met. *Example: A panel at a university that reviews all research proposals.*

Introspection:
observing one's own thoughts, feelings, or sensations. *Example: Trying to decide why you thought of a childhood memory while sitting in class.*

Naturalistic observation:
observing behavior in the environment in which the behavior typically occurs. *Example: Sitting in the mall and observing whether same sex-couples walk faster than mixed-sex couples do.*

Negative correlation:
a relationship in which increases in one variable correspond to decreases in a second variable. *Example: The older someone is, the slower they run.*

Population of interest:
the entire universe of animals or people that could be studied. *Example: All the people in the United States.*

Positive correlation:
a relationship in which increases in one variable correspond to increases in a second variable. *Example: The more you eat, the more you weigh.*

Predictive hypothesis:
an educated guess about the relationships among variables. *Example: Being male predicts that one is likely to like football.*

Psychoanalytic theory:
Sigmund Freud's view that emphasizes the influence of unconscious desires and conflicts on behavior. *Example: Freud's theory predicts that your choice of a mate is influenced by the unconscious feelings you have about your opposite-sex parent.*

Psychodynamic perspective:
focuses on internal unconscious mental processes, motives, and desires that may explain behavior. *Example: Presuming that dreams are influenced by our unconscious motives and desires.*

Psychology:
the scientific study of behavior and mental processes. *Example: A psychologist might study how people recall childhood memories.*

Quasi-experiment:

a research study that is not a true experiment because participants are not randomly assigned to the conditions. *Example: Comparing men and women on their levels of self-esteem.*

Random assignment:

participants have an equal chance of being placed in any condition of the study. *Example: Randomly assigning 50 participants to a condition where they sleep 8 hours a night and randomly assigning 50 participants to a condition where they sleep 4 hours a night to test the effects of sleep on test scores.*

Sample:

the portion of the population of interest that is selected for a study. *Example: Sampling 100 students to represent all the students at your school in a scientific study.*

Scientific method:

a systematic process used by psychologists for testing hypotheses about behavior. *Example: Deciding to study drug abuse, developing the theory that being exposed to drug abuse increases one's chance of later drug abuse, designing a survey to test this hypothesis, running the survey, collecting the survey data, and then using this data to see if they support or disconfirm your hypothesis.*

Sociocultural perspective:

focuses on societal and cultural factors that may influence behavior. *Example: Examining how standards of beauty may differ among people from the U.S., Central America, and Africa.*

Structuralism:

an early psychological perspective concerned with identifying the basic elements of experience. *Example: Asking how a person perceives the color of one flower as being red and another as being pink.*

Theory:

an explanation of why and how a behavior occurs. *Example: Predicting that whether or not you were abused as a child influences your adult level of self-esteem.*

Fill-in Review of the Chapter

Can you fill-in the missing terms for each of the sections of the chapter?

The Big Picture: What Do Psychologists Study?

Hurricane Katrina devastated the 1) _____ _____ of the United States.

Correcting Common Misconceptions About the Field of Psychology

Psychology is not just about giving people 2)_____.

Psychology is not just the study of 3)_____ _____.

Psychology is a 4)_____.

So, What Is Psychology?

Psychology is the scientific study of 5) _____ and 6) _____
_____.

Psychologists test their ideas using the 7) _____ _____.

Pseudoscientific findings sound persuasive, but they are not necessarily based on

8) _____ procedures.

The Origins of Psychology

9) _____is a perspective in psychology in which researchers attempt to study the mind by breaking it down into its essential components.

10) _____ stresses the idea that humans possess within themselves the resources to effect personal growth and development.

11) _____ psychology stresses the idea that unconscious motives and desires can affect our behavior.

12) _____, an early approach to psychology, stresses the importance of understanding the purpose or function of behavior.

J. B. Watson was affiliated with the perspective of 13) _____ in psychology.

Careers in Psychology

A 14) _____ psychologist would most likely study crime statistics in an attempt to discover what type of person is most likely to commit a crime.

Dr. Carlos is studying the best way to lay out a computer screen so that air traffic controllers can do their jobs with a minimum of errors. Dr. Carlos is conducting 15) _____research.

Most psychologists hold a 16) _____ degree.

Clinical or counseling psychologists are trained to do 17) _____ with clients.

Psychological Research: Goals, Hypotheses, and Methods

If you want to test a causal hypothesis, you must conduct a(n) 18)_____.

Naturalistic observations are especially helpful in helping psychologists fulfill the goal of 19) _____ behavior.

A 20) _____ would be an especially helpful research tool in allowing researchers to determine which products consumers like most.

An in-depth observation of one person is an example of a 21) _____ _____.

The ultimate goal of psychologists is to 22) _____ behavior.

There is a 23) _____ correlation between height and shoe size.

A weakness of surveys, case studies, and naturalistic observations is that they do not allow researchers to test 24) _____ hypotheses.

Ethical Issues in Psychological Research

At most institutions, researchers must have their research proposals reviewed by a(n) 25) _____ prior to conducting their studies.

Psychologists must obtain their participants' 26) _____ _____ before proceeding with their study.

In terms of the ethics involved in doing human participants research is that researchers can do no 27) _____ to the participants.

Use It or Lose It!

Would you have to use an experiment to test these hypotheses, or would some other type of study suffice? Answer yes or no.

Hypothesis	Would you have to use an experiment to test this hypothesis?
1. Taking drug X causes depression.	
2. Men tend to sleep more than women.	
3. Having low self-esteem predicts that you will also have lower grades.	
4. Outlining your chapters as you read increases your retention of the material.	
5. Smoking is associated with higher risk of lung cancer.	

Self-Check: Are You Getting the Big Picture?

After you have read and studied the chapter, see if you can answer the following quiz questions. Check your answers at the end of the chapter. If you miss a question, refer to your text and re-study the appropriate sections.

True or False Questions

Are these statements true or false?

1. Most psychologists study the causes of mental illness.
Choice T: True
Choice F: False

2. It is acceptable for psychologists to hurt their research participants, provided the psychologist is able to publish his or her results in a prestigious journal.
Choice T: True
Choice F: False

3. Introspection is the technique used primarily by the behaviorists to study the mind.
Choice T: True
Choice F: False

4. William James viewed behavior from the functionalist perspective.
Choice T: True
Choice F: False

5. If you do not hold a Ph.D., there are no jobs in psychology that you can hold.
Choice T: True
Choice F: False

6. A causal hypothesis is best tested using a naturalistic observation study.
Choice T: True
Choice F: False

7. Dr. Edwards predicts that the more education a person has, the more money he or she will earn. This hypothesis is an example of a predictive hypothesis.
Choice T: True
Choice F: False

8. "Drinking red wine protects your heart from heart disease" is an example of a causal hypothesis.
Choice T: True
Choice F: False

9. Dr. Santiago is a psychologist who works in a doctor's office. Her job is to work with clients to help manage their stress levels as they recover from serious illnesses. Dr. Santiago is most likely a behavioral psychologist.
Choice T: True
Choice F: False

10. A case study can be used to test predictive hypotheses.
Choice T: True
Choice F: False

Multiple Choice Questions

Can you choose the best answer for these questions?

1. Which of the following is not true about psychology?
A. Psychology is just common sense.
B. Psychology is the study of mental illness.
C. Psychology has no connection with everyday life.
D. All of the above

2. One of the biggest benefits of studying psychology is that:
A. it teaches you how to diagnose your friends' problems.
B. it teaches you critical thinking.
C. it allows you to know why people do what they do.
D. all of the above

3. The roots of psychology are:
A. medicine and law.
B. medicine and chemistry.
C. philosophy and medicine.
D. philosophy and chemistry.

4. Psychology became a science in:
A. ancient Greece.
B. ancient Rome.
C. the 1870s in Germany.
D. the 1870s in England.

5. The _____ perspective in psychology stresses the importance of looking at the purpose of behavior and mental processes.
A. functionalism
B. structuralism
C. psychoanalysis
D. behaviorism

6. _____ psychology is the study of mental processes such as thinking, memory, and problem solving.
A. Consumer
B. Cross-cultural
C. Cognitive
D. Clinical

7. Many modern psychologists follow the _____ approach to psychology, in that they do not adhere strictly to any one psychological perspective.
A. pragmatic
B. functional
C. common sense
D. eclectic

8. Which psychological approach analyzes whether or not a behavior helps an organism adapt to and survive in its environment?
A. evolutionary
B. structuralism
C. humanism
D. behaviorism

9. Dr. Lau is a psychologist who studies the brain's structure and function. Dr. Lau is approaching psychology from the _____ perspective.
A. cognitive
B. eclectic
C. biological
D. sociocultural

10. Dr. Steinberg is a psychologist whose research involves trying to determine the maximum number of words a person can hold in their mind at any one time. Dr. Steinberg is most likely engaged in what type of research?
A. basic
B. applied
C. correlational
D. cross-cultural

11. Dr. Cook is a psychologist who studies how people change over time. Dr. Cook is most likely a _____ psychologist.
A. cognitive
B. biological
C. social
D. developmental

12. Dr. Ringger is a psychologist who studies how psychological principles can be applied in the workplace. Dr. Ringger is most likely a(n) _____ psychologist.
A. organizational
B. clinical
C. social
D. health

13. Dr. Doyle-Portillo is a psychologist who studies how people interact with one another. Dr. Doyle-Portillo is most likely a _____ psychologist.
A. cross-cultural
B. social
C. behavioral
D. consumer

14. Dr. Pastorino is a psychologist who studies the most effective ways to teach a child to read. Dr. Pastorino is most likely a(n) _____ psychologist.
A. cognitive
B. educational
C. developmental
D. social

15. Dr. Jones wants to test the hypothesis that drinking alcohol impairs one's ability to remember information. What type of hypothesis is Dr. Jones interested in testing?
A. predictive
B. causal
C. correlational
D. biological

16. The first African American to earn a doctorate in psychology was:
A. Karen Horney.
B. Mary Calkins.
C. Gilbert Haven.
D. Sidney Beckham.

17. Today, who earns most of the doctorates in psychology?
A. men
B. women
C. African Americans
D. Asian Americans

18. As of the year 2000, most of the full professors in psychology were:
A. men.
B. women.
C. White women.
D. African American men.

19. Which of the following is not a goal of psychology?
A. to describe behavior
B. to change behavior
C. to explain behavior
D. to eliminate free will

20. A theory is:
A. an explanation of why a behavior occurs.
B. a statement of fact.
C. an untestable assumption.
D. a prediction.

21. For a hypothesis to be of use to a scientist, it must be:
A. true.
B. false.
C. testable.
D. untestable.

22. The hypothesis that the number of car accidents will increase during the summer months is an example of a_____ hypothesis.
A. causal
B. predictive
C. untestable
D. non-scientific

23. Dr. Ranstad conducted an experiment in which she randomly assigned her participants to one of two conditions. In the first condition, the participants studied some material for eight straight hours before taking an exam on the material. In the second condition, the participants studied the same material one hour a day for eight days and then took the exam on the material. Dr. Randstad then compared the exam scores for these two groups of participants. In this experiment, the independent variable is the:
A. number of questions missed on the exam.
B. condition under which the participants studied the material.
C. the sex of the subjects.
D. the room in which the participants took the exam.

24. Dr. Lee is studying aggression in children. Everyday, he goes to the local playground at 3pm, sits on the sidelines, and records the number of fights that break out, the sex of the children involved in the fights, and the duration of the fights. Dr. Lee is using which research method in his study?
A. an experiment
B. a case study
C. a naturalistic observation
D. a quasi-experiment

25. The necessary conditions for an experiment are:
A. controlled variables and random assignment of participants to groups.
B. confounding variables and random assignment of participants to groups.
C. manipulated variables and self-selection of participants to groups.
D. manipulated variables and a representative sample of participants.

Short-Answer Questions

Can you write a brief answer to these questions?

1. Why is it important to have a representative sample when conducting research?

2. What are the advantages and disadvantages of conducting experiments?

3. What is an IRB? Why is it important?

4. What are the ethical guidelines that govern research on human participants?

5. Dr. O'Neill is studying the effects of lack of sleep on exam performance. He randomly assigns 20 students to a condition where they read a chapter, sleep for 8 hours, and then take an exam over the chapter. Dr. O'Neill also randomly assigns 20 other students to a condition where they read the chapter, sleep for 4 hours, and then take the exam. Dr. O'Neill then compares the exam scores for the two groups of students.

   Is Dr. O'Neill's study an experiment? If so, what are the independent variable, dependent variable, and two possible confounding variables?

Label the Diagram

Can you fill in the missing information in this table?

Major Players	Psychological Perspectives
1. Wilhelm Wundt & Edward Titchener	
2.	Functionalism
3.	Psychodynamic
4. Carl Rogers & Abraham Maslow	
5. J. B. Watson & B. F. Skinner	

Big Picture Review

Can you fill in the following table with the appropriate psychological perspective that matches the descriptions of how a psychologist might view a person suffering from an anxiety disorder?

Approach	Perspective
1.	Anxiety is related to chemicals in the body or to genetics (heredity).
2.	Anxiety is an adaptive response that prepares one to respond to potential threats in the environment. This response helps humans survive because it warns them of danger and thereby helps them avoid situations or people that may harm them. However, in modern times, these threats tend to be ongoing: traffic jams, crowding, and the hectic pace of consumerism.
3.	Focuses on how anxious people think differently from nonanxious people. Anxious people may engage in more pessimistic thinking or worry that everything will go wrong.
4.	Anxiety is the product of unresolved feelings of hostility, guilt, anger, or sexual attraction experienced in childhood.

5.	Anxiety is a learned behavior much like Albert's fear of the white rat. It is a response that is associated with a specific stimulus or a response that has been rewarded.
6.	Anxiety is a product of a person's culture. In the United States more women than men report being anxious and fearful, and this gender difference results from different socialization experiences. Men in the United States are raised to believe that they must not be afraid, so they are less likely to acknowledge or report anxiety. Women do not experience this pressure to hide their fears, so they are more likely to tell others and to seek treatment.
7.	Anxiety is rooted in people's dissatisfaction with their real self (how they perceive themselves) as compared to their ideal self (how they want to be).
8.	Anxiety stems from various sources depending on the individual. One person may be prone to anxiety because many people in his family are anxious and he has learned to be anxious from several experiences. Another person may be anxious because she is dissatisfied with herself and believes that everything always goes wrong in her life.

Solutions

Each solution below is followed by its textbook page reference number and its corresponding chapter learning objective (LO) number. Items with a Big Picture LO help you build a Big Picture of psychology across the chapters you have studied so far.

Fill-in Review of the Chapter

1. Gulf Coast [p. 3; LO 2]
2. advice [p. 6; LO 1]
3. mental illness [p. 7; LO 1]
4. science [p. 3; LO 1]
5. behavior [p. 3; LO 2]
6. mental processes [p. 3; LO 2]
7. scientific method [p. 3; LO 2]
8. scientific [p. 8; LO 2]
9. Structuralism [p. 10; LO 3]
10. Humanism [p. 14; LO 3]
11. Psychodynamic [p. 17; LO 3]
12. Functionalism [p. 11; LO 3]
13. behaviorism [p. 12; LO 3]
14. forensic [p. 22; LO 4]
15. applied [p. 19; LO 4]
16. doctoral [p. 19; LO 4]
17. therapy [p. 23; LO 4]
18. experiment [p. 28; LO 6]
19. describing [p. 29; LO 5]
20. survey [p. 31; LO 7]
21. case study [p. 30; LO 7]
22. control [p. 26; LO 5]
23. positive [p. 31; LO 7]
24. causal [p. 32; LO 7]
25. IRB [p. 36; LO 8]
26. informed consent [p. 36; LO 8]
27. harm [p. 36; LO 8]

Use It or Lose It!

1. yes [p. 28; LO 6 & 7]
2. no [p. 28; LO 6 & 7]
3. no [p. 28; LO 6 & 7]
4. yes [p. 28; LO 6 & 7]
5. no [p. 28; LO 6 & 7]

Self-Check: Are You Getting the Big Picture?

True or False Questions

1. F [p. 7; LO 1]
2. F [p. 36; LO 8]
3. F [p. 10; LO 3]
4. T [p. 11; LO 3]

5. F [p. 19; LO 4]
6. F [p. 29; LO 7]
7. T [p. 28; LO 6]
8. T [p. 28; LO 6]

9. F [p. 17, 22; LO 4]
10. T [p. 30; LO 7]

Multiple Choice Questions

1. D [p. 6; LO 1]	10. A [p. 19; LO 4]	19. D [p. 26; LO 5]
2. B [p. 8; LO 2]	11. D [p. 21; LO 4]	20. A [p. 8; LO 6]
3. C [p. 9; LO 3]	12. A [p. 21; LO 4]	21. C [p. 27; LO 6]
4. C [p. 9; LO 3]	13. B [p. 21; LO 4]	22. B [p. 28; LO 6]
5. A [p. 11; LO 3]	14. B [p. 23; LO 4]	23. B [p. 33; LO 7]
6. C [p. 14; LO 4]	15. B [p. 28; LO 6]	24. C [p. 30; LO 7]
7. D [p. 17; LO 4]	16. C [p. 24; LO 3]	25. A [p. 32; LO 7]
8. A [p. 16; LO 4]	17. B [p. 25; LO 4]	
9. C [p. 15; LO 4]	18. A [p. 25; LO 4]	

Short-Answer Questions

Can you write a brief answer to these questions?

1. Why is it important to have a representative sample when conducting research? [p. 29; LO 7]

Because you will be using this sample to draw conclusions and make inferences about the entire population of interest, it is necessary for the people in your sample to be representative of the population. In other words, the participants in the sample must have approximately the same characteristics as the people in the population.

2. What are the advantages and disadvantages of conducting experiments? [p. 36; LO 7]

The major advantage of the experiment is that it allows you to establish cause and effect among your variables. Therefore, you can test hypotheses that look at the causes of behavior. With the knowledge gained from experiments, psychologists can satisfy two goals of psychology: explaining and changing behavior.

The disadvantages of using experiments include the fact that they do not always allow you to fulfill the goals of describing and predicting behavior; and at times, the need for experimental control forces psychologists to study behavior in highly artificial laboratory settings. In these cases, it may be questionable whether or not your research results will tell you much about behavior in the real world.

3. What is an IRB? Why is it important? [p. 36; LO 8]

An IRB is an institutional review board. IRBs are set up at research institutions to review plans for research studies before the studies are conducted. The purpose of these boards is to help ensure that all research is conducted within ethical guidelines and that participants' rights are upheld.

4. What are the ethical guidelines that govern research on human participants? [p. 36; LO 8]

Respect and concern for the dignity of participants must be upheld. Participants cannot be exposed to harm, risk, or danger; and if these conditions arise, the researcher must stop them. Participants must give their informed consent prior to the study. Participant data must be kept confidential. Deception should be limited, and all participants must be debriefed after their participation.

5. Dr. O'Neill is studying the effects of lack of sleep on exam performance. He randomly assigns 20 students to a condition where they read a chapter, sleep for 8 hours, and then take an exam over the chapter. Dr. O'Neill also randomly assigns 20 other students to a condition where they read the chapter, sleep for 4 hours, and then take the exam. Dr. O'Neill then compares the exam scores for the two groups of students.

Is Dr. O'Neill's study an experiment? If so, what are the independent variable, dependent variable, and two possible confounding variables? [p. 33; LO 7]

Yes, it is an experiment. It has a manipulated independent variable and random assignment. The independent variable is the amount of sleep the students received. The dependent variable is their exam score. Some possible confounding variables would be: sex, age, sleep disorders, intelligence levels, etc.

Label the Diagram

1. Structuralism [p. 10; LO 3]	4. Humanism [p. 14; LO 3]
2. William James [p. 11; LO 3]	5. Behaviorism [p. 12; LO 3]
3. Sigmund Freud [p. 12; LO 3]	

Big Picture Review

1. biological [p. 15; LO 4]	5. behavioral [p. 17; LO 4]
2. evolutionary [p. 16; LO 4]	6. sociocultural [p. 17; LO 4]
3. cognitive [p. 16; LO 4]	7. humanistic [p. 17; LO 4]
4. psychodynamic [p. XXX; LO 4]	8. eclectic [p. 17; LO 4]

2

How Does Biology Influence Our Behavior?

Learning Objectives

After studying each of the following sections of the chapter, you should be able to do these tasks.

Billions of Neurons: Communication in the Brain

1. Describe the basic structure of a neuron, including the axon, dendrites, and synapse.
2. Explain what an action potential is and describe how it moves down the axon and across the synapse.
3. Explain what excitation and inhibition are and how they occur at the synapse.

Neurotransmitters: Chemical Messengers in the Brain

4. List the major neurotransmitters and describe the functions they may influence.

The Structure of the Nervous System

5. Describe the major parts of the nervous system and what types of information they process.

The Brain and Spine: The Central Nervous System

6. Be able to locate the hindbrain, midbrain, and forebrain, list their parts, and explain what they do.

Techniques for Studying the Brain

7. Describe brain-imaging techniques and other ways we can study the brain, and explain their advantages and limitations.

The Endocrine System: Hormones and Behavior

8. Explain how the endocrine system works and list the endocrine glands.

Becoming Who We Are: The Influence of Genetics on Biology

9. Give an overview of the nature versus nature debate and list genetic and environmental factors in human development.
10. Give an overview of the theory of evolution and how the human nervous system may have developed through natural selection.

The Big Picture

The Big Picture: What Would We Be Without a Healthy Brain?

This chapter discusses the biological influences that affect our behavior. The story of Jean-Dominique shows us how crucial a healthy brain is to our ability to function normally. When Bauby lost the function of portions of his brainstem, he suffered locked-in syndrome and was a prisoner in his own body.

Billions of Neurons: Communication in the Brain

This section covers Learning Objectives 1-3. The cells of the nervous system that carry messages are called neurons. Neurons have dendrites at their head to receive signals from other neurons, a cell body with a nucleus, a long tail or axon that branches at its end, and axon bulbs that sit on the end of each axon branch. A synapse, or connection between neurons, occurs when the axon bulb of one neuron comes in close proximity to the dendrite of another neuron.

When neurons are at rest (not receiving or sending signals), the membrane on the axon is in a semi-permeable state in that it will not allow sodium to enter into the cell. Because sodium cannot enter into the cell at this time, the axon of the neuron is polarized with the inside of the axon being more negative than the outside of the cell. The magnitude of this resting potential difference is -70mv. When the neuron receives enough stimulation to move it to its threshold of excitation (-55mv), the axon's membrane becomes suddenly permeable to sodium and sodium floods into the cell. As sodium enters, it makes the cell rapidly more positive and the cell is said to fire a signal or action potential.

Once the action potential reaches the end of the axon, the neuron will release neurotransmitters into the synapse. These neurotransmitters will bind with receptors on the dendrites of some of the neurons on the other side of the synapse and cause either excitation or inhibition in those cells. Excitation makes the post-synaptic neurons more likely to fire action potentials by moving them closer to their threshold of excitation. Inhibition makes post-synaptic neurons less likely to fire action potentials by moving them away from their threshold of excitation. Both excitation and inhibition are necessary for normal functioning.

Neurotransmitters: Chemical Messengers in the Brain

This section covers Learning Objective 4. There are many neurotransmitters in the body. Some of the more important ones are: acetylcholine, dopamine, serotonin, norepinephrine, GABA, glutamate, endorphins, and substance P.

The Structure of the Nervous System

This section covers Learning Objective 5. In the body, the nervous system is divided into several sub-systems. The first division is between the central nervous system – the brain and spinal cord – and the peripheral nervous system, which is the remainder of the nervous system. The peripheral nervous system is sub-divided into the somatic and autonomic nervous systems. The somatic nervous system controls voluntary action in the body (e.g., muscle movement). The autonomic nervous system controls involuntary organ action in the body (e.g., heart rate). The autonomic nervous system is sub-divided into the parasympathetic and sympathetic nervous systems. The parasympathetic nervous system controls organ functioning during times of calm. The sympathetic nervous system controls organ function during times of stress or threat.

The Brain and Spine: The Central Nervous System

This section covers Learning Objective 6. The brain is the executive of the central nervous system. The brain contains approximately 100 billion neurons and many more glia cells that combine to form the structures of the brain. These structures can be divided into three main regions of the brain – the hindbrain, the midbrain, and the forebrain.

The hindbrain contains the medulla, pons, and cerebellum. These structures have basic life-sustaining functions; play a role in sensory processing; help balance our bodies; or help process motor skill memory. Even minor damage to the hindbrain can result in serious impairment or death – as is evidenced in the case of Jean-Dominique Bauby who suffered locked-in syndrome after having a stroke in the vicinity of his hindbrain.

The midbrain connects the lower structures of the hindbrain with the higher structures of the forebrain. One important midbrain structure is the reticular activating system or RAS. The RAS is important for maintaining arousal, regulating attention, and awakening from sleep. The RAS acts as something of an "on switch" for higher level brain structures.

The forebrain contains structures that influence higher-order processing in the brain – for example thinking and planning. The limbic system of the forebrain contains structures that influence emotion and motivation. These structures include the amygdala, septum, and hippocampus. The forebrain's diencephalon contains the thalamus and hypothalamus – structures that respectively influence sensory processing and motivation.

By far, the most sophisticated processing in the brain occurs in the cortex – the thin outer layer that covers the brain's surface. The cortex can be divided into four regions or lobes – the occipital lobe, the parietal lobe, the temporal lobe, and the frontal lobe. Of the total surface area of the cortex, about 25% has specific motor or sensory function and the other 75% is association cortex or areas where information is integrated and planning takes place. The occipital lobe contains the primary visual areas; the temporal lobe contains the auditory cortex; the parietal lobe contains the somatosensory cortex; and the frontal lobe contains the motor cortex.

Much of the brain's cortex is wired in a contralateral fashion, meaning that information coming from one side of the body is processed in the brain on the opposite side. For example, objects seen to the right side of the body are processed in the brain's left occipital lobe. The brain is also set up in a lateralized fashion, in that each hemisphere has somewhat different functions. One example of this lateralization is the location of language function in the brain. For most of us, language is located solely in the left hemisphere. Broca's area in the left frontal lobe allows us to produce speech. Wernicke's area in the left temporal lobe allows us to comprehend speech.

Techniques for Studying the Brain

This section covers Learning Objective 7. To determine what functions particular parts of the brain have, researchers must have ways of measuring and viewing the brain. To date, many technologies have been developed and used to study the brain. These include CAT scans and MRI that show the structure of the brain; PET scans and SPECT scans that show activity in the brain; functional MRIs that show detail and function in the brain; EEG and ERP machines that measure the electrical activity of the brain; and angiograms that show bloodflow in the brain. In animal studies, researchers may also produce lesions in the brain to see how such lesions change the animal's behavior. Stimulation of the brain can also tell researchers something about the function of specific brain areas. And single-cell recordings can tell researchers about the function of a single neuron in the brain.

The Endocrine System: Hormones and Behavior

This section covers Learning Objective 8. In the body there are two systems of communication that are very important influences on your mental processes and behavior – the nervous and endocrine systems. The endocrine system is a chemical system of communication that uses hormones to convey messages throughout the body. Because the endocrine system relies upon the circulatory system to carry its hormones throughout the body, this system is rather slow to react and long-lasting in its effects. The nervous system is an electro-chemical system of communication that uses electrical charges from ions to send messages throughout the body. Because the nervous system is electrical in nature, it is very fast to react and its effects are brief in comparison to the endocrine system.

Becoming Who We Are: The Influence of Genetics on Biology

This section covers Learning Objectives 9 & 10. We all have our own idiosyncrasies both in our bodies and in our behavior. We all develop into the people we are through a complex interaction of genetic (nature) and environmental (nurture) forces.

At conception, we inherit half our genes from each of our parents. Genes contain the DNA that is the blueprint for our development. According to the theory of natural selection, over many generations, genes that aid survival and reproduction remain in a species and genes that hinder survival and reproduction die out.

Throughout our lives our genes will direct the course of our physical development. However, the actual characteristics we end up with are not just a product of our genes. Our environment – the type of parents we had, the culture we grew up in, our diet and other factors – all interact with our genes to produce our actual characteristics.

Outlining the Big Picture

Chapter 2: How Does Biology Influence Our Behavior?

The Big Picture: What Would We Be Without a Healthy Brain?
Jean-Dominque Bauby's *The Diving Bell and the Butterfly*
Notes:

_____

_____

_____

_____

_____

_____

Billions of Neurons: Communication in the Brain (Learning Objectives 1-3)
The Anatomy of the Neuron
Signals in the Brain: How Neurons Fire Up
    Resting Potential
    The Action Potential and the Threshold of Excitation
    The Refractory Period
Jumping the Synapse: Synaptic Transmission
    Excitation
    Inhibition
    How Excitation and Inhibition Interact
Cleaning up the Synapse: Reuptake

Notes:

_____

_____

_____

_____

Neurotransmitters: Chemical Messengers in the Brain (Learning Objective 4)

The First Neurotransmitter: Acetylcholine
Parkinson's Disease and Schizophrenia: Dopamine
Playing a Part in Depression: Serotonin and Norepinephrine
Inhibiting and Exciting the Brain: GABA and Glutamate
Pain in the Brain: Endorphins and Substance P
Notes:

_____

_____

_____

_____

_____

The Structure of the Nervous System (Learning Objective 5)

Messages from the Body: The Peripheral Nervous System
Reaching Out: The Somatic Nervous System
Involuntary Actions: The Autonomic Nervous System
　　The Parasympathetic Nervous System
　　The Sympathetic Nervous System

Notes:

_____

_____

_____

_____

_____

_____

The Brain and Spine: The Central Nervous System (Learning Objective 6)
The Hindbrain
The Midbrain
The Forebrain
    The Limbic System
    The Diencephalon
The Cortex
    Lateralization and the Lobes of the Cortex
    The Left and Right Hemispheres
    The Corpus Callosum
    Spotlight on Diversity: Male-Female Differences in the Brain
    The Split-brain
The Specialization of Function in the Lobes of the Cortex
    The Frontal Lobe
    The Parietal Lobe
    The Occipital Lobe
    The Temporal Lobe
Notes:

_____

_____

_____

_____

_____

_____

Techniques for Studying the Brain (Learning Objective 7)
Notes:

_____

_____

_____

_____

_____

The Endocrine System: Hormones and Behavior (Learning Objective 8)
Notes:

_____

_____

_____

_____

_____

Becoming Who We Are: The Influence of Genetics on Biology (Learning Objectives 9 & 10)
Nature Versus Nurture and Interactionism
Twin Studies
Genetic Blueprint for Traits
The Evolution of Species: Natural Selection
Notes:

_____

_____

_____

_____

_____

_____

_____

Are You Getting the Big Picture?
Notes:

_____

_____

_____

_____

_____

_____

Seeing the Big Picture: A Mental Map of Chapter 2

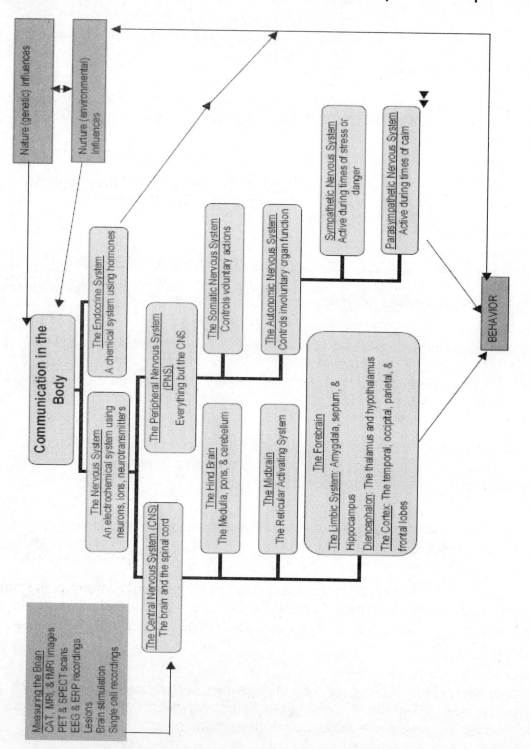

Nature (genetic) Influences

Nurture (environmental) Influences

Communication in the Body

The Endocrine System
A chemical system using hormones

The Nervous System
An electrochemical system using neurons, ions, neurotransmitters

The Peripheral Nervous System (PNS)
Everything but the CNS

The Somatic Nervous System
Controls voluntary actions

The Autonomic Nervous System
Controls involuntary organ function

Sympathetic Nervous System
Active during times of stress or danger

Parasympathetic Nervous System
Active during times of calm

BEHAVIOR

The Central Nervous System (CNS)
The brain and the spinal cord

The Hind Brain
The Medulla, pons, & cerebellum

The Midbrain
The Reticular Activating System

The Forebrain
The Limbic System: Amygdala, septum, & Hippocampus
Diencephalon: The thalamus and hypothalamus
The Cortex: The temporal, occipital, parietal, & frontal lobes

Measuring the Brain
CAT, MRI & fMRI images
PET & SPECT scans
EEG & ERP recordings
Lesions
Brain stimulation
Single cell recordings

Key Points of the Big Picture

Acetylcholine (ACh):
a neurotransmitter related to muscle movement and perhaps consciousness, learning, and memory. *Example: A loss of acetylcholine activity in the nervous system would, among other things, produce paralysis in the body.*

Action potential:
the neural impulse fried by a neuron when it reaches -55 mv. *Example: When you move your leg, action potentials carry the instructions from your brain to the muscles of your leg, allowing it to move.*

Adrenal cortex:
the outside part of the adrenal gland. It plays a role in the manufacture and release of androgens, and therefore influences sexual characteristics. *Example: Adrenal androgens influence the amount of facial hair a person has.*

Adrenal medulla:
the center part of the adrenal gland. It plays a crucial role in the functioning of the sympathetic nervous system. *Example: During an argument, your adrenal medulla may release adrenalin that increases heart rate and blood pressure.*

All-or-none fashion:
all action potentials are equal in strength and once a neuron begins to fire an action potential at -55mv, the action potential will fire all the way down the axon. *Example: Unless a neuron is cut or drugs are injected into it, the action potential will travel the entire length of the axon once it starts.*

Amygdala:
a part of the limbic system that plays a role in our emotions of fear and aggression. *Example: If you encounter an angry person on the street, your amygdala will help you process the situation and respond appropriately.*

Androgens:
a class of male hormones. *Example: Some men and women take testosterone, an androgen, to increase their lagging sex drive.*

Association cortex:
areas of the cortex that are involved in the association or integration of information from the motor-sensory areas of the cortex. *Example: When you decide to get up and walk across the room, you first use areas of your association cortex to plan how to execute this action prior to doing it.*

Auditory cortex:
a region of cortex found in the temporal lobe that governs our processing of auditory information in the brain. *Example: If you listen to a classical music concert on the radio, your auditory cortex will play a role in your perception of the music.*

Autonomic nervous system:
branch of the peripheral nervous system that primarily governs involuntary organ functioning and actions in the body. *Example: Right now, your autonomic nervous system is controlling the function of your internal organs.*

Axon:
the long tail-like structure that comes out of the soma of the neuron. Action potentials are fired down the axon and convey information from the soma to the synapse.

Broca's area:
a region in the left frontal lobe that plays a role in the production of speech. *Example: When you talk to your best friend, Broca's area ensures that he or she will be able to understand what you are saying.*

Cell body:
the part of the neuron that contains the nucleus and DNA.

Central nervous system (CNS):
the brain and the spinal cord.

Cerebellum:
a hindbrain structure that plays a role in balance of the body, muscle tone, and coordination of motor movements. *Example: When you bend over to tie your shoes, the cerebellum helps ensure that you don't topple over on your head.*

Cerebral cortex:
thin, wrinkled outer covering of the brain, in which very high-level processes like thinking, planning, language, interpretation of sensory data, and coordination of sensory and motor information take place. *Example: When recalling your cherished memories of childhood you likely use the cortex.*

Cerebral hemispheres:
right and left sides of the brain that to some degree, govern different functions in the body. *Example: As you take notes in class, the motor cortex on the opposite side of the brain from your dominate hand is controlling the movement of your hand.*

Corpus callosum:
a thick band of neurons that connect the right and left hemispheres of the brain. *Example: When typing, the actions of your right and left hands are coordinated in part because the corpus callosum allows information to pass back and forth between the two hemispheres.*

Dendrites:
branchlike structures on the head of the neuron that receive incoming signals from other neurons in the nervous system.

Diencephalon:
system in the forebrain that includes the thalamus and hypothalamus.

DNA:
the chemical, found in the nuclei of cells, that contains the genetic blueprint which guides development in the organism. *Example: Because each of us has a unique set of genes, forensic investigators can use DNA evidence to identify criminals.*

Dopamine:
neurotransmitter that plays a role in movement, learning, and attention. *Example: Drugs that increase dopamine action in the brain are used to treat people with Parkinson's disease.*

Endocrine glands:
organs of the endocrine system that produce and release hormones into the blood. *Example: After eating a big meal, your pancreas releases insulin to help lower your blood sugar and give your cells energy.*

Endorphins:
neurotransmitters that act as a natural painkiller. *Example: When Raj broke his finger, it didn't seem to hurt at first due to the release of endorphins in his body at the time of injury.*

Estrogens:
a class of female hormones. *Example: After menopause, many women take estrogen supplements to replace the estrogen their bodies no longer makes on it own.*

Excitation:
when a neurotransmitter depolarizes the postsynaptic cell and it becomes more likely to fire an action potential. *Example: When you smell a rose, the scent causes the neurons in your nasal passage to experience excitation. If enough excitation occurs, they fire action potentials and ultimately you perceive the smell of roses.*

Forebrain:
brain structures that govern higher-order mental processes. These structures include the limbic system, diencephalon, and cortex.

Fraternal twins:
twins that developed from two separate fertilized eggs and are no more genetically similar than normal siblings. *Example: Twins Joan and John must be fraternal twins because they are of different sexes.*

Frontal lobe:
Cortical area directly behind the forehead that plays a role in thinking, planning, decision making, language, and motor movement. *Example: When you read, you are using your frontal lobe to help you concentrate.*

Gamma amino butyric acid (GABA):
the body's chief inhibitory neurotransmitter, which plays a role in regulating arousal. *Example: To calm her down, doctors gave Brenna a tranquilizing drug that increased GABA action in her brain.*

Genes:
strands of DNA found in the nuclei of all living cells.

Genotype:
inherited genetic pattern for a given trait. *Example: The actual genes that you have for height are one of the factors that determined how tall you are.*

Glia cells:
brain cells that provide support functions for the neurons.

Glutamate:
the chief excitatory neurotransmitter in the brain, found at more than 50% of the synapses in the brain. *Example: You are probably using lots of glutamate right now as you read this sentence.*

Hindbrain:
primitive part of the brain that comprises the medulla, pons, and cerebellum. *Example: If you lost functioning in your hindbrain, you would die.*

Hippocampus:
part of the brain that plays a role in the transfer of information from short- to long-term memory. *Example: You will use your hippocampus to learn this material for your next psychology exam!*

Homeostasis:
an internal state of equilibrium in the body. *Example: You become thirsty when your body needs more water to maintain homeostasis of the amount of fluid surrounding your body tissues.*

Hormones:
chemical messengers of the endocrine system. *Example: Growth hormone helps you grow and repair damage in your body.*

Hypothalamus:
part of the diencephalon that plays a role in maintaining homeostasis in the body, involving sleep, body temperature, sexual behavior, thirst, hunger; also the point where the nervous system intersects with the endocrine system. *Example: When you get sleepy tonight, it will be due to the action of the hypothalamus.*

Identical twins:
twins that developed from a single fertilized egg and share 100% of their genes. *Example: The Olson twins are identical twins.*

Inhibition:
when a neurotransmitter further polarizes the post-synaptic cell it and becomes less likely to fire an action potential. *Example: Some drugs like Valium increase inhibition in the brain.*

Interactionism:
the perspective that our genes and environmental influences work together to determine our characteristics. *Example: Your level of intelligence is likely due to both nature (genes) and nurture (environment).*

Ions:
charged particles that play an important role in the firing of action potentials in the nervous system.

Limbic system:
a system of structures that govern certain aspects of emotion, motivation, and memory. Limbic system structures include the amygdala, septum, and hippocampus.

Medulla:
part of the hindbrain that controls basic, life-sustaining functions such as respiration, heart rate, and blood pressure. *Example: If your pet rabbit developed a tumor of the medulla, the rabbit would likely die.*

Midbrain:
brain structure that connects the hindbrain with the forebrain. *Example: Damage to the midbrain could cause an irreversible coma because the hindbrain could no longer communicate with the areas of the forebrain that maintain consciousness.*

Motor cortex:
a strip of cortex at the back of the frontal lobe that governs the execution of motor movement in the body. *Example: As you read these words, your motor cortex allows your eyes to move and scan the sentence.*

Motor neuron:
neurons that transmit commands from the brain to the muscles of the body. *Example: Motor neurons in the muscles of your face allow you to smile.*

Myelin:
fatty-waxy substance that insulates portions of some neurons in the nervous system.

Natural selection:
cornerstone of Darwin's theory of evolution, which states that genes for traits that allow an organism to be reproductively successful will be selected or retained in a species and genes for traits that hinder reproductive success will not be selected and therefore will die out in a species. *Example: If physical attractiveness leads to producing more healthy offspring, then humans should become more good-looking over the next few million years.*

Nature- nurture debate:
the degree to which biology (nature) or the environment (nurture) contributes to one's development. *Example: Are you smart because of your genes or because of your environment?*

Nervous system:
an electrochemical system of communication within the body that uses cells called neurons to convey information.

Neurons:
cells in the central nervous system that transmit information.

Neurotransmitters:
chemical messengers that carry neural signals across the synapse.

Norepinephrine (NOR):
neurotransmitter that plays a role in regulating sleep, arousal, and mood. *Example: A drug that lowers NOR in the brain might produce depression.*

Occipital lobe:
Cortical area at the back of the brain that plays a role in visual processing. *Example: You're using your occipital lobe right now to see these words.*

Parasympathetic nervous system:
branch of the autonomic nervous system most active during times of normal functioning. *Example: Unless you are upset right now, your parasympathetic nervous system is governing your organ function.*

Parietal lobe:
Cortical areas on the top sides of the brain that play a role in touch and certain cognitive processes. *Example: As you hold this book right now, your somatosenory cortex in the parietal lobe allows you to feel the book in your hands.*

Peripheral nervous system:
all of the nervous system except for the brain and spinal cord.

Phenotype:
actual characteristic that results from the interaction of the genotype and environmental influences. *Example: The exact color of your eyes.*

Pituitary gland:
master gland of the endocrine system that controls the action of all other glands in the body.

Pons:
hindbrain structure that plays a role in respiration, consciousness, sleep, dreaming, facial movement, sensory processes, and the transmission of neural signals from one part of the brain to another. *Example: As you read this page right now, the neural signals coming from your eyes first pass through your pons before reaching the occipital lobe of the brain.*

Postsynaptic neuron:
the neuron that is receiving the signal at a synapse in the nervous system

Presynaptic neuron:
the neuron that is sending the signal at a synapse in the nervous system

Refractory period:
brief period of time after which a neuron has fired an action potential in which the neuron is inhibited and unlikely to fire another action potential. *Example: Due to the refractory period, you can only fire the neurons that control the muscles of your arms and hands so fast. Therefore, there is a limit to how fast you can type a paper for your psychology class.*

Resting potential:
potential difference that exists in the neuron when it is resting (approximately -70 mv in mammals)

Reticular Activating System (RAS):
part of the midbrain that regulates arousal and plays an important role in attention, sleep, and consciousness. *Example: Your RAS helped you wake up this morning, energizing your frontal lobe to bring you to consciousness.*

Reuptake:
process through which unused neurotransmitters are recycled back into the vesicles. *Example: Think of reuptake as your body's own recycling program for neurotransmitters.*

Sensory neurons:
neurons that transmit information from the sense organs to the central nervous system. *Example: Without sensory neurons, you could not see, hear, smell, touch, or taste!*

Septum:
part of the limbic system that seems to be a pleasure center in the brain and may play a role in addictive behavior. *Example: Drugs like crack, methamphetamine, and heroin, may be addictive in part because of the action of the septum.*

Serotonin:
neurotransmitter that plays a role in many different behaviors including sleep, arousal, mood, eating, and pain perception. *Example: People who suffer from obsessive compulsive disorder, which is often characterized by the need to engage in repetitive actions, may have a lack of serotonin action in the brain.*

Somatic nervous system:
branch of the peripheral nervous system that governs sensory and voluntary motor action in the body. *Example: If you choose to turn the page of this book, you will use your somatic nervous system to execute the muscle movements needed to complete this action.*

Somatosensory cortex:
a strip of cortex at the front of the parietal lobe that governs our sense of touch. *Example: The pleasurable feeling of a kiss is processed in the somatosenory cortex of the brain.*

Split brain:
a brain that with its corpus callosum severed; sometimes done to control the effects of epilepsy in patients who do not respond to other therapies.

Sympathetic nervous system:
branch of the autonomic nervous system most active during times of danger or stress. *Example: If you were to see a rattlesnake while hiking, your sympathetic system would likely kick into high gear.*

Synapse:
the connection formed between two neurons when the axon bulb of one neuron comes into close proximity with the dendrite of another neuron.

Temporal lobes:

cortical areas directly below our ears that play a role in auditory processing and language. *Example: Whatever you are hearing right now is being processed in your temporal lobes.*

Thalamus:

part of the diencephalon that functions as a sensory relay station in the brain. *Example: Most of the sensory information coming from your eyes, ears, fingers, etc, travels through your thalamus before heading to your cortex.*

Threshold of excitation:

potential difference at which a neuron will fire an action potential (-55mv in humans).

Twin studies:

comparing the relative similarity of identical and fraternal twins to ascertain the relative contributions of genes and environment to our characteristics. *Example: Because having an identical twin with naturally blond hair predicts that you will have naturally blond hair, it's fair to assume that hair color is at least partly genetic.*

Visual cortex:

a region of cortex found at the back of the occipital lobe that processes visual information in the brain. *Example: A tumor in your occipital lobe might produce visual disturbances.*

Wernicke's area:

a region of the left temporal lobe that plays a role in the comprehension of speech. *Example: When you listen to your favorite TV show, Wernicke's area allows you to understand the actors' speech.*

Fill-in Review of the Chapter

Can you fill-in the missing terms for each section of the chapter? Items marked with an * encourage you to continue building the Big Picture of psychology by connecting the material in this chapter to material from previous chapters in the text.

The Big Picture: Where Would We Be Without a Health Brain?

Jean-Dominique Bauby suffered from a condition known as 1) _____.

This occurred because Bauby suffered brain damage to his 2) _____.

The story of Jean-Dominique Bauby represents the 3*) _____ research method from Chapter 1.

Billions of Neurons: Communication in the Brain.

The resting potential of a neuron is 4) _____.

As a neuron fires an action potential, the charge inside the neuron goes from being
5) _____ to being 6) _____ to being 7) _____ once again.

When a neuron experiences 8) _____ after receiving a signal from another neuron,
it becomes more likely to fire an action potential.

A 9) _____ is the connection that forms when the 10) _____ of one neuron
comes in close proximity to the 11) _____ _____ of another neuron.

Comparing differences in the brains of men and women would be an example of a(n)
12*) _____ _____ research design from Chapter 1.

Neurotransmitters: Chemical Messengers in the Brain

Lamar is suffering from Parkinson's disease. To help with his symptoms, Lamar's
doctors have prescribed a drug that 13) _____ the action of the neurotransmitter
14) _____ in his brain.

15) _____ is a neurotransmitter that plays a role in learning and memory as well as
16) _____ disease.

Dr. Lowe randomly assigns 20 people to receive a drug that lowers dopamine in the
brain and 20 people to receive a placebo. After six weeks on these treatments, the
participants are given a test of their memory to see if their memory was affected by the
treatment they received. In this experiment, the independent variable is
17*) _____ and the dependent variable is
18*) _____.

The Structure of the Nervous System

During times of calm, the 19) _____ nervous system controls our organ function.
During times of stress, the 20) _____ nervous system takes over the control of our
internal organs.

The 21) _____ nervous system is responsible for governing voluntary action and
sensation in the body.

The Brain and Spine: The Central Nervous System

Jamal was in a car accident in which he suffered damage to his 22) _____. After his accident, Jamal has trouble telling whether or not other people are angry.

In a 23) _____ _____ operation, doctors cut the 24) _____ _____ in an attempt to lessen the severity of epileptic seizures that affect both the right and left hemispheres of the brain.

Vision is to the 25) _____ lobe as 26) _____ is to the temporal lobe.

Male brains tend to be 27) _____ than female brains.

Males show more activation in the 28) _____ and 29)_____ of the brain when viewing sexually explicit material.

London Taxi cab drivers showed differences in the 30) _____ of the brain when compared to London bus drivers.

Techniques for Studying the Brain

Kelis has been having severe headaches lately and her doctors want to rule out the possibility that she may have a brain tumor. To do this, the doctors are most likely to order a(n) 31) _____ or a(n) 32) _____ scan for Kelis.

The Endocrine System: Hormones and Behavior

33) _____ are male hormones and 34) _____ are female hormones. Both of these types of hormones act as messengers in the body's 35) _____ system.

Becoming Who We Are: The Influence of Genetics on Biology

In the nature-nurture debate, the nature side of the argument claims that our traits and characteristics are largely due to the influence of our 36) _____.

Psychologists test the relative contributions of genes and environment by conducting 37) _____ _____.

From Chapter 1, like Charles Darwin, early functionalist psychologist 38*) _____ _____ was interested in the role that behavior played in our ability to survive and thrive in the world.

Use It or Lose It!

Can you fill in the following table with the location of damage in the brain that would produce the following behavioral symptoms?

Site of Brain Damage	Resulting Behavioral Symptoms
1.	paralysis on the right side of the body
2.	instant death
3.	inability to hear sounds coming from the right side of one's body
4.	inability to produce speech
5.	numbness on the left side of the body
6.	blindness
7.	inability to maintain a body temperature of 98.6 degrees
8.	lack of coordination and balance; trouble learning new motor skills
9.	inability to correctly read other people's emotions, especially when others are angry
10.	inability to learn new concepts or store new memories of the events in one's life

Self-Check: Are You Getting the Big Picture?

After you have read and studied the chapter, see if you can answer the following quiz questions. Check your answers at the end of the chapter. If you miss a question, refer to your text and re-study the appropriate sections.

True or False Questions

Are these statements true or false?

1. The reticular activating system controls hunger and thirst in the body.
Choice T: True
Choice F: False

2. The type of parents a child has is a nurture influence on the development of the child's brain.
Choice T: True
Choice F: False

3. Integration of information from the motor-sensory areas of the brain occurs in the association cortex.
Choice T: True
Choice F: False

4. A PET scan can give physicians or researchers a picture of which parts of the brain a person is using at a given point in time.
Choice T: True
Choice F: False

5. The midbrain connects the frontal lobe with the septum.
Choice T: True
Choice F: False

6. Concha suffered a stroke in her left temporal lobe. As a result, she will no longer be able to understand people when they speak to her, but she will be able to still speak Spanish.
Choice T: True
Choice F: False

7. Jean-Dominique Bauby likely suffered extensive damage to his frontal lobe, cerebellum and hypothalamus when he suffered the stroke that left him with locked-in syndrome.
Choice T: True
Choice F: False

8. At times, neurons fire action potentials that die out before they reach the synapse.
Choice T: True
Choice F: False

9. When a neurotransmitter causes inhibition in a post-synaptic cell, it causes the inside of the post-synaptic cell to become more negative.
Choice T: True
Choice F: False

10. Many anti-depressants work by increasing the reuptake of serotonin in the brain.
Choice T: True
Choice F: False

Multiple Choice Questions

Can you choose the best answer for these questions?

1. The part of the neuron that receives incoming signals from other neurons is the:
    A. axon.
    B. axon hillock.
    C. dendrite.
    D. cell body.

2. Randall suffered a severe brain injury when he fell while rock climbing. Since his accident, Randall has experienced severe disruptions in his sleep cycle. The likely site of Randall's brain injury is the:
    A. thalamus.
    B. hippocampus.
    C. hypothalamus.
    D. septum.

3. The _____ nervous system is most analogous to the auto-pilot feature on an airplane.
    A. peripheral
    B. central
    C. somatic
    D. autonomic

4. Yan had a stroke at age 55. Since his stroke, he can't seem to understand what people say to him, but has no paralysis. He can also produce speech, but he often says things that don't seem to make sense to others. For example, at dinner he may ask someone to pass him the umbrella instead of the salt. Which of the following brain structures was most likely damaged when Yan suffered his stroke?
    A. the left frontal lobe
    B. the right frontal lobe
    C. the left temporal lobe
    D. the right temporal lobe

5. The most common neurotransmitter in the healthy brain is:
    A. GABA.
    B. glutamate.
    C. serotonin.
    D. dopamine.

6. The motor cortex is found in the _____ lobe and the somatosensory cortex is found in the _____ lobe.
    A. frontal; parietal
    B. parietal; frontal
    C. temporal; parietal
    D. parietal; temporal

7. The diencephalon contains the _____ and the _____.
   - A. septum; hippocampus
   - B. amygdala; corpus callosum
   - C. pons; reticular activating system
   - D. thalamus; hypothalamus

8. The higher-order processes of thinking, planning, and the integration of sensory information occur in the brain's:
   - A. brainstem.
   - B. cortex.
   - C. cerebellum.
   - D. midbrain.

9. Juan and Juanita are twins. What kind of twins are they?
   - A. fraternal twins
   - B. identical twins
   - C. conjoined twins
   - D. We don't have enough information to say for sure.

10. The forebrain contains the:
    - A. cortex, midbrain, and brainstem.
    - B. RAS, limbic system, and corpus callosum.
    - C. limbic system, diencephalon, and cortex.
    - D. diencephalon, RAS, and midbrain.

11. Glia cells help neurons by doing all of the following except:
    - A. producing myelin.
    - B. maintaining the chemical environment of the neuron.
    - C. helping repair neural damage.
    - D. carrying neurotransmitters across the synapse.

12. The frontal lobe is responsible for all of the following except:
    - A. hearing.
    - B. language.
    - C. planning.
    - D. decision making.

13. An fMRI allows doctors to see:
    - A. the structure of the brain only.
    - B. which part of the brain is currently using the most radioactively tagged glucose.
    - C. which part of the brain is releasing the most energy from its oxygenated hemoglobin cells.
    - D. all of the above

14. _____ are natural painkillers in the brain.
    A. Endorphins
    B. Dopamine and serotonin
    C. Glutamates
    D. Hormones

15. The limbic system contains the:
    A. spinal cord and brainstem.
    B. amygdala, septum, and hippocampus.
    C. corpus callosum, thalamus, and hypothalamus.
    D. RAS, hippocampus, and amygdala.

16. Monique suffered brain damage in a car accident. After the accident she found that her memory for events that took place prior to the accident is fine, but she can no longer store new, permanent memories of what she experiences. Curiously, she is still able to learn new motor skills. For example, she recently learned to knit, but she doesn't remember going to knitting class. What part of Monique's brain was most likely damaged in her accident?
    A. the hypothalamus
    B. the frontal lobe
    C. the hippocampus
    D. the cerebellum

17. The _____ is thought to play a role in addictions.
    A. septum
    B. hippocampus
    C. amygdala
    D. hypothalamus

18. As an action potential begins to fire, what ion floods into the cell?
    A. potassium
    B. chloride
    C. sodium
    D. anions

19. _____ is the chief inhibitory neurotransmitter in the brain.
    A. Glutamate
    B. Endorphin
    C. Acetylcholine
    D. GABA

20. The_____ plays a role in the release of androgens in the body.
    A. adrenal cortex
    B. adrenal medulla
    C. pancreas
    D. thymus gland

21. A(n) _____ is a type of x-ray of the brain that is especially useful in helping doctors detect blood-flow problems in the brain.
    A. MRI
    B. fMRI
    C. EEG
    D. angiogram

22. Which part of the brain would be most likely to become active if a conscious person was touched on the right side of the face?
    A. the right frontal lobe
    B. the left frontal lobe
    C. the right parietal lobe
    D. the left parietal lobe

23. Look at the diagram below. If Nigel's brain were stimulated at the point marked by the "X" while he was conscious during brain surgery, what would likely happen?

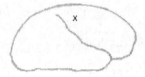

    A. He would feel pain on the right side of his body.
    B. He would feel pain on the left side of his body.
    C. There would be some movement on the right side of his body.
    D. There would be some movement on the left side of his body.

24. One of the effects of alcohol intoxication is that it impairs the function of the cerebellum. What symptom(s) does this impairment cause in a person?
    A. memory loss for events that occur while drunk
    B. lack of an ability to taste well
    C. loss of motor coordination and balance
    D. nausea and vomiting
    E. mood changes

25. The master gland of the endocrine system is the _____ gland.
    A. pineal
    B. thymus
    C. adrenal
    D. pituitary

Short-Answer Questions

Can you write a brief answer to these questions?

1. Think about our world today. What characteristics of humans would you expect to see in our species after the next 100,000 years of evolution? Why?

2. Shu Chen's doctor prescribed a drug for her that blocks the reuptake of dopamine in the brain. What effect will this drug cause at the synapse? For what condition did Shu Chen's doctor most likely prescribe this drug? What side effects would you expect to see in Shu Chen if she took too much of this drug?

Developing a Bigger Picture: Making Connections Across Chapters

An important aspect of learning is learning to see the "Big Picture" of the subject you are studying. As you learn about psychology, you should try to understand how the material from different chapters fits together to help you form a broad-based understanding of what psychology is all about. To help facilitate the development of this "Big Picture" in your mind, try to answer these questions using the knowledge you have learned in this chapter, as well as the other chapters referenced in the questions.

1. In Chapter 1, you learned about the use of experiments in psychological experiments. Using this knowledge, design an experiment to test the hypothesis that alcohol consumption reduces the intelligence of an adult rat.

2. In the preceding question, what ethical guidelines must you follow in your experiment?

3. In Chapter 1, you learned about functionalism as a school of thought in psychology. What questions would a functionalist ask in studying the brain?

4. In Chapter 1, you learned about the different perspectives in psychology. The content of Chapter 2 best illustrates which of these perspectives?

5. Could an experiment be conducted to test the hypothesis that men have larger frontal lobes than women do? Why or why not?

Label the Diagram

Can you label this picture of the brain with the appropriate terms?

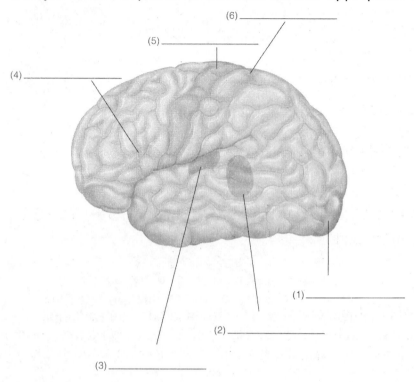

(6) _____

(5) _____

(4) _____

(1) _____

(2) _____

(3) _____

Big Picture Review

<table>
<tr><td colspan="3">Some Neurotransmitters, Their Functions, and Related Diseases and Clinical Conditions</td></tr>
<tr><th>Neurotransmitters</th><th>Functions</th><th>Related Diseases and Clinical Conditions</th></tr>
<tr><td>(1) _____</td><td>Excites skeletal muscles; Inhibits heart action; Memory</td><td>Alzheimer's disease</td></tr>
<tr><td>(2) _____</td><td>Movement; Learning; Attention; Motivation and reward</td><td>Parkinson's disease; Schizophrenia; Substance Abuse</td></tr>
<tr><td>(3) _____</td><td>Sleep; Arousal; Mood; Eating; Pain perception</td><td>Depression; Obsessive Compulsive Disorder; Some eating disorders; Chronic pain</td></tr>
<tr><td>(4) _____</td><td>Sleep; Arousal; Mood</td><td>Depression</td></tr>
<tr><td>(5) _____</td><td>Chief inhibitor; Regulates arousal</td><td>Some anxiety disorders; Some seizure disorders</td></tr>
<tr><td>(6) _____</td><td>Chief excitatory neurotransmitter; Many diverse functions</td><td>Neural death following head injuries</td></tr>
<tr><td>(7) _____</td><td>Suppression of pain; Eating; Cardiovascular functioning</td><td>Some indication of a link to mood</td></tr>
<tr><td>(8) _____</td><td>Carries pain signals</td><td>Some indication of a link to depression</td></tr>
</table>

Solutions

Each solution below is followed by its textbook page reference number and its corresponding chapter learning objective (LO) number. Items with a Big Picture LO help you build a Big Picture of psychology across the chapters you have studied so far.

Fill-in Review of the Chapter

1. locked-in syndrome [p. 46; LO 6]
2. brainstem or pons [p. 66; LO 6]
3. case study [p. 30; LO-Big Picture]
4. -70 mv [p. 52; LO 2]
5. negative [p. 52; LO 2]
6. positive [p. 52; LO 2]
7. negative [p. 52; LO 2]
8. excitation or depolarization [p. 52; LO 3]
9. synapse [p. 50; LO 1]
10. dendrite [p. 49; LO 1]
11. axon bulb [p. 49; LO 1]
12. quasi-experimental [p. 34; LO- Big Picture]
13. increases [p. 58; LO 4]
14. dopamine [p. 58; LO 4]
15. acetylcholine [p. 57; LO 4]
16. Alzheimer's [p. 57; LO 4]
17. level of the drug [p. 33; LO- Big Picture]
18. scores on memory test [p. 33; LO- Big Picture]
19. parasympathetic [p. 65; LO 5]
20. sympathetic [p. 65; LO 5]
21. somatic [p. 63; LO 5]
22. amygdala [p. 69; LO 6]
23. split-brain [p. 75; LO 6]
24. corpus callosum [p. 74; LO 6]
25. occipital [p. 73; LO 6]
26. hearing [p. 73; LO 6]
27. larger [p. 74; LO 6]
28. hypothalamus [p. 75; LO 6]
29. amygdala [p. 75; LO 6]
30. hippocampus [p. 70; LO 6]
31. MRI [p. 80; LO 7]
32. CAT [p. 80; LO 7]
33. androgens [p. 83; LO 8]
34. estrogens [p. 83; LO 8]
35. endocrine [p. 82; LO 8]
36. genes [p. 84; LO 9 & 10]
37. twin studies [p. 85; LO 9 & 10]
38. William James [p. 10; LO- Big Picture]

Use It or Lose It!

1. left motor cortex [p. 77; LO 6]
2. medulla [p. 66; LO 6]
3. left auditory cortex [p. 79; LO 6]
4. Broca's area [p. 73; LO 6]
5. right somatosensory cortex [p. 78; LO 6]
6. right and left visual cortex [p. 78; LO 6]
7. hypothalamus [p. 72; LO 6]
8. cerebellum [p. 67; LO 6]
9. amygdala [p. 69; LO 6]
10. hippocampus [p. 70; LO 6]

Self-Check: Are You Getting the Big Picture?

True or False Questions

1. F [p. 68; LO 6]
2. T [p. 84; LO 9]
3. T [p. 77; LO 6]
4. T [p. 80; LO 7]

5. F [p. 66; LO 6]
6. T [p. 73; LO 6]
7. F [p. 67; LO 6]
8. F [p. 52; LO 2]

9. T [p. 54; LO 3]
10. F [p. 59; LO 4]

Multiple Choice Questions

1. C [p. 49; LO 1]	10. C [p. 68; LO 6]	19. D [p. 59; LO 4]
2. C [p. 72; LO 6]	11. D [p. 48; LO 2]	20. A [p. 83; LO 8]
3. D [p. 63; LO 5]	12. A [p. 77; LO 6]	21. D [p. 81; LO 7]
4. C [p. 73; LO 6]	13. C [p. 81; LO 7]	22. D [p. 78; LO 6]
5. B [p. 60; LO 4]	14. A [p. 60; LO 4]	23. D [p. 77; LO 6]
6. A [p. 77; LO 6]	15. B [p. 68; LO 6]	24. C [p. 67; LO 6]
7. D [p. 68; LO 6]	16. C [p. 70; LO 6]	25. D [p. 82; LO 8]
8. B [p. 68; LO 6]	17. A [p. 69; LO 6]	
9. A [p. 85; LO 10]	18. C [p. 52; LO 2]	

Short-Answer Questions

Can you write a brief answer to these questions?

1. Think about our world today. What characteristics of humans would you expect to see in our species after the next 100,000 years of evolution? Why? [p. 86; LO 9 & 10]

Characteristics that survive in the human species for the next 100,000 years will be characteristics that help us survive and procreate in our environment. There are many possible answers here, but some possibilities are:

A genetic resistance to AIDS would be adaptive, especially if no cure is found in the near future. The ability to live in warmer environments might be beneficial due to global warming. The ability to think quickly and process information quickly might be beneficial as our technology increases and information overload becomes more and more of an issue. Genetic resistance to childhood cancers might also be seen in more people. Based on the current state of our world, these are just some of the possible changes we may see throughout our evolutionary future.

2. Shu Chen's doctor prescribed a drug for her that blocks the reuptake of dopamine in the brain. What effect will this drug cause at the synapse? For what condition did Shu Chen's doctor most likely prescribe this drug? What side effects would you expect to see in Shu Chen if she took too much of this drug? [p. 58; LO 4]

This drug will keep dopamine at the synapse for a longer period of time and in doing so will cause more reaction in the post-synaptic neuron than would normally occur. This drug would likely be prescribed for Parkinson's disease, a condition in which the person does not have enough dopamine in the brain. Side effects may include schizophrenic-like symptoms of hallucinations and delusions, which are associated with having too much dopamine action in the brain.

Developing a Bigger Picture: Making Connections Across Chapters

1. In Chapter 1, you learned about the use of experiments in psychological experiments. Using this knowledge, design an experiment to test the hypothesis that alcohol consumption reduces the intelligence of an adult rat. [p. 32; LO- Big Picture]

Here is one possible answer:

Randomly divide a group of 50 rats into two groups, a group that consumes .5 ounces of alcohol daily and a placebo group that consumes .5 ounces of flavored water a day. Keep the rats on this diet for 6 months. After 6 months, examine the rat's intelligence by measuring how long it takes the rat to learn to run through a maze.

2. In the preceding question, what ethical guidelines must you follow in your experiment? [p. 36; LO- Big Picture]

Because you wish to use animal subjects, you need to get IRB approval of your study. You must follow all laws concerning animals care and use. You must keep the animals clean, dry, fed, and as comfortable as possible in your study. You must minimize any pain to the animal, and you should only cause animal subjects discomfort if no suitable alternatives can be found. Any animal discomfort has to be offset by significant scientific gain.

3. In Chapter 1, you learned about functionalism as a school of thought in psychology. What questions would a functionalist ask in studying the brain? [p. 10; LO- Big Picture]

A functionalist would be concerned with the purpose or function of specific brain structures and mental abilities. Specifically he or she would be interested in how particular parts of the brain evolved through natural selection to help us survive and procreate in our environment.

4. In Chapter 1, you learned about the different perspectives in psychology. The content of Chapter 2 best illustrates which of these perspectives? [p. 15; LO- Big Picture]

Chapter 2 best illustrates the biological perspective because it emphasizes how our behavior is impacted by the biology of our bodies.

5. Could an experiment be conducted to test the hypothesis that men have larger frontal lobes than women do? Why or why not? [p. 34; LO- Big Picture]

No. Only a quasi-experiment could be done because you cannot randomly assign people to being male or female. Random assignment is required for a true experiment.

Label the Diagram

1. primary visual area [p. 73; LO 6]	4. Broca's area [p. 73; LO 6]
2. Wernicke's area [p. 73; LO 6]	5. primary motor area [p. 73; LO 6]
3. primary auditory area [p. 73; LO 6]	6. primary somatosensory area [p. 73; LO 6]

Big Picture Review

1. acetylcholine [p. 61; LO 4]	5. GABA [p. 61; LO 4]
2. dopamine [p. 61; LO 4]	6. glutamate [p. 61; LO 4]
3. serotonin [p. 61; LO 4]	7. endorphins [p. 61; LO 4]
4. norepinephrine [p. 61; LO 4]	8. substance P [p. 61; LO 4]

3

How Do We Sense and Perceive Our World?

Learning Objectives

After studying each of the following sections of the chapter, you should be able to do these tasks.

Measuring Sensation and Perception

1. Explain the concepts of absolute threshold, just noticeable difference (jnd), and signal detection used in measuring sensation and perception.

Vision: The World Through Our Eyes

2. Describe the physical properties of light – wavelength, amplitude, and the visible spectrum – and how they relate to human vision.
3. Describe the anatomy of the eye and the layers of the retina and how they function.
4. Explain how we adapt to light and dark, how we see color, and how the brain processes what we see.

Hearing: The World We Hear

5. Describe the physical properties of sound and how they relate to what we hear: pitch and loudness.
6. Be able to locate the outer, middle, and inner ear, list their major structures, and describe their roles in hearing.

Taste, Smell, Touch, and the Body Senses

7. Explain the processes involved in taste, smell, touch, and the body senses.

Perception: Interpreting Sensory Information

8. Describe top-down and bottom-up perceptual processing and explain the differences between them.
9. Give an overview of perceptual constancy theories and how we perceive depth.

How Accurate Are Our Perceptions?

10. Describe some of the common perceptual illusions we experience and explain their causes.
11. Explain how culture affects perception.

The Big Picture

The Big Picture: How Do We Take It All In?

In this chapter, we explore the ways in which we sense and perceive the world. Sensation is the act of transducing, or changing environmental energy into neural impulses, whereas perception is the interpretation of this sensory information. Everyday of our lives, we both sense and perceive our world. However, the opening story of Michael Watson shows us that we do not all sense and perceive the world in the same way. Watson's case is an extreme example of the uniqueness of our personal sensory and perceptual experiences. Watson's condition, synesthesia, led him to perceive tastes as shapes rather than flavors – an experience that most of us cannot relate to. Because Watson's neural pathways are not typical, neither is his sensation or perception. But, after studying this chapter you should have a good grasp on how the rest of us tend to sense and perceive the world.

Measuring Sensation and Perception

This section covers Learning Objective 1. Psychophysics is the study of how physical properties of energy relate to our sensation and perception of that energy. Among other things, psychophysicists study concepts like the absolute threshold, just noticeable difference, and signal detection for the various senses. Absolute threshold is the minimum intensity of a stimulus that can be detected 50% of the time. The just noticeable difference is the minimum change in intensity of a stimulus that can be detected 50% of the time. Signal detection is a method of measuring the relative proportions of hits, misses, and false alarms that occur when we are sensing the world. Signal detection helps psychophysicists get an unbiased view of our sensory capabilities.

Vision: The World Through Our Eyes

This section covers Learning Objectives 2-4. You learned that the eye allows us to transduce light energy into neural impulses. Light passes through the pupil and is focused on the retina by the lens of the eye. In the retina, specialized cells called rods and cones contain photopigments that become active when light hits them. The photopigments in rods are sensitive to all colors of light, whereas cones contain photopigments that are only sensitive to specific colors of light. Trichromatic theory states that one reason we see color is that we have cones in the retina that only respond to specific colors of light. Opponent-process theory says that another reason we see color is that we have dual-action cells in the visual system that can respond to only one of two colors of light at a time. Together, these two processes ensure that we can perceive color in the world.

When the photopigments of the rods and cones react to the light we see, the resulting neural messages are sent to the brain for further processing. They are first sent to the lateral geniculate nucleus of the thalamus and then to the occipital lobe of the cortex where interpretation or perception of the visual information occurs.

Hearing: The World We Hear

This section covers Learning Objectives 5 & 6. In audition (or hearing), our ears transduce sound waves into neural impulses. In the ear, sound waves set up vibrations in the ear drum, which are then transmitted through the bones of the middle ear to the cochlea of the inner ear. Inside the cochlea on the basilar membrane, hair cells begin to first vibrate and then to begin firing action potentials. These action potentials are thought to tell our brain which sounds we are hearing through several processes. Frequency and volley theories say that our brain can tell what pitch we are hearing by the rate at which the hair cells are firing action potentials. Place theory says that our brain understands pitch by looking at which region of the basilar membrane is firing the most action potentials. And, duplicity theory states that a combination of frequency and place theory is needed to explain our perception of pitch.

Taste, Smell, Touch, and the Body Senses

This section covers Learning Objective 7. Taste and smell are both chemical senses in which molecules from the substances we taste and smell are picked up by receptors in the nose and tongue, called odor receptors and taste buds respectively. When our odor receptors and taste buds are excited, we perceive smells and tastes. Currently, psychologists believe that the tongue has taste buds for only four or five distinct flavors and the nose has odor receptors that are sensitive to perhaps only a few hundred different smells.

Touch, pain, and temperature are sensed when specialized receptors in the skin are stimulated by pressure or temperature changes. Ultimately signals from these skin receptors are processed in the somatosensory cortex of the brain.

In addition to vision, hearing, taste, smell, and touch we also experience what are called the body senses – kinesthesis and vestibular sense. Kinesthesis uses feedback from our muscles, joints, and tendons to tell us where our body is located in space. While our vestibular sense uses feedback from the vestibular organs of the inner ear to give us our sense of balance. Both of these senses are necessary for us to execute graceful, controlled movements of our body.

Perception: Interpreting the Sensory Information

This section covers Learning Objectives 8 & 9. Information from all of our senses is ultimately interpreted or perceived in the cortex of the brain. Through the process of perception, we make sense of our sensory information. In general, there are two types of perceptual processes: top-down and bottom-up perceptual processes.

Top-down perceptual processing is perception that uses prior knowledge to interpret sensory information. For example, reading this text requires prior knowledge of English to perceive the marks on this page as meaningful words.

Bottom-up perceptual processing is perception that does not use prior knowledge. In bottom-up perception, the perception is built from the bottom-up using only the characteristics of the stimulus being perceived. An example of this type of processing would be seeing an object that does not look like anything you've seen before, such as a piece of abstract art that doesn't remind you of anything in particular.

Several processes in the brain and mind help us with our perception. For example, our brain corrects our perceptions for size, shape, and brightness to give us a constant view of the world. We see depth because retinal disparity gives us binocular depth perception and monocular depth cues tell us that certain objects in the world are farther away than others. The Gestalt rules of perception: figure-ground, closure, proximity, similarity, and good continuation explain how we organize our sensations into coherent perceptions of the world. And, feature detectors in the cortex fire only when we sense certain stimuli in the world. All of these processes together explain how we interpret what we see, hear, taste, smell, and touch.

How Accurate Are Our Perceptions?

This section covers Learning Objectives 10 & 11. Like most things, however, perception is not a perfect process. We do make perceptual mistakes at times. For example, the moon, Ponzo, and Mueller-Lyer illusions occur because of perceptual constancies in the brain. And, many times top-down processing can lead to errors in judgment – such as when personal biases affect the perception of eyewitnesses. Our perception is also affected by the culture in which we live. For example, people who live in non-carpentered areas of the world do not experience the Mueller-Lyer illusion like those of us who are used to seeing buildings with right angles in their design. Despite such issues, the majority of the time our sensory and perceptual systems work quite well.

Outlining the Big Picture

Chapter 3: How Do We Sense and Perceive Our World?

The Big Picture: How Do We Take It All In?
Richard Cytowic's *The Man Who Tasted Shapes*
Notes:

_____

_____

_____

_____

_____

_____

_____

Measuring Sensation and Perception (Learning Objective 1)
Absolute Thresholds
Signal Detection Theory
Just Noticeable Difference
Processing Without Awareness: Subliminal Stimulation of the Senses
Notes:

_____

_____

_____

_____

_____

_____

Vision: The World Through Our Eyes (Learning Objectives 2-4)
How Vision Works: Light Waves and Energy
    Measuring Light: Wavelength and Amplitude
    Properties of Light: Hue, Brightness, and Saturation
The Anatomy of the Outer Eye
    The Cornea, Pupil, Iris, and Lens
The Retina: Light Energy to Neural Messages
    The Anatomy of the Retina
    The Optic Nerve and the Blindspot
    The Rods and Cones
    Turning Light Energy Into Neural Messages
Adapting to Light and Darkness
How We See Color
    The Colors of Light
    The Trichromatic Theory of Color Vision
    Color Blindness
    The Opponent-Process Theory of Color Vision
    Trichromatic Theory or Opponent-Process Theory?
The Visual Pathways of the Brain
    The Optic Chiasm and Our Cross-Wired Brain
    Do Men and Women See the World Differently?

Notes:

_____

_____

_____

_____

_____

Hearing: The World We Hear (Learning Objectives 5 & 6)
How Hearing Works: Vibrating Sound Waves
The Anatomy and Function of the Ear
 The Outer Ear
 The Middle Ear
 The Inner Ear
The Auditory Pathways of the Brain
 Place Theory of Pitch Perception
 Frequency Theory of Pitch Perception
 Volley Theory of Pitch Perception
 Duplicity Theory: An Integration
Notes:

_____

_____

_____

_____

_____

Taste, Smell, Touch, and the Body Senses (Learning Objective 7)
Taste: Information from the Tongue
 Properties of Taste: The Four – or Five – Tastes
 The Anatomy and Function of the Tongue
 Taste Pathways in the Brain
 Spotlight on Diversity: What We Eat and What We Taste
Smell: Aromas, Odors, and a Warning System
 Olfactory Pathways: The Limits of Our Knowledge
 Pheromones

Touch: The Skin Sense
The Body Senses: Experiencing the Physical Body in Space
  Kinesthesis
  The Vestibular Sense
Notes:

_____

_____

_____

_____

Perception: Interpreting Sensory Information (Learning Objectives 8 & 9)
Using What We Know: Top-Down Perceptual Processing
Building a Perception "From Scratch": Bottom-up Perceptual Processing
Understanding What We Sense: Perceiving Shape, Size, and Brightness
Depth Perception: Sensing Our 3-D World with 2-D Eyes
  Binocular Depth Perception
  Monocular Depth Cues
Perceiving Form: The Gestalt Approach
Perceiving Form: Feature Detection Theory
Notes:

_____

_____

_____

_____

How Accurate Are Our Perceptions? (Learning Objectives 10 & 11)
Errors Due to Top-Down Processing: Seeing What We Expect to See
Errors Due to Perceptual Constancy: Tricks of the Brain
  The Moon Illusion
  The Ponzo Illusion
  The Mueller-Lyer Illusion

Cultural Factors in Perception
Notes:

_____

_____

_____

_____

_____

Are You Getting the Big Picture?
Notes:

_____

_____

_____

_____

_____

Seeing the Big Picture: A Mental Map of Chapter 3

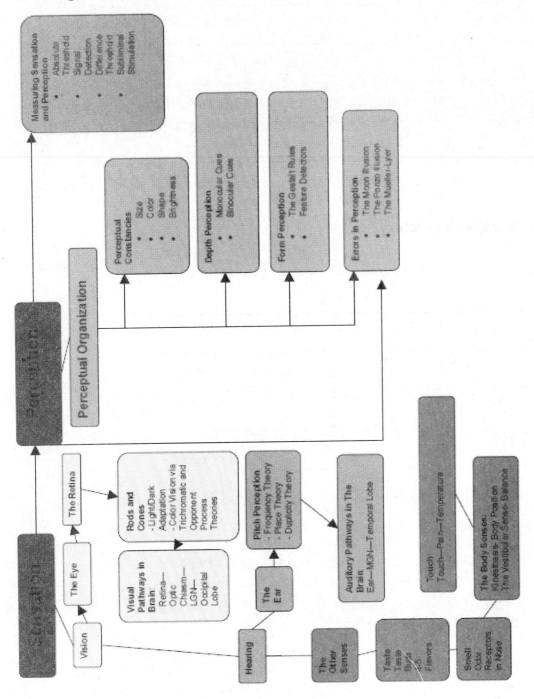

Key Points of the Big Picture

Absolute threshold:
the minimum intensity of a stimulus at which participants can identify its presence 50% of the time. *Example: The smallest amount of salt that you can taste on your popcorn 50% of the time would be your absolute threshold for tasting salt.*

Accommodation:
the process through which the lens is stretched or squeezed to focus light on the retina. *Example: When you read these words, your must first accommodate to bring them into focus.*

Amplitude:
a physical property of some energies that corresponds to the height of the wave peaks.

Attention:
conscious awareness; can be focused on events that are taking place in the environment or inside our minds. *Example: As you read this page, you are paying attention to its content, but you may also be tempted to pay attention to other things as well— such as a TV in the background.*

Auditory nerve:
the nerve that carries information from the inner ear to the brain.

Basilar membrane:
the structure in the cochlear duct, which contains the hair cells, which transduce sound waves into action potentials.

Binocular depth cues:
depth cues that utilize information from both eyes. *Example: The two slightly different images of this page that are projected onto each of your retinas.*

Blindspot:
the point where the optic nerve leaves the retina, where there are no rods or cones.

Bottom-up processing:
perception that is not guided by prior knowledge or expectations. *Example: When doing "Magic Eye 3-d" puzzles, you have to use bottom-up perception.*

Brightness:
the intensity of light; it corresponds to the amplitude of the light waves. *Example: Sunlight is brighter than a 20-watt lightbulb.*

Closure:
a Gestalt principle of perception that states that when we look at a stimulus, we have a tendency to see it as a closed in shape, rather than as lines. *Example: You would perceive a figure as a circle, even if it was slightly open at the top.*

Cochlea:
the curled, fluid-filled tube that contains the basilar membrane in the inner ear.

Color blindness:
a condition in which a person cannot perceive one or more colors due the lack of specific cones in the retina. *Example: John cannot distinguish between reds and greens due to his colorblindness.*

Cones:
the cells of the retina that are sensitive to specific colors of light and send information to the brain concerning the colors we are seeing.

Cycle:
a physical characteristic of energy defined as a wave peak and the valley that immediately follows it.

Dark adaptation:
the process through which our eyes adjust to dark conditions after having been exposed to bright light. *Example: You would experience this if your flashlight batteries died while hiking through the woods at night.*

Decibels (dB):
the unit of measure used to determine the loudness of a sound.

Dermis:
the inner layer of the skin.

Duplicity theory:
proposes that a combination of volley and place theory explain how our brain decodes pitch. *Example: Your brain uses both the location of maximum activation on your basilar membrane and the frequency at which your hair cells are firing to tell it what pitch you are hearing.*

Epidermis:
the outer layer of our skin that contains the touch receptors. *Example: Look at your arm. You are looking at your epidermis.*

Feature detection theory:
a theory of perception that proposes the existence of feature detectors or cortical cells that only fire when we see certain visual stimuli such as shapes, colors of light, or movements. *Example: A cat may have certain cortical cells that fire only when the cat sees a line oriented at a 45 degree angle to the right.*

Feature detectors:
specialized cells in the visual cortex that fire only when they receive input that indicates we are looking at a particular shape, color, angle, or other visual feature. *Example: The actual cortical cells that would fire when a cat sees a line oriented at a 45 degree angle to the right.*

Figure-ground:
a Gestalt principle of perception, which says that when we perceive a stimulus, we visually pull the *figure* part of the stimulus forward while visually pushing backward the background, or *ground*, part of the stimulus. *Example: If you look down at your hand lying on the desk top, your hand represents the figure and the desktop represents the ground.*

Frequency:
a physical characteristic of energy defined as the number of cycles that occur in a given unit of time. *Example: 9000 Hz, means 9000 cycles per second.*

Frequency theory:
proposes that our brain decodes pitch directly from the frequency at which the hair cells of the basilar membrane are firing. *Example: If you hear a 1000 Hz sound, your hair cells fire 1000 action potentials per second.*

Gestalt approach:
a psychological school of thought originating in Germany that proposed that the whole of a perception must be understood rather than trying to deconstruct perception into its parts.

Good continuation:
a Gestalt principle of perception that states that we have a preference for perceiving stimuli that seem to follow one another as being part of a continuing pattern. *Example: When you sign on the proverbial dotted line, you perceive it as a line – even though it is a series of dashes.*

Gustation:
the sense of taste. *Example: Tasting a yummy taco.*

Hair cells:
neurons that grow out of the basilar membrane and transduce sounds waves into action potentials.

Hue:
the color of a light. *Example: Red, blue, etc.*

Just noticeable difference (jnd):
the minimum change of intensity of a stimulus that participants can detect 50% of the time. *Example: The smallest amount of cinnamon added to your cinnamon toast that you would notice 50% of the time.*

Kinethesis:
our ability to sense the position of our body parts in relation to one another and in relation to space. *Example: When you bend over to tie your shoes, your vestibular sense informs your brain that your head is now upside down.*

Lateral geniculate nucleus (LGN):
the part of the thalamus that processes visual information en route to the cortex.

Lens:
the part of the eye that lies behind the pupil and focuses light rays on the retina.

Light adaptation:
the process through which our eyes adjust to bright light after having been exposed to darkness. *Example: If your sleeping partner were to suddenly turn on the bedroom lights, you would likely begin experiencing light adaptation.*

Lock-and-key theory:
proposes that olfactory receptors are excited by odor molecules in a fashion that is similar to how neurotransmitters excite receptor sites.

Loudness:
loudness is the psychophysical property of sound that corresponds to the amplitude of a sound wave. *Example: A truck horn will produce higher amplitude sound waves than a door bell will.*

Monocular depth cues:
depth cues that require information from only one eye. *Example: Drawing a house high on your canvas so that the viewer perceives it to be far away.*

Olfaction:
the sense of smell. *Example: Smelling food before you eat it is an important part enjoying a meal.*

Olfactory epithelium:
a special piece of skin at the top of the nasal cavity that contains the olfactory receptors.

Opponent-process theory:
proposes that we have dual-action cells beyond the level of the retina that signal the brain when we see one of a pair of colors. *Example: Explains why you might see green flashes of light after staring at a red stoplight for several minutes.*

Optic chiasm:
the point in the brain where the optic nerve from the left eye crosses over the optic nerve from the right eye.

Optic nerve:
the structure that conveys visual information away from the retina to the brain.

Papillae:
bumps on our tongue that many people mistake for taste buds.

Perception:
the process through which we interpret sensory information. *Example: You use your knowledge of English to help you perceive these words.*

Pheromones:
airborne chemicals that are released from glands and detected by the vomeronasal organs in some animals and perhaps humans. *Example: Humans may be able to sense the pheromones of potential sexual partners.*

Photopigments:
light-sensitive chemicals that create electrical changes when they come into contact with light.

Pitch:
the psychophysical property of sound that corresponds to the frequency of a sound wave. *Example: Sopranos sing at a higher frequency and therefore pitch than baritones do.*

Place theory:
proposes that our brain decodes pitch by noticing which region of the basilar membrane is most active. *Example: When listening to a soprano sing, specific regions of the basilar membrane would be most active. When listening to a baritone sing, different regions of the basilar membrane would be most active.*

Proximity:
a Gestalt principle of perception that states that we tend to group close objects together during perception. *Example: As you read this sentence, you use proximity to help you see where one word ends and another begins.*

Psychophysics:
the study of how the mind interprets the physical properties of stimuli. *Example: A psychophysicist might try to determine why some foods taste more intense than others.*

Pupil:
the hole in the iris through which light enters the eye. *Example: In dim conditions, your pupil dilates to allow in more light.*

Retina:
the structure at the back of the eye that contains cells that transduce light into neural signals. *Example: When you read these words, your retina is transducing the light bouncing off of this page into neural signals.*

Retinal disparity:
a binocular depth cue that uses the difference in the images projected on the right and left retinas to inform the brain about the distance of a stimulus. *Example: Seeing two slightly different images of your friend's face with each of your retinas.*

Rods:
the light-sensitive cells of the retina that pick up any type of light energy and convert it to neural signals. *Example: If you only had rods in your retina, your world would look like a black and white movie.*

Saturation:
the purity of light; pure light or saturated light consists of a single wavelength. *Example: A pure blue light, consisting of a single hue of blue, would be saturated.*

Sensation:
the process through which our sense organs transduce environmental energies such as light and sound into neural impulses. *Example: The fact that you can see this sentence is due to sensation.*

Signal detection:
a method of analyzing the relative proportions of hits and false alarms to eliminate the effects of response bias in a participant's detection of a stimulus. *Example: Thinking you heard thunder when you did not is a false alarm. Thinking you heard thunder, when indeed you did hear thunder is a hit. Psychologists would analyze the proportion of hits and false alarms you experience during a storm to determine exactly how sensitive you are to hearing thunder.*

Similarity:
a Gestalt principle of perception that states that we tend to group like objects together during perception. *Example: When viewing a TV screen or a computer monitor, you group the pixels on the screen together based on common color to help you perceive the image on the screen.*

Subliminal:
when the intensity of a stimulus is below the participant's absolute threshold and the participant is not consciously aware of the stimulus. *Example: An image flashed on a computer screen for only 1/10,000 of a second would be too brief to be consciously perceived.*

Taste buds:
the sense organs for taste that are found between the papillae on the tongue. *Example: Your taste buds allow you to perceive the flavor of your lunch.*

Top-down processing:
perception that is guided by prior knowledge or expectations. *Example: When you see your best friend, you use your knowledge of what he or she looks like to help you perceive their face.*

Transduction:
the process through which our sense organs convert environmental energies into neural impulses. *Example: When you smell baking bread, your nose must transduce the aroma into neural signals so that you can sense its smell.*

Trichromatic theory of color vision:
the idea that color vision is made possible by the presence of three different types of cones in the retina which react respectively to either red, green, or yellow light. *Example: When you look at a green light on a stoplight, your green cones will fire fastest, telling your brain that you are seeing a green light.*

Vestibular sense:
the sense of balance. *Example: You use your vestibular sense as you walk, turn your head, and so on. It keeps your brain informed of the orientation of your head.*

Visible spectrum:
the spectrum of light that humans can see. *Example: You can see red light, but you cannot sense X-rays.*

Volley theory:
proposes that our brain decodes pitch by noticing the frequency at which *groups* of hair cells on the basilar membrane are firing.

Wavelength:
a physical property of some energies that corresponds to the distance between the wave peaks.

Weber's law:
a psychophysical formula used to predict the jnd for a given stimulus: $\Delta I/I = k$ Where ΔI is the change in the stimulus required to produce a jnd, I is the original intensity of the stimulus, and k is a constant that varies for each of the five senses. *Example: k for*

weight is 1/40. If you pick up a 10lb weight, you would have to pick up an additional .25lbs to experience a jnd. On the other hand, if you pick up a 100lb weight, you would have to pick up an additional 2.5lbs to have a jnd.

Fill-in Review of the Chapter

Can you fill-in the missing terms for each section of the chapter? Items marked with an * encourage you to continue building the Big Picture of psychology by connecting the material in this chapter with to material from previous chapters in the text.

The Big Picture: How Do We Take It All In?

Michael Watson had a condition called 1)_____ which caused him to perceive shapes when he tasted different flavors.

Measuring Sensation and Perception

The minimum amount of stimulation that can be detected 50% of the time by a person is called the 2) _____ _____.

Sensory stimulation that occurs below a level of awareness is said to be 3)_____.

If k= 1/40 for weight and you are holding a 25lb weight, you would have to add 4)_____ pounds of weight to experience a jnd.

Vision: The World Through Our Eyes

5) _____ _____ states that we see color because we have cones in the 6)_____ that are maximally sensitive to particular wavelengths of light.

Negative afterimages are best explained by the 7)_____ theory of color vision.

8) _____ in the rods and cones of our eyes release electricity when struck by light.

The 9) _____ of the eye focuses light on the retina.

The LGN is part of the brain's 10*) _____.

A brain tumor in the 11*) _____ lobe of the brain would most likely disturb one's vision.

Hearing: The World We Hear

12) _____ _____ in the 13)_____ fire action potentials as they begin to vibrate in response to sound waves traveling through the auditory system.

Pitch is determined by a sound wave's 14) _____.

15) _____ theory integrates aspects of frequency and volley theory.

Hearing is processed in the 16*) _____ lobe of the cortex.

Hair cells grow from the 17) _____ _____ of the cochlea.

Taste, Smell, Touch, and the Other Body Senses

The basic tastes are 18) _____, 19)_____, 20)_____, 21)_____, and perhaps 22)_____.

According to Dr. Linda Bartoshuk, a person who has a large number of tastebuds on his or her tongue is a 23) _____.

24) _____ is a body sense that tells us where our body is in three-dimensional space, and the 25)_____ _____ is a body sense that helps us maintain our balance.

In addition to the vestibular organs, the 26*) _____ of the brain helps us maintain balance.

Transduction of smell occurs in the 27) _____ _____.

Perception: Interpreting Sensory Information

Juan was mowing his lawn when he spotted an object up ahead in the grass. At first, he thought the object was a large rock, but as he neared the object, he saw that it was a discarded tire that someone had thrown into his yard. Juan's perceptual error is most likely due to 28) _____ perceptual processing.

When listening to an unfamiliar piece of classical music, you would most likely rely on 29) _____ perceptual processing.

30) _____ _____ are specialized cells in the cortex that fire neural signals only when certain stimuli are perceived.

The 31) _____school of thought in psychology is most closely aligned with the study of form perception.

How Accurate Are Our Perceptions?

The 32) _____ illusion occurs when the moon looks larger on the horizon than it does when it is overhead.

The 33) _____ illusion has been shown to be less common in non-carpentered cultures.

Use It or Lose It!

Task	Answer
1. List the cells of the human retina.	
2. List the monocular depth cues.	
3. List the Gestalt rules of perception.	
4. List the opponent-process cells of the human visual system.	

Self-Check: Are You Getting the Big Picture?

After you have read and studied the chapter, see if you can answer the following quiz questions. Check your answers at the end of the chapter. If you miss a question, refer to your text and re-study the appropriate sections.

True or False Questions

Are these statements true or false?

1. We have at least four different types of cones in our retinas.
   Choice T: True
   Choice F: False

2. Women tend to suffer color blindness more than men.
   Choice T: True
   Choice F: False

3. According to Gestalt psychologists, humans have a preference for seeing closed in forms over seeing lines.
   Choice T: True
   Choice F: False

4. Almost all sensory information passes through the thalamus before being sent to the cortex of the brain.
   Choice T: True
   Choice F: False

5. Lock-and-key theory states that we have odor receptors in the olfactory epithelium that are stimulated by specific odor molecules.
   Choice T: True
   Choice F: False

6. All cone cells in the retina contain the same photopigment.
   Choice T: True
   Choice F: False

7. Many animals sense pheromones with their vomeronasal organ.
   Choice T: True
   Choice F: False

8. Pressure on the skin deforms the axonal membrane of our neurons that are sensitive to touch and allows negative ions to enter into the axon. These negative ions cause the neuron to begin firing action potentials that signal to the brain that we are experiencing the sense of touch.
   Choice T: True
   Choice F: False

9. Retinal disparity allows us to sense depth using binocular depth cues.
   Choice T: True
   Choice F: False

10. Figure-ground is a monocular depth cue.
    Choice T: True
    Choice F: False

Multiple Choice Questions

Can you choose the best answer for these questions?

1. On day while walking down a crowded city street, Jennifer thought she saw an old friend, only to find that she was mistaken. In signal detection theory terms, Jennifer's judgment would be considered to be a(n):
   A. correct rejection.
   B. hit.
   C. false alarm.
   D. miss.

2. In Weber's law, k represents:
   A. a constant.
   B. the original intensity of the stimulus.
   C. the change in the intensity of the stimulus.
   D. none of the above.

3. As light strikes the retina, the first layer of cells it encounters will be the:
   A. amacrine cells.
   B. bipolar cells.
   C. rods and cones.
   D. ganglion cells.

4. Gaylan just walked outside after having spent the last hour in a darkened theater watching a film. At first, he has trouble seeing because his retinal cells have a large supply of _____ built up and he undergoes _____.
   A. oxygen; dark adaptation
   B. photopigment; dark adaptation
   C. oxygen; light adaptation
   D. photopigment; light adaptation

5. The _____ cells of the retina only respond to certain colors of light.
   A. rod
   B. cone
   C. amacrine
   D. bipolar

6. Opponent-process cells are most likely to be found where in the visual system?
   A. the retina
   B. the sclera
   C. the rods
   D. the LGN

7. Reading your best-friend's handwriting is a challenge because his writing is very messy and many of his letters are not fully formed. In order to successfully read his writing, you most likely have to engage in what type of perceptual processing?
   A. top-down
   B. bottom-up
   C. Gestalt processing
   D. modified feature detection

8. A gymnast would have to have particularly well-developed abilities for which the following senses?
   A. hearing
   B. kinesthesis
   C. vestibular sense
   D. b & c

76

9. The skin on which part of your body has the highest number of touch receptors?
   A. the top of your forearm
   B. the back of your thigh
   C. your upper chest (if you are male)
   D. your fingertips

10. When experiencing age-related hearing loss, we tend to first lose our ability to hear higher frequency pitches. Which theory of hearing best explains this phenomenon?
    A. frequency theory
    B. place theory
    C. opponent-process theory
    D. volley theory

11. Frequency theory best explains how we perceive pitches up to:
    A. 150 Hz.
    B. 1000 Hz.
    C. 10,000 Hz.
    D. 15,000 Hz.

12. What cells will only fire when we see stimuli with specific shape and orientation in our world?
    A. amacrine.
    B. bipolar.
    C. opponent-process.
    D. feature detectors.

13. Which Gestalt rule of perception best explains why a rattlesnake that is hidden in the rocks is difficult for us to perceive while hiking up a mountain?
    A. similarity
    B. proximity
    C. good continuation
    D. closure

14. As Juan was walking down the road, he thought he saw a puddle of water up ahead on the sidewalk. As Juan neared the "puddle", he realized that it was actually a discarded jump rope lying on the ground. Which Gestalt rule of perception best explains why Juan first misperceived the jump rope as a puddle?
    A. closure
    B. good continuation
    C. similarity
    D. proximity

15. The _____ of light determines the _____ of the light we see.
    A. wavelength; brightness
    B. wavelength; hue
    C. amplitude; hue
    D. amplitude; saturation

16. The semicircular canals are part of our_____ system.
    A. visual
    B. taste
    C. vestibular
    D. touch

17. The olfactory epithelium likely contains _____ different types of odor receptors.
    A. four
    B. over one hundred
    C. over one thousand
    D. over ten thousand

18. The outer layer of the skin is called the:
    A. dermis.
    B. endodermis.
    C. epidermis.
    D. mesodermis.

19. Touch information is ultimately processed in the _____ lobe of the brain.
    A. occipital
    B. frontal
    C. temporal
    D. parietal

20. Pressure on our skin deforms the axonal membranes of our touch receptors and allows ions to enter into the neuron, causing the neurons to fire action potentials. This is an example of what process?
    A. sensation
    B. perception
    C. a & b
    D. none of the above

21. The cells on the basilar membrane that allow us to hear sound are called:
    A. papillae.
    B. rod cells.
    C. hair cells.
    D. ganglion cells.

22. Vicary's famous experiments on subliminal perception taught us what about the effectiveness of subliminal perception in persuading people to buy more snacks during a movie?
    A. It taught us nothing. It was largely a hoax.
    B. That subliminal perception can be a highly effective advertisement tool.
    C. That subliminal perception actually makes us more resistant to persuasion.
    D. That subliminal perception does not occur.

23. Research on sex differences in vision show that:
    A. women prefer simplistic color schemes.
    B. men prefer complex color schemes.
    C. men prefer warm colors to cool ones.
    D. women prefer warm colors to cool ones.

24. The frequency of a sound wave determines the _____ of the sound we perceive.
    A. loudness
    B. timbre
    C. pitch
    D. distortion

25. Going from the auditory canal to the oval window of the inner ear, the correct order of the ossicles is:
    A. stirrup, anvil, hammer.
    B. anvil, hammer, stirrup.
    C. hammer, anvil, stirrup.
    D. hammer, stirrup, anvil.

Short-Answer Questions

Can you write a brief answer to these questions?

1. Which theory best explains how we perceive pitch? Explain.

2. How is our sense of taste similar to our sense of vision?

3. No matter where you sit in a classroom, you always perceive that the blackboard (or white board) at the front of the room is rectangular in shape. Why is this true when the image the board projects onto your retina actually does change shape as you view the board from different locations in the room?

4. Why must artists use monocular depth cues to portray depth in a painting?

5. Does culture affect perception? Explain.

Developing a Bigger Picture: Making Connections Across Chapters

An important aspect of learning is learning to see the "Big Picture" of the subject you are studying. As you learn about psychology, you should try to understand how the material from different chapters fits together to help you form a broad-based understanding of what psychology is all about. To help facilitate the development of this "Big Picture" in your mind, try to answer these questions using the knowledge you have learned in this chapter, as well as the other chapters referenced in the questions.

1. In Chapter 1, you learned about the experimental method. Design a study to test the hypothesis that women more than men prefer warm colors to cooler colors.

2. In Chapter 2, you learned about the structures of the brain, including some that were important to sensation and perception. Based on what you have learned in Chapters 2 & 3, where in the brain would you look for a tumor in a patient who was experiencing strange visual symptoms?

3. In Chapter 12, you will read about prejudice and racism. Based on your current understanding of these topics, how might they affect a person's perceptual processes?

Label the Diagram

Can you label the cells shown in this picture of a cross-section of the retina?

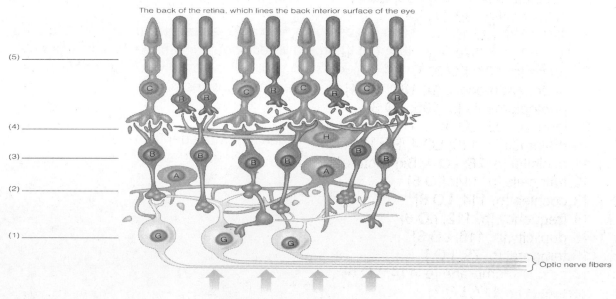

The back of the retina, which lines the back interior surface of the eye

(5) _____

(4) _____

(3) _____

(2) _____

(1) _____

Optic nerve fibers

Light rays entering from the outer eye

Big Picture Review

Theories of Pitch Perception

Theory	Description
(1) _____	Different pitches of sound activate specific regions of the basilar membrane more than others. Pitch perception occurs when the brain notices which portions of the basilar membrane are being most excited by incoming sound waves.
(2) _____	The hair cells of the basilar membrane fire action potentials at a rate equal to the frequency of the incoming sound wave. The brain determines pitch by noticing the rate at which the hair cells are firing. This theory only explains perception of pitches up to 1000 Hz, the maximum firing rate of a hair cell.
(3) _____	Similar to frequency theory, this theory states that groups of hair cells fire as teams to give us the perception of pitches over 1000 Hz. For example, three hair cells firing at 1000 Hz each together yield the perception of a 3000-Hz tone.
(4) _____	States that a combination of frequency and place information is used in pitch perception. Exactly how these sources of information are integrated in the brain is still being investigated.

Solutions

Self-Check: Are You Getting the Big Picture?

Fill-in Review of the Chapter

1. synesthesia [p.95; LO 7]
2. absolute threshold [p. 96; LO 1]
3. subliminal [p. 99; LO 1]
4. 1.6 [p. 98; LO 1]
5. trichromatic theory [p. 107; LO 4]
6. retina [p. 107; LO 3, 4]
7. opponent process [p. 108; LO 4]
8. photopigments [p. 105; LO 3]
9. lens [p. 102; LO 3]
10. thalamus [p. 110; LO 4, Big Picture]
11. occipital [p. 78; LO 4, Big Picture]
12. hair cells [p. 114; LO 6]
13. cochlea [p. 114; LO 6]
14. frequency [p. 112; LO 6]
15. duplicity [p. 116; LO 6]
16. temporal [p. 79; LO]
17. basilar membrane [p. 114; LO 6]
18. sweet [p. 117; LO 7]
19. salty [p. 117 LO 7]

20. sour [p. 117; LO 7]
21. bitter [p. 117; LO 7]
22. umami [p. 118; LO 7]
23. supertasters [p. 120; LO 7]
24. kinesthesis [p. 124; LO 7]
25. vestibular sense [p. 124; LO 7]
26. cerebellum [p. 67; LO 7, Big Picture]
27. olfactory epithelium [p. 121; LO 7]
28. top-down [p. 126; LO 8]
29. bottom-up [p. 127; LO 8]
30. feature detectors [p. 110; LO 8]
31. Gestalt [p. 130; LO 9]
32. moon [p. 134; LO 10]
33. Müller-Lyer [p. 136; LO 11]

Use It or Lose It!

1. Rods, cones, ganglion cells, amacrine cells, bipolar cells, horizontal cells [p. 104; LO 3]	4. red/green, yellow/blue, black/white [p. 108; LO 4]
2. Interposition, height on the horizon, relative size, texture gradient, aerial perspective, motion parallax, linear perspective [p. 129; LO 9]	
3. similarity, proximity, figure ground, good continuation, closure [p. 130; LO 8]	

True or False Questions

1. F [p. 107; LO 4]	6. F [p. 107; LO 4]
2. F [p. 108; LO 4]	7. T [p. 122; LO 7]
3. T [p. 130; LO 8]	8. F [p. 124; LO 7]
4. T [p. 71; LO 4]	9. T [p. 128; LO 9]
5. T [p. 121; LO 7]	10. F [p. 130; LO 9]

Multiple Choice Questions

1. C [p. 97; LO 1]	10. B [p. 115; LO 6]	19. D [p. 124; LO 7]
2. A [p. 98; LO 1]	11. B [p. 116; LO 6]	20. A [p. 93; LO 1]
3. D [p. 103; LO 3]	12. D [p. 110; LO 8]	21. C [p. 114; LO 6]
4. D [p. 106; LO 3, 4]	13. C [p. 131; LO 8]	22. A [p. 99; LO 1]

5. B [p. 103; LO 3, 4]	14. A [p. 130; LO 8]	23. D [p. 111; LO 2, 4]
6. D [p. 109; LO 4]	15. B [p. 101; LO 2]	24. C [p. 112; LO 5]
7. A [p. 126; LO 8]	16. C [p. 124; LO 7]	25. C [p. 113; LO 6]
8. D [p. 124; LO 7]	17. B [p. 121; LO 7]	
9. D [p. 123; LO 7]	18. C [p. 123; LO 7]	

Short-Answer Questions

1. Which theory best explains how we perceive pitch? Explain. [p. 116; LO 5, 6]

    Duplicity theory. Duplicity theory is a combination of frequency/volley theory and place theory. Neither frequency/volley nor place theory can adequately explain how we hear all levels of pitch. Frequency theory only explains perception of sounds up to 1000 Hz. Volley theory can explain how we perceive pitches beyond 1000 Hz, but it cannot explain why hair cells at different regions of the basilar membrane seem to be maximally excited by pitches of particular frequencies. Therefore, the best explanation of pitch comes from duplicity theory, which says that the brain uses both frequency and place information to help us perceive pitch.

2. How is our sense of taste similar to our sense of vision? [p. 119; LO 4, 7]

    It appears that in vision and taste respectively, perception of different colors and different flavors is due in part to specialized receptors that are maximally sensitive to specific colors or light or flavors. Our retinas have cones that respond maximally to red, green, or blue light and our tongue is equipped with specialized taste buds that maximally respond to either sweet, salty, sour, bitter, or perhaps umami flavors.

3. No matter where you sit in a classroom, you always perceive that the blackboard (or white board) at the front of the room is rectangular in shape. Why is this true when the image the board projects onto your retina actually does change shape as you view the board from different locations in the room? [p. 128; LO 9]

    You perceive a constant shape for the board because of shape constancy. Your brain actually steps in and corrects your perception to compensate for the different images the board projects on your retina as you move around the room. Because of this correction, you always perceive a constant rectangular shape for the board.

4. Why must artists use monocular depth cues to portray depth in a painting? [p. 129; LO 9]

    Viewed head-on, a painting is a flat surface that is the same distance from both of your eyes. Because there actually is no depth in a painting, the artist must use monocular depth cues to trick you into perceiving depth where depth does not actually exist. The retinal disparity used in binocular depth perception is only useful for judging how far the painting is away from you. It is not useful for perceiving depth in the flat surface of the painting.

5. Does culture affect perception? Explain. [p. 136; LO 10, 11]

Yes. Your culture can affect your knowledge of the world, which in turn can affect your expectations and your top-down perceptual processing. For example, if you are from a part of the world where black bear are very common, you might perceive a distant, large animal running through the woods as a bear. However, someone who grew up in the city may be quicker to realize that the animal is indeed just a large, black dog. Studies also show that cultural background can affect our susceptibility to certain perceptual illusions. For example, people who grew up in "non-carpentered" environments are less susceptible to the Müller-Lyer illusion than people who grew up in environments that had many rectangular structures.

Developing a Bigger Picture: Making Connections Across Chapters

1. In Chapter 1, you learned about the experimental method. Design a study to test the hypothesis that women more than men prefer warm colors to cooler colors. [p. 32; LO- Big Picture]

There are many ways to do this. Here is one:

You could randomly select a group of 50 men and 50 women to participate in your study. After they arrive at your lab, you could show the participants a series of color swatches containing some warm and some cool colors and ask them to rate how much they like the colors on a 1-10 scale (1=intense dislike and 10= intense liking). You could then calculate the average male and female ratings for the warm and cool colors to see if women preferred the warm ones more than the men did.

2. In Chapter 2, you learned about the structures of the brain, including some that were important to sensation and perception. Based on what you have learned in Chapters 2 & 3, where in the brain would you look for a tumor in a patient who was experiencing strange visual symptoms? [pp. 67, 71, 73, & 110; LO- Big Picture]

Some reasonable places to check for a tumor in the brain would be: the optic chiasm, where the optic nerves from the right and left eyes meet; the thalamus, a sensory relay station; the pons, which processes sensory information from the right and left sides of the body; and the occipital lobe where feature detectors allow visual perception to occur.

3. In Chapter 11, you will read about prejudice and racism. Based on your current understanding of these topics, how might they affect a person's perceptual processes?

Prejudices influence our expectations about the world. Because this is true, they can also affect our top-down perceptual processing. For example, if a racist believes that most criminals are people of color, then he or she might mistakenly perceive a criminal suspect to be a person of color—when in fact the suspect is White. This would be especially true if the racist person witnessed the crime under less than optimal circumstances—for only a brief period of time, in poorly lit conditions, from a great distance away, and so on. [p. 126; LO- Big Picture]

Label the Diagram

1. Ganglion cell [p. 104; LO 3]	4. Horizontal cell [p. 104; LO 3]
2. Amacrine cell [p. 104; LO 3]	5. Rod and cone receptors [p. 104; LO 3]
3. Bipolar cell [p. 104; LO 3]	

Big Picture Review

1. Place theory [p. 115; LO 5, 6]	4. Duplicity theory [p. 115; LO 5, 6]
2. Frequency theory [p. 115; LO 5, 6]	
3. Volley theory [p. 115; LO 5, 6]	

4

Consciousness: Wide Awake, in a Daze, or Dreaming?

Learning Objectives

After studying the chapter, you should be able to do these tasks.

Sleep, Dreaming, and Circadian Rhythm

1. Discuss why we sleep and what factors influence the amount of sleep we need.
2. Describe the sleep stages we progress through during a typical night of sleep.
3. Compare and contrast the different theories on dreaming.
4. Describe and distinguish among sleep disorders, including insomnia, narcolepsy, sleep apnea, sleepwalking, night terrors, and enuresis.

Hypnosis: Real or Imagined?

5. Detail the experience of hypnosis and explain several theories about how hypnosis occurs.
6. Distinguish between what hypnosis can and cannot do for you.

Psychoactive Drugs

7. Define tolerance and dependence, and explain how psychoactive drugs work.
8. Identify depressants, stimulants, and hallucinogens, and describe the effects these types of drugs have on behavior.

The Big Picture

The Big Picture: What Is Consciousness?

Consciousness includes the feelings, thoughts, and aroused states of which you are aware. This chapter discusses altered states of consciousness – when you are not fully awake, alert, or aware. In particular, this chapter focused on three altered states of consciousness: sleep, hypnosis, and the use of psychoactive drugs. The story of David Pelzer illustrates the intimate connection between biology, consciousness, and behavior. David's lack of sleep influenced his school achievement and later his job performance. His ability to engage in self-hypnosis mentally protected him from his mother's abuse. His parents' alcohol use demonstrates the effect of psychoactive drugs on cognition and behavior.

Sleep, Dreaming, and Circadian Rhythm

This section covers Learning Objectives 1-4. Sleep is a state of consciousness that most of us experience on a daily basis. Some of the hypothesized functions of sleep are that it restores our tissues and facilitates growth; aids our immune system; keeps us mentally alert; facilitates in the processing of memory; and enhances our mood states. Although it is hard to determine just how much sleep we need each night, most people will sleep 8-10 hours a night if undisturbed. Our schedule of sleep and wakefulness is called a circadian rhythm and it is regulated by the suprachiasmatic nucleus (SCN) of the hypothalamus. The SCN uses light levels to tell it when to release the sleep promoting hormone, melatonin, which regulates our circadian rhythm. Because the release of melatonin is determined by light levels, our sleep cycle can be altered if we experience a change in the amount of light we are exposed to—such as working a late shift under incandescent lights.

When we do go to sleep, our brain cycles through several stages of sleep which can be seen in the EEG waves of the brain. When we are awake but relaxed with our eyes closed, we emit alpha wave patterns. Upon falling asleep we enter into the first of four non-REM stages of sleep. This stage, stage 1, is characterized by theta waves which are slower and taller than waking state beta waves. Stage 2 is characterized by sleep spindles. Stage 3 is a transitional stage when delta waves appear. Delta waves are slower and taller than theta waves. The deepest stage of sleep, stage 4, is characterized by mostly delta waves, the release of growth hormone, and a deep state of unconsciousness. After about 30 minutes of deep sleep, our body begins to speed up again and we re-enter stages 3 & 2 of sleep before entering into REM sleep.

REM sleep is where we do most of our dreaming. REM is characterized by brain waves similar to waking state alpha and beta waves, major muscle paralysis, rapid eye movement, and dreaming. After spending some time in REM, we then re-enter the deeper stages of non-REM sleep and the cycle repeats itself about every 90 minutes throughout the night. However, as the night goes on, we tend to spend a larger proportion of this cycle in the REM stage. In a normal 8 hours of sleep, you will likely spend about 90 minutes dreaming in the REM stage of sleep.

To date, psychologists do not know for sure why humans dream. Sigmund Freud believed that dreams were the expression of the unconscious mind and that interpreting the meaning of one's dreams was an important part of psychotherapy. The continuity hypothesis suggests that dreaming is a way of coping with daily problems. Memory theory suggests that dreams serve to consolidate knowledge and discard trivial information. The threat simulation theory poses an evolutionary dream function. Dreams allow us to rehearse our responses to threatening situations. The activation-synthesis hypothesis states that dreams are merely a by-product of the random neural impulses generated in the brain during REM sleep.

Despite the importance of sleep to our health and well-being, not everyone is able to get a good night's sleep. Some people suffer from sleep disorders that include insomnia (trouble falling asleep or staying asleep), narcolepsy (falling asleep uncontrollably during the day), REM behavior disorder (REM sleep without muscle paralysis), sleep apnea (the cessation of breathing during sleep), sleep walking (walking during stage 4 sleep), night terrors (waking from stage 4 sleep in terror that was not caused by a nightmare), and enuresis (bed wetting).

Hypnosis: Real or Imagined?

This section covers Learning Objectives 5 and 6. Hypnosis is another state of consciousness. Hypnotized people exhibit alpha wave patterns (but do not go into non-REM or REM states) and they experience a heightened state of suggestibility. While hypnotized, people will tend to follow the directions of the hypnotist, but this does not mean that they become complete zombies while in this state of consciousness. In fact, some researchers question whether or not hypnosis is actually an altered state of consciousness at all.

Dissociation theory states that hypnosis is an altered state of consciousness in which part of the person's consciousness is dissociated or separated from the rest of their conscious mind. Others believe in the response set theory of hypnosis, which states that hypnotized people are merely just playing the role of a hypnotized person and that they have not entered into an altered state of consciousness at all. Regardless of whether or not hypnosis is an altered state, hypnosis has been shown to be helpful in reducing pain, reducing anxiety, and enhancing therapy and physical performance. Its use to cure addictions and recover memories is much more controversial and questionable.

Psychoactive Drugs

This section covers Learning Objectives 7 and 8. Another way of altering consciousness is to take psychoactive drugs. Alcohol and depressants (sedatives and barbiturates) tend to slow down the function of the central nervous system via their affect on the neurotransmitter GABA. These drugs can cause tolerance, dependence, withdrawal symptoms, and substance abuse.

Narcotics like the opiates (morphine, codeine, opium, and heroin) relieve pain and produce euphoria. These drugs are extremely addictive, causing dependence within a few weeks. The brain responds to continued opiate use by cutting back on its production of endorphins—so withdrawal from opiates may leave one without their body's natural pain fighting mechanisms and the absence of pleasurable feelings.

Stimulants are drugs that increase the activity of the central nervous system. Some stimulants are legal (nicotine and caffeine), while others are not (cocaine, crack, some amphetamines, and MDMA or Ecstasy). Stimulants work on several different neurotransmitters in the brain. Abuse of stimulants can lead to problems such as dependence, overdose, paranoia, depression, cardiac problems, and death.

Hallucinogens like marijuana, PCP, and LSD produce altered states of consciousness that involve distortions of our perceptions or hallucinations. The effects of these drugs on a person can be very unpredictable and have a lot to do with the mental state of the user at the time they use the drug. PCP users, in particular, can behave in very violent, destructive ways while under its influence.

Outlining the Big Picture

Chapter 4: Consciousness: Wide Awake, in a Daze, or Dreaming?

The Big Picture: What Is Consciousness?
Notes:

_____

_____

_____

_____

_____

Sleep, Dreaming, and Circadian Rhythm (Learning Objectives 1-4)
Functions of Sleep: Why Do We Sleep, and What If We Don't?
How Much Sleep Do We Need?
Circadian Rhythm and the Biological Clock
 "Weekend Lag" and Jet Lag
 Working the Night Shift
Stages of Sleep: What Research Tells Us
 The Four Stages of Non-REM Sleep
 REM Sleep: Dream On
A Typical Night's Sleep
Dreaming: The Night's Work
 Sigmund Freud's Interpretation of Dreams
 Dreams as Coping, Housekeeping, Evolutionary Defense or Just Biology
 at Work
 So, What Do Dreams Mean?
Sleep Disorders: Tossing and Turning – and More
 Insomnia: There is Help!
 Narcolepsy and Cataplexy
 Sleep Apnea and SIDS
 Sleepwalking: Wake Me Up!

Night Terrors and Enuresis
Gender and Ethnic Differences in Sleep
Notes:

_____

_____

_____

_____

_____

_____

Hypnosis: Real or Imagined? (Learning Objectives 5 and 6)

The Hypnosis Experience
    Hypnotic Susceptibility
Explaining Hypnosis: Is It an Altered State?
What Hypnosis Can and Cannot Do
Notes:

_____

_____

_____

_____

_____

Psychoactive Drugs (Learning Objectives 7 and 8)

Drug Tolerance, Dependence, and Substance Abuse
How Drugs Work: Biology, Expectations, and Culture
Alcohol and Other Depressants
    Health Effects of Alcohol
    Alcohol and Genetics
    Spotlight on Diversity: Alcohol and Ethnicity in the United States
    Social Costs of Alcohol Use
    Barbiturates and Sedatives
Opiates (Narcotics): Morphine, Codeine, Opium, and Heroin
Stimulants: Legal and Otherwise
    Caffeine: Java Jitters

Nicotine: A Really Bad Habit
Cocaine and Crack
Amphetamines
MDMA (Ecstasy)
Hallucinogens: Distorting Reality
Marijuana
PCP
LSD
Notes:

_____

_____

_____

_____

_____

Are You Getting the Big Picture?
Notes:

_____

_____

_____

_____

_____

Seeing the Big Picture: A Mental Map of Chapter 4

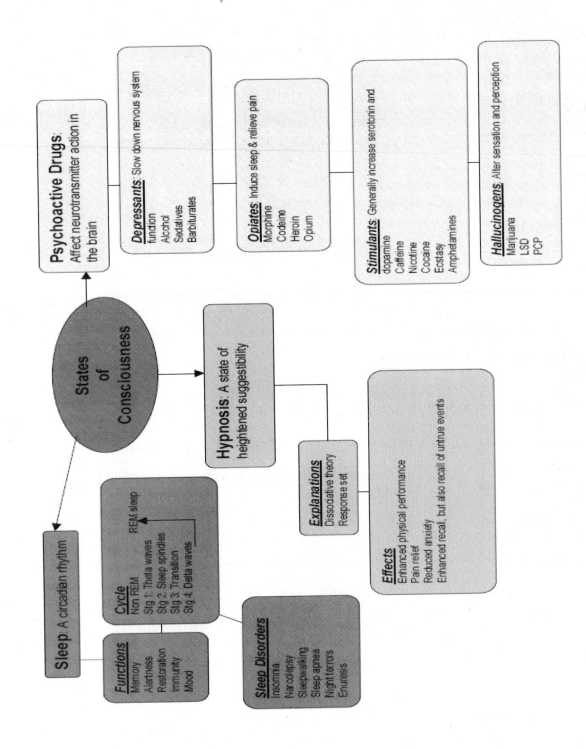

Psychoactive Drugs: Affect neurotransmitter action in the brain

Depressants: Slow down nervous system
function
Alcohol
Sedatives
Barbiturates

Opiates: Induce sleep & relieve pain
Morphine
Codeine
Heroin
Opium

Stimulants: Generally increase serotonin and dopamine
Caffeine
Nicotine
Cocaine
Ecstasy
Amphetamines

Hallucinogens: Alter sensation and perception
Marijuana
LSD
PCP

States of Consciousness

Hypnosis: A state of heightened suggestibility

Explanations
Dissociative theory
Response set

Effects
Enhanced physical performance
Pain relief
Reduced anxiety
Enhanced recall, but also recall of untrue events

Sleep: A circadian rhythm

Cycle
Non REM
Stg 1: Theta waves
Stg 2: Sleep spindles
Stg 3: Transition
Stg 4: Delta waves
REM sleep

Functions
Memory
Alertness
Restoration
Immunity
Mood

Sleep Disorders
Insomnia
Narcolepsy
Sleepwalking
Sleep apnea
Night terrors
Enuresis

Key Points of the Big Picture

Activation-synthesis theory:
suggests that dreams do not have symbolic meaning, but are the byproduct of the brain's random firing of neural impulses during REM sleep. *Example: You dream about elephants because the brain activated this memory, not because of any psychological meaning.*

Circadian Rhythm:
changes in bodily processes that occur repeatedly on approximately a 24-25-hour cycle. *Example: We alternate between wakefulness and sleepiness everyday.*

Consciousness:
feelings, thoughts, and aroused states of which we are aware. *Example: Being awake and not under the influence of drugs is a conscious state.*

Depressants:
drugs that inhibit or slow down normal neural functioning. *Example: Alcohol slows reaction time.*

Dissociation theory:
Hilgard's proposal that hypnosis involves two simultaneous states: a hypnotic state and a hidden observer. *Example: Being really absorbed in reading a book while still aware of everything that is going on around you.*

Enuresis:
a condition in which a person over the age of 5 shows an inability to control urination during sleep. *Example: Matt, age 7, wets the bed four times a week at night when he is asleep.*

Fetal Alcohol Syndrome (FAS):
a birth condition resulting from the mother's chronic use of alcohol during pregnancy that is characterized by facial and limb deformities, and mental retardation.

Hallucinogens:
drugs that simultaneously excite and inhibit normal neural activity, thereby causing distortions in perception. *Example: While on LSD (acid), Nelly feels like she is yellow and sees ants riding on horses.*

Hypnosis:
a state of heightened suggestibility. *Example: Myra believes hypnosis will work for her, so Myra is more likely to do what is suggested when she is hypnotized.*

Insomnia:
a sleep disorder in which a person cannot get to sleep and/or stay asleep. *Example: Patrick tries to go to sleep after the evening news, but often does not fall asleep until two or more hours later.*

Latent content:
the symbolic meaning of a dream according to Freudian theory. *Example: Dreaming about water suggests the birth or beginning of something.*

Manifest content:
what the dreamer recalls upon awakening, according to Freud. *Example: Recalling that you had a dream about water.*

Melatonin:
hormone in the body that facilitates sleep. *Example: Although not FDA approved, some people take melatonin to reduce the effects of jet lag.*

Microsleep:
brief episode of sleep that occurs in the midst of a wakeful activity. *Example: Seeming to zone out for a moment during class or while driving.*

Narcolepsy:
a rare sleep disorder in which a person falls asleep during alert activities during the day. *Example: In the middle of his golf swing, Reuben falls over. His partner notices that he is asleep.*

Nightmare:
a brief, scary REM-dream that is often remembered. *Example: Katelyn wakes up upset and remembers dreaming about a house fire.*

Night terror:
a very frightening non-REM sleep episode. *Example: Alberto screams while he is sleeping and looks terrified. In the morning, Alberto does not remember his fear.*

Non-REM sleep:
relaxing state of sleep in which the individual's eyes do not move. *Example: When we first go to sleep we are in non-REM sleep.*

Opiates:
painkilling drugs that depress some brain areas and excite others. *Example: Eric broke his leg and receives morphine in the hospital to reduce his pain.*

Psychoactive drugs:
substances that influence the brain and thereby the behavior of individuals. *Example: Caffeine, nicotine, and marijuana change our behavior and are therefore psychoactive drugs.*

REM behavior disorder:
a condition in which normal muscle paralysis does not occur, leading to violent movements during REM sleep. *Example: At times, Nick thrashes around while he is sleeping because his body does not produce the enzyme that inhibits this behavior.*

REM rebound:
loss of REM sleep is recouped by spending more time in REM on subsequent nights. *Example: Jenna has been staying up late to cram for her mid-terms. When her sleep pattern returns to normal she notices dreaming a lot more.*

REM sleep:
active state of sleep in which a person's eyes move. *Example: You can often notice the rapid eye movement of dogs and cats when they sleep.*

Response set theory of hypnosis:

asserts that hypnosis is *not* an altered state of consciousness, but a cognitive set to respond appropriately to suggestions. The intent to behave as a "hypnotized person" and the expectation that one will succeed in following the hypnotist's suggestion becomes a response set that triggers the hypnotic response automatically.

Sleep apnea:

a sleep disorder in which a person stops breathing during sleep. *Example: Prita often wakes up tired, despite sleeping 10 or more hours. She often wakes up her partner with her loud snoring throughout the night when she is trying to get air.*

Sleep disorder:

a disturbance in the normal pattern of sleeping. Example: Insomnia and sleep apnea are sleep disorders.

Sleepwalking:

a sleep disorder in which a person is mobile and may perform actions during Stage IV sleep. *Example: A few hours after he has gone to bed, Nelson gets up to go to the garage. His mother asks him what he is doing. He mumbles something incoherent and his mother realizes that he is asleep.*

Stimulants:

drugs that speed up normal brain functioning. *Example: Caffeinated drinks like coffee and tea help many people wake up in the morning.*

Substance abuse:

loss of control over one's drug use. *Example: Despite failed relationships, money problems, loss of jobs, and legal problems because of his drinking, Dennis continues to drink alcohol.*

Substance dependence:

a condition in which a person needs a drug in order to maintain normal functioning. *Example: If Jackie does not take her sedatives, she has panic attacks, and feels jittery all day.*

Suprachiasmatic nucleus:

a group of brain cells located in the hypothalamus that signal other brain areas when to be aroused and when to shut down.

Tetrahydrocannabinol (THC):

the active ingredient in marijuana that affects learning, short-term memory, coordination, emotion, and appetite.

Threat simulation theory (TST):

suggests that dreaming is an ancient biological defense mechanism that allows us to repeatedly simulate potentially threatening situations so that we can rehearse our responses to these events. *Example: Marquita's dream about being mugged will help prepare her if she is ever in this situation.*

Tolerance:
a condition in which after repeated use, more of a drug is needed to achieve the same effect. *Example: Doug needs to drink more beer now than he did two months ago in order to get a buzz.*

Withdrawal symptoms:
physical or behavioral effects that occur after a person stops using a drug. *Example: When Lindsey stopped smoking, she experienced insomnia, headaches, stomach upset, and irritability for four weeks.*

Fill-in Review of the Chapter

Can you fill-in the missing terms for each section of the chapter? Items marked with an * encourage you to continue building the Big Picture of psychology by connecting the material in this chapter to material from previous chapters in the text.

The Big Picture: What Is Consciousness?

According to psychologists, 1) _____ refers to the thoughts, feelings, and aroused states of which we are aware.

The story of David Pelzer represents the 2*) _____ _____ research method from Chapter 1.

Sleep, Dreaming, and Circadian Rhythm

If you are deprived of sleep, you are likely to experience brief periods of sleep during waking activity called 3) _____.

Sleep activates the release of growth hormone from the master gland in the brain called the 4*) _____ gland.

Sabrina tells her best friend of a dream in which she was flying over her place of employment dressed as a giant chicken. According to Freud, the events Sabrina relayed to her friend describe the 5) _____ content of her dream.

The threat simulation theory of dreaming is an example of the 6*) _____ psychological perspective introduced in Chapter 1.

7) _____ is a hormone that regulates the circadian rhythm of sleep.

Rick is asleep and dreaming that he is swimming and a giant shark is chasing him. Rick's partner reports that while having this dream Rick was wildly flailing around in bed as if he were really swimming. Rick was easily awakened from his dream. With symptoms like these, Rick is likely suffering from the sleep disorder called 8) _____ _____ _____.

Hypnosis: Real or Imagined?

The ability to become hypnotized is called 9) _____ _____.

In Hilgard's classic demonstration of hypnosis, participants were either hypnotized or not hypnotized and then instructed to submerge their arms in ice-cold water and press a key when they felt pain. Participants were timed to see how long they could tolerate the ice-cold water before pressing the key. In his experiment, the dependent variable was 10*) _____ _____ _____ _____.

Psychoactive Drugs

The amount of a drug required to produce its effect is called 11) _____.

12) _____ _____ _____ is a developmental disorder caused by maternal consumption of alcohol during pregnancy.

Benzodiazepines like valium belong to a class of drugs known as 13) _____.

Nicotine is a very powerful 14) _____.

The drug PCP affects the neurotransmitter 15*) _____ in the brain.

Use It or Lose It!

Can you identify the psychoactive drug that would produce the following behavioral effects?

Psychoactive Substance	Behavioral Effects
1.	Alertness and focused attention
2.	Blocks pain and produces dreamlike pleasure
3.	Increases sensitivity to taste; relaxation; altered perceptions
4.	Enhances mood and energy levels; increased feelings of warmth toward others
5.	Lowered inhibitions; impaired memory and motor coordination
6.	Distortion of senses; flashbacks
7.	Instant surge of arousal, pleasure, and optimism

Self-Check: Are You Getting the Big Picture?

After you have read and studied the chapter, see if you can answer the following quiz questions. Check your answers at the end of the chapter. If you miss a question, refer to your text and re-study the appropriate sections.

True or False Questions

Are these statements true or false?

1. In the United States, Latino/Hispanic Americans tend to drink more alcohol than European Americans.
True
False

2. Sleepwalking tends to occur during REM sleep.
True
False

3. The best-documented use of hypnosis is for recovering memories that have been buried in the unconscious since childhood.
True
False

4. During a state of hypnosis, the brain tends to emit higher levels of alpha waves.
True
False

5. When one becomes intoxicated with alcohol, his or her lack of inhibition and poor judgment skills is a result of depressed functioning in the cerebral cortex.
True
False

6. Long-term use of tranquilizers can actually increase your level of anxiety.
True
False

7. As we move from Stage IV sleep to REM sleep, brain waves get faster.
True
False

8. Obesity increases one's chances of developing sleep apnea.
True
False

9. Tyson has developed a daily routine of shooting up heroin every morning in his kitchen. After engaging in this routine for six months, it is possible that just entering into the kitchen may cause Tyson to begin craving heroin.
True
False

10. The most commonly reported sleep disorder is sleepwalking.
True
False

Multiple Choice Questions

Can you choose the best answer for these questions?

1. Which of the following is not a reason why we sleep each day?
    A. restoration of the body
    B. increase immunity to disease
    C. lower your blood pressure
    D. to keep your mind alert

2. Walter is 59 and Juan is 24. Given what you know about sleep, which of these men will likely require more sleep at night?
    A. Walter
    B. Juan
    C. Both will require the same amount.
    D. Both will require the same amount, but Walter will need more stage III sleep.

3. The part of the brain that governs the sleep cycle is the:
    A. suprachiasmatic nucleus.
    B. lateral hypothalamus.
    C. ventromedial hypothalamus.
    D. amygdala.

4. Given what you have learned about sleep, which of the following options is the best, if you are concerned with feeling and performing at your best?
    A. going to bed and getting up each day at the same time
    B. keeping a set schedule of going to bed and waking up during the week, but then sleeping late on the weekends
    C. going to bed and waking up at different times each day
    D. trying to sleep no more than five hours each night

5. Which of the following work shifts would be most difficult to adapt to?
    A. working a 9am to 5pm shift everyday
    B. working a 12am to 8am shift everyday
    C. working a 3pm to 11pm shift everyday
    D. working a 12am to 8am shift one week a month

6. Most dreams occur during _____ sleep.
    A. stage II
    B. stage III
    C. stage IV
    D. REM

7. The largest, slowest brain waves are:
    A. alpha waves.
    B. beta waves.
    C. delta waves.
    D. theta waves.

8. A complete cycle from non-REM to REM sleep takes about _____ minutes.
   A. 30
   B. 60
   C. 90
   D. 120

9. According to Sigmund Freud, dreams allow us to express our unconscious desires:
   A. after they are censored by our conscious mind.
   B. in an explicit, straightforward manner.
   C. in a conscious fashion.
   D. in symbolic form.

10. According to the activation-synthesis theory of dreams, dreams are:
   A. the expression of unconscious wishes and desires.
   B. the result of random activity in the cortex.
   C. completely devoid of meaning or relevance to our lives.
   D. a way to rehearse for threatening events.

11. Approximately _____ of Americans will suffer from a sleep disorder in their lifetime.
   A. 10%
   B. 25%
   C. 66%
   D. 95%

12. What sleeping disorder is related to sudden infant death syndrome (SIDS)?
   A. insomnia
   B. night terrors
   C. sleep apnea
   D. narcolepsy

13. Enuresis is more common in:
   A. males.
   B. females.
   C. children under age 4.
   D. children who have no biological relatives with enuresis.

14. Which of the following is a true statement about hypnosis?
   A. All people can be hypnotized.
   B. You can be hypnotized against your will.
   C. Hypnosis is definitely an altered state of consciousness.
   D. The skill of the hypnotist does not affect one's ability to be hypnotized.

15. Tanita now needs to take more cocaine to get high than she did when she first started using this drug. Tanita has developed_____ cocaine.
   A. an addiction to
   B. a withdrawal from
   C. a dependence on
   D. a tolerance for

16. To which of the following drugs can you develop a tolerance?
   A. cocaine
   B. alcohol
   C. LSD
   D. all of the above

17. Hallucinogens include all of the following, except:
   A. LSD.
   B. PCP.
   C. marijuana.
   D. Benzedrine.

18. The active ingredient in marijuana is:
   A. THC.
   B. MDMA.
   C. PCP.
   D. LSD.

19. Studies show that _____ plays a role in the majority of reported rapes and sexual assaults on college campuses.
   A. alcohol
   B. marijuana
   C. cocaine
   D. ecstasy

20. Which of the following is not a well-documented use of hypnosis?
   A. pain relief
   B. decrease anxiety
   C. age regression
   D. enhancing psychotherapy

21. Melanie takes a drug that blocks adenosine in her brain. This drug will cause Melanie to be more alert and will enhance her ability to focus. If she takes too much, it could cause irritability, nausea, and a racing heartbeat. Melanie is most likely taking _____.
   A. nicotine
   B. cocaine
   C. methamphetamine
   D. caffeine

22. The hidden observer is a part of which theory of hypnosis?
   A. dissociation theory
   B. response set theory
   C. activation synthesis theory
   D. threat simulation theory

23. Damian, a successful musician, has been smoking marijuana for 10 years. He feels that marijuana relaxes him and expands his mind, which makes him a more creative songwriter. In fact, he never attempts to write unless he has first smoked a joint. Damian has tried to stop smoking marijuana in the past, but has always returned to it because he fears losing his creativity. Damian most likely has _____ marijuana.
    A. substance dependence for
    B. withdrawal from
    C. a tolerance for
    D. both A & B

24. Stephanie has been using cocaine for several years now. If she stops taking cocaine, she will likely experience:
    A. nausea and diarrhea.
    B. hallucinations.
    C. depression and lack of energy.
    D. rapid heartbeat, shaking, and paranoia.

25. How a drug affects a person is a function of:
    A. his or her culture.
    B. his or her expectations about the drug.
    C. the properties of the drug.
    D. all of the above.
    E. B & C

Short-Answer Questions

Can you write a brief answer to these questions?

1. What advice would you give to a friend who is suffering from insomnia?

2. According to the research, what is hypnosis useful for?

3. Discuss the difference and similarities between substance dependence and substance abuse.

4. What are the physiological reactions to consuming alcohol?

5. What are the negative effects of using MDMA or Ecstasy?

Developing a Bigger Picture: Making Connections Across Chapters

An important aspect of learning is learning to see the "Big Picture" of the subject you are studying. As you learn about psychology, you should try to understand how the material from different chapters fits together to help you form a broad-based understanding of what psychology is all about. To help facilitate the development of this "Big Picture" in your mind, try to answer these questions using the knowledge you have learned in this chapter, as well as the other chapters referenced in the questions.

1. In this chapter, you learned that alcohol is a depressant that affects several parts of the brain including the brainstem and cortex. In Chapter 2, you learned about these structures in detail. Combining what you know about the brain and alcohol, what could happen to a person if he or she drank massive quantities of alcohol? Explain.

2. In Chapter 1, you learned about the different types of psychologists and the types of research questions they ask. Using this knowledge, answer the following question: what types of questions would a social psychologist ask about drug use?

3. In Chapter 1, you learned about the different research methods that psychologists use. Using this knowledge, design a study to test the hypothesis that having friends who use drugs increases the likelihood that a teenager will use drugs.

Label the Diagram

Can you identify the brain waves associated with each stage of sleep?

Stage of Sleep	Type of Brain Wave
Alert, wide awake, eyes open	1)
Awake, relaxed, eyes closed	2)
Stage I sleep	3)
Stage II sleep	4)
Stage III sleep	5)
Stage IV sleep	6)
REM sleep	7)

Big Picture Review

Identify whether each drug is a depressant, opiate, stimulant, or hallucinogen and indicate the main effects for each of the psychoactive drugs.

Substance	Type of Drug & Main Effects
Alcohol	1.
Barbiturates	2.
Benzodiazepines	3.
Codeine, Heroin, Morphine, Opium	4.
Caffeine	5.
Nicotine	6.
Cocaine	7.
MDMA	8.
Amphetamines	9.
Marijuana	10.
PCP	11.
LSD	12.

Solutions

Each solution below is followed by its textbook page reference number and its corresponding chapter learning objective (LO) number. Items with a Big Picture LO help you build a Big Picture of psychology across the chapters you studied so far.

Fill-in Review of the Chapter

1. consciousness [p. 143; LO-Big Picture]
2. case study [p. 30; LO-Big Picture]
3. microsleeps [p. 146; LO 1]
4. pituitary [p. 82; LO-Big Picture]
5. manifest [p. 156; LO 3]
6. evolutionary [p. 16; LO-Big Picture]
7. Melatonin [p. 150; LO 2]
8. REM behavior disorder [p. 154; LO 4]
9. hypnotic susceptibility [p. 162; LO 5]
10. time until felt pain [p. 33; LO-Big Picture]
11. tolerance [p. 166; LO 7]
12. Fetal alcohol syndrome [p. 171; LO 8]
13. sedatives [p. 173; LO 8]
14. stimulant [p. 175; LO 8]
15. glutamate [p. 181; LO-Big Picture]

Use It or Lose It!

1. caffeine [p. 175; LO 8]
2. opiates [p. 174; LO 8]
3. marijuana [p. 180; LO 8]
4. MDMA (Ecstasy) [p. 179; LO 8]
5. alcohol [p. 171; LO 8]
6. LSD [p. 181-182; LO 8]
7. cocaine [p. 177; LO 8]

Self-Check: Are You Getting the Big Picture?

True or False Questions

1. F [p. 172; LO 8]
2. F [p. 159; LO 4]
3. F [p. 164; LO 6]
4. T [p. 161; LO 5]
5. T [p. 170; LO 8]
6. T [p. 174; LO 8]
7. T [p. 154; LO 2]
8. T [p. 158; LO 4]
9. T [p. 167; LO 7]
10. F [p. 157; LO 4]

Multiple Choice Questions

1. C [p. 146-147; LO 1]	10. B [p. 156; LO 3]	19. A [p. 173; LO 8]
2. B [p. 148; LO 1]	11. D [p. 157; LO 4]	20. C [p. 163; LO 6]
3. A [p. 150; LO 2]	12. C [p. 159; LO 4]	21. D [p. 175; LO 8]
4. A [p. 150; LO 1]	13. A [p. 160; LO 4]	22. A [p. 162-163; LO 5]
5. D [p. 151-152; LO 1]	14. D [p. 162; LO 5]	23. A [p. 167; LO 7]
6. D [p. 154; LO 2]	15. D [p. 166; LO 7]	24. C [p. 177; LO 7]
7. C [p. 153; LO 2]	16. D [p. 168-181; LO 8]	25. D [p. 167-168; LO 7]
8. C [p. 155; LO 2]	17. D [p. 179; LO 8]	
9. D [p. 155; LO 3]	18. A [p. 180; LO 7]	

Short-Answer Questions

1. What advice would you give to a friend who is suffering from insomnia? [p. 157-158; LO 4]

   Keep a regular sleep/waking cycle. Avoid long naps during waking hours. Use your bed for sleep only. If you can't sleep after 10 minutes of trying, get up and do something else for a while, then try to sleep. Avoid caffeine, sleeping pills, alcohol, and tobacco. Exercise during the day, but avoid it right before bed time.

2. According to the research, what is hypnosis useful for? [p. 163-164; LO 6]

   Hypnosis has been shown to be useful for pain relief; decreasing anxiety; enhancing physical performance; and enhancing psychotherapy. Hypnosis has not been shown to be very useful for curing addictions, age-regression, or recovering lost memories (because recovered memories may be false).

3. Discuss the difference and similarities between substance dependence and substance abuse. [p. 167; LO 7]

   In both substance dependence and substance abuse, one must take a drug to avoid unpleasant physical and behavioral withdrawal symptoms. Some people may have substance dependence because they continue to take a drug to avoid the unpleasant withdrawal symptoms. Substance abuse implies that a person has lost control over his or her drug use.

4. What are the physiological reactions to consuming alcohol? [p. 170-172; LO 8]

   Alcohol is a depressant that affects GABA sites in the brain. Depression of the cortex leads to lessened inhibitions and poor judgments. Motor processes are also affected as the brainstem is depressed. Reaction time is lengthened, balance and coordination degrade, and sexual performance suffers. Alcohol also inhibits your ability to form new memories and disrupts REM sleep.

5. What are the negative effects of using MDMA or Ecstasy? [p. 179; LO 8]

   Possible negative effects of MDMA include: insomnia, teeth-clenching, nausea, increased heart rate and blood pressure, paranoia, confusion, depression, drug craving, overheating, cardiac complications, kidney failure, seizures, strokes, and psychoses.

Developing a Bigger Picture: Making Connections Across Chapters

1. In this chapter, you learned that alcohol is a depressant that affects several parts of the brain including the brainstem and cortex. In Chapter 2, you learned about these structures in detail. Combining what you know about the brain and alcohol, what could happen to a person if he or she drank massive quantities of alcohol? Explain. [p. 66-68; LO-Big Picture]

   Death would be a real possibility. Alcohol is a brainstem depressant. If structures like the pons, RAS, and medulla are depressed too far, the person could lose consciousness and stop breathing.

2. In Chapter 1, you learned about the different types of psychologists and the types of research questions they ask. Using this knowledge, answer the following question: what types of questions would a social psychologist ask about drug use? [p. 21; LO-Big Picture]

   While there are many possible answers to this question, social psychologists would be interested in how social interactions relate to drug use. Here are a few examples of the type of questions they might ask: Does having friends who abuse drugs increase the probability that a teenager will also abuse drugs? Does involvement in after school activities and clubs reduce the likelihood that a student will use drugs? Do certain professions have higher incidences of drug use? Do people who use drugs take higher doses when taking drugs with others as opposed to when they are alone?

3. In Chapter 1, you learned about the different research methods that psychologists use. Using this knowledge, design a study to test the hypothesis that having friends who use drugs increases the likelihood that a teenager will use drugs. [p. 30-31; LO-Big Picture]

   In this case, it would be unethical and impractical to conduct an experiment. You cannot experimentally control who a person is friends with nor would you want to purposely increase a person's likelihood of abusing drugs. Therefore, you must do some other type of study. One option would be to do a survey (correlational research) in which you ask high school students if they use drugs and if they have friends who use drugs. This would give you an indication if there is a relationship between having friends who do drugs and a person's likelihood of abusing drugs.

Label the Diagram [p. 153; LO 2]

Stage of Sleep	Type of Brain Wave
Alert, wide awake, eyes open	1. Beta waves
Awake, relaxed, eyes closed	2. Alpha waves
Stage I sleep	3. Theta waves
Stage II sleep	4. Sleep spindles
Stage III sleep	5. Delta waves appear
Stage IV sleep	6. Mostly Delta waves
REM sleep	7. Beta-like waves

Big Picture Review [p. 167-168; LO 8]

1. Alcohol: depressant; relaxation; lowered inhibitions; impaired reflexes, motor coordination, and memory
2. Barbiturates; depressant; anxiety relief; euphoria; severe withdrawal symptoms
3. Benzodiazepines: depressant; anxiety relief; irritability; confusion; depression; sleep problems
4. Codeine, heroin, opium, morphine: opiates; euphoria; pain control; constipation; loss of appetite
5. Caffeine: stimulant; alertness, insomnia; loss of appetite; high blood pressure
6. Nicotine: stimulant; alertness; calmness; loss of appetite
7. Cocaine: stimulant; increased energy; excitation; insomnia; loss of appetite; mood swings; delusions; paranoia; heart problems
8. MDMA: stimulant; increased insight and emotion; muscle tension; sleep problems; anxiety; paranoia
9. Amphetamines: stimulant; increased alertness and energy; insomnia; loss of appetite; delusions; paranoia
10. Marijuana: hallucinogen; relaxation; altered perceptions; sleep problems; paranoia; amotivation
11. PCP: hallucinogen; euphoria; unpredictable moods; hostility
12. LSD: hallucinogen; altered perceptions; distortion of senses; panic reactions; flashback effects

5

How Do We Learn?

Learning Objectives

After studying each of the following sections of the chapter, you should be able to do these tasks.

Defining Learning: In and Beyond the Classroom

1. Define learning.

Orienting and Habitutation: Learning to Ignore

2. Define and give examples of orienting reflexes, habituation, and dishabituation.

Classical Conditioning: Learning Through the Association of Stimuli

3. Describe Pavlov's paradigm of classical conditioning.
4. Define classical conditioning and discuss the factors that affect it.
5. Explain how classical conditioning occurs in humans.
6. Describe the process through which classically conditioned responses are removed.

Instrumental and Operant Conditioning: Learning from the Consequences of Our Actions

7. Explain how classical conditioning and instrumental/operant conditioning differ.
8. Explain the Law of Effect and the experiments that led to its discovery.
9. Describe the contributions that B. F. Skinner made to the study of instrumental/operant conditioning.
10. Describe the phases of instrumental/operant conditioning.
11. Describe the factors that affect the process of instrumental/operant conditioning.
12. Describe generalization, discrimination, and shaping as they relate to instrumental/operant conditioning.
13. Describe the decisions that must be made when applying instrumental/operant conditioning in the real world.

Social Learning or Modeling

14. Describe Albert Bandura's Bobo doll experiments.
15. Describe social learning theory.
16. Describe the role that cognition plays in social learning.

The Big Picture

The Big Picture: Learning to Live

Many would have predicted that Peter was destined for a much better life when he was adopted by a loving couple in the United States. But for Peter, adjusting to life with his new family in the United States required a great deal of learning that was guided by his interactions with peers, parents, teachers and so on.

Defining Learning: In and Beyond the Classroom

This section covers Learning Objective 1. Learning is a relatively permanent change in behavior or behavior potential as a result of experience. Although learning is always the result of experience, there are several different types of experiences that can lead to learning. In this chapter, we covered four of them—habituation, classical conditioning, operant conditioning, and social learning.

Orienting and Habitutation: Learning to Ignore

This section covers Learning Objective 2. Habituation occurs when we learn to stop responding to repetitive stimuli. For example, you habituate when you learn to stop paying attention to sound of the television while you are trying to study. Habituation is a beneficial type of learning because it allows us to have orienting reflexes—a tendency to automatically orient your senses towards unexpected, novel stimuli—without being a slave to them. Without the capacity for habituation, you would have no choice but to pay attention to all stimuli you encounter in the world.

Classical Conditioning: Learning Through the Association of Stimuli

This section covers Learning Objectives 3-6. Classical conditioning is a type of learning that occurs when you learn to associate an originally neutral stimulus with an unconditioned stimulus, which has the power to elicit an unconditioned response. Because of this association, the neutral stimulus loses its neutrality and becomes a conditioned stimulus that now has the power to elicit the conditioned response. This type of learning was first discovered by Ivan Pavlov as he studied the digestive process in dogs. He found that a dog would naturally salivate (UR) when presented with food (US) but not when presented with a sound (NS). However, when Pavlov repeatedly paired the sound and the food together, the dog soon came to salivate (CR) when it heard the sound (CS)—even though the dog was not presented with food. The dog had been conditioned or taught to respond to the sound the same way it did to food.

Classical conditioning is a valuable type of learning that can explain how we learn to have specific emotional and physiological responses to stimuli we encounter in the world. For example, the famous Little Albert experiments clearly showed that humans can acquire phobias through classical conditioning. And, a special type of classical conditioning that is frequently seen in everyday life, taste aversion, illustrates our ability to become classically conditioned to avoid foods that have made us ill in the past.

Instrumental and Operant Conditioning: Learning from the Consequences of Our Actions

This section covers Learning Objectives 7-13. A third type of learning is operant or instrumental conditioning. In operant or instrumental conditioning, we learn through the consequences of our actions. This type of learning was first discovered by E. L. Thorndike in his work with cats in puzzle boxes. Thorndike found that a cat locked in a puzzle box would learn through trial and error to preferentially emit responses that were most likely to lead to escape from the box. Thorndike summed up instrumental conditioning in the law of effect—or the idea that random behaviors that lead to reward are strengthened and random behaviors that lead to punishment are weakened.

In the 1950s, American psychologist B. F. Skinner renamed instrumental conditioning "operant conditioning" and furthered our study of this type of learning with his invention of the Skinner box, a chamber in which a rat or pigeon can be quickly conditioned through reward or punishment.

Using Skinner boxes, researchers have studied many of the variables that affect operant conditioning including the type of consequence that follows the behavior and the schedule of reinforcement used. Skinner boxes have also allowed researchers to examine the different phases of operant conditioning such as acquisition, extinction, spontaneous recovery, reacquisition, generalization, and discrimination.

Social Learning or Modeling

This section covers Learning Objectives 14-16. The final type of learning discussed in this chapter is social learning or modeling. This type of learning was first studied by Albert Bandura. Bandura discovered that it is possible for us to learn a new behavior even though we have not directly engaged in the behavior. Classical and operant conditioning both require that you actually engage in the behavior as part of the learning process, but in real life there are abundant situations in which we learn without actually ever engaging in the behavior. For example, you could watch a person knitting on TV and learn to knit without ever picking up needle and yarn. In this example, you would learn to knit through observation or modeling of the TV model's behavior.

Albert Bandura demonstrated the power of modeling in his famous Bobo doll experiments in which young children learned to be aggressive by watching a film of an adult model beating up a plastic Bobo doll. These experiments showed that we do learn by watching others, and that our willingness to actually engage in behaviors we've seen in others is influenced by the expected consequences of those behaviors.

Bandura's social learning or modeling is an important bridge between the strict behaviorism of classical and operant conditioning and cognitive psychology. This is true because Bandura proposed that for modeling to occur, you must observe another's behavior, store a memory of it, later retrieve that memory, and then choose whether or not to actually execute that behavior. In other words, unlike the other types of learning discussed in this chapter, modeling necessitates the acknowledgment that cognitive processes play an important role in learning.

Outlining the Big Picture

Chapter 5: How Do We Learn?

The Big Picture: Learning to Live
Bruce D. Perry's *The Boy Who Was Raised as a Dog.*
Notes: _____

_____

_____

_____

_____

Defining Learning: In and Beyond the Classroom (Learning Objective 1)
Notes: _____

_____

_____

_____

_____

Orienting and Habituation: Learning to Ignore (Learning Objective 2)
Habituation as an Adaptive Asset
Dishabituation
Practical Applications of Habituation
Notes: _____

_____

_____

_____

_____

_____

_____

Classical Conditioning: Learning Through the Association of Stimuli (Learning Objectives 3-6)
The Elements of Classical Conditioning
Factors Affecting Classical Conditioning
> *Relationship in Time: Contiguity*
> *Consistency and Reliability: Contingency*
Real-World Classical Conditioning: What Responses Can Be Classically Conditioned in Humans?
> *Classical Conditioning of Emotional Responses*
> *Classical Conditioning of Physiological Responses: The Special Case of Taste Aversion*
Extinction of Classically Conditioned Responses
Notes:

_____

_____

_____

_____

_____

_____

Instrumental and Operant Conditioning: Learning from the Consequences of Our Actions (Learning Objective 7-13)
E. L. Thorndike's Law of Effect
> *Unlocking the Puzzle of Learning*
> *Random Actions and Reinforcement*
> *Positive and Negative Reinforcement*
> *Positive and Negative Punishment*
> *Spotlight on Diversity: A Japanese View of Reinforcement*
How Classical and Instrumental Conditioning Differ
B. F. Skinner and Operant Responses
Acquisition and Extinction
Schedules of Reinforcement
> *Continuous Schedules of Reinforcement*
> *Ratio Schedules of Reinforcement*
> *Interval Schedules of Reinforcement*
Discrimination and Generalization

Discrimination
Generalization
Shaping New Behaviors
Decisions That Must Be Made When Using Operant Conditioning
    Punishment or Reinforcement?
    Choosing a Reinforcer that Is Reinforcing
    Primary and Secondary Reinforcers
The Role of Cognition in Learning
Notes:

_____

_____

_____

_____

_____

_____

Social Learning or Modeling (Learning Objectives 14-16)
Albert Bandura and The Bobo Doll Experiments
Social Learning Theory and Cognition
Notes:

_____

_____

_____

_____

_____

_____

Are You Getting the Big Picture?
Notes:

_____

_____

_____

_____

_____

_____

Seeing the Big Picture: A Mental Map of Chapter 5

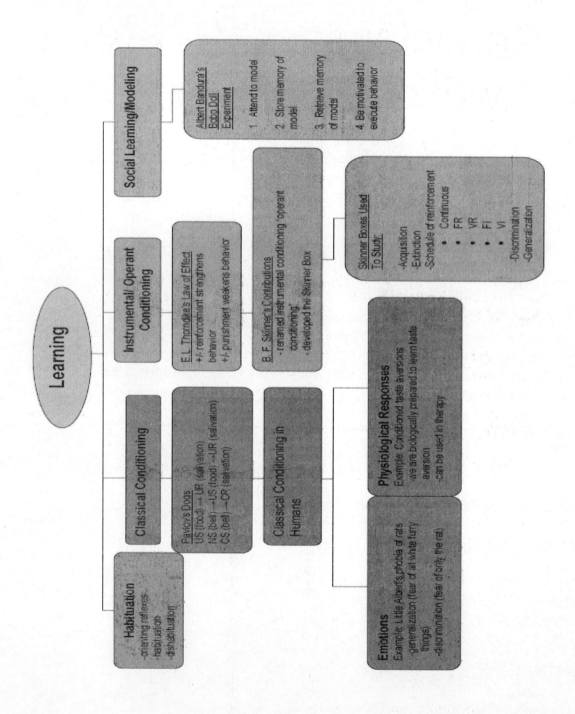

Key Points of the Big Picture

Acquisition:
the process of learning a conditioned response or behavior. *Example: Learning to study in hopes of making good grades.*

Aversion therapy:
a type of therapy that uses classical conditioning to condition people to avoid certain stimuli. *Example: Having smokers sit together in a small room and smoke until they get nauseated may condition them to become nauseated at the smell of cigarettes.*

Behaviorism:
a psychological perspective that emphasizes the study of observable behavior over the study of the mind.

Classical conditioning:
learning that occurs when a neutral stimulus is repeatedly paired with an unconditioned stimulus; because of this pairing, the neutral stimulus becomes a conditioned stimulus with the same power as the unconditioned stimulus to elicit the response in the organism. *Example: Being conditioned to fear dogs after having been bitten by one.*

Cognitive map:
a mental representation of the environment. *Example: Being able to draw a map of your home town.*

Conditioned response (CR):
the response elicited by a conditioned stimulus in an organism. *Example: Feeling afraid when you see a dog because you associate dogs with the pain of a dog bite.*

Conditioned stimulus (CS):
a stimulus that elicits a conditioned response in an organism. *Example: The sight of a dog causes you to feel fear because you associate dogs with the pain of a dog bite.*

Contiguity:
the degree to which two stimuli follow one another in time. *Example: Seeing a bee and immediately being stung by it. Being stung is contiguous with seeing the bee.*

Contingency:
the degree to which the presentation of one stimulus is contingent upon the presentation of the other. *Example: Hearing screeching tires is followed by the impact of a car accident.*

Continuous reinforcement:
a schedule of reinforcement in which the organism is rewarded for every instance of the desired response. *Example: A salesman receives a percentage of every pairs of shoes he sells.*

Counterconditioning:
using classical conditioning to remove an undesired conditioned response in an organism. *Example: Conditioning a person with a fear of flying to feel relaxed on an airplane.*

Dishabituation:
to begin re-responding to a stimulus to which one had been habituated. *Example: After tuning out the frequent noise of a railroad track that runs by your house, you once again respond to the sound the train when a train with a squeaking wheel passes your home one day.*

Extinction burst:
a temporary increase in a behavioral response that occurs. *Example: A child may beg harder for candy when her mother begins to ignore the child's pleas for candy.*

Extinction:
the removal of a conditioned response. *Example: A child stops begging for candy when she realizes that her pleas are not going to cause her mother to give her some candy.*

Fixed interval schedule:
schedule of reinforcement in which the organism is rewarded for the first desired response in an xth interval of time. *Example: Waiting for a bus that runs on a regular 15-minute schedule. It doesn't matter if you arrive at the bus stop right after the previous bus leaves or just before your bus comes— either way, you can only catch the bus once in a 15-minute interval.*

Fixed ratio schedule:
schedule of reinforcement in which the organism is rewarded for every xth instance of the desired response. *Example: A saleswoman receives a bonus for every five new accounts she signs with the company.*

Habituation:
the tendency of an organism to ignore repeated stimuli. *Example: Learning to ignore the sound of the air conditioner in your bedroom.*

Insight:
a new way of looking at a problem that leads to a sudden understanding of how to solve it. *Example: All of a sudden, you realize how to solve a math problem you've been working on for days.*

Instrumental conditioning:
a type of learning in which the organism learns through the consequences of its behavior. *Example: Learning to ask questions in class because asking questions leads to better understanding of the material and better grades.*

Latent learning:
learning that cannot be directly observed in an organism's behavior. *Example: Knowing how to build a house after watching a television show, but never actually doing it.*

Law of Effect:
a principle discovered by E. L. Thorndike, which states that random behaviors that lead to positive consequences will be strengthened and random behaviors that lead to negative consequences will be weakened. *Example: If you lose $25 at poker, you'll be less likely to gamble on poker again. If you play the lottery and win $25, you'll be more likely to buy more lottery tickets.*

Learning:
a relatively permanent change in behavior or behavior potential as a result of experience. *Example: Learning to knit a sweater.*

Negative punishment:
weakening a behavior by removing something pleasant to the organism's environment. *Example: A child has to give up a toy after willfully disobeying her parents.*

Negative reinforcement:
reinforcing a behavior by removing something unpleasant from the environment of the organism. *Example: A woman stops nagging her husband when he picks up his wet towels from the bathroom floor.*

Neutral stimulus (NS):
a stimulus that does not naturally elicit an unconditioned response in an organism. *Example: The color brown does not normally elicit nausea in the average person.*

Operant behavior:
behavior that operates on the environment to cause some sort of consequence to occur. *Example: Going to work to get paid.*

Orienting reflex:
the tendency of an organism to orient its sense towards unexpected stimuli. *Example: Looking up when a student comes into the classroom after class has started.*

Partial reinforcement schedule:
a schedule of reinforcement in which the organism is rewarded for only some instances of the desired response. *Example: A parent only occasionally rewards a child for making his bed.*

Positive punishment:
weakening a behavior by adding something unpleasant to the organism's environment. *Example: Your boss reprimands you for telling a dirty joke at work.*

Positive reinforcement:
Strengthening a behavior by adding something pleasant to the environment of the organism. *Example: Receiving an award at work for selling the most merchandise one month.*

Primary reinforcer:
a reinforcer that is reinforcing in and of itself. *Example: Sex, food, a warm blanket when you are cold.*

Punishment:
the weakening of a response that occurs when a behavior leads to an unpleasant consequence. *Example: Failing your psychology exam because you didn't read the chapter in the textbook makes it less likely that you will fail to read the book in the future.*

Reinforcement:
the strengthening of a response that occurs when the response is rewarded. *Example: Receiving a hug from your significant other for studying hard and passing your psychology exam makes it more likely that you will study hard in the future.*

Respondent behavior:
behavior that is emitted in response to some stimulus. *Example: Blinking when air is puffed in your eye.*

Schedule of reinforcement:
the frequency and timing of the reinforcements that an organism receives. *Example: The conditions under which an employee receives an employee bonus for selling merchandise.*

Secondary reinforcer:
a reinforcer that is reinforcing only because they lead to a primary reinforcer. *Example: Money, grades, poker chips in Las Vegas.*

Shaping:
using operant conditioning to build a new behavior in an organism by rewarding successive approximations of the desired response. *Example: Slowly conditioning your dog to sit up by rewarding him for behaviors that are closer and closer to sitting up.*

Skinner box:
a device created by B. F. Skinner to study operant behavior in a compressed timeframe; in a Skinner box, an organism is automatically rewarded or punished for engaging in certain behaviors.

Social learning:
learning through the observation and imitation of others' behavior. *Example: A baby chimpanzee learns to crack nuts with a rock by watching its mother do so.*

Spontaneous recovery:
during extinction, the tendency for a conditioned response to reappear and strengthen over a brief period of time before re-extinguishing. *Example: After having conquered your fear of flying, all of a sudden you feel intense fear when your plane hits a bit of turbulence.*

Stimulus discrimination:
responding only to particular stimuli. *Example: Being only afraid of pit-bull dogs.*

Stimulus generalization:
responding in a like fashion to similar stimuli. *Example: Being afraid of all big dogs.*

Taste aversion:
classical conditioning that occurs when an organism pairs the experience of nausea with a certain food and becomes conditioned to feel ill at the sight, smell, or idea of the food. *Example: Feeling nauseated at the idea of drinking alcohol after a getting drunk and throwing up one night.*

Token economy:
a system of operant conditioning in which subjects are reinforced with tokens that can be later cashed in for primary reinforcers. *Example: Earning points in school for following the rules when these points can be cashed in for prizes later.*

Unconditioned response (UR):
the response that is elicited by an unconditioned stimulus. *Example: Salivation is an unconditioned response to having lemon juice on your tongue.*

Unconditioned stimulus (US):
a stimulus that naturally elicits a response in an organism. *Example: Lemon juice on the tongue is an unconditioned stimulus for salivation.*

Variable interval schedule:
a schedule of reinforcement in which the organism is rewarded for the first desired response in an average xth interval of time. *Example: Waiting for a bus that is known for not being on time.*

Variable ratio schedule:
a schedule of reinforcement in which the organism is rewarded on average for every xth instance of the desired response. *Example: Playing the lottery.*

Fill-in Review of the Chapter

Can you fill-in the missing terms for each section of the chapter? Items marked with an * encourage you to continue building the Big Picture of psychology by connecting the material in this chapter with the material from previous chapters in the text.

The Big Picture: Learning to Live

Ultimately, Peter was helped by his peers who modeled proper behavior for him. This is an example of 1) _____ learning.

Defining Learning: In and Beyond the Classroom

Learning is a relatively permanent change in 2) _____ or 3) _____ as a result of experience.

Orienting and Habitutation: Learning to Ignore

4) _____ is learning to ignore repetitive stimuli.

5) _____ occurs when you resume responding to a stimulus to which you had previously habituated.

When your cat turns to look in the direction of the can opener as you are preparing his dinner, he is emitting in an 6) _____ _____.

Classical Conditioning: Learning Through the Association of Stimuli

A stimulus that naturally and reliably elicits a response in an organism is called a(n) 7)_____ _____.

In Pavlov's experiment, food was the 8) _____ _____.

If you are afraid of bees after having been stung as a child, your fear is likely the result of 9) _____ conditioning.

The 10*) _____ of the brain most likely plays a role in the conditioning of fear.

11) _____ and 12)_____ responses can be classically conditioned in humans.

Instrumental and Operant Conditioning: Learning from the Consequences of Our Actions

When playing a slot machine in Las Vegas, you are being reinforced on a 13) _____ _____ schedule of reinforcement.

The author of the Law of Effect was 14) _____.

Being told that you do not have to pay a fine because you returned your library book on time is an example of 15) _____ _____.

Having to pay a fine because you returned your library book late is an example of 16) _____ _____.

According to Japanese researcher, Yukata Haruki, the types of reinforcement are external reinforcement, self-reinforcement, internal reinforcement, and 17) _____ _____.

Knowing how to find your way from your home to your school is an example of what Edward Tolman called a 18) _____ _____.

Money is a good example of a 19) _____ reinforcer, while food is a good example of a 20) _____ reinforcer.

One major problem with 21) _____ is that it doesn't teach the correct behavior to the organism.

Social Learning or Modeling

If a child watches his mother paint a room and then mimics this by smearing shampoo on the bathroom walls, his behavior is an example of 22) _____ learning.

Bandura's famous experiments are called the 23) _____ _____ experiments, and they are an example of the 24*)_____ research method.

Use It or Lose It!

Can you fill in the following table with the type of learning that is exampled in these scenarios?

Type of Learning	Scenario
1.	Juan's wife gives him a kiss after he does the dishes.
2.	Willie doesn't ride his bike to school today because last time he did he fell and skinned his knee.
3.	Micah feels happy when he sees Kelly because last week Kelly shared her candy with him.
4.	Julie learned to knit by watching her grandmother knit.
5.	Shu Chen has lived near the airport for six years. Now she is not bothered by the sound of the planes taking off.
6.	Eddie goes to work to earn money.
7.	Lucas feels nauseous when he thinks of burritos after getting sick on fiesta night at the cafeteria.
8.	Gerri gets up early to get to class on time.

Self-Check: Are You Getting the Big Picture?

After you have read and studied the chapter, see if you can answer the following quiz questions. Check your answers at the end of the chapter. If you miss a question, refer to your text and re-study the appropriate sections.

True or False Questions

Are these statements true or false?

1. J. B. Watson was very concerned with the way that thoughts and feelings impact our behavior in the real world.
   Choice T: True
   Choice F: False

2. Kevin is attempting to teach his daughter to ride a bicycle. Of the different types of learning discussed in this chapter, classical conditioning is the method that is most likely to work for Kevin in this situation.
   Choice T: True
   Choice F: False

3. In Pavlov's original experiment, the conditioned response was salivation in the dog.
   Choice T: True
   Choice F: False

4. Taste aversion is a unique form of classical conditioning in that we tend to learn it very quickly and the interval of time between the presentation of the US and the NS/CS is unusually brief.
   Choice T: True
   Choice F: False

5. Jamal's father told him that he has to mow the yard on Saturday as punishment for forgetting to take out the trash last night. Jamal's father is using operant conditioning to control Jamal's behavior.
   Choice T: True
   Choice F: False

6. Peter, the boy from the Big Picture, was able to learn from his peers primarily through habituation.
   Choice T: True
   Choice F: False

7. B. F. Skinner wanted to rename classical conditioned behavior, "respondent behavior."
   Choice T: True
   Choice F: False

8. In operant conditioning, extinction occurs when the reinforcement for a behavior is removed.
   Choice T: True
   Choice F: False

9. If you want to build a response that is strong and very resistant to extinction, then you should use a continuous schedule of reinforcement.
   Choice T: True
   Choice F: False

10. You are a parent who wants to use operant conditioning to teach your child to study harder. All things being equal, you will have the most success if you use punishment instead of reinforcement to control your child's studying behavior.
    Choice T: True
    Choice F: False

Multiple Choice Questions

Can you choose the best answer for these questions?

1. When an organism is first placed on an extinction schedule, often its rate of responding temporarily increases. For example, if a rat has been conditioned to receive a pellet every time it presses a bar and the feeding mechanism runs out of pellets, the rat will initially increase the rate at which it presses the bar. This increase in bar presses is known as a(n)_____.
   A. acquisition response
   B. spontaneous recovery
   C. extinction burst
   D. re-acquisition response

2. Daniella is afraid of spiders. It doesn't matter whether she sees a garden spider or a black widow, she responds by screaming and running away. Daniella's behavior best illustrates a(n) _____.
   A. modeled behavior
   B. extinction burst
   C. stimulus generalization
   D. stimulus discrimination

3. Shu Chen was in a tornado that destroyed her apartment building. Now every time there is a thunder storm Shu Chen finds that she feels tense. Her palms sweat, her heart beats faster, and she finds it difficult to breathe. Shu Chen's behavior best illustrates what type of learning?
   A. habituation
   B. classical conditioning
   C. operant conditioning
   D. social learning

4. Jared was watching Batman on TV. Later that afternoon Jared was seen tying his jacket around his shoulders like a cape and pretending to be Batman. Jared's behavior best illustrates which type of learning?
   A. habituation
   B. classical conditioning
   C. operant conditioning
   D. social learning

5. LaDonna raised her hand and asked a question in class. As a result, her teacher smiled at her and thanked her for the question. Now LaDonna is more willing to ask questions in class. LaDonna's behavior best illustrates which type of learning?
   A. habituation
   B. classical conditioning
   C. operant conditioning
   D. social learning

6. Aversion therapy uses _____ to help clients overcome certain problems, such as alcoholism.
   A. habituation
   B. classical conditioning
   C. operant conditioning
   D. social learning

7. Roberto's former girlfriend wore blackberry perfume. She left Roberto last month. Now when Roberto smells blackberries, he feels sad. In this example, the US is:
   A. Roberto's girlfriend.
   B. the smell of blackberries.
   C. Roberto's loss of his girlfriend.
   D. Roberto's sadness at the loss of his girlfriend.

8. Roberto's former girlfriend wore blackberry perfume. She left Roberto last month. Now when Roberto smells blackberries, he feels sad. In this example, the CS is:
   A. Roberto's girlfriend.
   B. the smell of blackberries.
   C. Roberto's loss of his girlfriend.
   D. Roberto's sadness at the loss of his girlfriend.

9. To stop himself from feeling sad when smelling blackberries, Roberto buys some blackberry room freshener for his apartment. Everyday, he sprays the freshener in his apartment in the hope that he will soon stop feeling sad when he smells blackberry scent. Roberto is attempting to accomplish _____ of his response to blackberries.
   A. acquisition
   B. generalization
   C. discrimination
   D. extinction

10. James has a fear of snakes. To help with this problem, James' therapist trains him to pair relaxation techniques with successively more life-like encounters with snakes in the hopes that eventually James will be able to hold a snake while remaining relaxed. In this scenario, James' therapist is using a(n) _____ approach to help James.
    A. counter-conditioning
    B. operant conditioning
    C. aversion therapy
    D. habituation

11. "Behaviors that lead to positive consequences are more likely to be repeated and behaviors that lead to negative consequences are less likely to be repeated" is a statement of:
    A. the principle of habituation.
    B. the process of classical conditioning.
    C. the Law of Effect.
    D. the phenomenon of stimulus generalization.

12. Although she fed her cat canned food in the past, for the last two years Madge has fed her cat only dry food. Yet, tonight as Madge is using the can opener to open a can of green beans, her cat comes running and meowing for canned food. Which of the following phenomena best explain why Madge's cat would behave this way?
    A. extinction burst
    B. extinction
    C. stimulus generalization
    D. spontaneous recovery

13. Manny wants to use negative reinforcement to encourage students to come to class on time. To do this, he could:
    A. make late students stay after class.
    B. give late students more homework to do.
    C. allow on-time students to skip a homework assignment.
    D. give on-time students 5 extra credit points.

14. Herman just received a $100 fine for driving 95 mph on the interstate. The speeding ticket is an example of:
    A. positive punishment.
    B. negative punishment.
    C. classical conditioning.
    D. negative reinforcement.

15. One of B. F. Skinner's major contributions to the study of behavior was:
    A. the idea of punishment.
    B. the term instrumental conditioning.
    C. the puzzle box.
    D. none of the above.

16. In psychological terms, a sudden realization that allows you to solve a problem is referred to as _____.
    A. insight
    B. inspiration
    C. intuition
    D. none of the above

17. _____learning does not have an immediately observable effect on a person's behavior.
    A. Hidden
    B. Social
    C. Latent
    D. Cognitive

18. Betty gets paid a $50 bonus for every 100th pair of shoes that she sells at her job in a shoe store. Betty is being reinforced on which schedule of reinforcement?
    A. continuous
    B. fixed interval
    C. fixed ratio
    D. variable ratio

19. Josefina gets paid once a month at her job as a teacher. Josefina is being reinforced on which schedule of reinforcement?
    A. fixed interval
    B. variable interval
    C. fixed ratio
    D. variable ratio

20. The train Phillip takes to work is notorious for being off schedule. It's supposed to run every 10 minutes, but it's often late or early. If catching the train is viewed as reinforcement, then Phillip is being reinforced on which schedule of reinforcement?
    A. fixed interval
    B. variable interval
    C. fixed ratio
    D. variable ratio
    E. continuous

21. Berta is an animal trainer in Hollywood. On her next film, she has to teach a pig to dance. Which of the following techniques would most likely allow Berta to accomplish this task?
    A. habituation
    B. stimulus generalization
    C. shaping
    D. social learning

22. Gabe is a first grade teacher. Every time one of his students behaves all day long, Gabe gives the student a gold star. After a student has accumulated five stars, he or she can spend an extra 10 minutes at recess. Which learning technique(s) is Gabe using with his students?
    A. operant conditioning
    B. secondary reinforcement
    C. a token economy
    D. all of the above

23. Albert Bandura's Bobo doll experiments indicated all of the following except:
    A. You must engage in a behavior to truly know how to do it.
    B. Children can learn by watching others.
    C. Learning can be latent.
    D. Reinforcement and punishment are not necessary for learning to occur.

24. The available research on social learning indicates that social learning can occur:
    A. in children as young as 12 months.
    B. only when children are old enough to understand the implications of a behavior.
    C. only when we perceive that we will be rewarded if we engage in the behavior.
    D. only when we have an opportunity to repeatedly view the model, such as on a weekly TV show.

25. Which of the following is not a primary reinforcer?
    A. food
    B. water
    C. an "A" on an exam
    D. feeling proud of receiving a promotion at work

Short-Answer Questions

Can you write a brief answer to these questions?

1. A friend is having trouble getting her boyfriend to be on time for their dates. What advice would you give her about using learning theory to teach her boyfriend to be more on time?

2. Give an original example of negative reinforcement.

3. Give an original example of classical conditioning and be sure to label all the components.

4. Name some professions in which the ability to habituate would be helpful.

5. What factors affect the quality of classical conditioning?

Developing a Bigger Picture: Making Connections Across Chapters

An important aspect of learning is learning to see the "Big Picture" of the subject you are studying. As you learn about psychology, you should try to understand how the material from different chapters fits together to help you form a broad-based understanding of what psychology is all about. To help facilitate the development of this "Big Picture" in your mind, try to answer these questions using the knowledge you have learned in this chapter, as well as the other chapters referenced in the questions.

1. Using the information you learned about ethics in Chapter 1, what recommendations would you have for making the Little Albert experiments more ethical?

2. Using what you learned about the history of psychology in Chapter 1, explain the significance of the discovery of classical and operant conditioning to the development of psychology as a field of science.

3. Given what you have learned in Chapters 1, 2, and 5, give an example of a question that a biological psychologist might ask about learning.

Label the Diagram

Can you label the components of classical conditioning on this figure from your text book?

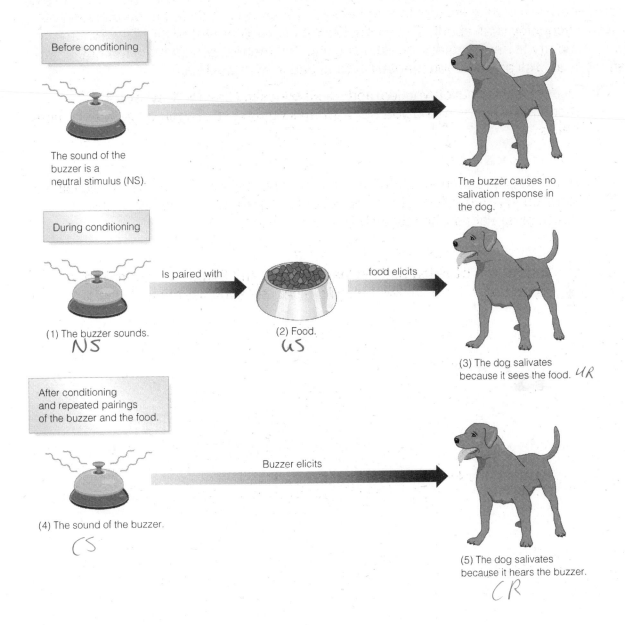

Before conditioning

The sound of the buzzer is a neutral stimulus (NS).

The buzzer causes no salivation response in the dog.

During conditioning

Is paired with

food elicits

(1) The buzzer sounds.
NS

(2) Food.
US

(3) The dog salivates because it sees the food. UR

After conditioning and repeated pairings of the buzzer and the food.

Buzzer elicits

(4) The sound of the buzzer.
CS

(5) The dog salivates because it hears the buzzer.
CR

Big Picture Review

The Four Types of Consequences of Behavior

Reinforcement increases the likelihood of a behavior; punishment decreases it.

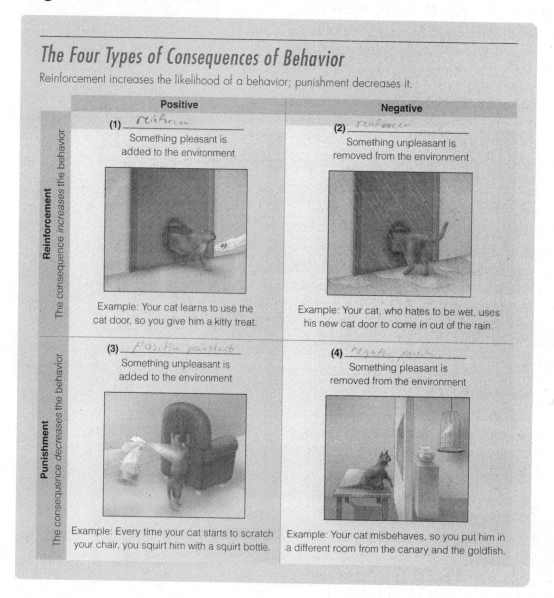

	Positive	Negative
Reinforcement The consequence *increases* the behavior	**(1)** _reinforcer_ Something pleasant is added to the environment	**(2)** _reinforcer_ Something unpleasant is removed from the environment
	Example: Your cat learns to use the cat door, so you give him a kitty treat.	Example: Your cat, who hates to be wet, uses his new cat door to come in out of the rain.
Punishment The consequence *decreases* the behavior	**(3)** _Positive punishment_ Something unpleasant is added to the environment	**(4)** _negative punisher_ Something pleasant is removed from the environment
	Example: Every time your cat starts to scratch your chair, you squirt him with a squirt bottle.	Example: Your cat misbehaves, so you put him in a different room from the canary and the goldfish.

Solutions

Each solution below is followed by its textbook page reference number and its corresponding chapter learning objective (LO) number. Items with a Big Picture LO help you build a Big Picture of psychology across the chapters you have studied so far.

Fill-in Review of the Chapter

1. social [p. 190, 229; LO 16, Big Picture]
2. behavior [p. 191; LO 1]
3. behavior potential [p. 191; LO 1]
4. Habituation [p. 194; LO 2]
5. Dishabituation [p. 196; LO 2]
6. orienting reflex [p. 193; LO 2]
7. unconditioned stimulus [p. 198; LO 3-5]
8. unconditioned stimulus [p. 198; LO 3-5]
9. classical [p. 202; LO 3-5]
10. amygdala [p. 69, LO 5; Big Picture]
11. Emotional [p. 202; LO 5]
12. physiological [p. 202; LO 5]
13. variable ratio [p. 218; LO 13]
14. E. L. Thorndike [p. 210; LO 8]
15. negative reinforcement [p. 212; LO 11, 13]
16. negative punishment [p. 212; LO 11, 13]
17. alien reinforcement [p. 213; LO 13]
18. cognitive map [p. 227; LO 16]
19. secondary [p. 225; LO 11, 13]
20. primary [p. 225; LO 11, 13]
21. punishment [p. 222; LO 13]
22. social [p. 229; LO 15]
23. Bobo doll [p. 228; LO 14]
24. experimental [p. 32; LO 14, Big Picture]

Use It or Lose It!

1. Operant Conditioning [p. 209; LO 7]
2. Operant Conditioning [p. 209; LO 7]
3. Classical Conditioning [p. 200; LO 7]
4. Social Learning [p. 229; LO 15]
5. Habituation [p. 194; LO 2]
6. Operant Conditioning [p. 209; LO 7]
7. Classical Conditioning [p. 200; LO 7]
8. Operant Conditioning [p. 209; LO 7]

Self-Check: Are You Getting The Big Picture?

True or False Questions

1. F [p. 226; LO 4, Big Picture]	6. F [p. 189, 194; LO 2, 15, Big Picture]
2. F [p. 202; LO 7]	7. T [p. 215; LO 9]
3. T [p. 199; LO 3]	8. T [p. 216; LO 10]
4. F [p. 206; LO 5]	9. F [p. 217; LO 10, 11]
5. T [p. 209; LO 7]	10. F [p. 222; LO 13]

Multiple Choice Questions

1. C [p. 216; LO 10]	10. A [p. 204; LO 6]	19. A [p. 219; LO 11, 13]
2. C [p. 203; LO 12]	11. C [p. 210; LO 8]	20. B [p. 220; LO 11, 13]
3. B [p. 202; LO 4]	12. D [p. 208; LO 10]	21. C [p. 221; LO 12]
4. D [p. 229; LO 15]	13. C [p. 212; LO 11]	22. D [p. 225; LO 13]
5. C [p. 209; LO 7]	14. B [p. 212; LO 11]	23. A [p. 228; LO 14]
6. B [p. 207; LO 6]	15. D [p. 214; LO 9]	24. A [p. 229; LO 15]
7. C [p. 198; LO 5]	16. A [p. 226; LO 16]	25. C [p. 225; LO 11]
8. B [p. 199; LO 5]	17. C [p. 227; LO 16]	
9. D [p. 207; LO 6]	18. C [p. 218; LO 11,13]	

Short-Answer Questions

Can you write a brief answer to these questions?

1. A friend is having trouble getting her boyfriend to be on time for their dates. What advice would you give her about using learning theory to teach her boyfriend to be more on time? [pp. 209-228; LO 1, 5, 7-13, 15]

There are many possible correct answers to this question. One would be to advise her to use operant conditioning on her boyfriend. She should avoid punishment and positively or negatively reinforce him when he is on time. She could do something as simple as thanking him for being on time, or being extra nice to him when he arrives on time. When he is late, she should then withhold whatever reinforcer she is using, but avoid being punishing because punishment can cause negative emotions.

2. Give an original example of negative reinforcement. [p. 212; LO 11]

There are many possible answers here. All correct answers should remove some unpleasant or aversive stimulus as a means of rewarding the organism. For example, your partner does the dishes. So, you tell him/her that he/she doesn't have to take the trash out.

3. Give an original example of classical conditioning and be sure to label all the components. [p. 220; LO 4, 5]

One possible answer to this question would be learning to feel happy when you smell baking turkey because it reminds you of your mother's home at Thanksgiving dinner. Here the US is your beloved mother; the NS/CS is the smell of cooking turkey; and the US/UR is feeling happy.

4. Name some professions in which the ability to habituate would be helpful.

[p. 194; LO 2]

Any workplace that involves many distractions would be one in which habituation would come in handy-- for example a daycare, a noisy factory, the New York Stock Exchange, a telemarketing phone room, a prison, and so on.

5. What factors affect the quality of classical conditioning? [pp. 200-201; LO 4, 5]

    Contiguity and contingency between the US and the NS/CS are both important if strong conditioning is to occur. Contiguity means that typically the NS/CS must be presented close in time to the US for the organism to be conditioned. Contingency means that in order for conditioning to occur, the organism must usually perceive that the presentation of the NS/CS means that the US is going to be presented.

Developing a Bigger Picture: Making Connections Across Chapters

1. Using the information you learned about ethics in Chapter 1, what recommendations would you have for making the Little Albert experiments more ethical? [pp. 36, 203; LO 14, Big Picture]

    Some possible responses to this question include having Albert's mother sign an informed consent form; use an adult participant instead of a child; condition a positive emotion instead of fear; scrap the entire experiment; or use an animal subject.

2. Using what you learned about the history of psychology in Chapter 1, explain the significance of the discovery of classical and operant conditioning to the development of psychology as a field of science. [pp. 12-14, 200, & 209; LO 3, 8, Big Picture]

    The discovery of classical and operant conditioning paved the way for behaviorism in the early part of the 1900s. Both of these theories allowed psychologists to explain behavior without having to discuss mental processes like thoughts, feelings, and so on. This freed psychologists to focus their attention on observable behaviors that could be measured objectively and to ignore cognitive processes, which were more difficult to measure scientifically.

3. Given what you have learned in Chapters 1, 2, and 5, give an example of a question that a biological psychologist might ask about learning. [pp. 15, 70, & 188-230; LO 1-13, Big Picture]

    There are many correct answers to this question. One example is that a biological psychologist might ask whether or not the hippocampus plays a role in the process of acquiring a classically conditioned response.

Label the Diagram

1.	NS [p. 199; LO 3]
2.	US [p. 199; LO 3]
3.	UR [p. 199; LO 3]
4.	CS [p. 199; LO 3]
5.	CR [p. 199; LO 3]

Big Picture Review

1. positive reinforcement [p. 211; LO 11]
2. negative reinforcement [p. 211; LO 11]
3. positive punishment [p. 211; LO 11]
4. negative punishment [p. 211; LO 11]

6

How Does Memory Function?

Learning Objectives

After studying each of the sections of the chapter, you should be able to do these tasks.

The Functions of Memory: Encoding, Storing, and Retrieving

1. Explain the functions of memory.
2. Tell the difference between implicit and explicit use of memory.

The Traditional Three Stages Model of Memory

3. Describe the three stages model of memory.
4. Describe the function and characteristics of sensory, short-term, and long-term memory.
5. Describe the newer conception of working memory and how it relates to the three-stage model's concept of short-term memory.

Long-term Memory: Permanent Storage

6. Explain how information is organized in long-term memory.
7. Describe the different types of long-term memory and their characteristics.

Retrieval and Forgetting: Random Access Memory?

8. Explain retrieval processes in memory.
9. Describe and give examples of the various theories of forgetting in long-term memory.

Is Memory Accurate?

10. Describe the accuracy of memory and its implications for eyewitness memory.

Improving Your Memory: Tips to Remember

11. Describe ways in which to improve your memory.

The Biology of Memory

12. Discuss what is known about the biology of memory.

The Big Picture

The Big Picture: The Real Rain Man: Does Extraordinary Memory Come at a Price?

For Kim Peek, memory has been both a blessing and a curse. He can memorize phone books and symphonies, but he must relearn how to brush his teeth each day and he cannot think analytically about the very topics of which he knows so many details. His memory abilities are amazing and inadequate at the same time. By studying people like Kim, we gain greater understanding and appreciation for the awesome powers and fragility of the human mind.

The Functions of Memory: Encoding, Storing, and Retrieving

This section covers Learning Objectives 1-2. In this chapter, you learned about how your memory works—a practical topic that should improve your academic success! But, you don't just use your memory in the classroom. In everyday life, you constantly use your memory in both a conscious, explicit fashion (e.g., remembering an old friend's name) and an unconscious, implicit fashion (e.g., remembering how to drive a car). To date, psychologists have spent more time studying the function of explicit memory than implicit memory.

The Traditional Three Stages Model of Memory

This section covers Learning Objectives 3-6. One early theory of how memory works is the three stages model of memory. According to this model, memory is stored in a sequence of three stages: sensory memory, short-term memory, and long-term memory.

Sensory memory is the first stage of memory, in which brief sensory impressions are stored for the things we encounter in the world. There are three types of sensory memory: iconic (visual), echoic (auditory), and haptic (touch). Of these, the most is known about the function of iconic and echoic sensory memory. In iconic sensory memory, icons or pictures of what we see are stored in memory for only about half a second. In this brief time, the mind extracts information about what we have seen from the icon and sends it on to short-term memory for further processing. Echoic memory stores an echo or sound recording of what we have heard for about two seconds, during which time, information about what we have heard is extracted and sent to short-term memory for processing. The transfer of information from sensory to short-term memory is relatively effortless and requires only that you pay attention to the information in sensory memory.

Short-term memory is the second stage of memory. It is thought to have both a limited capacity and duration. According to the three-stage model of memory, short-term memory holds about 7±2 bits of information for about 20 sec. It is a temporary stage of memory where information is stored before it is moved into long-term memory. According to the three stage model, the key to getting information from short-term to long-term memory is to keep it in short-term memory as long as you through maintenance rehearsal or repeating the information over and over again to yourself.

However, research has shown that maintenance rehearsal is not a good way of moving information into long-term memory. A better way is to use elaborative rehearsal that involves forming mental associations between the information you are trying to store and the information you already have stored in long-term memory. Taking a levels-of-processing approach, researchers have demonstrated that the harder you think about information and the more deeply you process it, the better your long-term memory for that information will be.

Today, modern theories of memory question the three-stage model's conception of short-term memory. In particular, these models question the idea that you can always hold 7+2 items in short-term memory and whether information must pass sequentially through the three stages of memory. One modern theory, the working memory model proposes that the stages of memory work in more of a parallel fashion than a serial fashion. In this model, working memory and short-term memory are parts of long-term memory. Working memory works to move information in and out of long-term memory and short-term memory is the part of working memory that briefly stores the information you are using at any particular moment in time.

Working memory is also thought to contain other components, including a central executive and two slave systems called the phonological loop and the visuo-spatial sketchpad. The central executive is the part of working memory that controls your attention. It also controls the phonological loop, which processes auditory information and the visuo-spatial sketchpad, which processes visual and spatial information.

Long-term Memory: Permanent Storage

This section covers Learning Objective 7. If information is processed deeply enough, it will be moved into long-term memory by the working memory system. Long-term memory is your permanent memory storage stage. There are different types of long-term memory. Declarative memory is memory that is easily put into words. Semantic memory and episodic memory are both types of declarative memory. Semantic memory is memory for concepts. Episodic memory is your autobiographical memory for events in your life.

Procedural memory or your memory for skills is long-term memory that is not easily put into words. Procedural memory is often executed implicitly, whereas declarative is more frequently processed explicitly. Procedural memories are also tend to be more long-lasting that declarative memories—especially under conditions in which the memory has not been used very frequently or recently. Studies of amnesia victims like H.M. support the idea that procedural memory is a separate form of memory.

Long-term memory is thought to be organized into general knowledge structures called schemata. Schemata contain the information we have learned about our world including knowledge about concepts, people, places, activities and so on. Your schemata are arranged in conceptual hierarchies or categories that allow you to use your memory efficiently.

Retrieval and Forgetting: Random Access Memory?

This section covers Learning Objectives 8-9. Retrieval of information for long-term memory involves using probes or cures to contact and retrieve memory traces that have been stored in long-term memory. There are two types of retrieval processes: recall and recognition. In recall, the retrieval probes are weak and contain little information. In recognition, the retrieval probes or cues are very strong and contain a great deal of information. Generally recognition is easier to accomplish than recall.

Whether or not you successfully retrieve information from long-term memory is a function of the memory's availability (presence) and accessibility (being retrievable) in memory. As such, there are times when we are unable to retrieve memories and forgetting occurs. Decay theory predicts that forgetting will occur when memory traces for memories that are not routinely accessed decay and eventually disappear. This theory, however, is controversial.

Interference is a more accepted explanation of forgetting. In proactive interference memory traces for older memories block the accessibility of newer memory traces. In retroactive interference, newer memory traces block the accessibility of older memory traces in long-term memory. Another type of forgetting, cue-dependent forgetting, occurs when we try to retrieve memories in a context that is different from the context in which we originally stored the memory trace—for example, trying to remember the name of a classmate when you see him downtown may be more difficult than trying to remember his name when you are in school.

Sigmund Freud's idea of repression is a final, controversial explanation of forgetting. According to Freud, memories for traumatic or threatening events can be repressed into the unconscious and therefore become inaccessible for retrieval. So far, researchers have been unable to determine whether or not repression is a viable explanation for forgetting.

Is Memory Accurate?

This section covers Learning Objective 10. Even though forgetting is a frequent occurrence, often we do successfully retrieve memories. But, how accurate are your retrieved memories? Research has shown that in many instances retrieved memories contain inaccurate details. This is due to the fact that memory is both reconstructive (based on actual events) and constructive (based on your expectations). In other words, you do not store all the details of the events in your life and when you later retrieve memories of these events, you tend to fill in the missing details based on your expectations of what likely happened. Most of the time, any inaccuracies in your memory are of little consequence. However in circumstances like eyewitness testimony these inaccuracies could be of extreme importance.

Improving Your Memory: Tips to Remember

This section covers Learning Objective 11. As students, information on how to improve the accuracy of you memory should be of great interest to you. Here are several bits of advice from psychologists: pay attention in class; don't cram for exams; use elaborative rehearsal; overlearn material; and use mnemonics or memory devices.

The Biology of Memory

This section covers Learning Objective 12. A final topic in this chapter looks at the biology of memory. As you learned in this chapter, as well as Chapter 2, the hippocampus plays a crucial role in the storage of declarative memory traces. Brain imaging studies have also indicated that the frontal lobe may play a role in the storage of declarative memory. Procedural memories do not seem to be processed by the hippocampus, but there is evidence that motor skill memory is processed in the cerebellum and in specific regions of the cortex.

Outlining the Big Picture

Chapter 6: How Does Memory Function?

The Big Picture: The Real Rain Man: Does Extraordinary Memory Come at a Price? Fran Peek's *The Real Rain Man.*
Notes:

_____

_____

_____

_____

_____

The Functions of Memory: Encoding, Storing, and Retrieving (Learning Objectives 1-2)
Explicit and Implicit Memory
Notes:

_____

_____

_____

_____

_____

_____

The Traditional Three Stages Model of Memory (Learning Objectives 3-6)
Sensory Memory: Where It All Begins
    Visual Sensory Memory: Iconic Memory
    Auditory Sensory Memory: Echoic Memory
    Transferring Information from Sensory to Short-term Memory
Short-term Memory: Where Memories are Made (and Lost)
    The Capacity of Short-Term Memory: Seven (Plus or Minus Two)
    The Duration of Short-Term Memory: It's Yours for 30 Seconds
    How We Transfer Information from Short-Term to Long-Term Memory
    Elaborative Rehearsal
    Levels of Processing
Does Short-term Memory Really Exist?
    The Serial Position Curve, Primacy and Recency
The Working Memory View: Parallel Memory
    The Central Executive
Notes:

_____

_____

_____

_____

_____

Long-term Memory: Permanent Storage (Learning Objective 7)
The Capacity of Long-term Memory
Encoding in Long-term Memory
Organization in Long-term Memory
Types of Long-term Memory
    Spotlight on Diversity: Gender and Autobiographical Memory.
Amnesia: What Forgetting Can Teach Us about Memory
Notes:

_____

_____

_____

_____

_____

_____

_____

Retrieval and Forgetting: Random Access Memory? (Learning Objectives 8-9)
Recognition and Recall
When Retrieval Fails: Forgetting
Notes:

_____

_____

_____

_____

_____

Is Memory Accurate? (Learning Objective 10)
Memory Is Not a Videotape
Eyewitness Memory
Notes:

_____

_____

_____

_____

_____

Improving Your Memory: Tips to Remember (Learning Objective 11)
Pay Attention
Do Not Cram for Exams
Use Elaborative Rehearsal
Use Overlearning
Mnemonics Make Your Memory Mighty
    Acronyms
    Acrostics
    Peg Word System
    Method of Loci

The SQ3R Method
Notes:

_____

_____

_____

_____

The Biology of Memory (Learning Objective 12)
Notes:

_____

_____

_____

_____

Are You Getting the Big Picture?
Notes:

_____

_____

_____

_____

Seeing the Big Picture: A Mental Map of Chapter 6

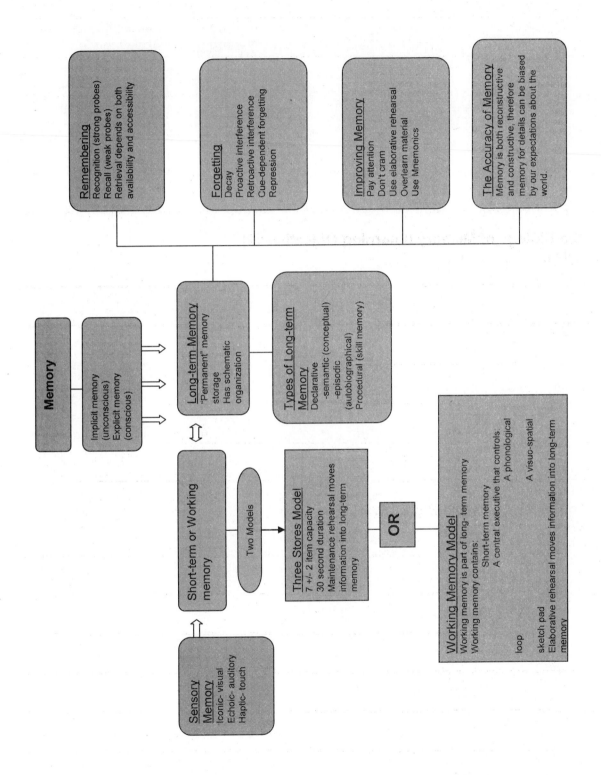

Key Points of the Big Picture

Anterograde amnesia:
a type of amnesia in which one is unable to store new memories in long-term memory. *Example: After a head injury, Jeremy cannot learn new concepts or store new episodic memories.*

Attention:
conscious awareness; can be focused on events that are taking place in the environment or inside our minds. *Example: As you read this page, you are focusing your attention on these words.*

Central executive:
the attention-controlling component of working memory. *Example: To focus your attention on this page, your central executive must direct your memory resources to accomplish this task.*

Chunking:
the process of using one's limited short-term memory resources more efficiently by combining small bits of information to form larger bits of information or chunks. *Example: Recalling your phone number as being three numbers instead of ten— "312" "555" "1257".*

Consciousness:
feelings, thoughts, and aroused states of which we are aware. . *Example: Your awareness that you are currently reading this page.*

Constructive memory:
memory that utilizes knowledge and expectations to fill in the missing details in our retrieved memory traces. *Example: Later using your expectations of what material is supposed to be in a study guide to help you fill in the missing details of what you read on this page.*

Cue-dependent forgetting:
a type of forgetting that occurs when one cannot recall information in a context other than the context in which it was encoded. *Example: Not being able to recall the name of your classmate when you run into her at the store, but being able to recall her name at school.*

Decay theory:
a theory of forgetting that proposes that memory traces that are not routinely activated in long-term memory will decay away. *Example: If you do not routinely think about the content of this chapter, it will disappear from your long term memory.*

Declarative memory:
a type of long-term memory that encompasses memories that are easily verbalized including episodic and semantic memories. *Example: Memories of psychology and being in psychology class are declarative memories.*

Distributed practice:
spreading one's study time across a series of study sessions. *Example: Studying your psychology for one hour everyday.*

Dual-coding system:
a system of memory that encodes information in more than one type of code or format. *Example: Storing the sound of the word "dog" and the visual image of the word "dog".*

Echoic memory:
sensory memory for auditory information. *Example: Storing the exact sound of your professor's last statement for a very brief period of time.*

Elaborative rehearsal:
forming associations or links between information one is trying to learn with information already stored in long-term memory so as to facilitate the transfer of this new information into long-term memory. *Example: Thinking about how the material in this chapter relates to the material you learned in Chapters 1-5.*

Encoding:
the act of inputting information into memory. *Example: Right now, you are encoding these words.*

Episodic memory:
long-term, declarative memory for autobiographical events. *Example: Your memory of what you did this morning.*

Explicit memory:
the conscious use of memory. *Example: On test day, you will consciously try to recall the answers to your professor's questions.*

Flashbulb memory:
an unusually detailed and seemingly accurate memory for an emotionally charged event. *Your memory of where you were when you first heard about the shootings at Virginia Tech, 9/11, etc.*

Iconic memory:
sensory memory for visual information. *Example: Storing the exact image of these words in your memory for very brief period of time.*

Implicit memory:
the unconscious use of memory. *Example: As you write notes, you are not consciously retrieving memories of how to write, you are retrieving this information implicitly.*

Levels-of-processing model:
a model that predicts that information which is processed deeply and elaboratively will be best retained in and recalled from long-term memory. *Example: If you engage in elaborative rehearsal of this material, you will have a better chance of recalling it on exam day.*

Long-term memory (LTM):
a system of memory that works to store memories for a long time, perhaps even permanently. *Example: Your memories of childhood are stored in your long term memory.*

Maintenance rehearsal:
repeating information over and over again so as to keep it in short-term memory for an extended period of time. *Example: Attempting to study this material by reading the chapter over and over.*

Massed practice:
cramming or attempting to learn large amounts of information in a single session of study. *Example: Cramming for your next psychology exam by studying all night the night before the test.*

Memory traces:
the stored code that represents a piece of information that has been encoded into memory. *Example: The long term memories you will store for this material.*

Mnemonic device:
a cognitive procedure or mental trick that is designed to improve one's memory. *Example: "SSL", sensory, short term, and long term— the order in which memory traces are encoded.*

Overlearning:
improving memory for material that is already known by continuing to rehearse it. *Example: Continuing to study this material even after you think you know it pretty well.*

Phonological loop:
in the working memory model, the part of working memory that processes the phonological, or sound, qualities of information. *Example: The phonological loop processes the sounds of these words as you read them.*

Primacy effect:
the tendency for people to recall words from the beginning of a list better than words that appeared in the middle of the list. *Example: You will likely remember what you read at the beginning of the chapter better than the middle of the chapter, unless you take action to study the middle material.*

Proactive interference:
a type of forgetting that occurs when older memory traces inhibit the retrieval of newer memory traces. *Example: On the first day of a new semester, you might find yourself heading toward the classroom in which you had class last semester.*

Procedural memory:
long-term memory for skills and behaviors. *Example: Knowing how to drive a car.*

Recall:
A type of retrieval process in which the probe or cue does not contain much information. *Example: Knowing the name of an old friend you meet at the store.*

Recency effect:
the tendency for people to recall words from the end of a list better than words that appeared in the middle of the list. *Example: If you listening to your professor list your homework assignments for the weekend, you are most likely to recall the last item he or she mentions.*

Recognition:
a type of retrieval process in which the probe or cue contains a great deal of information, including the item being sought. *Example: Meeting an old friend at the store and recognizing that you know him, but not being able to recall from where you know him or what his name is.*

Reconstructive memory:
memory that is based on the retrieval of memory traces that contain the actual details of the events that we have experienced. *Example: Accurately recalling the events of the last hour.*

Repression:
a type of forgetting proposed by Sigmund Freud in which memories for events, desires, or impulses that we find threatening are pushed into an inaccessible part of the mind called the unconscious. *Example: If you were to have caused a car accident due to carelessness, you might repress your memories of the event into your unconscious.*

Retrieval:
the process of accessing information in memory and pulling it into consciousness. *Example: Recalling the meaning of these words you are reading.*

Retroactive interference:
a type of forgetting that occurs when newer memory traces inhibit the retrieval of older memory traces. *Example: Being able to recall your current phone number, but not being able to recall your last phone number.*

Retrograde amnesia:
a type of amnesia in which one is unable to retrieve previously stored memories from long-term memory. *Example: Not being able to recall events prior to suffering a head injury, but still being able to remember events after the time of the injury.*

Schema:
an organized, generalized knowledge structure in long-term memory. *Example: Your stored knowledge of what happens when you go to the doctor is an example of a schema for an event.*

Semantic encoding:
encoding memory traces in terms of the meaning of the information being stored. *Example: Storing the knowledge that a dog is an animal.*

Semantic memory:
long-term, declarative memory for conceptual information. *Example: Your stored knowledge of psychology.*

Sensory memory:

a system of memory that very briefly stores sensory impressions so that we can extract relevant information from them for further processing in memory. *Example: Storing the image of these words in your sensory memory before moving this information into short term/ working memory.*

Short-term memory (STM):

a system of memory that is limited in both capacity and duration; in the three stages model of memory, short-term memory was seen as the intermediate stage between sensory memory and long-term memory. *Example: Holding a list of the items you need to buy at the store in your memory as you look for a pen and paper to write them down.*

Storage:

the place where information is retained in memory. *Example: Hopefully, you will process and store this information in your long term memory so that you can later retrieve it on exam day.*

Visuo-spatial sketchpad:

in the working memory model, the part of working memory that processes the visual and spatial aspects of information. *Example: The visuo-spatial sketch pad are processing the visual characteristics of these words you are reading.*

Working memory:

a multi-faceted component of long-term memory that contains short-term memory, a central executive, a phonological loop, and a visuo-spatial sketchpad; the function of working memory is to access, move, and process information that we are currently using. *Example: Hopefully, the content of this definition are in your working memory.*

Fill-in Review of The Chapter

Can you fill-in the missing terms for each section of the chapter? Items marked with an * encourage you to continue building the Big Picture of psychology by connecting the material in this chapter to material from previous chapters in the text.

The Big Picture: The Real Rain Man: Does Extraordinary Memory Come at a Price?

Kim Peek has damage to the 1*) _____ of his brain which prevents him from learning many procedural memories such as brushing his teeth.

Kim Peek seems to have a great capacity for memorizing conceptual memories. Psychologists refer to conceptual memory as 2) _____ long term memory.

The Functions of Memory: Encoding, Storing, and Retrieving

Conscious is to 3) _____ memory as unconscious is to 4) _____ memory.

The functions of memory are 5) _____, 6) _____, and 7) _____.

The Traditional Three Stages Model of Memory

You use your iconic memory to store 8) _____ or brief visual sensory impressions of what you are seeing.

An echo lasts for up to 9) _____.

According to the three stages model of memory, the capacity of short-term memory is about 10) _____ small bits of information.

Information in short-term memory is encoded in a 11) _____ or 12) _____ form.

One way to store more information in short-term memory is to use 13) _____.

Information can remain in short-term memory for about 14) _____. To keep information in short-term memory for a longer period of time, you would have to use 15) _____ _____.

Long-term Memory: Permanent Storage

The memory of going to the movies with your friends last weekend is an example of 16) _____ memory.

Most long-term memories are encoded in a 17) _____ _____.

Retrieval and Forgetting: Random Access Memory?

Retrieving the phone number of the pizza place without looking in the phonebook is an example of a 18) _____ retrieval task.

Meeting an old friend in the store are realizing that the person is someone you know is an example of a 19) _____ retrieval task.

Being able to recall your new class schedule, but unable to recall your schedule from last year is likely due to 20) _____ interference.

Not recalling the name of your professor when you see her in the grocery store is an example of forgetting due to a change in 21) _____.

Is Memory Accurate?

22) _____ memory is memory that is based on the details of the actual events. Whereas 23) _____ memory is memory that is based in part on your expectations of what happened during the event.

Improving Your Memory: Tips to Remember

SQ3R is a 24) _____ device that helps improve memory for what you have read.

An 25) _____ is a sentence made with words that begin with the first letters of the words on a list that you are trying to remember.

The Biology of Memory

The 26*) _____ of the brain helps to move declarative information from short term to long term memory.

The 27*) _____ of the brain seems to help us learn new procedural memories.

Use It or Lose It!

Can you fill in the following table with the appropriate answers to these questions?

Answer	Scenario
1.	You moved the clock in your room to a new location, but you persist in looking towards its old location when you wish to see what time it is. Why?
2.	This question is likely in which stage of your memory right now?
3.	What you learned about the brain in Chapter 2 is likely in which stage of your memory right now?
4.	What is the best type of rehearsal to use in studying for your next psychology exam?
5.	If you recall the first things your professor said during a lecture, but can't recall the material that followed, this would be an example of what memory phenomenon?
6.	Shoving an unpleasant memory into one's unconscious is called what?

7.	What type of rehearsal is best for keeping information in short term memory?
8.	When a person suffers from Alzheimer's disease, which component of working memory is thought to falter?

Self-Check: Are You Getting the Big Picture?

After you have read and studied the chapter, see if you can answer the following quiz questions. Check your answers at the end of the chapter. If you miss a question, refer to your text and re-study the appropriate sections.

True or False Questions

Are these statements true or false?

1. Information in sensory memory will automatically pass to short-term memory. It is not necessary for you to do anything to accomplish this transfer.
   Choice T: True
   Choice F: False

2. Information in long-term memory can be encoded in visual, acoustic, or semantic code.
   Choice T: True
   Choice F: False

3. The results of many serial position experiments support the idea that short-term memory actually exists.
   Choice T: True
   Choice F: False

4. The case study of K.F., the man who suffered brain damage in a motorcycle accident, is more consistent with the three stages model of memory than the working memory model of memory.
   Choice T: True
   Choice F: False

5. The fact that humans can engage in top-down perceptual processing is more consistent with the working memory model of memory than the three stages model of memory.
   Choice T: True
   Choice F: False

6. If you are given a list of words to remember, you are more likely to remember words from the end of the list than from any other part of the list.
   Choice T: True
   Choice F: False

7. When taking an exam in your psychology class, it is primarily your semantic memory that is being tested.
   Choice T: True
   Choice F: False

8. When using your working memory, the phonological loop must process the auditory aspects of the information before the visuo-spatial sketch pad can process its visual aspects.
   Choice T: True
   Choice F: False

9. A schema is a generalized knowledge structure that allows you to organize your long-term memory traces.
   Choice T: True
   Choice F: False

10. Researcher Penelope Davis' work indicates that women are better than men at recalling all types of childhood memories.
    Choice T: True
    Choice F: False

Multiple Choice Questions

Can you choose the best answer for these questions?

1. While driving her car, Rosa is able to shift from one gear to another without thinking about where the gears are located. This is possible because Rosa is using her memory in a(n) _____ or _____ fashion.
   A. conscious; explicit
   B. unconscious; explicit
   C. conscious; implicit
   D. unconscious; implicit

2. If information is lost from sensory memory, it is:
   A. gone from the memory system.
   B. retrievable if you think hard.
   C. stored in long-term memory in an implicit form.
   D. usable in an implicit, but not an explicit from.

3. Which of the following methods of study would be most likely to result in memory traces that can be easily retrieved on exam day?
    A. Reading and underlining the chapter.
    B. Reading and underlining the chapter four times.
    C. Outlining the material in the chapter.
    D. Looking over your notes and re-reading the chapter.

4. Susanna and her husband are watching a TV show on moose. Suddenly Susanna recalls that moose lose the fur on their horns every year. Susanna's recollection of this fact is due to her _____ memory.
    A. episodic
    B. procedural
    C. semantic
    D. sensory

5. Of the following students, who is most likely to make a good grade on the upcoming history exam?
    A. Ramone, who studies 1 hour each day for 8 days.
    B. Marla, who studies 8 hours on 1 day.
    C. Jack, who doesn't study at all.
    D. Terrell, who studies 2 hours each day for 3 days.

6. Procedural memories differ from declarative memories in that they:
    A. are not easily verbalized.
    B. tend to be executed implicitly.
    C. tend to be long-lasting.
    D. all of the above

7. People, like H.M. who suffer from anterograde amnesia often:
    A. have damage to their cerebellum.
    B. can still store new autobiographical memories.
    C. can still store new procedural memories.
    D. a & c

8. Lorena was in a car accident and sustained some head injuries. She can now store new memories, but she cannot recall events that occurred prior to her accident. Lorena is suffering from:
    A. anterograde amnesia.
    B. retrograde amnesia.
    C. cerebellum damage.
    D. b & c

9. When studying for an exam, if you really want to do well, you should use a(n) _____ test to determine whether or not you really know the material.
    A. implicit memory
    B. recognition
    C. recall
    D. a or b

10. "If you do not routinely access and retrieve memory traces, over time they will fade away," is a statement of which theory of forgetting?
     A. decay theory
     B. interference theory
     C. proactive interference theory
     D. cue-dependent forgetting theory

11. The best reasons to doubt that memory traces decay over time come from studies that show that:
     A. explicit memories do not change over time.
     B. recall doesn't diminish over time.
     C. recognition doesn't diminish over time.
     D. none of the above

12. You recently moved to a new address. Now you find that you frequently put down your old zip code when addressing your monthly bills. This memory lapse is most likely the result of:
     A. cue-dependent forgetting.
     B. retroactive interference.
     C. proactive interference.
     D. memory trace decay.

13. Two months ago, you were given a new membership number at your gym. Now you are filling out an application for a new locker at your gym and you mistakenly put down your old membership number. This mistake is likely the result of:
     A. proactive interference.
     B. retroactive interference.
     C. anterograde amnesia.
     D. repression.

14. You always study your psychology at a particular desk in the library. Today when taking a psychology exam, you were frustrated to find that you couldn't remember the name of the person who discovered classical conditioning. Immediately after leaving the exam, you went to the library, and as soon as you sat down at your favorite desk, Ivan Pavlov's name popped into your head. You original inability to recall Pavlov's name during the exam is most likely an example of:
     A. memory trace decay.
     B. a lack of availability.
     C. interference.
     D. cue-dependent forgetting.

15. Belinda's high school science teacher taught her a mnemonic for remembering the planets of the solar system. Now that she is in college, her professor taught the class a new mnemonic for this task. Belinda now finds that she can no longer recall the mnemonic she learned in high school. Belinda's forgetting is most likely due to:
     A. cue-dependent forgetting.

B. proactive interference.

C. retroactive interference.

D. a lack of memory trace availability.

16. The fact that your memory would probably be best if you took your exams while seated in the same desk that you normally listen to lectures is consistent with the:

A. Freudian idea of repression.

B. encoding specificity principle.

C. serial position curve.

D. none of the above

17. If you miss a question on your history exam, it is least likely to be a result of:

A. proactive interference.

B. retroactive interference.

C. cue-dependent forgetting.

D. repression.

18. The work of Elizabeth Loftus on eyewitness testimony shows that eyewitness memory is:

A. remarkably accurate.

B. always faulty.

C. often faulty.

D. completely reconstructive.

19. Recent studies on false memories suggest that:

A. children are more susceptible to having false memories.

B. adults are more susceptible to having false memories.

C. adults and children are equally susceptible to having false memories.

D. neither children nor adults are likely to have false memories for past events in their lives.

20. According to the levels of processing approach to memory, which of the following would likely produce the best memory for a list of words?

A. Determining whether or not the words are printed in capital letters.

B. Determining whether or not the words rhyme with the word "fish".

C. Determining whether or not the words are printed in red ink.

D. Determining the definition of the words.

21. Recently researchers have suggested that which part of working memory is malfunctioning when a person suffers from attention deficit/hyperactivity disorder?

A. the phonological loop

B. the visuo-spatial sketch pad

C. short-term memory

D. the central executive

22. If you are having trouble committing more information to long-term memory, it is likely due to:
    - A. a lack of space in long-term memory.
    - B. a lack of space on the visuo-spatial sketch pad.
    - C. a lack of attention.
    - D. interference.

23. A seemingly crystal-clear, detailed memory for an emotionally charged event is called a:
    - A. episodic memory.
    - B. semantic memory.
    - C. repressed memory.
    - D. flashbulb memory.

24. The_____ may play a role in the formation of memories for emotionally charged events.
    - A. hypothalamus
    - B. basal ganglia
    - C. amygdala
    - D. thalamus

25. The fact that people tend to recall more words from the end of a list than from the middle of the list is referred to as the:
    - A. primacy effect.
    - B. recency effect.
    - C. encoding specificity effect.
    - D. none of the above.

Short-Answer Questions

Can you write a brief answer to these questions?

1. What is the function of sensory memory?

2. Why are recognition tests typically easier than recall tests of memory?

3. You are a defense attorney defending a client accused of armed robbery. You are convinced that your client is innocent despite the fact that an eyewitness says that your client was the one who committed a robbery. To help your client, what would you tell the jury about the accuracy of eyewitness?

4. Why does elaborative rehearsal help improve memory?

5. What are the differences between the traditional three stages view of short-term memory and the working memory model?

Developing a Bigger Picture: Making Connections Across Chapters

An important aspect of learning is learning to see the "Big Picture" of the subject you are studying. As you learn about psychology, you should try to understand how the material from different chapters fits together to help you form a broad-based understanding of what psychology is all about. To help facilitate the development of this "Big Picture" in your mind, try to answer these questions using the knowledge you have learned in this chapter, as well as the other chapters referenced in the questions.

1. Of the different techniques you learned about in Chapter 2 for studying the brain, which of them would be most useful for determining which part of the brain is used for storing memory for auditory stimuli?

2. The story of Kim Peek seems to indicate that extraordinary memory for facts comes at the expense of the ability to reason well. Thinking back to Chapter 1, in which you learned about research methods, why can't we draw firm conclusions about how our memory works based solely on Kim's case?

3. Using what you learned in Chapter 4 about sleep and dreams, explain why cramming for exams in all-night study sessions is not a good idea if you want to be academically successful.

Label the Diagram

Can you label the different types of memory in the working memory model?

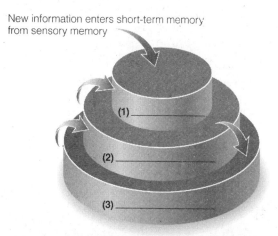

New information enters short-term memory from sensory memory

(1)_____

(2)_____

(3)_____

The Big Picture Review

Can you fill in the missing information on this table of the differences between the traditional Three Stages Model of Memory and the Working Memory Model?

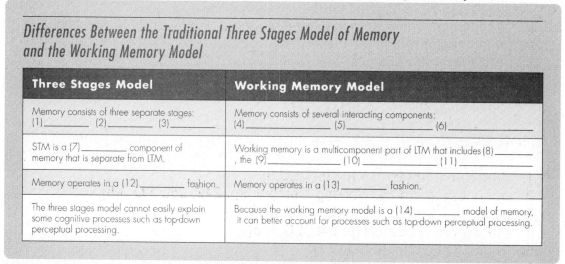

Differences Between the Traditional Three Stages Model of Memory and the Working Memory Model

Three Stages Model	Working Memory Model
Memory consists of three separate stages: (1)_____ (2)_____ (3)_____	Memory consists of several interacting components: (4)_____ (5)_____ (6)_____
STM is a (7)_____ component of memory that is separate from LTM.	Working memory is a multicomponent part of LTM that includes (8)_____, the (9)_____ (10)_____ (11)_____
Memory operates in a (12)_____ fashion.	Memory operates in a (13)_____ fashion.
The three stages model cannot easily explain some cognitive processes such as top-down perceptual processing.	Because the working memory model is a (14)_____ model of memory, it can better account for processes such as top-down perceptual processing.

Solutions

Each solution below is followed by its textbook page reference number and its corresponding chapter learning objective (LO) number. Items with a Big Picture LO help you build a Big Picture of psychology across the chapters you have studied so far.

Fill-in Review of The Chapter

1. cerebellum [p. 238; LO 7, 12, Big Picture]
2. semantic [p. 258; LO 7, Big Picture]
3. explicit [p. 240; LO 2]
4. implicit [p. 240; LO 2]
5. encoding [p. 239; LO 1]
6. storage [p. 239; LO 1]
7. retrieval [p. 239; LO 1]
8. icons [p. 242; LO 3, 4]
9. 2 seconds [p. 244; LO 4]
10. 5 to 9 [p. 246; LO 4]
11. visual [p. 246; LO 4]
12. acoustic [p. 246; LO 4]
13. chunking [p. 247; LO 4]
14. 30 seconds [p. 247; LO 4]
15. maintenance rehearsal [p. 248; LO 4]
16. episodic [p. 258; LO 7]
17. semantic code [p. 256; LO 4]
18. recall [p. 264; LO 8]
19. recognition [p. 264; LO 8]
20. retroactive [p. 266; LO 9]
21. context [p. 266; LO 9]
22. Reconstructive [p. 270; LO 10]
23. constructive [p. 270; LO 10]
24. mnemonic [p. 275; LO 11]
25. acrostic [p. 275; LO 11]
26. hippocampus [pp. 276, 70; LO 12]
27. cerebellum [pp. 278, 67; LO 12]

Use It or Lose It!

1. Proactive interference [p. 266; LO 9]
2. Short term memory/ working memory [pp. 242, 252; LO 3-5]
3. Long term memory [p. 242; LO 3, 4]
4. Elaborative rehearsal [p. 248; LO 4, 5]
5. Primacy effect [p. 250; LO 7]
6. Repression [p. 267; LO 9]
7. Maintenance rehearsal [p. 248; LO 4]
8. Central executive [p. 253; LO 5]

Self-Check: Are You Getting the Big Picture?

True or False Questions

1. F [p. 242; LO 4]	6. T [p. 256; LO 4]
2. T [p. 256; LO 5, 6]	7. T [p. 258; LO 7]
3. T [p. 250; LO 4, 5]	8. F [p. 253; LO 5]
4. F [p. 251; LO 4, 5]	9. T [p. 257; LO 6]
5. T [p. 251; LO 5]	10. F [p. 259; LO 7]

Multiple Choice Questions

1. D [p. 240; LO 2]	10. A [p. 265; LO 9]	19. A [p. 268; LO 10]
2. A [p. 242; LO 3, 4]	11. C [p. 266; LO 9]	20. D [p. 248; LO 4, 5]
3. C [p. 248; LO 5, 6, 8]	12. C [p. 266; LO 9]	21. D [p. 253; LO 5]
4. C [p. 258; LO 7]	13. A [p. 266; LO 9]	22. C [p. 255; LO 3-5]
5. A [p. 274; LO 11]	14. D [p. 266; LO 9]	23. D [p. 269; LO 10]
6. D [p. 261; LO 7]	15. C [p. 266; LO 9]	24. C [p. 270; LO 12]
7. C [p. 262; LO 7, 12]	16. B [p. 266; LO 9]	25. B [p. 250; LO 4]
8. B [p. 262; LO 9]	17. D [p. 267; LO 9]	
9. C [p. 264; LO 8]	18. C [p. 271; LO 10]	

Short-Answer Questions

1. What is the function of sensory memory? [p. 242; LO 3, 4]

   Sensory memory is the stage of memory where sensory impressions of the things you see, hear, and touch are stored for a very brief period of time. The time that the sensory impression is stored in sensory memory allows the mind to extract the important aspects of the impression that need to be retained. If you are paying attention, these aspects are then sent on for further processing in working memory.

2. Why are recognition tests typically easier than recall tests of memory? [p. 264; LO 8]

   Recognition tests are easier because in recognition, the probe or cue contains a great deal of information. For example, in a multiple-choice question, the question or cue actually contains the answer you are searching for in memory. In recall tasks, the cue is relatively weak and contains little information. For instance, in an essay question the question does not typically contain the answer. For this reason, to do well on a recall task you must have the information well organized and elaborated in memory if you are to have much chance of recalling it.

3. You are a defense attorney defending a client accused of armed robbery. You are convinced that your client is innocent despite the fact that an eyewitness says that your client was the one who committed a robbery. To help your client, what would you tell the jury about the accuracy of eyewitness? [p. 270; LO 10]

   You should tell the jury that memory is not like a video recorder. We do not store all the details of the events we experience in memory. As a result, when we retrieve memories from long-term memory our memory is both reconstructive and constructive. Constructive memory means that we fill in the missing details of our memories using the expectations we have about the world and our schemata. In filling in the missing details, it is very possible for us to make mistakes without even realizing that our memory is faulty. Therefore, it is very possible that the eyewitness only thinks he or she saw your client at the scene of the crime, when in reality your client was not present at the time.

4. Why does elaborative rehearsal help improve memory? [p. 248; LO 4, 5, 6]

   Elaborative rehearsal helps improve memory because it forces you to associate the new information you are trying to learn to information that you already have stored in long-term memory. In doing this, you end up processing the information very deeply, which encodes the new information in long-term memory in a much more accessible form than you would typically get with maintenance rehearsal. The more accessible a memory trace is, the easier it is to retrieve.

5. What are the differences between the traditional three stages view of short-term memory and the working memory model? [pp. 242, 252; LO 5]

   The traditional three stages model of short-term memory proposes that information must pass sequentially from sensory to short-term to long-term memory. In this traditional view, short-term memory is a single system and it is separate from long-term memory.

   In contrast, the working memory model proposes that your memory systems work in a parallel fashion rather than a series. In this view, working memory and short-term memory are parts of long-term memory. Working memory is a multi-component system that moves information into and out of long-term memory. Its components include short-term memory and a central executive that directs the action of two slave systems: the phonological loop and the visuo-spatial sketch pad. These slave systems respectively process the auditory and visual/spatial aspects of the memory traces we store. In this model, all the components of working memory may be active at the same time instead of information passing sequentially from one memory stage to the next.

Developing a Bigger Picture: Making Connections Across Chapters

1. Of the different techniques you learned about in Chapter 2 for studying the brain, which of them would be most useful for determining which part of the brain is used for storing memory for auditory stimuli? [p. 80; LO 4, Big Picture]

   fMRI and PET scans would be the most useful because they show anatomical structure, as well as which parts of the brain are most active at any particular moment in time. A participant could be given a piece of music to memorize while being scanned with one of these technologies to see which parts of the brain the participant is using during the act of memorizing the auditory stimulus.

2. The story of Kim Peek seems to indicate that extraordinary memory for facts comes at the expense of the ability to reason well. Thinking back to Chapter 1, in which you learned about research methods, why can't we draw firm conclusions about how our memory works based solely on Kim's case? [p. 30; LO- Big Picture]

   Kim's story represents a case study. Case studies are not controlled experiments, and no cause and effect relationships can be established based on the results of uncontrolled studies. Also, case studies are based on a single participant's experiences. It is always possible that Kim's brain and memory do not work in exactly the same fashion as the average person's do.

3. Using what you learned in Chapter 4 about sleep and dreams, explain why cramming for exams in all-night study sessions is not a good idea if you want to be academically successful. [p. 147; LO- Big Picture]

   All-night study sessions deprive you of sleep. Lack of sleep, particularly REM sleep, has been shown to interfere with your brain's ability to process memory. Also, lack of sleep leads to fatigue, which leads to difficulty in focusing your attention. Without the ability to concentrate and pay attention, memory processing will be further adversely affected. The end result is that you will likely not do your best after a sleepless night of cramming for an exam. It would be much better to study ahead of time and sleep well the night before the exam.

Label the Diagram

1.	Short-term memory [p. 252; LO 5]
2.	Working memory [p. 252; LO 5]
3.	Long-term memory [p. 252; LO 5]

Big Picture Review

1. sensory [p. 254; LO 5]	8. short-term memory [p. 254; LO 5]
2. short-term memory [p. 254; LO 5]	9. central executive [p. 254; LO 5]
3. long-term memory [p. 254; LO 5]	10. phonological loop [p. 254; LO 5]
4. sensory memory [p. 254; LO 5]	11. visuospatial sketch pad [p. 254; LO 5]
5. working memory [p. 254; LO 5]	12. serial [p. 254; LO 5]
6. long-term memory [p. 254; LO 5]	13. parallel [p. 254; LO 5]
7. single [p. 254; LO 5]	14. parallel [p. 254; LO 5]

7

Cognition, Language, and Intelligence: How Do We Think?

Learning Objectives

After studying each of the following sections of the chapter, you should be able to do these tasks.

Thinking: How We Use What We Know

1. Describe the process of thinking and the manner in which we represent knowledge in our memory.

Problem Solving: Where Does Our Thinking Get Us?

2. Describe the different types of problems we are faced with and the ways in which we may try to solve them.
3. Describe common obstacles to problem solving.

Reasoning, Decision making and Judgment

4. Describe the processes of making decisions and judgments.
5. Discuss the availability and representativeness heuristics and how they may bias our decisions and judgments.

Language: Essential to Thought and Action

6. Describe how children acquire language.
7. Explain the usefulness of language.
8. Describe current research on the issue of nonhuman language.

Defining and Measuring Intelligence

9. Describe historical and modern attempts to measure intelligence, and some of the advantages and disadvantages of these methods.
10. Describe the various ways that researchers have conceptualized intelligence.
11. Describe the nature versus nurture debate as it applies to intelligence.

The Big Picture

The Big Picture: A Life Without Language?

In this chapter, you learned about three important topics in psychology: cognition, language, and intelligence. All of these processes are essential to our everyday functioning and to a large extent they are interdependent. The case of Ildefonso clearly demonstrated that his lack of language impacted his cognitive processes and his ability to adapt to his environment. As you study this chapter, attempt to see how your own cognitive processes (i.e., thinking, problem solving, decision making, reasoning, and judgment) interact with your linguistic abilities and give rise to your intelligence.

Thinking: How We Use What We Know

This section covers Learning Objective 1. Thinking is the use of knowledge to accomplish a goal. Knowledge is stored in the form of mental representations, or bits of memory that can be either visual images or conceptual in nature. Studies that examine the nature of visual mental representations have shown that they are influenced by the actual characteristics of the stimulus, as well as the verbal interpretation we place on them. For example, researcher Steven Kosslyn showed that our cognitive maps of the world are not entirely accurate because they are influenced by our expectations about the world.

It appears that our conceptual knowledge of the world is stored in a verbal or propositional form in memory, and that it is organized into hierarchical categories. Superordinate categories contain broad, general information (e.g., animal). Basic level categories contain intermediate levels of information and is the level at which you tend to most often think about the world (e.g., dog). And subordinate categories contain the most specific detailed level of information (e.g., toy poodle).

We acquire these categories from an early age as we observe our world. Some concept categories exist as formal categories. Formal categories are ones in which clear rules exist for which concepts belong in the category and which do not (e.g., items are clearly animal or not). However, not all concepts fit cleanly into categories. Natural categories evolve in a less rigid, rule-driven fashion and as such often have somewhat fuzzy boundaries. For example, the category "hip-hop music" is a natural category as there are no hard and fast rules about the defining characteristics of this type of music. Instead the degree to which a concept is similar to the prototype or most typical member of a category is used to judge category membership.

Problem Solving: Where Does Our Thinking Get Us?

This section covers Learning Objectives 2-3. One of the most important uses of your conceptual knowledge is problem solving. Some problems are well structured in that they have a clear solution. Well-structured problems can be solved using algorithms or heuristics. Algorithms always lead to the correct solution, but heuristics are short cuts that may or may not lead to the right answer. Therefore, if you have time and you know the algorithm, it is your best bet. However, not all problems have known algorithms. Ill-structured problems have no clear solution path, so the only way to solve ill-structured problems is through the use of heuristics. In solving ill-structured problems, insight, incubation, and creativity may be very important tools in overcoming common blocks to problem solving, such as functional fixedness and mental sets.

Reasoning, Decision making and Judgment

This section covers Learning Objectives 4-5. Reasoning, decision making, and judgment are also activities that require the use of conceptual knowledge. Reasoning is drawing conclusions that are based on certain assumptions about the world. Deductive reasoning involves reasoning from the general to the specific and inductive reasoning involves the opposite— reasoning from the specific to the general.

Decision making involves choosing from a series of options. When making decisions, we tend to pay attention to the possible outcomes of our decisions and the probability of obtaining these outcomes, which is somewhat dependent on how the options are presented or framed.

Judgments are a type of problem solving in which you must determine the likelihood of a certain event. Often when making judgments, we rely upon heuristics like availability and representativeness—sometimes to such a degree that we ignore actual probabilities or base rate information.

Language: Essential to Thought and Action

This section covers Learning Objectives 6-8. The human capacity for language is truly one of our more remarkable characteristics. Language is essential to everyday communication as well as to your thought processes. Much of the conceptual knowledge stored in your mind is stored in a verbal format. It is difficult to imagine what thinking must be like for people like Ildefonso who have no linguistic abilities.

Some researchers believe that humans are born with an innate ability to develop language—a language acquisition device (LAD). Others disagree, stating that language is merely a device children use to fulfill the need to communicate with others. Determining which perspective is correct is difficult, in that it is impossible to tease apart nature's and nurture's influences on language development in normal children.

Normal children all go through the same stages of language development (i.e., cooing, babbling phonemes, uttering morphemes, first words, telegraphic speech, and full sentences) at roughly the same ages. But this does not necessarily mean that these similarities are due to genetic or biological forces. Similar environmental exposure to language could account for the development of language in children.

However, studies of challenged children, such as the deaf children in Nicaragua, do seem to shed some light on this question. These deaf children also seem to develop a form of language, despite the fact that they are never exposed to that language. This argues strongly for the idea that the ability to develop language is innate.

Once a child acquires language, it becomes an indispensable part of everyday life. Humans use language to transmit culture from generation to generation. We use language to communicate with each other, learning culturally specific pragmatic rules to help facilitate communication. Some even argue that language actually determines how you think about and perceive the world—and idea called the Whorfian or linguistic relativity hypothesis. However, the research has not supported this view. Rather, the available data seem to indicate that rather than determining our thoughts and perceptions, language merely influences them.

Given that language is so important to our lives, some have wondered whether language is a uniquely human attribute. Although very controversial, some researchers now believe that other species (i.e., bonobos, dolphins, and African gray parrots) have at least limited linguistic abilities. More research is needed to determine what, if any language skills these species have.

Defining and Measuring Intelligence

This section covers Learning Objectives 9-11. Cognition and language are mental abilities that allow us to adapt to our environment and accomplish goals—in other words, they underlie what psychologists refer to as intelligence. The study of intelligence and how to measure it has been ongoing for quite some time. In the mid-1800s, Francis Galton was one of the first people to attempt to measure intelligence. For Galton, intelligence was an inherited trait that was associated with certain physical traits like having keen senses and quick reaction time. Therefore, Galton believed that intelligence could be objectively measured by measuring particular physical traits. However, this idea soon fell out of favor.

In 1904, the French government appointed Alfred Binet and Théodore Simon to find a way to measure the intelligence of French school children. In doing this, Binet and Simon defined intelligence in terms of cognitive abilities that allowed people to define and satisfy a purpose or goal. They then developed a test to measure children's intelligence in terms of mental age or the age that reflects the child's mental abilities in comparison to the average child.

Soon after Binet and Simon developed their test in France, American psychologist, Lewis Terman, completed an American revision of the test called the Stanford-Binet. Terman also developed the idea of the intelligence quotient or IQ score, which is calculated by dividing your mental age by your chronological age and multiplying by 100. Since Terman developed the Stanford-Binet test, it has undergone five revisions.

In the 1930s David Wechsler developed his own intelligence tests. The Wechsler tests furthered the measurement of intelligence by creating subscales to measure different aspects of intelligence and abandoning the idea of mental age. Instead of using mental age as a benchmark for determining IQ, Wechsler compared individual's performance on his test to the performance of the average person. Because the Wechsler tests are designed so that the average person will score 100, people with scores above 100 have above average IQs and those scoring below 100 have below average IQs. Today there are three separate Wechsler tests: the WPPSI for children aged 2 1/2-7; the WISC for children aged 6-16; and the WAIS for those over age 15.

With all these intelligence tests to choose from, how do psychologists determine what a good test of intelligence is? Two important criteria for determining this are the reliability and validity of the test. Reliability is the degree to which the test yields consistent scores, and validity is the degree to which the test actually measures the characteristic it was designed to measure. Subsequently, a good test of intelligence is one that actually measures intelligence and one in which people tend to score about the same on repeated testing.

Today many psychologists are stilled engaged in trying to determine exactly what intelligence is. The idea that intelligence is a single factor ("g") has been questioned by many. Raymond Cattell argued that "g" does exist, but has two different forms: crystallized intelligence (knowledge) and fluid intelligence (speedy and efficient mental processing).

Howard Gardner rejects the idea of "g" in favor of the notion that humans possess multiple intelligences. To date, he has proposed nine different intelligences: linguistic, spatial, logical-mathematical, musical, bodily-kinesthetic, interpersonal, intrapersonal, naturalistic, and existential.

In his triarchic theory of intelligence, Robert Sternberg argues that intelligence is made up of three separate cognitive abilities: practical intelligence, creative intelligence, and analytical intelligence.

Daniel Goleman has called into question the idea that intelligence is based solely on cognitive abilities. Goleman proposes that how far you get in life is not just a function of mental abilities. It is also a function of how well you can control your emotional states. For Goleman, an emotionally intelligent person is one who is a confident, ethical, and adaptable—the type of person who sets goals and does not let minor obstacles derail their progress. To help identify such people, John Mayer, Peter Salovey, and David Caruso have developed a test of emotional intelligence, the *Mayer-Salovey-Caruso Emotional Intelligence Test,* or *MSCEIT*.

As you can see, there is still a good deal of controversy about what intelligence is. Likewise, there is still some controversy over where intelligence comes from. Is your intelligence a product of your genes (nature) or is it the product of your environment (nurture)? Throughout the history of psychology people have argued both sides of the nature-nurture debate when discussing intelligence, but today most psychologists believe that the data best support an interactionist perspective on intelligence. Your intelligence seems to be a product of both nature and nurture influences.

The last topic addressed in this chapter was the question of whether or not men and women differ in intelligence. Again, there is some controversy over this issue. It appears that men and women do not differ with respect to overall intelligence or "g", but when you examine gender differences in multiple intelligences, some differences emerge. However in interpreting these differences you must keep in mind that the differences are small; the differences depend on how the variables were measured in the study; gender differences can vary by age, culture, and race; and gender differences can be the result of bias in intelligence testing. To sum up, males and females are probably more alike in intelligence than they are different.

Outlining the Big Picture

Chapter 7: Cognition, Language, and Intelligence: How Do We Think??

The Big Picture: What Would Life Be Without Language?
Susan Schaller's *A Man Without Words*: The story of Ildefonso, a deaf man who didn't know that language existed.

Notes:
_____
_____
_____
_____
_____

Thinking: How We Use What We Know (Learning Objective 1)
Visual Images: How Good Is the Mental Picture?
    The Limits of the Mental Picture
Concepts: How We Organize What We Know
    Organizing Concepts into Categories
    Formal and Natural Categories
Notes:
_____
_____
_____
_____
_____

Problem Solving: Where Does Our Thinking Get Us? (Learning Objectives 2-3)
Well-structured Problems: The Answer Is Out There
Algorithms and Heuristics: The Long and Short of Problem Solving
Ill-structured Problems: The Answer May Be Out There
Creativity: Overcoming Obstacles to Problem Solving
    Functional Fixedness
    Mental Sets
Notes:
_____
_____
_____

_____

_____

_____

_____

Reasoning, Decision making, and Judgment (Learning Objectives 4-5)
Deductive and Inductive Reasoning
Decision making: Outcomes and Probabilities
Judgments: Estimating the Likelihood of Events
      The Availability Heuristic
      The Representativeness Heuristic
Notes:

_____

_____

_____

_____

_____

_____

Language: Important to Thought and Action (Learning Objectives 6-8)
How Humans Acquire Language
      Spotlight on Diversity: The Spontaneous Development of a Language in Nicaragua
      Cooing and Babbling: Baby Steps to Learning One or More Languages
      From "Mama" and "Dada" to Full Conversations
The Function of Language in Culture and Perception
      Language and the Development of Culture
      Linguistic Relativity: Language Directs Our Thoughts
      The Modern View: Language Influences Our Thoughts
Language in Other Species: Are We the Only Speakers?
      Bonobos: Matata and Kanzi
      Talking Parrots and Dolphins
      Can Other Animals Really Use Language?
Notes:

_____

_____

_____

_____

_____

_____

_____

Defining and Measuring Intelligence (Learning Objectives 9-11)
Measuring Intelligence by Abilities and IQs
 Alfred Binet: Measuring Intelligence by Measuring Cognitive Abilities
 Lewis Terman: The Intelligence Quotient and the Stanford-Binet
 David Wechsler's Intelligence Scales
 Testing the Test: What Makes a Good Intelligence Test?
The Nature of Intelligence: The Search Continues
 Intelligence as a Single Factor
 Intelligence as a Collection of Abilities
 A New Spin: Howard Gardner's Multiple Intelligences
 Robert Sternberg's Triarchic Theory of Intelligence
 Daniel Goleman's Theory of Emotional Intelligence
So, What Is Intelligence After All?
Nature, Nurture, and IQ: Are We Born Intelligent or Do We Learn to Be?
 Twin Studies: Nature and Nurture
 Interpreting Intelligence Studies
 Gender and Intellectual Abilities: Are We Really All that Different?
Notes:

_____

_____

_____

_____

_____

_____

Are You Getting the Big Picture?
Notes:

_____

_____

_____

_____

Seeing the Big Picture: A Mental Map of Chapter 7

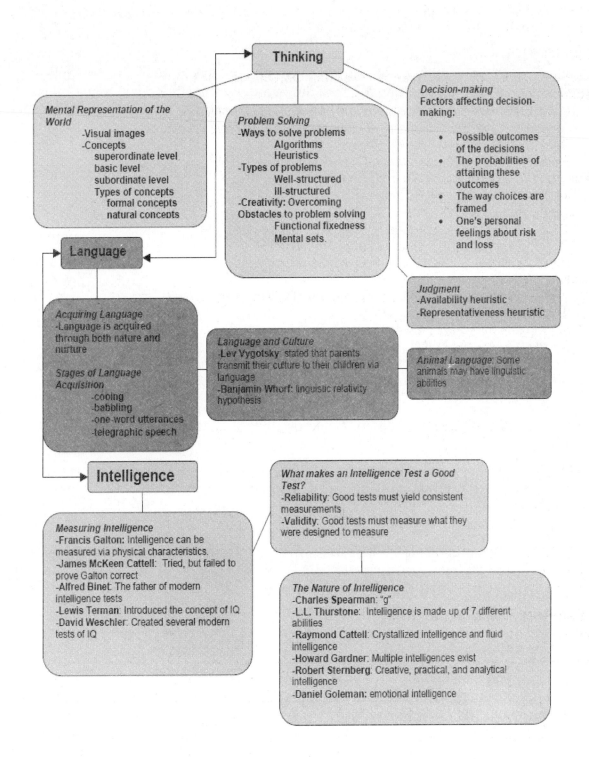

Thinking

Mental Representation of the World
-Visual images
-Concepts
   superordinate level
   basic level
   subordinate level
   Types of concepts
      formal concepts
      natural concepts

Problem Solving
-Ways to solve problems
   Algorithms
   Heuristics
-Types of problems
   Well-structured
   Ill-structured
-Creativity: Overcoming
Obstacles to problem solving
   Functional fixedness
   Mental sets.

Decision-making
Factors affecting decision-making:

- Possible outcomes of the decisions
- The probabilities of attaining these outcomes
- The way choices are framed
- One's personal feelings about risk and loss

Judgment
-Availability heuristic
-Representativeness heuristic

Language

Acquiring Language
-Language is acquired through both nature and nurture

Stages of Language Acquisition
-cooing
-babbling
-one-word utterances
-telegraphic speech

Language and Culture
-Lev Vygotsky: stated that parents transmit their culture to their children via language
-Benjamin Whorf: linguistic relativity hypothesis

Animal Language: Some animals may have linguistic abilities

Intelligence

What makes an Intelligence Test a Good Test?
-Reliability: Good tests must yield consistent measurements
-Validity: Good tests must measure what they were designed to measure

Measuring Intelligence
-Francis Galton: Intelligence can be measured via physical characteristics.
-James McKeen Cattell: Tried, but failed to prove Galton correct
-Alfred Binet: The father of modern intelligence tests
-Lewis Terman: Introduced the concept of IQ
-David Weschler: Created several modern tests of IQ

The Nature of Intelligence
-Charles Spearman: "g"
-L.L. Thurstone: Intelligence is made up of 7 different abilities
-Raymond Cattell: Crystallized intelligence and fluid intelligence
-Howard Gardner: Multiple intelligences exist
-Robert Sternberg: Creative, practical, and analytical intelligence
-Daniel Goleman: emotional intelligence

Key Points of the Big Picture

Algorithm:
a method of solving a particular problem that always leads to the correct solution. *Example: Counting the pennies in your piggy bank to see how much money you have.*

Availability heuristic:
a heuristic in which we use the ease with which we can recall instances of an event in memory to help us estimate the frequency of the event. *Example: Judging that it rains more often in Georgia than it does in your home state, because it was raining last week when you visited Georgia.*

Babbling:
the combination of vowel and consonant sounds uttered by infants beginning around 4 months of age. *Example: Ma, Ma, Ma…*

Basic level category:
the intermediate level of categorization that seems to be the level that we use most to think about our world. *Example: Cars*

Cognition:
the way in which we use and store information in memory. *Example: Thinking, planning, decision making, memory, problem solving, etc.*

Cognitive map:
a mental representation of the environment. *Example: Your mental representation of the building in which you have psychology class.*

Concept:
mental category that contains related bits of knowledge. *Example: Fruit, cars, history, etc.*

Cooing:
the vowel sounds made by infants beginning at 2 months of age. *Example: "oo", "aa", etc.*

Creativity:
the ability to combine mental elements in new and useful ways. *Example: Using needle and thread reattach the ear piece to your sunglasses.*

Crystallized intelligence:
abilities that rely on knowledge, expertise, and judgment. *Example: Knowing cultural customs, psychology, math, language, etc.*

Cultural bias:
the degree to which a test puts people from other cultures at an unfair disadvantage because of the culturally specific nature of the test items. *Example: An analogy question like "Merlot is to red and Chardonnay is to _____", meant to measure general intelligence, would be cultural biased against people who have little knowledge of wine.*

Decision making:
making a choice from among a series of alternatives. *Example: Deciding which major to pursue in college.*

Deductive reasoning:
reasoning from the general to the specific. *Example: Guessing that Mike must be a good swimmer because he is a scuba diver and scuba divers must be good swimmers.*

Exemplar:
a mental representation of an actual member of a category. Example: A mental representation of an actual car you saw on the highway.

Fluid intelligence:
abilities that rely on information-processing skills such as reaction time, attention, and working memory. *Example: Being able to quickly learn to play a new video game is an example of having well-developed fluid intelligence.*

Formal concept:
concept that is based on learned, rigid rules that define certain categories of things. *Example: Food is an example of a formal concept. To be food, the item must be edible and have nutritional value.*

Functional fixedness:
being able to only see objects in their familiar roles. *Example: Only being able to see a sewing machine as being useful for sewing.*

Generalized intelligence (g):
Charles Spearman's notion that there is a general level of intelligence that underlies our separate abilities. *Example: Your intelligence quotient or IQ is a measure of your level of generalized intelligence.*

Grammar:
the rules that govern the sentence structure in a particular language. Example: In English, adjectives precede the nouns that they modify.

Heuristic:
a shortcut or rule-of-thumb that may or may not lead to a correct solution to the problem. *Example: Guessing how much money you have in your piggy bank by feeling how much it weighs.*

Ill-structured problem:
a problem for which an algorithm is not known. *Example: Trying to find the best way to cure AIDS.*

Incubation:
a period of not thinking about the problem that helps one solve the problem. *Example: If you can't solve a math problem, try setting it aside for some time while you move on to other things. Perhaps this will allow you to discover the correct way to solve the problem.*

Inductive reasoning:
reasoning from the specific to the general. *Example: Noticing that among your friends, those who love Indian food also tend to like sushi, and deciding that in general people who like Indian food will also like sushi.*

Insight:
a new way of looking at the problem that leads to a sudden understanding of how to solve it. *Example: Suddenly realizing that the solution to your problem of how to dig a hole without a shovel is to use the claw end of a hammer as a digging tool.*

Intelligence:
abilities that allow you to adapt to adapt to your environment and behave in a goal-directed way. *Example: A farmer knowing how to diagnose diseases in his livestock is exhibiting intelligence.*

Intelligence quotient:
one's mental age divided by one's chronological age times 100. *Example: An IQ of 100 means that your mental age and chronological age are the same.*

Judgment:
the act of estimating the probability of an event. *Example: Judging that it is okay to leave your car unlocked because crime is rare in your area.*

Knowledge:
information stored in our long-term memory about the world and how it works. *Example: Knowing how to study effectively for an exam.*

Language:
a well-developed, syntactical verbal system for representing the world. *Example: English, Spanish, Sanskrit, Polish, etc.*

Mental age:
the age that reflects the child's mental abilities in comparison to the average child of the same age. *Example: A 10-year-old child who thinks at the level of the average 12-year-old, has a mental age of 12 years.*

Mental representation:
memory traces that represent objects, events, people, and so on, which are not present at the time. *Example: The memory you have for your father's face.*

Mental set:
the tendency to habitually use methods of problem solving that have worked for you in the past. *Example: Studying for an exam in the way that you studied for your last exam because you made an "A" on that exam.*

Morpheme:
the smallest unit of sound in a language that has meaning. *Example: the suffix, "-ed", means past.*

Multiple intelligences:
the idea that we possess different types of intelligence rather than a single, overall level of intelligence. *Example: An entertainer might be high in musical intelligence, but low in interpersonal intelligence.*

Natural concept:
concept that develops naturally as we live our lives and experience the world. *Example: Your category for "cool" people.*

Overextension:
when a child uses one word to symbolize all manners of similar instances. *Example: calling all birds a parakeet.*

Phonemes:
the smallest unit of sound in a language. *Example: The sound for "ph" in English.*

Pragmatics:
the rules of conversation in a particular culture. *Example: In the United States, it is polite to pause to allow the other person to respond after you have asked him/her a question.*

Prototype:
our concept of the most typical member of the category. *Example: If you close your eyes and think of an apple, you are most likely thinking of your prototype.*

Reasoning:
drawing conclusions about the world based on certain held assumptions. *Example: Judging that you need to be cautious when walking alone at night in a city because you have recently read that this city is experiencing an increase in crime.*

Reliability:
the degree to which a test yields consistent measurements of a trait. *Example: Every time you measure Juan's intelligence with your new intelligence test, you get approximately the same score for him. This indicates that your test is reliable.*

Representativeness heuristic:
a heuristic in which we rely on the degree to which something is representative of a category, rather than the base rate, to help us judge whether or not it belongs in the category. *Example: You decide that Sally must be a mother because she is very nurturing and loves kids— qualities you associate with mothers.*

Subordinate category:
the lowest level of categorization, which contains concepts that are less general and more specific than those at the basic level. *Example: Siamese cat.*

Superordinate category:
the highest, most general level of a concept. *Example: Animals.*

Telegraphic speech:
two-word sentences that children begin to utter at 20-26 months. *Example: Doggie bad.*

Thinking:
the use of knowledge to accomplish some sort of goal. *Example: Pondering where the best place to eat dinner is.*

Triarchic theory of intelligence:
a theory of intelligence that proposes that intelligence is composed of *analytical*, *practical*, and *creative* abilities that help us successfully adapt to our environment.

Underextension:
when a child inappropriately restricts her use of a word to a particular case. *Example: Using the word cat to only describe the family pet.*

Validity:
the degree to which test measures the trait that it was designed to measure. *Example: A test that is designed to measure intelligence should actually measure intelligence.*

Well-structured problems:
problems for which there is a clear pathway to the solution. *Example: To figure out how much tile you need for your bathroom, you need to measure and calculate the area of the walls you wish to tile.*

Whorfian hypothesis/Linguistic relativity hypothesis:
the theory that one's language can directly determine or influence one's thoughts. *Example: The idea that a French-speaking person's view of the world is influenced by the fact that he speaks French.*

Fill-in Review of the Chapter

Can you fill-in the missing terms for each section of the chapter? Items marked by an * encourage you to continue building the Big Picture of psychology by connecting the material in this chapter to material from previous chapters in the text.
Chapter 7: Cognition, Language, and Intelligence: How Do We Think??

The Big Picture: A Life Without Language?

Ildefonso was unique because he did not have 1) _____.

As such, Ildefonso would have had to use pictures for his 2) _____ _____ of knowledge.

Thinking: How We Use What We Know

3) _____ is the use of knowledge to accomplish some goal.

We store bits of knowledge in memory as 4) _____ _____.

A(n) 5) _____ is the most typical member of a natural category.

Fruit is an example of a 6) _____ concept category.

A mental representation of your hometown is an example of a(n) 7) _____ _____.

"Dog" is an example of a(n) 8) _____.

Problem Solving: Where Does Our Thinking Get Us?

9) _____ is a period of time in which you do not think about a problem that could actually help you discover a solution.

Thinking of a needle as only a tool for sewing is an example of 10) _____ _____.

Finding a solution to the problem of global warming is an example of a(n) 11) _____ problem.

Determining how much carpet you need to cover your dining room floor is an example of a(n) 12) _____ problem.

Dave keeps trying to solve his calculus problem in the same fashion, even though it isn't yielding the correct answer. Dave is exhibiting a(n) 13) _____ _____.

Reasoning, Decision making and Judgment

When you must choose from a list of alternatives, you are engaged in the cognitive process of 14) _____ _____.

Judging that Raul must be an athlete because he has well-developed muscles is an example of the 15) _____ heuristic.

The fact that train travel declines immediately after a well-publicized train wreck is most likely due to the public's use of the 16) _____ heuristic.

Deciding based on your interactions with nurses that women make better nurses than men is an example of 17) _____ reasoning.

Creativity is associated with high levels of 18) _____ thinking.

Language: Essential to Thought and Action

The smallest unit of sound in a language that has meaning is a(n) 19) _____.

20) _____ occurs when babies begin to combine vowel and consonant sounds in meaningless utterances.

21) _____ are the rules that govern conversation in a culture.

Two brain areas that are essential to the processing of language are 22*) _____ and 23*) _____.

The idea that language influences knowledge is known as the 24) _____ _____ hypothesis.

The idea that humans are born with a language acquisition device (LAD) is most consistent with the 25*) _____ side of the nature-nurture debate.

183

Defining and Measuring Intelligence

Billie is 6 years-old, but here intelligence test scores indicate that she can think on the level of an 8-year-old. Billie's 26) _____ _____ is eight years.

27) _____ intelligence is our accumulation of knowledge.

According to Daniel Goleman, self-control, self-confidence, and conscientiousness are components of your 28) _____ _____.

Use It or Lose It!

Can you identify the researchers who might say these things?

Researcher	Statement
1.	"Humans possess three different types of intelligence."
2.	"Humans possess at least nine different intelligences."
3.	"Humans possess different levels of emotional intelligence."
4.	"Humans possess different levels of general intelligence or 'g'."
5.	"Mental age has little relevance in adulthood."

Self-Check: Are You Getting the Big Picture?

After you have read and studied the chapter, see if you can answer the following quiz questions. Check your answers at the end of the chapter. If you miss a question, refer to your text and re-study the appropriate sections.

True or False Questions

Are these statements true or false?

1. Although controversial, some researchers believe that linguistic abilities have been demonstrated in Bonobo chimpanzees, African gray parrots, dolphins, and German Shepard dogs.
   Choice T: True
   Choice F: False

2. Research shows that humans store very accurate, detailed cognitive maps of the world in their long-term memory.
   Choice T: True
   Choice F: False

3. The concept "mammal" is an example of a formal concept.
   Choice T: True
   Choice F: False

4. The concept "friend" is an example of a natural concept.
   Choice T: True
   Choice F: False

5. Deaf children in China, but not Nicaragua, have been found to develop spontaneous sign language.
   Choice T: True
   Choice F: False

6. Well-structured problems can be solved using either an algorithm or a heuristic.
   Choice T: True
   Choice F: False

7. Finding a cure for cancer or AIDS is an example of a well-structured problem.
   Choice T: True
   Choice F: False

8. Someone high in divergent thinking can quickly generate many different ideas.
   Choice T: True
   Choice F: False

9. People high in divergent thinking are more likely to encounter functional fixedness.
   Choice T: True
   Choice F: False

10. Francis Galton believed that intelligence is learned or acquired through experience and that an enriching environment could greatly enhance one's level of intelligence.
    Choice T: True
    Choice F: False

Multiple Choice Questions

Can you choose the best answer for these questions?

1. Some common obstacles to problem solving include:
   A. mental sets.
   B. functional fixedness.
   C. Incubation.
   D. a & b

2. Inductive reasoning is reasoning from the _____ to the _____.
   A. general; specific
   B. specific; general
   C. concrete; abstract
   D. abstract; concrete

3. Based on the research, which indicates that harsh physical punishment leads to a lack of empathy in children, Dr. Martinez predicts that Sonja is not very empathetic because he knows that Sonja was harshly punished as a child. Dr. Martinez's prediction about Sonja is an example of:
   A. inductive reasoning.
   B. deductive reasoning.
   C. the use of an algorithm.
   D. the use of a heuristic.

4. Benjamin tends to frame choices in terms of loss aversion. Based on what you know about decision making, which of the following choices would you most expect Benjamin to make?
   A. To invest his retirement funds in a safe investment that does not yield high returns.
   B. To invest his retirement funds in a risky investment that yields high returns.
   C. To avoid making decisions about investment because he finds it too stressful.
   D. To make illogical decisions about how to invest his retirement money.

5. You attend a party where some of the guests are lawyers, librarians, doctors and nurses. You meet a woman named Betty there. Betty is 52. She has gray hair that she wears in a bun. She is dressed conservatively in a skirt, blouse, and sweater. She also has a pair of reading glasses hanging from a chain around her neck. If you use the representativeness heuristic, you will most likely make the judgment that Betty is a _____.
   A. lawyer
   B. nurse
   C. librarian
   D. doctor

6. Of the following types of concept categories, which one has the most fuzzy or unclear boundaries?
   A. natural concepts
   B. formal concepts
   C. superordinate categories
   D. basic level categoriets

7. Tabitha is trying to determine how much flour to buy for her holiday baking needs. She decides that because she needed five pounds last year, she will need 6 pounds this year since she has one more family to bake for this year. Which of the following problem solving strategies is Tabitha using?
   A. an algorithm
   B. a heuristic
   C. the representativeness heuristic
   D. the availability heuristic

8. When someone is stuck in a mental set while trying to solve a problem, they lack the required _____ to find a solution.

    A. functional fixedness
    B. deductive reasoning
    C. inductive reasoning
    D. insight

9. Chanita goes off to college in St. Paul, Minnesota. She finds the people there to be very nice. On the basis of her experience in St. Paul, Chanita decides that Minnesotans in general are nice people. Chanita's reasoning is an example of:
    A. deductive reasoning.
    B. inductive reasoning.
    C. algorithm use.
    D. decision making.

10. According to Noam Chomsky, humans acquire language because:
    A. we are operantly conditioned by our parents to learn language.
    B. language development is a completely biological process that requires no learning whatsoever.
    C. we have an innate tendency to acquire the language we hear spoken around us when we are very young children.
    D. we are born with latent knowledge of our native language already stored in our brains.

11. The case of the Nicaraguan deaf children discussed in your text suggests that:
    A. children learn language through modeling and operant conditioning.
    B. language development is completely biological and requires no exposure to spoken language.
    C. there are some innate aspects to the development of language.
    D. deaf children are completely unable to acquire language.

12. Once a child has begun_____, she has the ability to produce the basic phonemes of her native language.
    A. cooing
    B. babbling
    C. speaking
    D. using telegraphic speech

13. Communication between parent and child is first accomplished when the parent learns to interpret the child's:
    A. cooing.
    B. babbling.
    C. preverbal gestures.
    D. morphemes.

14. When Ildefonso used the word "green" to refer to anything that dealt with the U.S. Border Patrol, he was exhibiting a(n) _____ in his language.
    A. overextension
    B. underextension
    C. phoneme
    D. heuristic

15. "Your language directly determines or influences your thoughts" is a statement of the:
    A. strong form of the Whorfian hypothesis.
    B. weak form of the Whorfian hypothesis.
    C. strong form of the linguistic relativity hypothesis.
    D. a & c
    E. none of the above

16. Kanzi the Bonobo chimpanzee learned language after:
    A. watching researchers attempt to teach her mother language.
    B. being trained by researchers to learn language.
    C. listening to humans speaking language around her.
    D. listening to spoken language on the radio that the zookeepers played each day.

17. The best time to learn a second language is_____.
    A. before late adulthood
    B. before middle adulthood
    C. before young adulthood
    D. before adolescence

18. If a 7-year-old child performs at the level of the average 9-year-old on the Stanford-Binet intelligence test, the child would have an IQ of approximately _____.
    A. 100
    B. 119
    C. 129
    D. 140

19. In his approach to measuring intelligence, David Wechsler abandoned the idea of:
    A. IQ.
    B. trying to measure the intelligence of adults.
    C. mental age.
    D. using subscales to measure different mental abilities.

20. On the Wechsler tests of intelligence, a score of 100 indicates a(n) _____ level of intelligence.
    A. above average
    B. average
    C. below average
    D. extremely low

21. You are a psychologist who needs to measure the IQ of a 4-year-old boy. Which of the following tests would be most appropriate for this task?
    A. WISC-III
    B. WAIS-III
    C. WPPSI-III
    D. Daniel Goleman's test of EQ

22. Dr. Li developed a new test of one's ability to spell correctly. To examine the effectiveness of his test, Dr. Li gives it to a group of school children and then correlates their test score with their grades in spelling class. Dr. Li finds that those children who scored the highest on his test also scored highly in spelling. He also finds that those children who scored poorly on his test, scored low in spelling. Based on these findings, Dr. Li's new test appears to have _____.

    A. reliability
    B. validity
    C. reliability and validity
    D. no merit

23. Fredric can read, solve math problems, and learn material very quickly. People are always saying that Fredric is a "quick study". Based on what you know about intelligence, Fredric is most likely to be high in _____ intelligence.

    A. interpersonal
    B. practical
    C. creative
    D. fluid

24. Eduardo, a Central American farmer, can tell when it is going to rain by watching the behavior of his pigs. According to Robert Sternberg, Eduardo's ability to predict the weather in this manner is an example of _____ intelligence.

    A. naturalistic
    B. practical
    C. creative
    D. analytical

25. When parents are asked to rate the intelligence of their children, they usually rate their:

    A. daughters higher in overall intelligence.
    B. sons higher in verbal intelligence.
    C. daughters higher in spatial intelligence.
    D. sons higher in overall intelligence.

Short-Answer Questions

Can you write a brief answer to these questions?

1. When we store mental images, do we store visual images that are exact replicas of the things we see in the world?

2. What would the superordinate and subordinate categories be for the concept, "car"?

3. What is "g"?

189

4. Give an original example of deductive reasoning.

5. According to the availability heuristic, if you ask someone in the United States on July 4th to estimate the number of days it snows each year, he or she should underestimate this figure. Why?

Developing a Bigger Picture: Making Connections Across Chapters

An important aspect of learning is learning to see the "Big Picture" of the subject you are studying. As you learn about psychology, you should try to understand how the material from different chapters fits together to help you form a broad-based understanding of what psychology is all about. To help facilitate the development of this "Big Picture" in your mind, try to answer these questions using the knowledge you have learned in this chapter, as well as the other chapters referenced in the questions.

1. Using what you learned about learning in Chapter 5, how can learning theory explain how children acquire language?

2. In Chapter 4, you learned about sleep and in Chapter 6 you learned about memory. Using this knowledge, answer this question: How might long-term, chronic sleep deprivation affect one's level of intelligence?

3. Using what you learned about memory in Chapter 6 and what you learned about problem solving in Chapter 7, can you further explain why spacing out your study time or distributed practice works better than cramming for exams?

Label the Diagram

What are the names of the multiple intelligences proposed by Howard Gardner?

Intelligence	Description	Examples
(1) _____	The ability to learn and use languages	An author has good command of language and can express ideas well in written form.
(2) _____	The ability to recognize and manipulate patterns of space	A surveyor is very good at judging distances. A seamstress designs a pattern for a jacket.
(3) _____	The ability to attack problems in a logical manner, solve mathematical problems, and in general exhibit scientific thought	A psychologist can develop and test theories in a scientific manner. A physician examines a patient and makes a diagnosis.
(4) _____	The ability to perform, compose, and appreciate music	A songwriter can create unique melodies and perform them.
(5) _____	The ability to use one's body to solve problems and create products	A gymnast can perform intricate maneuvers on the balance beam.
(6) _____	The ability to understand the intentions, motivations, and desires of others	A manager is good at working with others, and can inspire others to perform at their optimal level of performance.
(7) _____	The ability to understand oneself	A student knows what she wants in terms of her career and future life, and she uses this information to choose an appropriate major.
(8) _____	Paying attention to nature and understanding environmental issues	A homemaker recycles her trash and avoids using household cleaners that are harmfull to the environment.
(9) _____	Being concerned with "ultimate" issues; seeking higher truths	A philosophy student ponders the meaning of life.

Big Picture Review

Based on the research you read in your text, are men or women better at these tasks?

Task	On average, are males or females better at this task?
• anagrams	1.
• detecting touch, taste, odor, and sound at low levels of intensity	2.
• fine motor skill tasks like tracing the mirror image of a stimulus on a piece of paper	3.

• foreign languages	4.
• general knowledge	5.
• knowledge about literature	6.
• knowledge about math, geography, and science	7.
• making judgments about moving objects—for example, judging how far away a moving object is	8.
• mechanical reasoning	9.
• mental rotation tasks	10.
• most subject areas at school	11.
• motor skills that involve aiming, such as throwing a baseball or darts	12.
• proportional reasoning	13.
• quantitative reasoning	14.
• reading comprehension	15.
• scientific reasoning	16.
• searching for letters within lines of text	17.
• spelling	18.
• synonym generation	19.
• tongue twisters	20.
• verbal analogies	21.
• verbal fluency	22.
• writing	23.

Solutions

Each solution below is followed by its textbook page reference number and its corresponding chapter learning objective (LO) number. Items with a Big Picture LO help you build a Big Picture of psychology across the chapters you have studied so far.

Fill-in Review of the Chapter

1. language [p. 286; LO 1, Big Picture]
2. mental representation [pp. 286, 288; LO 1, Big Picture]
3. Thinking [p. 288; LO 1]
4. mental representations [p. 288; LO 1]
5. prototype [p. 293; LO 1]
6. natural [p. 292; LO 1]
7. cognitive map [p. 290; LO 1]
8. concept [p. 291; LO 1]
9. Incubation [p. 299; LO 3]

10. functional fixedness [p. 298; LO 3]
11. ill-structured [p. 296; LO 2]
12. well-structured [p. 295; LO 2]
13. mental set [p. 298; LO 3]
14. decision making [p. 300; LO 4]
15. representativeness [p. 302; LO 5]
16. availability [p. 301; LO 5]
17. inductive [p. 300; LO 4]
18. divergent [p. 298; LO 3]
19. morpheme [p. 307; LO 6]
20. Babbling [p. 306; LO 6]
21. Pragmatics [p. 307; LO 6]
22. Broca's area [p. 73; LO 6, Big Picture]
23. Wernicke's area [p. 73; LO 6, Big Picture]
24. linguistic relativity/ Whorfian hypothesis [p. 308; LO 6]
25. nature [p. 84; LO 6, Big Picture]
26. mental age [p. 313; LO 9]
27. Crystallized [p. 318; LO 10]
28. emotional intelligence [p. 320; LO 10]

Use It or Lose It!

1. Robert Sternberg [p. 319; LO 9-10]
2. Howard Gardner [p. 318; LO 9-10]
3. Daniel Goleman [p. 320; LO 9-10]
4. Charles Spearman [p. 317; LO 9-10]
5. David Wechsler [p. 314; LO 9-10]

Self-Check: Are You Getting the Big Picture?

True or False Questions

1. F [p. 309; LO 8]	6. T [p. 295; LO 2]
2. F [p. 289; LO 1]	7. F [p. 295; LO 2]
3. T [p. 292; LO 1]	8. T [p. 298; LO 3]
4. T [p. 292; LO 1]	9. F [p. 298; LO 3]
5. F [p. 305; LO 6]	10. F [p. 313; LO 9]

Multiple Choice Questions

1. D [p. 298; LO 3]	10.C [p. 304; LO 6]	19.C [p. 314; LO 9]
2. B [p. 300; LO 4]	11.C [p. 305; LO 6]	20.B [p. 314; LO 9]
3. B [p. 300; LO 4]	12.B [p. 306; LO 6]	21.C [p. 314; LO 9]
4. B [p. 301; LO 4]	13.C [p. 306; LO 6]	22.B [p. 315; LO 9]
5. C [p. 302; LO 5]	14.A [p. 307; LO 6]	23.D [p. 318; LO 10]
6. A [p. 292; LO 1]	15.D [p. 308; LO 7]	24.B [p. 319; LO 10]
7. B [p. 295; LO 2]	16.A [p. 310; LO 8]	25.D [p. 323; LO 10, 11]
8. D [p. 297; LO 3]	17.D [p. 306; LO 6]	
9. B [p. 300; LO 4]	18.C [p. 314; LO 9]	

Short-Answer Questions

1. When we store mental images, do we store visual images that are exact replicas of the things we see in the world? [p. 289; LO 1]

No, at least not all the time. Mental rotation and visual scanning tasks often seem to indicate that our mental pictures are accurate copies of what we have seen. However, other studies refute this. For example, when people view ambiguous figures, they are sometimes unable to later mentally reinterpret the figure in a manner that is different from how they interpreted it at encoding. In other words, if they interpreted the figure as a rabbit when they first saw it, they cannot later think of the picture and see it as a duck. If they had an exact copy of the picture stored in memory, they should be able to reinterpret it later on.

2. What would the superordinate and subordinate categories be for the concept, "car"? [p. 292; LO 1]

The superordinate category would be "vehicle". A subordinate category would be something like "Toyota Camry".

3. What is "g"? [p. 317; LO 9, 10]

The idea of "g" was first proposed by Charles Spearman in the early 1900s when he argued that test scores of different mental abilities tend to correlate because there is a general level of intelligence, "g", which underlies these abilities.

4. Give an original example of deductive reasoning. [p. 300; LO 4]

There are many correct answers to this question. Here's one: Reasoning that because caring people tend to work for charities, your friend Leo must be a caring person because he works for a charity.

5. According to the availability heuristic, if you ask someone in the United States on July 4th to estimate the number of days it snows each year, he or she should underestimate this figure. Why? [p. 301; LO 5]

Because when judging the likelihood of an event, we tend to use the ease with which we can recall a memory of the event to help us judge how likely the event is. During the middle of the summer, retrieving a memory of a snowy day will be harder than it might be during the winter months. This lack of ease will likely bias a person to underestimate the frequency with which it snows. Alternately, if you asked a person to estimate yearly snow fall in the winter, the availability heuristic would likely bias him or her to overestimate how often it snows.

Developing a Bigger Picture: Making Connections Across Chapters

1. Using what you learned about learning in Chapter 5, how can learning theory explain how children acquire language? [pp. 197-230 & 303-312; LO 6, Big Picture]

   Learning theory would predict that children acquire language through modeling the language they hear spoken around them. It would also predict that adults who have contact with the child reinforce the child's correct attempts at language and that they ignore or perhaps even punish the child's incorrect attempts at language. Through this process of reward and punishment, the adults shape the development of language in the child.

2. In Chapter 4, you learned about sleep and in Chapter 6 you learned about memory. Using this knowledge, answer this question: How might long-term, chronic sleep deprivation affect one's level of intelligence? [pp. 146-148, 244-275, & 313-324; LO 10, Big Picture]

   Chronic sleep deprivation could possibly affect your mind's ability to consolidate long-term memories. It would also produce fatigue that could reduce your ability to concentrate, which would further affect your ability to encode new memories and make it harder to learn. If you are unable to store, process, and retrieve information in an efficient manner, you may end up lacking necessary knowledge, and your ability to solve problems may be reduced. If your ability to solve problems is reduced, you may be less able to function in your environment—which by some definitions would mean that you could be considered to be less intelligent.

3. Using what you learned about memory in Chapter 6 and what you learned about problem solving in Chapter 7, can you further explain why spacing out your study time or distributed practice works better than cramming for exams? [pp. 244-275 & 294-299; LO 2, 3, Big Picture]

   In Chapter 7, you learned how incubation can be beneficial when you are trying to solve a difficult problem. If you try to cram a large amount of knowledge into your mind in one setting, you will not give yourself time to incubate. Without time to incubate, you may find yourself unable to solve problems that you would otherwise be able to solve-- if you just gave yourself more time. By spacing out your study time over a series of days, you ensure that you are not handicapping yourself. With distributed practice, it will be easier for you to reach your full potential as a student.

Label the Diagram

1.	Linguistic [p. 319; LO 10]
2.	Spatial [p. 319; LO 10]
3.	Logical-mathematical [p. 319; LO 10]
4.	Musical [p. 319; LO 10]
5.	Bodily-Kinesthetic [p. 319; LO 10]
6.	Interpersonal [p. 319; LO 10]
7.	Intrapersonal [p. 319; LO 10]
8.	Naturalistic [p. 319; LO 10]
9.	Existential [p. 319; LO 10]

Big Picture Review

1. female [p. 324; LO 11]
2. female [p. 324; LO 11]
3. female [p. 324; LO 11]
4. female [p. 324; LO 11]
5. male [p. 324; LO 11]
6. female [p. 324; LO 11]
7. male [p. 324; LO 11]
8. male [p. 324; LO 11]
9. male [p. 324; LO 11]
10. male [p. 324; LO 11]
11. female [p. 324; LO 11]
12. male [p. 324; LO 11]
13. male [p. 324; LO 11]
14. male [p. 324; LO 11]
15. female [p. 324; LO 11]
16. male [p. 324; LO 11]
17. female [p. 324; LO 11]
18. female [p. 324; LO 11]
19. female [p. 324; LO 11]
20. female [p. 324; LO 11]
21. male [p. 324; LO 11]
22. female [p. 324; LO 11]
23. female [p. 324; LO 11]

8

Motivation and Emotion: What Guides Behavior?

Learning Objectives

After studying each of the following sections of the chapter, you should be able to do these tasks.

Theories About Motivation

1. Describe how psychologists define motivation.
2. Describe the different theoretical ways of conceptualizing motivation.

Hunger and Thirst: What Makes Us Eat and Drink?

3. Describe the feedback our bodies use to regulate hunger.
4. Explain what is known about why some people become obese.
5. Describe bulimia, anorexia, and binge eating disorder and explain their possible causes.
6. Describe the feedback in the body that leads to thirst.

The Puzzle of Destructive Motivation

7. Describe the role that motivation may play in drug-taking behavior.

Theories and Expression of Emotion

8. Describe the various theoretical perspectives on emotion.
9. Describe how we express our emotional states through facial expressions.

The Big Picture

The Big Picture: What Happens When Motives Go Astray?

In this chapter, you learned about the processes of motivation and emotion. Motivation is a catalyzing force that drives and directs our behavior, and emotion is a complex reaction that you have to some internal or external event. Both motivation and emotion are important psychological forces in your everyday life.

Motivation is essential for life because without it, you wouldn't know when to engage in necessary behaviors like eating, drinking water, sleep, and so on. However, as you learned in the cases of Marya Hornbacher and Toren Volkmann, motivation can also be problematic if we feel motivated to engage in destructive behaviors like abusing alcohol or bingeing and purging.

Theories About Motivation

This section covers Learning Objectives 1-2. Because of the importance of motivation, psychologists have long been interested in understanding exactly what does and does not motivate our behavior. One of the first psychologists to examine motives was William James. James believed that motives were inborn instincts that directed our behavior. This approach soon fell out of favor because the list of proposed instincts kept getting longer and longer, and it was impossible to rule out the possibility that some of our "instincts" were actually learned behaviors.

Drive theory was another early approach to understanding motivation. Drive-reduction theories state that motivation stems from a desire to reduce an aversive internal state or drive. Primary drives (e.g., hunger and thirst) motivate us to maintain certain bodily processes at homeostasis. Negative feedback loops in the body keep tabs on these bodily processes and send feedback to the brain. Using this feedback, the brain will initiate a drive-state when we are lacking in some biological need (e.g., we will feel hunger when our blood-sugar levels drop).

However, not all motives are related to survival or bodily processes. We also experience the motivation to achieve, be close to others, and so on. These drives, called secondary drives, are thought to be learned through experience.

Drive theory does a good job of explaining some of our motivation—particularly the concept of primary drives. However, drive theory does not explain all of our motivation. For example, Marya's motivation to be anorexic does not fit with the idea of drive reduction, which would predict that Marya would eat to satisfy her hunger.

Incentive theories of motivation state that many of our behaviors are motivated by the desire to obtain incentives. Incentives can be extrinsic (e.g., money or social approval) or intrinsic (e.g., pride or increased self-esteem).

Looking at the drive-reduction and incentive theories of motivation, you can see that not all motives are created equal. Some motivations like hunger are needed for survival, whereas other motives like wanting to please a friend with a nice gift are more socially based. Abraham Maslow believed that you tend to prioritize such motives along a hierarchy of need. According to Maslow, you seek to satisfy basic human needs followed by psychological needs and self-fulfillment needs. In other words, a starving person is more concerned with finding food than with realizing her potential as a human. Hunger takes precedence.

Hunger and Thirst: What Makes Us Eat and Drink?

This section covers Learning Objectives 3-6. Because hunger is one of the most important motivations, psychologists have spent considerable time trying to understand the biological mechanisms that give rise to it. Hunger works on a negative feedback loop system, and there are many sources in the body that provide this feedback. The stomach contractions signal hunger and special receptors in the walls of the stomach keep tabs on how much nutrient you have eaten. The liver monitors the balance between glucose and glycogen in the body and uses this information to indicate to the brain whether or not you need to eat. Hormones from the endocrine system also play a role in hunger. Ghrelin is released by the stomach and stimulates us to eat. When we have eaten enough food, cholecystokinin (CCK) is released by the small intestines and tells the brain to shut off hunger. Leptin is released from your fat cells and allows the brain to keep tabs on how much stored fat you have in your body. This information may allow the brain to regulate long-term eating behavior.

The brain itself plays a large role in initiating and stopping hunger. Glucoreceptors in the brain monitor your blood-sugar levels and signal hunger when these levels drop. The lateral hypothalamus is one part of the brain that is believed to turn on hunger, although other "on switches" are also thought to exist. The ventromedial hypothalamus (VMH) is thought to play an indirect role in satiety—possibly through its influence on insulin release in the body.

Surprisingly, not all hunger is initiated from within the body. Hunger can be initiated by just seeing or smelling food. You also can be conditioned to feel like eating in particular situations. For example, most holidays (especially in Western cultures) are associated with large amounts of food. Because of these traditions, you may become conditioned to associate eating with the experience of positive emotions. As a result, you may begin to eat when you wish to feel good.

Emotional eating when you actually do not require fuel can lead to obesity—a growing problem in many cultures. Restrictive dieting has also been shown to lead to binge eating that can put the pounds back on a dieter. However, not all obese people are to blame for their weight. There are also biological factors involved in obesity. Some obese people have genetically low metabolisms or efficient digestive systems that cause them to gain weight even though they eat and exercise just a thin people do. Some obese people have problems with insulin that cause them to gain weight. The *Spotlight on Diversity* in this chapter discusses racial differences in obesity and some of the genetic reasons for these differences.

Although a major problem for many people, obesity is not considered to be a psychological disorder, but there is a mental disorder called binge-eating disorder in which people binge on food without engaging in some compensatory means of avoiding weight gain. People suffering from binge-eating disorder are often overweight. Anorexia and bulimia are other serious mental conditions in which people experience severe disturbances of their eating behavior. People with anorexia starve themselves, exercise a great deal, and experience severe, often life-threatening weight loss and a distorted body image. Bulimics tend to binge and purge or restrict their eating to counteract the effects of the binge. The case of Marya Hornabacher profiled her life-long struggle with both anorexia and bulimia.

Both anorexia and bulimia are thought to stem from many causes. In Western societies, a cultural emphasis on an unrealistically thin standard of beauty for women is thought to play a role in the development of eating disorders among women. Other factors may include genetics and personality factors.

The motivation to eat is critical for survival, but an even more crucial motive is the motivation to drink fluids. Death due to dehydration will occur sooner than death due to starvation. Like hunger, thirst is considered to be a primary drive that seeks to maintain homeostasis in the body. In the body, thirst is initiated when the hypothalamus notices an intracellular drop in fluid or when specialized cells in your heart, kidneys, or blood vessels notice a drop in your blood pressure.

The Puzzle of Destructive Motivation

This section covers Learning Objective 7. As you learned in the case of Toren Volkmann, not all motivation directs us to behave in ways that are good for us. At times, people can be motivated to behave in self-destructive ways, such as binge drinking. Operant conditioning may explain why some people begin taking illegal drugs, in that these drugs may act as positive or negative reinforcers; but the opponent-process theory of motivation explains why people continue to abuse drugs. According to this theory, as a person continues to abuse a drug, his body will attempt to physiologically counteract the effect of the drug by engaging in an opponent-process. If the drug is a stimulant, the opponent process will lower the user's physiological arousal. If the drug is a depressant, the opponent-process will increase arousal in the body. If the user continues to use drugs over a period of time, the action of the opponent-process will cause the user to develop a tolerance to the drug and larger and larger doses will be required to produce the desired effect. As tolerance develops, so can physical dependence that results in unpleasant withdrawal symptoms if the user stops taking the drug. At the height of his alcoholism, Toren could not function without consuming alcohol.

Theories and Expression of Emotion

This section covers Learning Objectives 8-9. Motivation catalyzes and directs your behavior, and it can be either intrinsic or extrinsic. On the other hand, your emotional reactions to events are usually (but not always) brought about by events outside your body; and may include physiological reactions, behavioral reactions, facial expressions, cognition, or affective responses. Psychologists have developed several theories to explain the nature and function of our emotions.

One of the earliest of these theories is the James-Lange theory. According to the James-Lange theory, emotion is the pattern of physiological arousal you experience in response to some event. In this view, every emotion you experience is associated with its own unique pattern of physiological arousal.

Walter Cannon criticized the James-Lange theory on three points. First, he argued that some emotions seem to have very similar patterns of arousal that would not allow you to distinguish among them. Second, it is possible to be aware that you are experiencing an emotion before you feel any physiological arousal in your body. And finally, the James-Lange theory cannot account for the fact that artificially created states of arousal do not give rise to emotions. Correspondingly, the Cannon-Bard theory of emotion states that emotion originates in the brain and not in the body's physiological reaction to an event.

Despite Cannon's criticisms of the James-Lange theory, using modern equipment to measure minute changes in the body, researchers have found some support for the idea that emotions have their own unique physiological patterns of arousal in the body. Another approach that emphasizes the role of the body in emotion is the facial-feedback hypothesis. According to this theory, feedback from the muscles of the face informs the brain of the emotional state you are experiencing.

However, Cannon was not the only researcher to suggest that the brain has something to do with emotion. In their two-factor theory of emotion, Stanley Schachter and Jerome Singer argue that emotion is a product of both physiological arousal in the body and cognitive interpretation of the situation in the brain. According to this theory, when you experience emotion, your body becomes physiologically aroused. You then use situational cues to help you interpret which emotion is causing this arousal. In different situations, the same physiological arousal could be interpreted as different emotions.

Another theory that recognizes the importance of cognition in emotion is Richard Lazarus's cognitive-mediational theory. In this view, your cognitive interpretation or appraisal of the situation influences the emotion you feel. There is little doubt that appraisals can affect the emotions you feel, but are appraisals a necessary part of emotion? Some, like Robert Zajonc believe that thought is not a necessary part of emotion. Zajonc has demonstrated that people have preferences for certain objects even though they don't even know what the objects are—a fact that makes any sort of cognitive appraisal about the object difficult or impossible. Zajonc also demonstrated the mere-exposure effect, or the fact that you tend to like things that you have been exposed to more than things that you have not encountered before.

Regardless of where emotions originate in your mind and/or body, it is clear that you have the capacity to experience a wide range of emotions. Whether or not humans have basic emotions that are independent of cultural background is the subject of some debate. Even if basic emotions do exist, determining which emotions are basic promises to be an even more controversial task.

Outlining the Big Picture

Chapter 8: Motivation and Emotion: What Guides Behavior?

The Big Picture: What Happens When Motives Go Astray?
Marya Hornbacher's *Wasted:* One woman's life-long struggles with eating disorders.
Chris and Toren Volkmann, *From Binge to Blackout: A Mother and Son Struggle with Teen Drinking*
Notes:

_____

_____

_____

_____

_____

_____

_____

Theories About Motivation (Learning Objectives 1-2)
Motivation as an Instinct
Motivation as a Drive
Arousal Theories of Motivation
Incentive Theories of Motivation
Maslow's Hierarchy of Needs
Notes:

_____

_____

_____

_____

Hunger and Thirst: What Makes Us Eat and Drink? (Learning Objectives 3-6)
Hunger and Feedback in the Body
　　Hunger Feedback from the Stomach
　　Hunger Feedback from the Liver
　　Hunger Feedback from Hormones
　　Hunger Feedback from Fat Cells
　　Hunger Regulation in the Brain
　　Other Cues that Influence Eating: Culture and Consumerism
Obesity: Nature and Nurture, Again
　　Behavioral Factors in Obesity
　　Culture and Weight-Based Prejudice
　　The Battle of the Bulge: Why Is Dieting So Hard?
　　Biological Factors in Obesity
　　Spotlight on Diversity: Obesity in White and Black American Adolescent
　　Females
Eating Disorders: Bulimia Nervosa, Anorexia Nervosa, and Binge Eating Disorder
　　Bulimia Nervosa
　　Anorexia Nervosa
　　Bing Eating Disorder
Thirst

Notes:

_____

_____

_____

_____

_____

_____

The Puzzle of Destructive Motivation (Learning Objective 7)
Notes:

_____

_____

_____

_____

_____

_____

Theories and Expression of Emotion (Learning Objectives 8-9)
The James-Lange Theory of Emotion
     Walter Cannon's Criticisms of the James-Lange Theory
     Some Validation of the James-Lange Theory
The Facial-Feedback Hypothesis
The Schacter-Singer Two-Factor Theory of Emotion
Lazarus's Cognitive-Mediational Theory of Emotion
Communicating Emotions: Culture, Gender, and Facial Expressions
Notes:

_____

_____

_____

_____

_____

_____

_____

Are You Getting the Big Picture?
Notes:

_____

_____

_____

_____

_____

Are You Getting the Big Picture: A Mental Map of Chapter 8

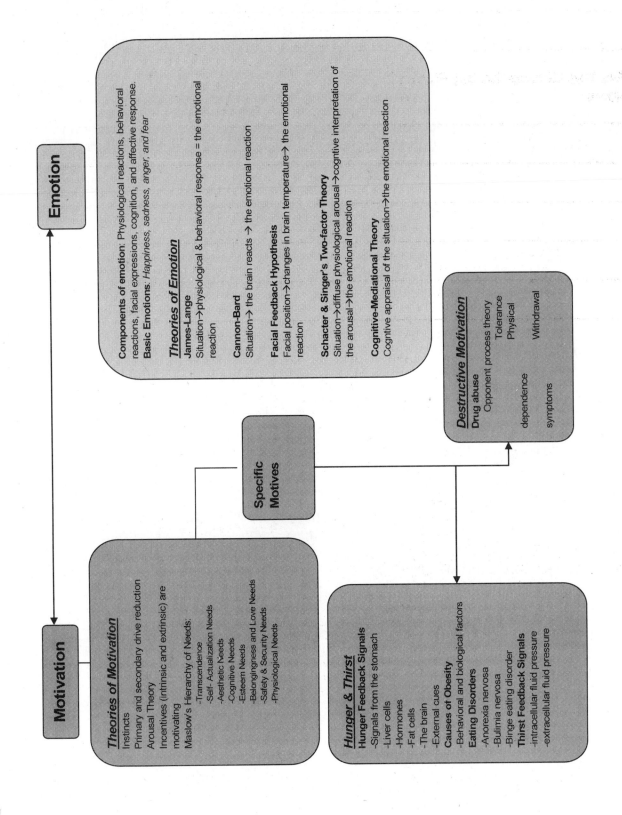

Emotion

Components of emotion: Physiological reactions, behavioral reactions, facial expressions, cognition, and affective response.
Basic Emotions: *Happiness, sadness, anger, and fear*

Theories of Emotion

James-Lange
Situation→physiological & behavioral response = the emotional reaction

Cannon-Bard
Situation → the brain reacts → the emotional reaction

Facial Feedback Hypothesis
Facial position→changes in brain temperature→ the emotional reaction

Schacter & Singer's Two-factor Theory
Situation→diffuse physiological arousal→cognitive interpretation of the arousal→the emotional reaction

Cognitive-Mediational Theory
Cognitive appraisal of the situation→the emotional reaction

Motivation

Theories of Motivation
Instincts
Primary and secondary drive reduction
Arousal Theory
Incentives (intrinsic and extrinsic) are motivating
Maslow's Hierarchy of Needs:
-Transcendence
-Self- Actualization Needs
-Aesthetic Needs
-Cognitive Needs
-Esteem Needs
-Belongingness and Love Needs
-Safety & Security Needs
-Physiological Needs

Specific Motives

Destructive Motivation
Drug abuse
Opponent process theory
Tolerance
Physical
dependence   Withdrawal
symptoms

Hunger & Thirst
Hunger Feedback Signals
-Signals from the stomach
-Liver cells
-Hormones
-Fat cells
-The brain
-External cues
Causes of Obesity
-Behavioral and biological factors
Eating Disorders
-Anorexia nervosa
-Bulimia nervosa
-Binge eating disorder
Thirst Feedback Signals
-intracellular fluid pressure
-extracellular fluid pressure

Key Points of the Big Picture

Affective component of emotion:
the subjective experience of what you are *feeling* during the emotion. *Example: You feel happy when you see your boyfriend or girlfriend.*

Anorexia nervosa:
a mental health disorder in which a person has an intense fear of gaining weight, even though he or she is actually underweight. This irrational fear motivates the person to lose unhealthy amounts of weight through self-starvation. *Example: Marya Hornbacher suffered from anorexia and starved herself nearly to death.*

Basic emotion:
a proposed set of innate emotions common to all humans from which other higher-order emotions may stem. *Example: Happiness, sadness, fear, and so on.*

Bulimia nervosa:
a mental health disorder in which a person alternately binges on large quantities of food and then engages in some inappropriate compensatory behavior to avoid weight gain. *Example: Many college students suffer from bulimia and are unable to stop themselves from bingeing and purging food.*

Cannon-Bard theory:
a theory of emotion that states that emotions originate in the brain not the body. *Example: You know you are afraid, even before you feel your heart pounding.*

Cholecystokinin (CCK):
a hormone released by the small intestines that plays a role in hunger regulation. *Example: When you eat a big meal, your small intestines release CCK to help shut off your hunger.*

Cognitive-mediational theory:
a theory of emotion which states that our cognitive appraisal of a situation determines what emotion we will feel in the situation. *Example: If you believe that your friend failed to answer your question because she is ignoring you, you are likely to feel anger. If you feel that she failed to answer you because she didn't hear you, you will probably not feel angry.*

Drive:
an uncomfortable internal state that motivates us to reduce this discomfort through our behavior. *Example: You feel hunger when you need fuel, sleepy when you need sleep.*

Drive reduction theory:
theory of motivation that proposes that motivation seeks to reduce internal levels of drive. *Example: To eat to relieve hunger, sleep to relieve sleepiness.*

Emotion:
a complex reaction to some internal or external event that involves physiological reactions, behavioral reactions, facial expressions, cognition, and affective responses. *Example: Happiness, sadness, guilty, pride, etc.*

Extracellular fluid:
the level of fluid found in the spaces outside the cells of the body, which is used to regulate thirst.

Extrinsic motivation:
motivation that comes from outside our person. *Example: Going to work to earn money.*

Facial feedback hypothesis:
a theory which states that our emotional state is affected by the feedback our brain gets from facial muscles. *Example: If you smile right now, it should improve your mood. If you frown, it should decrease your mood.*

Ghrelin:

a hunger stimulating hormone produced by the stomach

Glucose:
the form of sugar that our body burns as a fuel.

Glycogen:
a starchy molecule that is produced from excess glucose in the body; it can be thought of as our body's stored energy reserves.

Hierarchy of needs:
Maslow's theory that humans are motivated by different motives, some of which take precedence over others. *Example: If you were starving right now, studying for your next psychology exam to make a good grade would not be the most important thing on your mind.*

Homeostasis:
an internal state of equilibrium in the body. *Example: Being neither hungry or stuffed, but rather having just the right amount of fuel in our body to meet your biological needs.*

Incentives:
a goal or desire that we are motivated to fulfill. *Example: Working hard in school to help yourself one day get the career you want.*

Instinct:
innate impulse from within a person that directs or motivates behavior. *Example: The instinct to step back when you get to close to the edge of a cliff while hiking.*

Intracellular fluid:
the level of fluid found inside the cells of the body, which is used to regulate thirst.

Intrinsic motivation:
motivation that comes from within the person. *Example: Your desire to do well on your next psychology exam simply to please yourself.*

James-Lange theory:
a theory of emotion that defines an emotion as a unique pattern of physiological arousal. *Example: The pattern of physiological arousal you are experiencing right now also defines the emotion you are currently experiencing.*

Lateral hypothalamus (LH):
a region of the hypothalamus once thought to be the hunger center in the brain.

Leptin:
a hormone released by adipose cells in the body that plays a role in the regulation of hunger.

Mere exposure effect:
the idea that the more one is exposed to something, the more they grow to like it. *Example: If you see a person everyday at school, over time you may begin to like that person a bit more.*

Motive:
a tendency to desire and seek out positive incentives or rewards and to avoid negative outcomes . *Example: Your desire to achieve will be a primary determinant of how well you do on your next psychology exam.*

Negative feedback loop:
a system of feedback in the body that monitors and adjusts our motivation level so as to maintain homeostasis. *Example: When you become dehydrated, you feel thirsty. When you take in enough water, your thirst abates.*

Neuropeptide y:
the most powerful hunger stimulant known.

Obese:
having a body mass index of 30 or over.

Opponent process theory:
a theory of motivation that states that the body will counteract the effects of ingested drugs by adjusting its arousal level in a direction opposite that of the drug's effect. *Example: If you abuse alcohol, a depressant, your brain will increase its level of arousal to counteract the effects of the alcohol.*

Physical dependence:
a condition that occurs when a person is motivated to continue taking a drug because to stop taking the drug would result in painful withdrawal symptoms. *Example: When a smoker tries to stop smoking, he/she will experience painful physical symptoms of withdrawal. The person is therefore motivated to continue smoking so as to avoid the painful withdrawal symptoms.*

Primary drive:
a drive that motivates us to maintain homeostasis in certain biological processes within the body. *Example: Hunger, thirst, sleepiness, and so on.*

Secondary drive:
learned drive that is not directly related to biological needs. *Example: Need for achievement, need for power, the need to be valued by others, and so on.*

Sensation seekers:
people who, by trait, tend to seek out arousing activities. *Example: Sensation seekers may include people such as extreme athletes, explorers, people who seek out dangerous professions, and people who experiment with other risky behaviors.*

Set point:
the theory that our body has a particular weight or set point that it seeks to maintain. *Example: Your current body weight may represent your set point.*

Tolerance:
a condition in which after repeated use, more of a drug is needed to produce the same effect. *Example: If you abuse alcohol, soon it will take more and more alcohol for you to become intoxicated.*

Two-factor theory:
a theory that states that emotions result when we cognitively interpret our physiological reactions in light of the situation. *Example: If you feel aroused while viewing a bar fight, you will be more likely to attribute this feeling to anger than to joy.*

Ventromedial hypothalamus (VMH):
a region of the hypothalamus that plays an indirect role in creating a feeling of satiety.

Withdrawal:
an unpleasant physiological state that results when one stops taking a drug to which he or she has built up a tolerance. *Example: When a smoker tries to stop smoking, he/she will experience painful physical symptoms.*

Self-Check: Are You Getting the Big Picture?

After you have read and studied the chapter, see if you can answer the following quiz questions. Check your answers at the end of the chapter. If you miss a question, refer to your text and re-study the appropriate sections.

Fill-in Review of The Chapter

Can you fill-in the missing terms for each section of the chapter? Items marked with an * encourage you to continue building the Big Picture of psychology by connecting the material in this chapter to material from previous chapters in the text.

The Big Picture: What Happens When Motives Go Astray?

Toren Volkmann suffered from the shakes, insomnia, and an inability to focus his attention when he didn't drink. These 1) _____ symptoms were due to dependence on alcohol.

Toren also found that he needed to drink more and more alcohol to feel its effects. This phenomenon is known as 2) _____.

Marya Hornbacher suffered from 3) _____ _____and 4) _____ _____, two very serious eating disorders.

Theories About Motivation

Research suggests that people high in sensation seeking have low levels of 5) _____ _____ in their brains.

Getting paid to engage in your favorite hobby would provide 6) _____ motivation for engaging in the hobby.

The motivation to do well in psychology class is an example of a(n) 7) _____ drive.

Abraham Maslow believed that 8) _____ is the highest level of motivation that humans experience.

When a mother cat takes care of her young, this behavior is likely motivated by a(n) 9) _____.

Hunger and Thirst: What Makes Us Eat and Drink?

Hunger and thirst are examples of 10) _____ _____ that must be satisfied to maintain 11) _____ in the body.

12) _____ is the form of sugar that your body burns for fuel.

13) _____ is a hormone that is secreted by the body's fat cells.

14) _____ is a hormone secreted by the stomach that stimulates hunger.

When you have taken in enough food to meet your energy requirements, your small intestines release 15) _____ shut off your hunger.

The 16) _____ hypothalamus plays a role in turning on hunger.
The 17) _____ hypothalamus plays a role in shutting off hunger.

Thirst is regulated in part by pressure receptors in your heart, kidneys, and 18) _____ _____, which monitor your 19) _____fluid levels.

Loss of blood would likely cause a person to feel motivated to 20) _____.

The Puzzle of Destructive Motivation

Dave is dependent on the heroin he injects daily. Dave has noticed that just seeing a needle makes him feel a bit high. This unusual reaction is likely due to the action of classical conditioning. The sight of the needle is acting as a 21*) _____ _____ that elicits the 22*) _____ _____ of feeling high.

When a person who is dependent on drugs experiences withdrawal symptoms, he is motivated to take more drugs to relieve the discomfort. Because the drug acts as a(n) 23*) _____ reinforcer, making him feel better, the person is likely to continue taking the drugs and deepening his dependence.

Theories and Expression of Emotion

The idea that the configuration of your facial muscles informs your brain about the emotional state you are experiencing is called the 24) _____ _____ _____.

According to Walter Cannon, emotion originates in the 25) _____.

According to the cognitive-mediational theory of emotion, your 26) _____ _____ of a situation is a powerful determinant of the emotion you feel in that situation.

27) _____ _____ are emotional states that are common to all people, regardless of their culture.

According to the 28) _____ _____ theory of emotion, we use the context in which we find ourselves to help us interpret our level of physiological arousal and determine which emotion we are feeling.

A(n) 29) _____ is our interpretation of a situation that influences the emotion we feel in the situation.

According to the 30) _____ _____ effect, the more we experience something, the better we tend to like it.

Use It or Lose It!

Would these bits of feedback increase or decrease your hunger?

Feedback	Hunger Increases or Decreases
A large amount of leptin is released by fat cells in your body.	1.
CCK is released by your small intestines.	2.
Ghrelin is released by your stomach.	3.
Gylcogen is being converted into glucose in your liver.	4.
Glucose is being converted into glycogen in your liver.	5.

211

Glucose levels have dropped in your brain.	6.
Your stomach is empty.	7.
You smell your favorite food cooking.	8.

True or False Questions

Are these statements true or false?

1. Motivational processes that are regulated by negative feedback loops are ones in which activity is raised and lowered so as to maintain homeostasis in the body.
   Choice T: True
   Choice F: False

2. The need for achievement is an example of a secondary drive.
   Choice T: True
   Choice F: False

3. Cross-cultural studies suggest that regardless of their cultural background, humans have a standard set of basic emotions.
   Choice T: True
   Choice F: False

4. In general, humans perform their best when they are highly aroused.
   Choice T: True
   Choice F: False

5. According to the drive theory of motivation, secondary drives are learned when we associate certain things like money and approval with satisfaction of our primary drives.
   Choice T: True
   Choice F: False

6. Physical dependence occurs when you cannot survive without a drug.
   Choice T: True
   Choice F: False

7. Opponent-process theory does a good job of explaining why someone would be motivated to try an illegal drug for the first time.
   Choice T: True
   Choice F: False

8. The experience of emotion contains physiological reactions, behavioral reactions, facial expressions, cognition, and affective responses to the situation.
   Choice T: True
   Choice F: False

9. New technologies for precisely measuring physiological responses in the brain and body have provided recent support for the James-Lange theory of emotion.
   Choice T: True
   Choice F: False

10. One of Walter Cannon's criticisms of the James-Lange theory of emotion was that sometimes our body's physiological response to a situation precedes our subjective emotional reaction to the situation.
Choice T: True
Choice F: False

Multiple Choice Questions

Can you choose the best answer for these questions?

1. To help regulate your thirst, intracelluar fluid levels in the body are monitored in the _____.
   A. hypothalamus
   B. amygdala
   C. cortex
   D. heart

2. The fact that two people can be side by side in the same situation, yet experience different emotions is most consistent with the _____ theory of emotion.
   A. James-Lange
   B. Schacter-Singer
   C. cognitive-mediational
   D. facial feedback

3. Which of the following is not thought to be a basic human emotion?
   A. happiness
   B. sadness
   C. pride
   D. fear

4. Which of the following characteristics has not been found to correlate with having an eating disorder?
   A. being female
   B. being a perfectionist
   C. having a personality disorder
   D. being the middle child

5. Which of these eating disorders is more likely to be seen in female college students than it is in non-college students?
   A. bulimia nervosa
   B. anorexia nervosa
   C. both anorexia and bulimia nervosa
   D. compulsive overeating disorder

6. Joel sustained head injuries in a tornado five years ago. Prior to his injury, Joel was grossly overweight. However, afterwards Joel lost so much weight that his wife was convinced that he had become anorexic. Based on what you know about eating, where would you expect to find damage in Joel's brain?
    A. the left frontal cortex
    B. the ventromedial hypothalamus
    C. the lateral hypothalamus
    D. the ventricles

7. A person who characteristically takes risks and engages in exciting activities is likely to score high in _____.
    A. need for self-actualization
    B. need for transcendence
    C. sensation seeking
    D. all of the above

8. Which of the following behaviors would drive-reduction theory have the most trouble explaining?
    A. drinking water on a hot summer day
    B. eating a big supper after having skipped your lunch
    C. putting an extra blanket on the bed during the winter
    D. consuming alcohol on New Year's Eve

9. According to arousal theories of motivation, we all perform best:
    A. when highly aroused.
    B. when slightly aroused.
    C. when moderately aroused.
    D. at our optimal level of arousal.

10. Your motivation to study hard and make good grades is best explained by which theory of motivation?
    A. instinct theory
    B. drive-reduction theory
    C. an incentive theory
    D. the lowest level of Maslow's hierarchy

11. Wanting to do well on a term paper to make yourself feel proud is an example of :
    A. a primary drive.
    B. extrinsic motivation.
    C. intrinsic motivation.
    D. transcendence.

12. Abraham Malsow's theory of motivation cannot explain which of the following behaviors?
    A. A starving man who steals a loaf of bread.
    B. A middle-aged, middle class woman who is looking for love.
    C. A man who lives in a very dangerous part of town, whose primary concern is finding a job that makes him feel important.
    D. A woman who has food, a safe place to live, love, and high self-esteem, yet still feels unfulfilled in her life.

13. Juan eats a very large salad for lunch. Mona has a cheeseburger. And Abe has a piece of pizza. Knowing what you do about hunger feedback in the body, who will get hungry soonest?
    A. Juan
    B. Mona
    C. Abe
    D. Due to homeostatic regulation, all three will feel hunger at about the same time.

14. Which of the following statements is untrue about hunger feedback in the body?
    A. Specialized cells in the stomach measure the quality of the food we eat.
    B. Cells in the intestines release CCK as part of hunger regulation.
    C. The brain has receptors for glycogen that allow it to monitor how much energy we have in our bloodstream.
    D. Our fat cells release leptin which allows our brain to keep tabs on how much stored fuel we have in or bodies.

15. If you destroy the lateral hypothalamus of a rat, what will happen to the rat?
    A. It will die immediately.
    B. If left alone, it will starve to death.
    C. Its set point will increase, and the rat will gain weight.
    D. Its weight will fluctuate wildly over a period of about a month before stabilizing at a new, lower set point.

16. Which of the following statements about the role that cholecystokinin (CCK) plays in hunger regulation is correct?
    A. Giving a person CCK is not enough by itself to stop hunger.
    B. CCK is a powerful hormone that can shut off hunger immediately, regardless of how much you have eaten.
    C. Taking CCK actually increases your level of hunger.
    D. Taking CCK has absolutely no effect on your level of hunger.

17. The brain has leptin receptors:
    A. near the ventricles.
    B. in the hypothalamus.
    C. both a & b
    D. neither a or b

18. If an obese rat is injected with leptin, what happens?
    A. It dies.
    B. It gains weight.
    C. It loses weight.
    D. Nothing.

19. What does destruction of the ventromedial hypothalamus appear to do to the body?
    A. It causes the body to stop producing CCK.
    B. It causes the body to stop releasing insulin.
    C. It causes the body to release more insulin.
    D. It causes the body to release more leptin.

20. External cues for hunger, such as the smell of popcorn, can:
    A. only increase hunger in thin people.
    B. only increase hunger in people who are already hungry.
    C. only increase hunger in overweight people.
    D. increase hunger in people of all weights.

21. A BMI of _____ indicates that you are obese.
    A. 20
    B. 25
    C. 30
    D. 35

22. Which of the following statements is true?
    A. Inefficient digestion is a leading cause of obesity.
    B. All obese people have low metabolic rates.
    C. Drastic reduction in caloric intake can raise your metabolic rate.
    D. People on restrictive diets are more likely to engage in binge eating.

23. Successful dieting should include:
    A. a moderate reduction in calories that leads to slow weight loss.
    B. exercise.
    C. a permanent commitment to healthier eating.
    D. all of the above

24. The typical American diet is:
    A. unhealthy.
    B. healthy.
    C. no better or worse than the diet of most cultures.
    D. far better than the diet found in European countries.

25. In the National Heart, Lung, and Blood Institute Growth and Health Study (NGHS), what was found to be the strongest demographic or lifestyle predictor of obesity in Black girls?
    A. their mother's education level
    B. the family income
    C. eating more
    D. how much TV they watched

Short-Answer Questions

Can you write a brief answer to these questions?

1. Why did instinct theory fall out of favor as an explanation for motivation?

2. According to the Schacter-Singer theory of emotion, why is it not such a good idea to take a blind date to the library if you really want him or her to find you attractive and exciting?

3. According to the opponent-process theory of motivation, what would likely happen to a methamphetamine addict, if he or she tries to stop taking this drug?

4. What role does the liver play in regulating hunger?

5. How can you explain the fact that eating disorders like anorexia and bulimia are more common among women from Western, industrialized cultures?

Developing a Bigger Picture: Making Connections Across Chapters

An important aspect of learning is learning to see the "Big Picture" of the subject you are studying. As you learn about psychology, you should try to understand how the material from different chapters fits together to help you form a broad-based understanding of what psychology is all about. To help facilitate the development of this "Big Picture" in your mind, try to answer these questions using the knowledge you have learned in this chapter, as well as the other chapters referenced in the questions.

1. Based on what you learned about the brain in Chapter 2, which parts of the brain play a significant role in the processing of emotion?

2. Using what you learned in Chapter 1, design a study to test the hypothesis that liquid diets are more effective than low-carbohydrate diets in causing people to lose weight.

3. Using the information you learned in Chapter 3 concerning the senses of taste and smell, develop a plan for keeping persons suffering from the early stages of Alzheimer's disease motivated to eat.

Label the Diagram

Can you label the different levels of Maslow's Hierarchy of Needs?

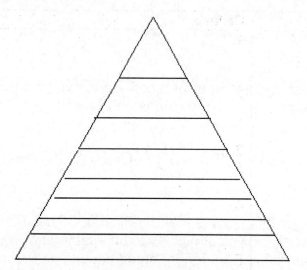

Big Picture Review

Can you fill in the diagnostic criteria for these eating disorders?

Disorder	Criteria
Bulimia Nervosa	1. 2. 3. 4. 5.
Anorexia Nervosa	6. 7. 8. 9.
Binge-eating Disorder	10.

Solutions

Each solution below is followed by its textbook page reference number and its corresponding chapter learning objective (LO) number. Items with a Big Picture LO help you build a Big Picture of psychology across the chapters you have studied so far.

Fill-in Review of The Chapter

1. withdrawal [pp.333 & 360; LO 7, Big Picture]
2. tolerance [p. 360; LO 7, Big Picture]
3. anorexia nervosa [p. 333; LO 5]
4. bulimia nervosa [p. 333; LO 5]
5. monoamine oxidase [p. 337; LO 2]
6. extrinsic [p. 339; LO 2]
7. secondary [p. 336; LO 2]
8. transcendence [p. 340; LO 2]
9. instinct [p. 334; LO 2]
10. primary drives [p. 335; LO 2]
11. homeostasis [p. 335; LO 2]
12. Glucose [p. 343; LO 3]
13. Leptin [p. 344; LO 3]
14. Ghrelin [p. 343; LO 3]
15. CCK [p. 344; LO 3]
16. lateral [p. 345; LO 3]
17. ventromedial hypothalamus [p. 345; LO 3]
18. blood vessels [p. 358; LO 8]
19. extracellular [p. 358; LO 8]
20. drink [p. 358; LO 8]
21. conditioned stimulus [p. 199; LO 7, Big Picture]
22. conditioned response [p. 199; LO 7, Big Picture]
23. negative [p. 212; LO 7, Big Picture]
24. facial feedback hypothesis [p. 365; LO 8]
25. brain [p. 364; LO 8]
26. cognitive appraisal [p. 367; LO 8]
27. Basic emotions [p. 368; LO 9]
28. cognitive-mediational [p. 367; LO 8]
29. appraisal [p. 367; LO 8]
30. mere exposure [p. 367; LO 8]

Use It or Lose It!

1. Decrease [p. 344; LO 3]
2. Decrease [p. 344; LO 3]
3. Increase [p. 343; LO 3]
4. Increase [p. 344; LO 3]
5. Decrease [p. 344; LO 3]

6. Increase [p. 345; LO 3]	
7. Increase [p. 343; LO 3]	
8. Increase [p. 346; LO 3]	

Self-Check: Are You Getting the Big Picture?

True or False Questions

1. T [p. 335; LO 3]	6. F [p. 360 LO 7]
2. T [p. 336; LO 2]	7. F [p. 359; LO 7]
3. F [p. 368; LO 9]	8. T [p. 362; LO 8]
4. F [p. 336; LO 2]	9. T [p. 364; LO 8]
5. T [p. 336; LO 2]	10. F [p. 363; LO 8]

Multiple Choice Questions

1. A [p. 358; LO 6]	10. C [p. 339; LO 2]	19. C [p. 346; LO 3, 4]
2. C [p. 367; LO 8]	11. C [p. 339; LO 2]	20. D [p. 346; LO 3, 4]
3. C [p. 368; LO 8, 9]	12. C [p. 340; LO 2]	21. C [p. 348; LO 4]
4. D [p. 356; LO 5]	13. A [p. 343; LO 3]	22. D [p. 350; LO 4]
5. A [p. 354; LO 5]	14. C [p. 345; LO 3]	23. D [p. 351; LO 4]
6. C [p. 345; LO 3, 4]	15. B [p. 345; LO 3]	24. A [p. 352; LO 4]
7. C [p. 337; LO 2]	16. A [p. 344; LO 3]	25. D [p. 353; LO 4]
8. D [p. 335; LO 2]	17. C [p. 344; LO 3]	
9. D [p. 336; LO 2]	18. C [p. 345; LO 3, 4]	

Short-Answer Questions

Can you write a brief answer to these questions?

1. Why did instinct theory fall out of favor as an explanation for motivation? [p. 334; LO 2]

   Instinct theory fell out of favor for two reasons. First, the number of proposed instincts became so large that the theory really wasn't useful anymore. Taken to its logical extreme, almost any behavior could be seen as an instinct. Even more problematic was the fact that it is nearly impossible to determine whether motivations are truly instincts or whether they are actually learned behaviors.

2. According to the Schacter-Singer theory of emotion, why is it not such a good idea to take a blind date to the library if you really want him or her to find you attractive and exciting? [p. 366; LO 8]

   According to Schacter-Singer, emotion is a product of diffuse physiological arousal that is then interpreted in light of the situation. Because the library is not a very arousing place for many people, the danger is that your date may attribute his or her lack of arousal to a lack of attraction for you. If this happens, you may not get a second date. A better choice for a first date would be an amusement park!

3. According to the opponent-process theory of motivation, what would likely happen to a methamphetamine addict, if he or she tries to stop taking this drug? [p. 359; LO 7]

While taking methamphetamine, the body would engage in an opponent-process to counteract the effects of the drug. Given that methamphetamine is a stimulant, this would mean that the body would lower its baseline level of physiological arousal. When the person stops using methamphetamine, he or she will likely experience symptoms of physiological depression as a result.

4. What role does the liver play in regulating hunger? [p. 343; LO 3]

When the liver begins to convert glucose into glycogen, this indicates that you have taken in too much nutrient and the liver will signal the brain to stop eating. When the liver begins to convert stored glycogen into glucose, indicating that you are beginning to burn up your stored energy reserves, the liver will signal the brain to initiate hunger.

5. How can you explain the fact that eating disorders like anorexia and bulimia are more common among women from Western, industrialized cultures? [p. 355; LO 5]

Women in these cultures are more exposed to cultural standards of beauty that are unrealistically thin. This causes many young women to want to look like the unrealistically thin women in magazines and on TV-- a desire that many cannot achieve without drastic dieting and exercise. This can lead to anorexia. Bulimia may result from living in a cultural where women are expected to achieve impossible standards of thinness, while living in a culture that also encourages overeating and eating unhealthy foods. Some women are tempted to have their cake and eat it too—by consuming large quantities of food and then purging it or dieting drastically to avoid weight gain. The result can be bulimia.

Developing a Bigger Picture: Making Connections Across Chapters

1. Based on what you learned about the brain in Chapter 2, which parts of the brain play a significant role in the processing of emotion? [pp. 68-70, & 77; LO- Big Picture]

The limbic system structures of the amygdala and septum play a role in the processing of fear and aggression. In particular, the amygdala plays a role in our processing of emotion-evoking stimuli in social situations. The pre-frontal cortex also plays a role in our ability to regulate our emotions. Recall how Phineas Gage lost the ability to regulate his behavioral expression of emotions when the connections between his prefrontal cortex and his limbic system were severed.

2. Using what you learned in Chapter 1, design a study to test the hypothesis that liquid diets are more effective than low-carb diets in causing people to lose weight. [pp. 32-39; LO- Big Picture]

    Because this hypothesis is a causal hypothesis, you must use an experiment to test it. There are many different ways to design such an experiment. One would be to record the weight of some overweight people and then randomly assign them to one of two groups. In the first group, the participants follow a liquid diet for six weeks. In the other, the participants follow a low-carbohydrate diet for six weeks. At the end of the six week period, the participants are weighed and their weight change is recorded. If your hypothesis has merit, then you should see that the average weight loss in the liquid diet group is greater than the weight loss in the low-carbohydrate group.

3. Using the information you learned in Chapter 3 concerning the senses of taste and smell, develop a plan for keeping persons suffering from the early stages of Alzheimer's disease motivated to eat. [pp. 117-123; LO- Big Picture]

    As you learned in Chapter 3, loss of the ability to smell is thought to be one of the early signs of Alzheimer's disease. You also learned that your sense of taste depends heavily on your ability to smell. Therefore, people suffering from Alzheimer's disease may experience a loss of appetite because their loss of smell and taste may make food less attractive to them. To combat this, you may wish to make food more strongly flavored. Or, you might attempt to increase its aroma by using spices that release strong scents. A final strategy might be to attempt to compensate for the lack of perceived flavor in food by increasing its visual appeal. Towards this end, you could use colorful foods and attractive placement of food on the plate.

Label the Diagram

ANSWERS
FROM THE TOP TO THE BOTTOM
transcendence needs [p. 340; LO 2]
self-actualization needs [p. 340; LO 2]
aesthetic needs [p. 340; LO 2]
cognitive needs [p. 340; LO 2]
esteem needs [p. 340; LO 2]
belongingness and love needs [p. 340; LO 2]
safety and security needs [p. 340; LO 2]
physiological needs [p. 340; LO 2]

Big Picture Review

All answers [p. 357; LO 5]

Bulimia Nervosa

1. Recurrent episodes of bingeing in which the person eats unusually large amounts of food. The person must have the sense of being unable to control his/her eating during these binges.

2. Recurrent inappropriate compensatory behavior aimed at preventing weight gain (e.g., purging; enemas; misuse of laxatives, diuretics, or other medicines; fasting; excessive exercise).

3. Bingeing and inappropriate compensatory behaviors must both occur, on average, twice a week for a period of at least three months.

4. Self-evaluation is unduly influenced by one's body shape or weight.

5. These behaviors do not occur exclusively during episodes of anorexia nervosa.

Anorexia Nervosa

6. Refusal to maintain a minimally normal body weight (usually defined as 85% of the normal weight for one's height).

7. Intense fear of gaining weight, even though underweight.

8. A disturbed perception of one's body weight or shape, denial of the seriousness of one's low weight, or undue influence of one's body weight or shape on his/her self-evaluation.

9. In females, having missed at least three consecutive menstrual periods.

Binge Eating Disorder

10. Recurrent episodes of binge eating (as defined for bulimia nervosa) without regularly engaging in inappropriate compensatory behaviors to avoid weight gain.

9

How Do People Grow, Change, and Develop?

Learning Objectives

After studying each of the following sections of the chapter, you should be able to do these tasks:

Nature–Nurture Revisited: Biology and Culture

1. Explain the nature-nurture issue.

Prenatal Development: Conception to Birth

2. Identify and describe the three stages of prenatal development – germinal, embryonic, and fetal – and explain the importance of a positive prenatal environment.

Infancy and Childhood

3. Describe major physical changes that infants and children experience as their brains and bodies develop.
4. Describe the perceptual abilities of infants and how these abilities develop in the first weeks and months of life.
5. Compare and contrast Piaget's and Vygotsky's theories of cognitive development.
6. Compare and contrast Kohlberg's and Gilligan's theories of moral reasoning.
7. Define temperament and distinguish among the three temperamental styles of infants.
8. Describe behaviors that indicate that an attachment has been formed, distinguish among different attachment patterns, and describe the three parenting styles that Baumrind documented.
9. Describe Erikson's theory of psychosocial development as it applies to infants and children.

Adolescence and Adulthood

10. Describe the physical changes that occur in adolescence and adulthood.
11. Describe cognitive changes in adolescence and adulthood.
12. Detail Erikson's psychological transitions in adolescence and adulthood.

13. Describe the varieties of social relations in adolescence and adulthood.
14. Describe the new roles and responsibilities of being a parent.
15. Explain the stages of career choice, the predictable changes people experience in occupational development, and the factors that influence adjustment to retirement.

Death and Dying

16. Describe how people cope psychologically with their own impending death and the death of their loved ones.

The Big Picture

The Big Picture: The Changes and Challenges of Life

This chapter discusses what developmental psychologists have learned about how we change and develop through life. The story of Hongyong Lee illustrates the complex interplay of development with circumstance and culture. From childhood to old age, developmental processes influenced how Hongyong thought of herself and her abilities. Such thinking also influenced her values and goals in terms of what she wanted to be. She searched for personal meaning in her life and questioned her purpose on earth. Her story nicely captures how physical, cognitive, and social aspects of development make each person unique.

Nature–Nurture Revisited: Biology and Culture

This section covers Learning Objective 1. One of the primary issues in the study of development is the nature-nurture issue—the degree to which development is the product of our genes (nature) or the environment (nurture). Recall that it is not really a case of nature *or* nurture. Rather, it is the *interaction* of these two forces that play a role in developmental processes.

Prenatal Development: Conception to Birth

This section covers Learning Objective 2. The study of development begins at conception when the sperm and ovum come together to form the zygote. The first 14 days after conception define the germinal period of development. After conception, the zygote begins to undergo cell division and implants into the wall of the uterus.

The period of the embryo, from about 2 weeks to the 8th week of the pregnancy, is when most of the major systems in the body—the circulatory system, nervous system, digestive system, and so on—begin to develop. Because the period of the embryo is when these critical systems are laid down, the developing embryo is especially sensitive to the effects of teratogens— chemicals, diseases, drugs, and so on that can disrupt development and cause birth defects.

During the final stage of prenatal development, the fetal stage, from 9 weeks until birth, the developing child is referred to as a fetus. The major developments of the fetal stage are continued growth and maturation.

Infancy and Childhood

This section covers Learning Objectives 3-9. The average newborn or neonate weighs about seven pounds, but quickly undergoes rapid physical growth and development. The brain forms neural connections, myelinates pathways, and prunes unneeded connections during childhood and adolescence. In terms of motor development, infants are born with reflexes that help them survive. As infants use these reflexes to interact with the world, they form neural connections that ultimately allow them to engage in voluntary actions like walking, prehension (grasping), writing, and so on. Throughout childhood, physical development of gross motor skills is followed by fine motor skill development.

Perceptual abilities also rapidly improve as the brain develops during infancy. At birth, babies tend to be very near sighted, yet by 6 months they seem to have developed some level of depth perception. Babies prefer looking at complex stimuli, such as faces and by 3 months, can discriminate their mother's face from those of strangers. Babies react to sound in the womb and soon after birth, can recognize their mother's voice, locate sounds, discriminate consonant sounds, and prefer sounds that are rhythmic, soft, and higher pitched. Babies prefer sweet tastes, have an acute sense of smell that allows them to discriminate their mother's breast odor, and are very responsive to touch.

Psychologist Jean Piaget studied the cognitive development of children and proposed that children develop generalized knowledge structures called schemas that reflect what we know about the world. Schemas help us interpret our world through a process called assimilation. And through accommodation, we change or modify our schemas as we experience new things in our world. Our ability to form and use schemas becomes more sophisticated as we pass through several stages of cognitive development. In the sensorimotor stage, from birth to 2 years of age, we progress from being unable to form schemas to having object permanence or the ability to store mental representations of our world. In the preoperational stage, from approximately age 2 to age 6 or 7, children engage in symbolic thought, but they are illogical. Preoperational children exhibit centration (they can only focus on one aspect of an object at one time) and they are not capable of conservation (understanding that something is the same even if its appearance changes). In the concrete operations stage, from age 6 or 7 to age 12, children acquire conservation and become logical. Yet, they are only able to reason logically about concrete problems—that is objects that children can see and touch—or have seen and touched in the past. By age 12, many children enter Piaget's final stage called formal operations in which abstract scientific logic and problem solving skills develop.

Piaget recognized that a child's environment can influence cognitive development, but it was Russian psychologist Lev Vygotsky who really focused our attention on how culture and thinking influence each other. For Vygotsky, social interactions—especially those involving conversation with others—are a critical influence on our cognitive development. Such interaction also helps children develop as they work on tasks within their zone of proximal development, or tasks that they cannot do on their own but can accomplish with the help of adults or older peers.

Children's improving mental abilities also facilitate moral reasoning skills. According to Lawrence Kohlberg, children pass through three levels of moral reasoning. At the preconventional level, children base their understanding of right and wrong on their ability to avoid punishment or gain reward. At the conventional level, children base their understanding of right and wrong on the rules of their society or culture. At the postconventional level, people base their judgments of right and wrong on contractual or universal principles of morality that lead to internal standards of right and wrong. Studies show that people often reach Kohlberg's conventional level but few people progress to the post-conventional level. Cross-cultural studies indicate that Kohlberg's theory applies best to Western, industrialized cultures. There is also controversy over possible gender differences in moral reasoning. Carol Gilligan argues that males and females reason differently about morality.

We also develop in a social sense forming attachments and developing our personality. We are born with one of three basic temperaments or our general way of dealing with the world. Easy going children are outgoing and have fairly regular patterns for eating and sleeping. Difficult children are irregular in their sleep and eating patterns and do not readily accept new people or situations. Slow-to-warm up children are moderately regular in their sleep and eating patterns and approach new people and situations with initial wariness and caution.

A child's temperament and the parents' responses to this temperament influence the parent–child bond, called attachment that is typically established by 8-9 months of age. Parents establish attachments by holding and caressing their children. Stranger anxiety and separation anxiety are two indications that a child has securely attached to his or her caregiver. In the U.S., the most common attachment style is secure, but some children may exhibit insecure attachments such as resistant and avoidant attachments. It is widely believed that the quality of our first attachments sets the stage for our future social relationships.

Parenting style also can influence our social development. Diana Baumrind identified three distinct styles of parenting. An authoritarian parent sets high standards and expects children to adhere to rigid rules. Permissive parents are warm and affectionate but place few demands and few rules on the child. An authoritative parent is warm and affectionate. Family rules are set in a democratic manner and when rules are broken, authoritative parents are least likely to resort to physical punishment, instead using non-violent means of controlling children's behavior. Research shows that authoritative parenting is associated with the best outcomes for children.

Healthy personality development often requires a goodness-of-fit between a parent's style and a child's temperament. This goodness-of-fit is just one factor that influences how well children weather psychosocial transitions. According to Erik Erikson, we each pass through a series of eight crises in our lives, and how well we resolve these crises affects the development of our personality. In childhood, these crises are: trust vs. mistrust; autonomy vs. shame and doubt; initiative vs. guilt; and industry vs. inferiority.

Adolescence and Adulthood

This section covers Learning Objectives 10-15. Physical changes that occur after childhood are rarely as dramatic as they are in adolescence. Puberty, the process of sexual maturation, begins for females shortly after age 10 and age 12 for boys. Puberty initiates the development of sexual characteristics that are related to reproduction (e.g., the development of the testes or ovaries). For girls, puberty results in menarche or their first menstrual cycle, whereas boys begin to experience erections and ejaculation of semen. Research indicates that early blooming females and late blooming males find adolescence to be more stressful than late blooming females and early blooming males. However, in the long run it may be the early blooming females and late blooming males who psychologically fare the best in adulthood.

During adolescence, brain changes tend to begin at the back of the brain in the cerebellum and move toward the frontal lobe. The cerebellum experiences increased neural growth and connections as the teenager prepares to deal with his or her new taller, heavier body. Throughout this process of brain development, the frontal lobes are the last part of the adolescent brain to develop, which may explain why teenagers' judgment is not always sound.

Throughout adulthood we continue to experience physical change. Physical strength, stamina, coordination, and dexterity peak in early adulthood. In middle age, we begin to see declines in these areas that continue throughout late adulthood. A similar pattern is seen for sensory abilities like vision and hearing. These changes occur for all of us, but genetics, diet, exercise, and lifestyle influence how quickly and severely we experience such declines.

Sexual maturation also continues as females experience menopause around age 50 and they are no longer able to bear children. Males experience an andropause, or reduction in male hormone production, after age 60. Andropause slows men's sexual response and reduces their sperm count, but this normally does not prevent men from siring children throughout their life span.

Cognitive changes also occur during and after adolescence. Adolescents reach formal operations and are able to engage in abstract and scientific reasoning. While this is a decidedly beneficial ability to have, it also gives rise to egocentrism as teenagers' newfound, abstract thoughts are mostly focused on themselves. This leads teenagers to believe in what psychologists call an imaginary audience—the idea that everyone is focused on you. Adolescents also often endorse a personal fable, feeling as if they are so special that they are immune to dangers to which others fall prey—such as contracting HIV through unprotected sex or getting into a car accident after drinking and driving.

After adolescence, we experience what is called postformal thought in which we become less dualistic and more relativistic in our thought. Dualistic thought, or seeing the world in terms of two categories—right and wrong—good and bad, is characteristic of adolescent cognitive processing. In adulthood, we become less black and white and begin to see that many judgments depend upon the circumstances of the situation. Memory changes also occur during adulthood as our reaction time lengthens, working memory declines, and recall memory declines. Many of these declines may be related to a reduction in fluid intelligence, our ability to quickly process information, which occurs as we age. However, crystallized intelligence (i.e., knowledge and judgment) does not decrease with age and many of the cognitive declines we do face may be slowed by remaining mentally active and regularly exercising our mental abilities.

Psychosocial changes also occur in adolescence and adulthood. During adolescence, we come to understand who we are by forming an identity. Psychologist James Marcia identified four identity statuses that we may experience during this time. In diffusion, one does not have an identity, nor is he or she searching for one. In moratorium, one is trying on different identities without committing to any one of them. In foreclosure, one allows others such as parents or peers to determine his or her identity. And in achievement, one commits to an identity that he or she has decided on after much thought and exploration.

After achieving an identity in adolescence, young adults face intimacy vs. isolation—the challenge of finding intimacy in life through friends and/or romantic partners. The crisis of middle age is generativity vs. stagnation or the challenge of finding ways to make meaningful contributions to the world. According to Erikson, all of the preceding crises set the stage for the final crisis in late adulthood—integrity vs. despair when we look back on our successes and failures to determine if we have lived a good and worthwhile life.

The social relationships and social roles we fulfill during adulthood impact the types of transitions we experience. Dating, singlehood, cohabitation, marriage, divorce, parenting, choosing and building a career, and retirement are some of the activities that challenge our ability to cope during adulthood.

Death and Dying

This section covers Learning Objective 16. According to pioneer researcher Elizabeth Kubler-Ross, when a person is first told he or she is dying, one enters into a state of denial. As one becomes sicker, denial diminishes and the next stage of anger begins. For some, anger gives way to bargaining in which the person attempts to strike a deal with a supreme being, the doctors, fate, and so on in attempt to extend their lives. After the bargaining stage, depression may set in. The final stage is acceptance in which the dying person comes to terms with his or her own death. Subsequent research has confirmed Kubler-Ross' stages, but not all dying people go through these stages in order and not everyone goes through all of the stages. Many factors affect how one approaches his or her death including coping style, the circumstances of one's life and illness, and the quality of social support one experiences.

Bereavement is the experience of losing a loved one and grief is our emotional reaction to that loss. Typically the first stage of grief, impact, is one of shock and disbelief. The confrontation stage follows as the acute pain of the loss is felt. Next, the grieving person enters into the accommodation phase in which he or she comes to grips with the loss and begins to get back to a normal routine of life. However, the grieving process is very individual. The time it takes a person to reach accommodation can be relatively short or it may take years. Some may never actually recover from a loss—especially if it involves the loss of a child.

Outlining the Big Picture

Chapter 9: How Do People Grow, Change, and Develop?

The Big Picture: The Changes and Challenges of Life
Notes:

_____

_____

_____

_____

_____

Nature-Nurture Revisited: Biology and Culture (Learning Objective 1)
Notes:

_____

_____

_____

_____

_____

Prenatal Development: Conception to Birth (Learning Objective 2)
Germinal Stage
Embryonic Stage
Fetal Stage
The Emotional Effects of Miscarriage on Women and Men
The Importance of a Positive Prenatal Environment
Notes:

_____

_____

_____

_____

_____

_____

_____

Infancy and Childhood (Learning Objectives 3-9)
Physical Development: Growing, Moving, and Exploring
    Brain Development
    Reflexes and Motor Development
Cognitive Development: Perception and Thinking
    Perceptual Development
    Piaget's Theory of Cognitive Development
    Vygotsky's Theory of Cognitive Development: Culture and Thinking
Moral Reasoning: How We Think About Right and Wrong
    Kohlberg's Theory of Moral Reasoning
    Gilligan's Theory: Gender and Moral Reasoning
Psychosocial Development: Temperament, Attachment, and Erikson's First Four Stages
    Temperament: The Influence of Biology
    Attachment: Learning about Relationships
    Parenting Styles
    Erikson's Stages of Psychosocial Development: The Influence of Culture
Notes:

_____

_____

_____

_____

_____

_____

Adolescence and Adulthood (Learning Objectives 10-15)
Physical Changes: Maturation and Aging
    Puberty: Big Changes, Rapid Growth
    Brain Changes in Adolescence and Adulthood
    Physical Changes from Early to Later Adulthood
    Gender and Reproductive Capacity
Cognitive Changes in Reasoning and Mental Abilities
    Formal Operations Revisited

Postformal Thought
Changes in Memory and Mental Abilities
Psychosocial Transitions: Personality, Relationships, and Work
Erikson's Psychosocial Stages of Adolescence and Adulthood
Social Relations in Adolescence and Adulthood
Parenting
Spotlight on Diversity: The Culture of Fatherhood
Adult Development and the World of Work
Notes:

_____

_____

_____

_____

_____

Death and Dying (Learning Objective 16)
Reactions to Death: Kubler-Ross's Stages
Bereavement and Grief: How We Respond to Death
Notes:

_____

_____

_____

_____

_____

Are You Getting the Big Picture?
Notes:

_____

_____

_____

Seeing the Big Picture: A Mental Map of Chapter 9

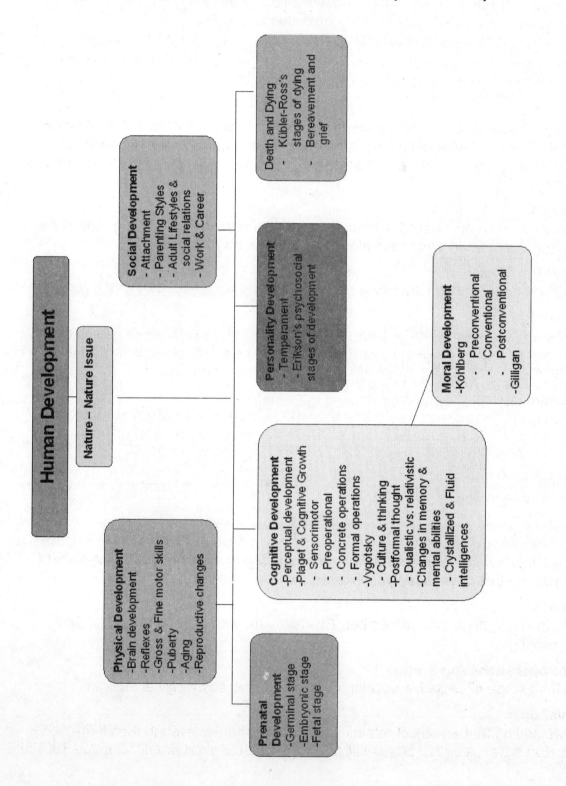

Human Development

Nature – Nature Issue

Social Development
- Attachment
- Parenting Styles
- Adult Lifestyles & social relations
- Work & Career

Death and Dying
- Kübler-Ross's stages of dying
- Bereavement and grief

Personality Development
- Temperament
- Erikson's psychosocial stages of development

Moral Development
-Kohlberg
- Preconventional
- Conventional
- Postconventional
-Gilligan

Physical Development
-Brain development
-Reflexes
-Gross & Fine motor skills
-Puberty
-Aging
-Reproductive changes

Cognitive Development
-Perceptual development
-Piaget & Cognitive Growth
- Sensorimotor
- Preoperational
- Concrete operations
- Formal operations
-Vygotsky
- Culture & thinking
- Postformal thought
- Dualistic vs. relativistic
-Changes in memory & mental abilities
- Crystallized & Fluid intelligences

Prenatal Development
-Germinal stage
-Embryonic stage
-Fetal stage

Key Points of the Big Picture

Accommodation:
the process by which a schema is changed, modified, or created anew in order to understand something new in the environment. *Example: A child's schema for fish changes after seeing a porpoise at the local aquarium.*

Achievement:
according to Marcia and Erikson, an identity state in which a commitment to personal values that have been adequately explored is attained. *Example: After working for different political organizations and attending many rallies, a youth registers for one political party.*

Assimilation:
the process by which an existing schema is used to understand something new in the environment. *Example: A child describes all things that swim as fish.*

Attachment:
the emotional bond between caretaker and infant that is established by 8 or 9 months.

Authoritarian parent:
a parenting style characterized by high levels of control and low levels of affection. *Example: A mother who does not demonstrate affection to her son, tells him to clean his room from top to bottom each weekend or else he will be punished.*

Authoritative parent:
a parenting style characterized by moderate levels of control and affection. Example: *A mother and son sit down and discuss what chores he is capable of and willing to do. They discuss what the consequences will be if he does not do his chores.*

Bereavement:
the experience of losing a loved one.

Centration:
the act of focusing on only one aspect or feature of an object. *Example: A young child looks at a photograph of her father when he was younger and states, "Dad, it doesn't look like you. I have never seen you in a red shirt."*

Cognition:
the ability to know, think, and remember. *Example: memory, problem solving, and decision making*

Concrete operations:
Piaget's third stage of cognitive development, characterized by logical thought.

Conservation:
the understanding that an object retains its original properties even though it may look different. *Example: A ball of clay is still the same amount even when it is rolled flat into a pancake.*

Critical period:
in prenatal development, a time when genetic and environmental agents are most likely to cause birth defects. *Example: Rubella (German measles) has more serious birth defects or can cause miscarriage when the mother contracts this virus early in her pregnancy.*

Crystallized intelligence:
abilities that rely on knowledge, expertise, and judgment. *Example: Playing games like Trivial Pursuit and Jeopardy rely on one's crystallized intelligence.*

Development:
changes in behavior and/or abilities. *Example: Progressing from sitting to crawling to walking to running characterize physical development.*

Diffusion:
an identity status in which a person has not explored or committed to any person values. *Example: Mandy does not have any standards for friendship and hangs out with whoever is around or available.*

Down Syndrome:
a genetic birth disorder resulting from an extra 21st chromosome, characterized by distinct facial features and a greater likelihood of heart defects and mental retardation.

Dualistic thinking:
reasoning that divides situations and issues into right and wrong categories. *Example: Lying is always bad so you should never tell a lie no matter what the circumstance.*

Egocentrism:
the belief that everyone thinks as you do. *Example: My favorite ice cream is chocolate so everyone must like chocolate ice cream.*

Embryonic stage:
the second stage of prenatal development, lasting from the 2nd through the 8th week.

Fetal Alcohol Syndrome (FAS):
a birth condition resulting from the mother's chronic use of alcohol during pregnancy; it is characterized by facial and limb deformities, and mental retardation.

Fetal stage:
the stage of prenatal development from the 9th week through the 9th month.

Fine motor skills:
motor behaviors involving the small muscles of the body. *Examples: Writing, threading a needle, turning the pages of a book.*

Fluid intelligence:
abilities that rely on information-processing skills such as reaction time, attention and working memory. *Example: Putting together a puzzle or solving math problems quickly.*

Foreclosure:
according to Marcia, an identity status in which the individual prematurely commits to personal values before exploration is complete. *Example: Ted becomes a firefighter because all the males in his family have always been firefighters.*

Formal operations:
Piaget's final stage of cognitive development, characterized by the ability to engage in abstract thought.

Germinal stage:
the first stage of prenatal development from conception to fourteen days.

Grief:
one's emotional reaction to the death of a loved one. *Example: Crying and sobbing after losing a loved one.*

Gross motor skills:
motor behaviors involving the large muscles of the body. *Examples: Running, punching, kicking, dancing*

Imaginary audience:
the belief held by adolescents that everyone is watching what they do. *Example: Teenagers' belief that everyone will notice and be grossed out by a pimple on their face.*

Menarche:
a girl's first menstruation.

Menopause:
the period when a female stops menstruating and is no longer fertile.

Moral reasoning:
how you decide what is right and what is wrong. *Example: Everyone else speeds so you reason that speeding is okay.*

Moratorium:
according to Marcia, an identity status in which the individual actively explores personal values. *Example: Jameka is visiting many different religious faiths to determine which one is best for her.*

Nature-nurture issue:
the degree to which biology (nature) or the environment (nurture) contributes to one's development.

Neonate:
the first 28 days of life; a newborn.

Object permanence:
the understanding that an object continues to exist even when it is not present. *Example: Knowing that your car is still in the parking lot even when you are in the mall and cannot see it.*

Permissive parent:
a parenting style characterized by moderate levels of affection but low levels of control. *Example: Jeff lets his young children decide when they will go to bed and what they will eat for breakfast.*

Personal fable:
the belief held by adolescents that they are unique and special. *Example: Michelle and Chuck do not use any form of birth control because they believe teenage pregnancy happens to other people and won't happen to them.*

Postformal thought:
the idea that a correct solution (or solutions) may vary, depending on the circumstances. *Example: There are some situations where lying is wrong and there are some situations where telling a lie is appropriate.*

Preoperational stage:
Piaget's second stage of cognitive development, characterized by the use of symbols and illogical thought.

Private speech:
Vygotsky's term describing when young children talk to themselves to guide their own actions. *Example: Morgan is talking to his bear as they are putting together a puzzle.*

Puberty:
the process of sexual maturation.

Reflex:
an automatic response to a specific environmental stimulus. *Example: In the palmar reflex, if you tickle the palm of an infant (stimulus), the baby will respond by flexing his or her fingers.*

Relativistic thinking:
the idea that in many situations there is not necessarily one right or wrong answer. *Example: Clara understands that not everyone is depressed for the same reason. Some people are depressed because of biological factors while others may be depressed due to social and psychological factors.*

Scaffolding:
a process in which initially adults initially offer guidance and support in helping a child to reason, solve a problem or master a task; as the child becomes more proficient and capable, the adult helps less and less until the child can master it on his or her own. *Example: When teaching a child to ride a bike a parent may at first hold onto the bike and run with the bike as the child pedals. As the child masters balance the parent helps less and less.*

Schema:
a mental idea, concept, or thought. *Example: Having an image for a dog or a horse.*

Sensorimotor stage:
Piaget's first stage of cognitive development in which infants learn schemas through their senses and motor abilities.

Separation anxiety:
the fear an infant expresses when separated from the major caretaker. *Example: When Dustin's mom drops him off at daycare, Dustin screams and cries when his mother leaves.*

Stranger anxiety:
the distress an infant expresses when faced with unfamiliar people. *Example: Sheila stays close to her dad and hides her face when he introduces her to the zookeeper.*

Symbolic thinking:
the understanding that an object can be represented with a symbol such as bodily gestures or language. *Example: Miguel rides a broom and calls it his "horsey".*

Temperament:
a person's general pattern of attention, arousal, and mood that is evident at birth.

Teratogen:
an environmental substance that has the potential to harm the developing organism. *Examples: alcohol, bleach, over-the-counter medications*

Zone of proximal development (ZPD):
according to Vygotsky, the gap between what a child is already able to do and what he or she is not yet capable of doing. Example: *Miriam can put her shoes on but does not know how to tie her shoes. This is Miriam's zone of proximal development.*

Zygote:
a fertilized egg.

Fill-in Review of the Chapter

Can you fill-in the missing terms for each section of the chapter? Items marked with an * encourage you to continue building the Big Picture of psychology by connecting the material in this chapter to material from previous chapters in the text.

The Big Picture: The Changes and Challenges of Life

Hongyong Lee's story is a powerful example of 1) _____ or the changes we experience in our abilities.

Focusing on how Hongyong Lee's behavior resulted from her learning experiences emphasizes the 2*) _____ perspective.

Nature-Nurture Revisited: Biology and Culture

3) _____ refers to the genetic influences that direct your development and
4) _____ refers to the environmental influences that direct your development.

Prenatal Development: Conception to Birth

Cells form into organs and systems during the 5) _____ stage of prenatal development.

By 6) _____ weeks, the developing fetus has developed enough to reach the age of viability.

7) _____ are environmental factors, such as German measles or cleaning fluids that may cause birth defects.

The 8) _____ stage of development is a critical period during which teratogens may cause many different types of birth defects.

Infancy and Childhood

At birth, an infant's brain has billions of neurons, but the coating on axons called 9*) _____ is incomplete.

10) _____ serve as the foundation for behaviors such as walking, eating, crying, smiling, and grasping

Using utensils such as a fork or a spoon are examples of 11) _____ motor skills.

Infants prefer 12) _____ tastes.

Carmella sees a truck on the highway and says, "Look at the big car." Carmella's statement is an example of 13) _____.

Peter has four nickels in his pocket. His sister has a dollar. Peter thinks he has more than his sister because it looks like and feels like more. Peter is most likely in Piaget's 14) _____ stage of development.

Zahara can pull her pants on but has not yet mastered how to button them. This difference between what Zahara can and cannot do is called her 15) _____.

Huang feels that downloading music from his computer is okay because all of his friends do it. Huang is most likely at Kohlberg's 16) _____ stage of moral reasoning.

As a baby, Maurice cried a lot, did not approach new people and situations, and had an irregular pattern of eating and sleeping. Maurice's temperament is best described as 17) _____.

While at the pediatrician's office, Cecile remains close to her dad and does not explore the toys in the corner. She shows extreme distress when her dad momentarily leaves to fill out medical forms and appears to be angry with him when he returns. Cecile most likely has a(n) 18) _____ attachment style.

Diana Baumrind's investigation on parenting styles used the 19*) _____ research method.

Preschoolers' curiosity reflects their resolution of Erikson's psychosocial crisis called 20) _____.

Adolescence and Adulthood

21) _____ is a girl's first menstrual period.

During adolescence, brain development begins in the 22) _____ which is necessary for 23*)_____.

The 24) _____ of the brain is among the last parts of the brain to fully develop during adolescence and young adulthood.

Although men do not experience a "male menopause," they too undergo hormonal changes after age 60 termed 25) _____.

Teenagers begin to think abstractly during Piaget's 26) _____ stage of cognitive development.

Melissa reasons that there is not just one cause of drug addiction and that there are many factors leading to addiction. Melissa's reasoning illustrates 27) _____.

Completing crossword puzzles and playing *Wheel of Fortune* relies on people's 28) _____ intelligence.

Marco is not sure what career path he wants to pursue so he is taking courses in several different areas such as biology, architecture, and communication. Marco is most likely in Marcia's identity status of 29) _____.

According to Erik Erikson, the last crisis we face in life is 30) _____.

People in the 31) _____ are more likely to return home to live with their parents after having moved out on their own.

Young people enter the workforce and begin to learn about jobs firsthand in the 32) _____ phase of career development.

Parents' marital satisfaction tends to 33) _____ when their children reach early adolescence.

Death and Dying

A famous man once promised God that he would build a children's hospital if God would let him recover from a life-threatening illness. In making this promise, the man appeared to be in the 34) _____ stage of Elizabeth Kubler-Ross' theory.

The 35) _____ phase of grieving begins when we first learn that a loved one has died.

Use It or Lose It!

Can you identify Piaget's cognitive stage of development from the behaviors given?

Behavior	Cognitive Stage
Logical thought related to tangible objects and/or experiences	1.
Obtains object permanence	2.
Abstract thought	3.
Illogical thinking	4.
Develops schemes through motor abilities	5.
Imaginary audience	6.
Conservation is attained	7.
Begins to use language to symbolically represent objects	8.

Self-Check: Are You Getting the Big Picture?

After you have read and studied the chapter, see if you can answer the following quiz questions. Check your answers at the end of the chapter. If you miss a question, refer to your text and re-study the appropriate sections.

True or False Questions

Are these statements true or false?

1. All the available studies show that compared to their female partners, men experience less grief after miscarriage brings a pregnancy to an end.
True
False

2. Fetal alcohol syndrome (FAS) is the leading cause of mental retardation in children.
True
False

3. When a newborn infant grasps her father's finger, it is a gesture of her attachment to her father.
True
False

4. Of the different styles of parenting, authoritarian parenting seems to result in the best developmental outcomes for most children.
True
False

5. Studies show that by adulthood most people reach the conventional stage of moral reasoning.
True
False

6. After age 65, most people report that their health is beginning to fail.
True
False

7. The U.S. has the highest rate of cohabitation in the world.
True
False

8. Being prepared for the changes that will occur during puberty and having a supportive family tend to help teens adjust psychologically to puberty.
True
False

9. All people finish grieving within a year.
True
False

10. Postformal thought involves dualistic thinking.
True
False

Multiple Choice Questions

Can you choose the best answer for these questions?

1. Basil believes that genes are mostly responsible for development. Basil is emphasizing the _____.
   A. nurture side of the nature-nurture issue
   B. nature side of the nature-nurture issue
   C. influence of the environment
   D. influence of unconscious desires

2. During prenatal development, all body systems begin to form during the:
   A. germinal stage.
   B. embryonic stage.
   C. fetal stage.
   D. last trimester.

3. Frank stole some bananas to feed his younger siblings and stop them from crying. Because Frank's theft resulted in a positive outcome, he concluded that his actions were moral. Frank's reasoning most closely matches which of Kohlberg's stages of moral reasoning?
   A. preconventional
   B. conventional
   C. postconventional
   D. none of the above

4. Our brain undergoes a pruning of unnecessary synapses during:
   A. the last trimester of pregnancy.
   B. childhood.
   C. early adolescence.
   D. B & C

5. Which of the following activities most involves fine motor skill development?
   A. hitting a baseball with a bat
   B. running
   C. cutting out a paper doll with scissors
   D. running and throwing a ball to your pet dog

6. Breastfed newborns can discriminate the odor of their mother's breast from that of another woman as early as:
   A. 3 days after birth.
   B. 3 weeks after birth.
   C. 3 months after birth.
   D. 6 months after birth.

7. Which of the following is the best example of accommodation?
   A. On seeing a deer for the first time, a child believes it is a dog.
   B. When first learning to drink milk from a glass, a child tries sucking the milk.
   C. After her first trip to a zoo, a child learns about elephants and tigers.
   D. A child sees a man with long hair and believes he is a woman.

8. Two-month-old Elba has been shaking her mother's car keys like a rattle when her mother takes the keys away and hides them in a drawer. According to Piaget, how will Elba likely respond?
   A. Elba will cry for approximately one hour.
   B. Elba will cry for about 15 minutes.
   C. Elba won't cry for long because she will forget the keys exist.
   D. Elba will forget the keys for the moment. But as soon as she sees the keys again, she will remember them and want to play.

9. According to Piaget, 4-year-old Jack should exhibit all of the following traits, except which one?
   A. centration
   B. egocentrism
   C. a lack of conservation
   D. abstract thought

10. Monika cries when her mother leaves her with the babysitter while she goes to the grocery store. When she returns, Monika stops crying and crawls over to her mother for comfort. Monika's behavior best exemplifies which style of attachment?
    A. secure
    B. resistant
    C. avoidant
    D. disorganized

11. Little Miguel has a difficult temperament and his parents have an authoritarian parenting style. Which of the following is most likely to be true?
    A. Miguel and his parents will have a goodness-of-fit.
    B. Miguel and his parents will not have a goodness-of-fit.
    C. Miguel's parents will never bond with him.
    D. Miguel will never attach to his parents.

12. Adolescent mood swings seem to be mostly due to:
    A. raging hormones.
    B. changing social environments.
    C. lack of cerebellar development in the brain.
    D. all of the above.

13. Visual acuity peaks in our:
    A. teens.
    B. early 20s.
    C. early 30s.
    D. mid-40s.

14. Which of the following people tend to have a difficult time adjusting during adolescence?
    A. early maturing girls and early maturing boys
    B. early maturing girls and late maturing boys
    C. late maturing girls and early maturing boys
    D. late maturing girls and late maturing girls

15. Adolescents acquire the ability to think _____ as they reach Piaget's formal operations stage.
    A. concretely
    B. logically
    C. abstractly
    D. conservatively

16. What do teenagers have in common with preoperational children (i.e., children aged 2-6 or 7)?
    A. They are both egocentric.
    B. They are both logical.
    C. They are both abstract in their thought.
    D. All of the above

17. Marla is 15 years old. Lately she has been taking longer and longer to get ready for school in the morning because she is obsessed with wearing just the right outfit. Marla is likely doing this because she is suffering from which adolescent phenomena?
    A. personal fable
    B. imaginary audience
    C. hypothetico-deductive reasoning
    D. postformal thought

18. Dave is 15 and Dean is 55. Which of the following statements is most likely to be true about how Dave and Dean think about the world?
    A. Dave is likely to engage in relativistic thinking. Dean is likely to engage in dualistic thinking.
    B. Dean is likely to engage in relativistic thinking. Dave is likely to engage in dualistic thinking.
    C. Dave is likely to engage in abstract thinking. Dean is likely to engage in concrete thinking.
    D. None of the above is true.

19. Juanita is 15-yrs-old. In the last six months, she has tried out for the swim team, decided to become a mariachi musician, and took up an interest in interior design. After a period of trial, she abandoned each of these pursuits. Juanita seems to be in which of Marcia's identity states?
    A. diffusion
    B. foreclosure
    C. moratorium
    D. achievement status

20. Which of the following is likely to decline with age?
    A. crystallized intelligence
    B. fluid intelligence
    C. recognition memory
    D. all of the above

21. Compared to Whites, which ethnic group(s) begin(s) to date at a later age?
    A. Asian-Americans
    B. African-Americans
    C. Hispanic-Americans
    D. A & C

22. After learning that she has a terminal disease, Maleka lost all interest in her usual activities. Maleka is most likely in which Kubler-Ross stage?
    A. denial
    B. bargaining
    C. depression
    D. anger

23. Today, fathers who are involved in their children's upbringing report:
    A. high levels of stress.
    B. high satisfaction with their lives.
    C. having no roles models as co-parents in their children's lives.
    D. all of the above

24. 7-yr-old Lyle wants to be a firefighter. Which stage of Ginzberg's career choice is Lyle at?
    A. the fantasy stage
    B. the tentative stage
    C. the realistic stage
    D. the implementation stage

25. 45-yr-old Wanda has worked at the same firm for the last 20 years. She doesn't make a great deal of money, but she loves her job and wouldn't think of leaving the company. Which phase of career development is Wanda most likely at?
    A. specification
    B. implementation
    C. establishment
    D. maintenance

Short-Answer Questions

Can you write a brief answer to these questions?

1. Using what you have learned about development, explain why early educational interventions (e.g., Headstart), which provide enriching environments for underprivileged children early in life, are beneficial for cognitive development.

2. Describe the temperaments that Alexander Thomas and Stella Chess observed in infants.

3. Dave's teenage son has recently made a string of very poor decisions. For example, he allowed an intoxicated friend to give him a ride home from a party. Using what you know about development, why would an otherwise intelligent boy do something like this?

4. Belinda was just told that she is terminally ill. According to Elizabeth Kubler-Ross, how is Belinda likely to react during her remaining time on earth?

5. How does having a child change a couple?

Developing a Bigger Picture: Making Connections Across Chapters

An important aspect of learning is learning to see the "Big Picture" of the subject you are studying. As you learn about psychology, you should try to understand how the material from different chapters fits together to help you form a broad-based understanding of what psychology is all about. To help facilitate the development of this "Big Picture" in your mind, try to answer these questions using the knowledge you have learned in this chapter, as well as the other chapters referenced in the questions.

1. In Chapter 7, you learned about cognitive structures called concepts. Using this knowledge, explain how Jean Piaget would describe what a concept is.

2. Using what you learned in Chapter 1, design a study to test the hypothesis that infants who are read to by adults are more likely to develop language faster than children who are not read to.

3. Using what you've learned about operant conditioning and social learning in Chapter 5, explain how these processes could influence a teenager's identity development.

4. Given the cognitive abilities of a 5-yr-old child, how might 5-yr-old Juan conceptualize the death of his pet parakeet?

Label the Diagram

Can you label Marcia's different states of identity formation?

Exploration

	Present	Absent
Commitment — Present	(1) _____ (successful achievement of a sense of identity)	(2) _____ (unquestioning adoption of parental or societal values)
Commitment — Absent	(4) _____ (active struggling for a sense of identity)	(3) _____ (absence of struggle for identity, with no obvious concern about it)

Big Picture Review

Identify Erik Erikson's Psychosocial Stages of Development

Erikson's Stages of Psychosocial Development

AGE	STAGE	DEVELOPMENTAL CHALLENGE
birth–1 year	(1) _____	Sense of security
1–3 years	(2) _____	Independence
3–6 years	(3) _____	Trying new things
6–12 years	(4) _____	Sense of mastery and competence
Adolescence	(5) _____	Sense of self, personal values, and beliefs
Young adulthood	(6) _____	Commit to a mutually loving relationship
Middle adulthood	(7) _____	Contributing to society through one's work, family, or community services
Late adulthood	(8) _____	Viewing one's life as satisfactory and worthwhile

Solutions

Each solution below is followed by its textbook page reference and its corresponding chapter learning objective (LO) number. Items with a Big Picture LO help you build a Big Picture of psychology across the chapters you have studied so far.

Fill-in Review of the Chapter

1. development [p. 375, LO 1]
2. behavioral [p. 17; LO-Big Picture]
3. Nature [p. 378; LO1]
4. nurture [p. 378; LO 1]
5. embryonic [p. 380; LO 2]
6. twenty-four [p. 380; LO 2]
7. Teratogens [p. 382; LO 2]
8. embryonic [p. 382; LO 2]
9. myelin [p. 49; LO-Big Picture]
10. Reflexes [p. 385; LO 3]
11. fine [p. 386; LO 3]
12. sweet [p. 388; LO 4]
13. assimilation [p. 389; LO 5]
14. preoperational [p. 391; LO 5]
15. zone of proximal development [p. 395; LO 5]
16. conventional [p. 396; LO 6]
17. difficult [p. 398; LO 7]
18. resistant [p. 400; LO 8]
19. correlational [p. 30; LO-Big Picture]
20. initiative versus guilt [p. 402-403; LO 9]
21. Menarche [p. 405; LO 10]
22. cerebellum [p. 406; LO 10]
23. balance and coordination [p. 67; LO-Big Picture]
24. prefrontal cortex [p. 406-408; LO 10]
25. andropause [p. 409; LO 10]
26. formal operations [p, 410; LO 11]
27. postformal thought [p. 412; LO 11]
28. crystallized [p. 414; LO 11]
29. moratorium [p. 416; LO 12]
30. integrity versus despair [p. 418; LO 12]
31. boomerang generation [p. 423; LO 13]
32. implementation [p. 425; LO 15]
33. decrease [p. 423; LO 14]
34. bargaining [p. 428; LO 16]
35. impact [p. 429; LO 16]

Use It or Lose It! [LO 5]

1. concrete operations [p. 393]
2. sensorimotor [p. 390]
3. formal operations [p. 393]
4. preoperational [p.391]

5. sensorimotor [p. 389-390]
6. formal operations [p. 411]
7. concrete operations [p. 392]
8. preoperational [p. 391]

Self-Check: Are You Getting the Big Picture?

True or False Questions

1. F [p. 381; LO 2]
2. T [p. 383; LO 2]
3. F [p. 385; LO 3]
4. F [p. 400-401; LO 8]
5. T [p. 396; LO 6]

6. F [p. 409; LO 10]
7. F [p. 419-420; LO 13]
8. T [p. 405; LO 10]
9. F [p. 430; LO 16]
10. F [p. 412; LO 11]

Multiple Choice Questions

1. B [p. 378; LO 1]	10. A [p. 399; LO 8]	19. C [p. 416; LO 11]
2. B [p. 380; LO 2]	11. B [p. 401; LO 8]	20. B [p. 414; LO 12]
3. A [p. 395-396; LO 6]	12. D [p. 405-406; LO 10]	21. D [p. 418; LO 13]
4. D [p. 384; LO 3]	13. B [p. 408; LO 10]	22. C [p. 428; LO 16]
5. C [p. 386; LO 3]	14. B [p. 406; LO 10]	23. D [p. 424; LO 14]
6. A [p. 388; LO 4]	15. C [p. 410; LO 11]	24. A [p. 425; LO 15]
7. C [p. 389; LO 5]	16. A [p. 410; LO 5 & 11]	25. D [p. 426; LO 15]
8. C [p. 389-390; LO 5]	17. B [p. 411; LO 11]	
9. D [p. 391-393; LO 5]	18. B [p. 412; LO 11]	

Short-Answer Questions

1. Using what you have learned about development, explain why early educational interventions (e.g., Headstart), which provide enriching environments for underprivileged children early in life, are beneficial for cognitive development. [p. 384-385; LO 3 & 5]

   By providing an enriching environment for children, these programs foster development of synapses in the brain. They also provide children with opportunities to explore their environment and foster cognitive development through Piaget's stages. These programs also give the child a chance to work with more skilled adults and peers within their zone of proximal development to acquire skills faster.

2. Describe the temperaments that Alexander Thomas and Stella Chess observed in infants. [p.397-398; LO 7]

   Easy infants are pleasant, have regular eating and sleeping patterns, and are open to changes in their environment. Difficult infants are fussy, exhibit negative emotions, have irregular sleep and eating patterns, and react poorly to changes in their environment. Slow-to-warm-up infants are in between these two extremes. They take a while to warm up to new people and places, exhibit some negative emotions, and are somewhat irregular in their sleep and eating patterns.

3. Dave's teenage son has recently made a string of very poor decisions. For example, he allowed an intoxicated friend to give him a ride home from a party. Using what you know about development, why would an otherwise intelligent boy do something like this? [p. 406 & 410; LO 10 & 11]

   Teenagers have just passed into Piaget's stage of formal operations, and although they are now capable of abstract, logical thought, they are not always very good at it. One common adolescent trait is egocentrism. Teenagers feel very special now that they are capable of adult-like thought. One result of this egocentrism is a phenomenon called personal fable, in which the teenager feels invincible. This may explain why Dave's son felt safe riding with a drunk driver. Another possible reason teenagers sometimes make poor decisions is due to immature brain development in the prefrontal cortex, which plays a role in impulse control and decision-making. It is possible that without adequate brain development teenagers may have trouble making logical decisions.

4. Belinda was just told that she is terminally ill. According to Elizabeth Kubler-Ross how is Belinda likely to react during her remaining time on earth? [p. 428-429; LO 16]

   Kubler-Ross found that terminally ill patients often pass through stages of denial, anger, bargaining, depression, and acceptance as they deal with their impending death. Belinda may experience any number of these stages, in any order—as dying is to some extent a process unique to each individual.

5. How does having a child change a couple? [p. 422-423; LO 14]

   Having a child brings less sleep, less free time, and less time together as a couple. It forces couples to juggle responsibilities and time pressures. Sometimes, it forces couples to redefine the division of labor in their relationship, which may lead to lowered marital satisfaction. As children age, parent-child conflicts may arise from time to time, and marital dissatisfaction may peak during the children's adolescence. However, tensions usually begin to ease as children work through their own adolescent development and parents negotiate allowing their children more adult freedom.

Developing a Bigger Picture: Making Connections Across Chapters

1. In Chapter 7, you learned about cognitive structures called concepts. Using this knowledge, explain how Jean Piaget would describe what a concept is. [p. 291; LO-Big Picture]

    For Piaget, concepts are schemes or schemas that we use to mentally represent our world. As we experience the world, we encode incoming information in memory in the form of schemes or concepts so that we can later use this information to guide our behavior and our perception of the world.

2. Using what you learned in Chapter 1, design a study to test the hypothesis that infants who are read to by adults are more likely to develop language faster than children who are not read to. [p. 27; LO-Big Picture]

    Given the way the hypothesis is written, your study only needs to test a predictive hypothesis. As such, your design does not have to be an experiment (although it could be if you wish). One way to test this hypothesis is to survey parents of 3 year-olds and ask them how often they read to their child during infancy and at what age their child began to speak. Then you can correlate the number of hours per week the parent read to the child with the age at which the child began to speak. If your hypothesis has merit, the age should decrease as the number of hours increases.

3. Using what you've learned about operant conditioning and social learning in Chapter 5, explain how these processes could influence a teenager's identity development. [p. 216-230; LO-Big Picture]

    During adolescence, teenagers often pass through the different states of identity formation including diffusion, foreclosure, moratorium, and achievement. At all of these stages, except perhaps diffusion where the person is unconcerned with identity issues, operant conditioning and social learning may impact identity.

    For example, authoritarian parents or peers may punish a child for trying on new identities of which they disapprove. In this fashion, the child may end up in a state of foreclosure, adopting the identity others prescribe for him or her. On the other hand, a child in moratorium may use reinforcement and punishment from others to help guide his or her choice of a final identity.

    Reward and punishment may also come without social interaction. For example, a child who gets hurt while trying out for football may be less inclined to pursue an athletic identity.

    Social learning also plays a big role in identity formation. Children will tend to model the identities of people they admire (e.g., sports figures, celebrities, parents, popular peers, etc.).

4. Given the cognitive abilities of a 5-yr-old child, how might 5-yr-old Juan conceptualize the death of his pet parakeet? [p. 391-393; LO-Big Picture]

A 5-yr-old child is in Piaget's preoperational stage. During this stage children are egocentric and lack conservation skills. Because of this, Juan may believe that his own behavior caused the death of his pet. For example, Juan may believe that because he failed to say goodnight to his pet the night before it died, he caused his pet to die from sadness. He may also not really understand what death actually means for his pet. He may believe that the animal is temporarily away somewhere and could return someday— much as people return from extended vacations or as cartoon characters sometimes return to life after being "killed".

Label the Diagram [p. 415; LO 12]

Marcia's states of identity formation
1. achievement
2. foreclosure
3. diffusion
4. moratorium

Big Picture Review [p. 403; LO 9 & 12]

STAGE
1. Trust vs. Mistrust
2. Autonomy vs. Shame and Doubt
3. Initiative vs. Guilt
4. Industry vs. Inferiority
5. Identity vs. Role Confusion
6. Intimacy vs. Isolation
7. Generativity vs. Stagnation
8. Ego Integrity vs. Despair

10

How Do Gender and Sexuality Affect Our Behavior?

Learning Objectives

After studying each of the following sections of the chapter, you should be able to do these tasks:

Gender Identity and Gender Differences

1. Explain sexual differentiation.
2. Explain gender-schema theory.
3. Describe how nature and nurture influence gender-role behavior and gender identity.
4. Explain gender differences in cognitive abilities and in personality.

Sexual Behavior and Attitudes: And the Survey Says . . .

5. Detail changes in sexual attitudes and behaviors gathered through the survey method over the past fifty years.

Sexual Orientation

6. Distinguish between sexual orientation and sexual behavior, and analyze the research investigating the causes of sexual orientation.

Sexual Arousal and Response

7. Explain the biological and psychological components of sexual desire, and outline the phases of the sexual response cycle in men and women.

Sexual Disorders

8. Discriminate between the various sexual dysfunctions and paraphilias, and explain nature's and nurture's role in causing these disorders.

Sexual Coercion

9. Define the various forms of sexual coercion, and describe how they might be prevented.

Sexually Transmitted Infections

10. Discriminate among the various sexually transmitted infections, their causes, modes of transmission, and treatment options.

The Big Picture

The Big Picture: How Do We Develop a Gender and Sexual Identity?

By age two, most toddlers can identify whether they are male or female. This is one of the first steps in developing a gender identity or the personal experience of being male or female. For example, early in life Maya Angelou's ideas about gender compelled her to seek out dominant men because at the time, her concept of womanhood included being submissive to a husband.

Gender, in turn affects our sexuality or the ways in which we express ourselves sexually. Maya Angelou wondered about her sexual orientation, experienced a teenage pregnancy, danced in a strip joint, and felt coerced into becoming a prostitute. Maya Angelou's life experiences powerfully illustrate the influence of gender and sexuality on one's behavior.

Gender Identity and Gender Differences

This section covers Learning Objectives 1-4. Males are born with an XY chromosomal pattern and females are born with an XX pattern. These chromosomes contain the genes that will direct the development of our sexual anatomy, a process known as sexual differentiation. By the 7th week of pregnancy, these chromosomes begin to direct the developing embryo to differentiate into either a male or a female being. If something goes wrong in the differentiation process, such as a hormonal error, hermaphroditism (having both male and female genitalia) or pseudohermaphroditism (having ambiguous internal or external genitalia) can occur.

The process of sexual differentiation results in a person being labeled as male or female at birth. This gender label then sets the stage for gender-role development. Gender refers to our feelings about our biological make-up or assigned sex. Gender roles are the collection of traits that our society typically associates with being males or female. Children under the age of 6 typically do not have gender permanence or an understanding that gender is permanent. But even before age 6, children are acquiring a gender. Nature or genetics may play a role in the development of gender in children, but nurture or environmental influences are also powerful forces. Gender-schema theory states that we learn to be masculine or feminine through the processes of social learning and operant conditioning. As we observe men and women and experience reinforcement for behaving in gender appropriate ways, we begin to form schemas for gender in our minds. Parents, teachers, peers, and the media all play a role in guiding our understanding of gender as these schemas are forming.

Because sexual differentiation affects our sexual appearance, it also impacts the development of our gender identity. Looking like a boy tends to foster the development of a masculine or male gender identity. Looking like a girl tends to foster the development of a feminine or female gender identity. Hermaphrodites and pseudohermaphrodites that are surgically altered to resemble one sex and raised as a member of that sex, often develop a gender identity that is consistent with their assigned sex. This indicates that environment plays a role in gender identity. However, in such cases, the child usually receives sex hormones appropriate for their assigned sex, so it is possible that biology also plays a role in gender identity. All in all, it is most likely that gender identity results from a combination of environmental and biological factors.

Do men and women behave differently? Do they have different abilities? Common stereotypes in our society say yes, but what does the research say? Research on gender differences is complex and difficult to interpret. Some studies show that females have better verbal skills, but this edge is small and getting smaller as time goes on. Some studies show that males are better at math, but this varies significantly with the age of the participants and the type of measure being used. Males do seem to have better visual-spatial skills, but gender differences in academic success tend to be small and insignificant. Psychologists have also examined the influence of gender on personality. Such research suggests that females are more extraverted, anxious, trusting, and nurturing than males. Males tend to be more assertive and tough-minded and to have more self-esteem than females.

Sexual Behavior and Attitudes: And the Survey Says . . .

This section covers Learning Objective 5. People's sexual attitudes and behavior have long been of interest to psychologists. Alfred Kinsey conducted his famous exploration of American sexuality in the 1930s and 1940s. Today, psychologists still try to keep up with the changing attitudes and behavior that are part of our sexual lives.

Masturbation or sexual self-stimulation is a common sexual activity despite being historically frowned upon by many. Today, most people report that they have masturbated at some point, but males tend to report higher frequencies of masturbation than females. Masturbation is also more common among European-Americans, single people, and the educated.

Sexual fantasy is a mental image or thought that is arousing to a person. Most adults engage in fantasy at some point in time and despite popular belief, fantasy is not related to having an unsatisfactory sex life. Men tend to fantasize more than women and women tend to have more romantic fantasies compared to men.

Sex with others can include sexual intercourse, oral sex, premarital sex, extramarital sex, or sex with multiple partners. Societal attitudes about these sexual activities often represent a double standard, with men being given more sexual freedom than females.

In the U.S., the average rate of sexual intercourse is about once a week, with a similar pattern indicated worldwide from Pfizer's global study on sexual behavior. Oral sex has become quite prevalent, and the majority of young and educated married people report having engaged in it. However, ethnic differences show that oral sex is less common among African-Americans. Anal sex is less common, but growing in popularity.

Sexual activity is something that is seen across nearly the entire lifespan. Young children engage in self-exploratory and self-stimulating activities such as "playing doctor". Adolescents engage in kissing, petting, masturbation, with roughly two-thirds of U.S. teenagers having intercourse by age 18. Adults also engage in a wide variety of sexual behavior throughout their lives. Kinsey found that by age 60, the vast majority of men and women are still sexually active.

Sexual Orientation

This section covers Learning Objective 6. Sexual orientation, one's attraction for members of the same (homosexual), other sex (heterosexual) or both sexes (bisexual), can impact one's sexual behavior. Yet, sexual orientation is not as fixed as these three terms suggest. Heterosexuality and homosexuality more often represent endpoints on a broad spectrum of behaviors that Kinsey identified as a continuum of sexual orientation. Moreover, sexual orientation may change over time, with women reporting greater change in orientation than men.

Negative attitudes about homosexuality make it difficult to accurately determine how common homosexuality is, but recent data suggest that 4-6% of males and 2-4% of females identify as being exclusively homosexual. However, attitudes towards homosexuality in the United States may be changing. Today it is more common to see positive portrayals of homosexuality in the media and some corporations now extend benefits to same-sex partners of employees. But, not all people view homosexuality as an acceptable variation of human sexuality. Homophobia, or prejudice against homosexuals and bisexuals, is still widespread.

The question of what causes sexual orientation is a topic of intense inquiry and at times, debate. Many people mistakenly equate gender and sexual orientation. Being gay or straight doesn't necessarily correlate with gender identity. A gay man can be masculine, and a heterosexual man can be feminine. A few studies have suggested that early gender-related activities may be a predictor of later sexual orientation for *some* people. But, there is at this time no compelling reason to believe that gender-related activities (e.g., playing with dolls or trucks) can cause one's sexual orientation. It also appears that family dynamics do not cause sexual orientation.

Having failed to find evidence that environment is a universal cause of homosexuality researchers have looked for possible biological mechanisms. Twin studies and familial studies indicate that genetics may play some role, but the exact nature of that role has not been specified. Similarly, research on prenatal factors also indicates a possible interaction between nature and nurture. At this time, no one can say for sure what causes our sexual orientation.

Sexual Arousal and Response

This section covers Learning Objective 7. Sexual arousal, or a heightened state of sexual interest and excitement, is something that most humans experience at some point in time. Sexual desire or libido is a normal part of the human condition. In humans, testosterone is the hormone that regulates libido for both men and women although other hormones may also play a role. Libido can also be influenced by external stimuli such as visual cues, sounds, scents, and touches. Some areas of the body, erogenous zones, are particularly responsive to such stimulation.

When we engage in sexual activity, we go through what is called the sexual response cycle: excitement, plateau, orgasm, and resolution. As one progresses from excitement to plateau, there is an initial increase in physiological arousal that levels off somewhat in the plateau phase. During orgasm, arousal reaches its peak and orgasm occurs. For males, orgasm also involves ejaculation. Following orgasm, males and females enter the resolution phase in which arousal declines. For males, this phase includes a refractory period during which they are incapable of experiencing another orgasm or ejaculation.

Sexual Disorders

This section covers Learning Objective 8. Most people experience sexual problems from time to time, but some of us suffer from sexual disorders. Sexual dysfunctions are problems in sexual desire or sexual response. These include hypoactive disorder (persistent disinterest in sex) and sexual aversion disorder (persistent disgust and aversion to sex). Disorders of sexual arousal include male erectile dysfunction (inability to achieve or sustain an erection) and female arousal disorder (difficulty becoming sexually aroused or sufficiently lubricated in response to sexual stimulation). Orgasmic disorders include male or female orgasmic disorder (difficulty or inability to achieve orgasm) and premature ejaculation (persistent or recurrent trouble ejaculating with very little sexual stimulation). Sexual pain disorders include dyspareunia (pain during sexual intercourse that affects both men and women) and vaginismus (involuntary vaginal contractions that make sexual intercourse difficult).

A second class of sexual disorders is the paraphilias. People with paraphilias become sexually aroused by objects or situations that are not typically arousing for most people. Non-coercive paraphilias include fetishism (being aroused by inanimate objects) and transvestism (becoming sexually aroused by wearing clothes of the opposite gender). Coercive paraphilias include voyeurism (becoming sexually aroused by watching unsuspecting others who are naked, disrobing, or engaged in sexual activity), pedophilia (being sexually aroused by children), sexual sadism (achieving sexual satisfaction by causing pain or humiliation in others), and sexual masochism (achieving sexual satisfaction from being humiliated or receiving pain).

Sexual Coercion

This section covers Learning Objective 9. In addition to the coercive paraphilias, some other sexual behaviors are coercive in nature. These include sexual harassment (forcing unwanted sexual overtures on another), child sexual abuse (subjecting children to sexual advances like fondling or sexual intercourse), and rape and date rape (having sex with a person against his or her will).

Sexually Transmitted Infections

This section covers Learning Objective 10. Sometimes engaging in sexual activity can lead to a sexually transmitted infection or STI. Across the world, STIs are widespread. Anyone who is sexually active is at risk of contracting one, but unprotected sex and sex with multiple partners can increase your chances of contracting one. STIs fall into three categories: bacterial (Chlamydia, gonorrhea, and syphilis), viral (genital herpes, genital warts, and HIV/AIDS), and parasitic (pubic lice and scabies). Some of these like Chlamydia can be easily cured, but others such as HIV/AIDS are serious, incurable diseases. When it comes to STIs, prevention is the best medicine.

Outlining the Big Picture

Chapter 10: How Do Gender and Sexuality Affect Our Behavior?

The Big Picture: How Do We Develop a Gender and Sexual Identity?
Notes:

_____

_____

_____

_____

_____

_____

Gender Identity and Gender Differences (Learning Objectives 1-4)
Sexual Differentiation: How Do We Develop Our Sexual Anatomy?
Gender and Gender Role Development
       Nature and Nurture Influences on Gender-Role Behavior
Gender Identity: The Influence of Nature and Nurture
Gender Differences: Do Males and Females Think and Act Differently?
   Cognitive Abilities
   Personality Factors
Notes:

_____

_____

_____

_____

_____

_____

Sexual Behavior and Attitudes: And the Survey Says... (Learning Objective 5)
Masturbation and Sexual Fantasy
Sex with a Partner
  Spotlight on Diversity: Sexuality in Youth and Age
Notes:

_____

_____

_____

_____

_____

_____

Sexual Orientation (Learning Objective 6)
Sexual Orientation and Sexual Behavior
Attitudes toward Gay Males and Lesbians: Differing Views across the World
What Causes One's Sexual Orientation? The Influence of Biology and the
      Environment
Notes:

_____

_____

_____

_____

_____

_____

Sexual Arousal and Response (Learning Objective 7)
Sexual Desire: A Mixture of Chemicals, Thoughts, and Culture
The Sexual Response Cycle
Notes:

_____

_____

_____

_____

_____

Sexual Disorders (Learning Objective 8)
Sexual Dysfunctions: Problems in Sexual Desire or Response
  Disorders of Sexual Desire
  Disorders of Sexual Arousal
  Orgasmic Disorders
  Sexual Pain Disorders
Paraphilias: Sexually Aroused by an Object or Situation
Internet Sexual Addictions
Notes:

_____

_____

_____

_____

_____

Sexual Coercion (Learning Objective 9)
Sexual Harassment: Unwelcome Comments, Gestures, or Contact
Child Molestation and Sexual Abuse: Short- and Long-Term Effects
Rape: Forcing Sex on Someone
  Attitudes and Beliefs about Rape
  Date Rape
Notes:

_____

_____

_____

_____

_____

_____

Sexually Transmitted Infections (Learning Objective 10)
Prevalence of STIs: Will I Get an STI?
Risk Factors: Age, Gender, Ethnicity, and Behavior
Types of STIs: Bacterial, Viral, and Parasitic
Notes:

_____

_____

_____

_____

_____

Are You Getting the Big Picture?
Notes:

_____

_____

_____

_____

_____

Seeing the Big Picture: A Mental Map of Chapter 10

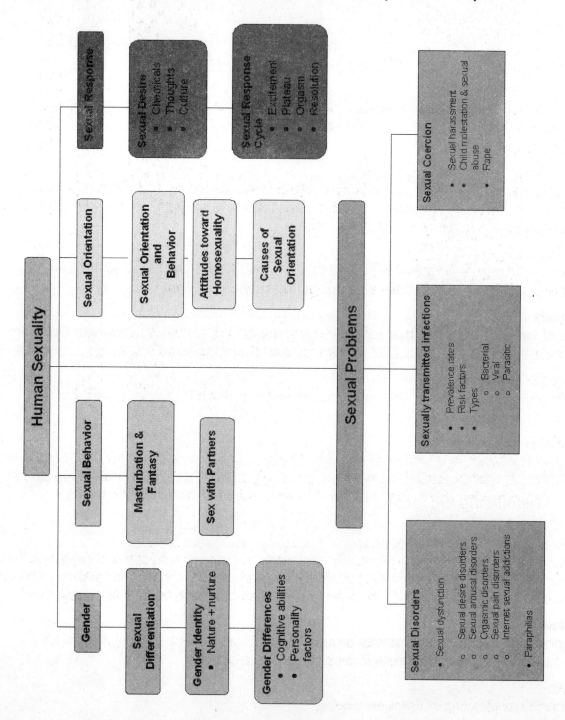

Key Points of the Big Picture

Bisexual:
one who is sexually attracted to members of both sexes. *Example: Anne has been attracted to and dated both males and females in her adulthood.*

Date rape:
a form of acquaintance rape in which a person is forced or threatened to engage in sexual activity with a social escort. *Example: On their third date, Robert forced Juno to perform oral sex on him.*

Dyspareunia:
a disorder characterized by painful sexual intercourse. *Example: For the past six months, every time MayLing starts to have sexual intercourse with her partner, she experiences shooting pains in her pelvic region.*

Erogenous zones:
areas of the skin that are sensitive to touch. *Example: Keanu gets sexually aroused when his partner licks his earlobes, an erogenous zone for Keanu.*

Estrogens:
a class of female hormones that regulate many aspects of sexuality. *Example: Estrogen levels increase during puberty and pregnancy and decrease at menopause.*

Excitement phase:
the first stage of the sexual response cycle in which males get erections and females produce vaginal lubrication.

Exhibitionism:
a paraphilia in which one is sexually aroused by the fantasies or the behavior of exposing his or her genitals to some unsuspecting person. *Example: A car pulled up to ask Henrietta for directions. The man in the car was an exhibitionist who had his trousers and underwear down to show Henrietta his genitals.*

Female sexual arousal disorder:
persistent difficulty in becoming sexually excited or sufficiently lubricated in response to stimulation. *Example: Although Consuelo desires sexual activity with her partner, she often does not produce vaginal lubrication even when her partner stimulates her clitoris.*

Fetishism:
a paraphilia characterized by sexual arousal to inanimate objects. *Example: Jonah needs to feel lacy undergarments in order to get an erection.*

Gender:
the experience of being male or female

Gender identity:
one's personal experience of being male or female.

Gender permanence:
the understanding that one's gender will not change. *Example: Terrence identifies himself as male and understands that as a male he cannot get pregnant – he will always be a male.*

Gender roles:
society's expectations for how males and females should behave. *Example: Traditional gender roles assume that males are assertive, brave, and dominant, and females are gentle, submissive, and anxious.*

Gender-schema theory:
the idea that gender roles are acquired through modeling and reinforcement processes that work together with a child's mental abilities. *Example: Andres sees that boys get rewarded and girls get punished for being rough and active. Andres now has the idea or scheme that only boys should be rough and active.*

Hermaphrodite:
a person who develops both fully formed testicular and ovarian tissue.

Heterosexual:
one who is sexually attracted only to members of the other sex. *Example: Sofia has always been attracted to men but never to women.*

Homophobia:
prejudicial attitudes against homosexuals and homosexuality. *Example: Believing that gay teachers should not be hired to teach young children is a homophobic attitude.*

Homosexual:
one who is sexually attracted only to members of the same sex. *Example: Gary has always been attracted to other males and has never felt sexual desire for females.*

Hypoactive sexual desire disorder:
a persistent disinterest in sex and sexual activities. *Example: Since her rape, Marquita has had no interest in any form of sexual activity.*

Libido:
one's physical desire, or drive, to have sex. *Example: People who have a low libido may take medication to increase their physical desire to have sex.*

Male erectile dysfunction:
the persistent inability to sustain or attain an erection sufficient to complete sexual activity. *Example: For the past eight months, Raphael has not been able to keep his erection during sexual activity with his partner.*

Masturbation:
sexual self-stimulation.

Orgasmic disorder:
a lack of orgasm or a persistent delay in reaching orgasm despite adequate stimulation. *Example: Penelope gets excited and produces lubrication when engaged in sexual activity with her partner, but she cannot climax.*

Orgasm phase:
the third stage of the sexual response cycle in which the pelvic and anal muscles contract.

Ovaries:
the organs in a female's body that produce eggs, or ova.

Paraphilia:
sexual arousal in response to an unusual object, situation, or unconsenting person. *Examples: fetishism, exhibitionism, voyeurism*

Pedophilia:
a paraphilia in which one is sexually aroused by fantasies of or engaging in sexual activity with a prepubescent child. *Example: James gets an erection when he imagines engaging in sexual activity with a nine-year-old girl.*

Plateau phase:
the second stage of the sexual response cycle in which excitement peaks.

Premature ejaculation:
persistent or recurrent ejaculation with minimal sexual stimulation before the person wishes it. *Example: Jeff frequently feels that he cannot hold off his orgasm and ejaculates before he wants to.*

Pseudohermaphrodite:
a person who develops ambiguous internal or external sexual anatomy. Example: *Margo was born with what looks like an enlarged clitoris or a very small penis.*

Rape:
the threat or use of force to obtain sex. *Example: While walking to work one night, Tricia was jumped on by a man who held her down and had sexual intercourse with her.*

Refractory period:
a time during the resolution phase in which males are incapable of experiencing another orgasm or ejaculation. *Example: Forty-year old Corbin used to be able to have sexual intercourse and ejaculate several times in one day. Now, he must wait a few hours before engaging in sexual activity again in order to be able to ejaculate because of his longer refractory period.*

Resolution phase:
the final stage of the sexual response cycle in which the body returns to homeostasis. *Example: After having sexual intercourse, Kate's breathing, heart rate, and blood pressure returned to normal levels.*

Sex:
our biological makeup, starting with our chromosomes (XX for female, XY for male) and proceeding to our internal and external genitalia.

Sexual arousal:
a heightened state of sexual interest and excitement. *Example: While watching sexually explicit movies, Keenan got an erection and was sexually aroused.*

Sexual aversion disorder:
a persistent disgust and aversion toward sexual activity. *Example: Marta is repulsed when her partner, who she loves, tries to initiate sexual contact.*

Sexual coercion:
sexual behaviors that are non-consenting, abusive, or forcible. *Examples: sexual harassment, rape, child molestation*

Sexual desire:
one's motivation and interest in engaging in sexual activity. *Example: Matilda is not interested in engaging in sexual activity all that frequently; she has low sexual desire.*

Sexual differentiation:
the process by which males and females develop their sexual anatomy. *Example: When the embryo develops testes or ovaries this is a part of the sexual differentiation process.*

Sexual disorder:
a persistent sexual problem that causes a person a great deal of distress and interferes with his/her ability to function sexually. *Examples: sexual dysfunction disorders such as sexual aversion disorder and paraphilias such as exhibitionism or voyeurism.*

Sexual dysfunction:
a persistent problem with sexual desire, arousal or satisfaction. *Examples: premature ejaculation, hypoactive sexual disorder, male erectile dysfunction*

Sexual fantasy:
a mental thought or image that is sexually arousing to a person. *Example: When Phan imagines that he is having sexual intercourse with Jessica Alba, he gets sexually excited.*

Sexual harassment:
the repeated use of unwanted verbal comments, gestures or physical contact of a sexual nature against another person in a subordinate position. *Example: Lulu's boss often puts his arm around her waist and makes comments about her chest cleavage despite Lulu's repeated requests for him to stop.*

Sexuality:
the ways we express ourselves as sexual beings. *Example: How you dress, walk, and flirt with others are expressions of your sexuality.*

Sexually transmitted infection (STI):
an infection that is passed from one person to another primarily through sexual contact. *Example: Two weeks ago, Rupert did not use a condom when he had sex with someone he met at a club. Rupert now has contracted gonorrhea.*

Sexual masochism:
a paraphilia in which a person desires to be humiliated or receive pain in order to attain sexual pleasure. *Example: Johanna gets sexually aroused when her partner forcibly slaps her buttocks.*

Sexual orientation:
one's sexual attraction for members of the same and/or other sex.

Sexual sadism:
a paraphilia in which a person achieves sexual satisfaction by inflicting pain or humiliation on a sex partner. *Example: Darshun gets an erection when he hits his partner with a whip and the person grimaces in pain.*

Testes:
the organs in a male's body that produce both sperm and testosterone.

Testosterone:
a male hormone that plays a role in many aspects of sexuality, including sexual desire. *Example: Medications that increase one's sex drive often have this effect by increasing testosterone levels.*

Transsexual:
a person whose gender identity is opposite to his or her chromosomal sex. *Example: Despite being born with a penis and testes, Maggie, who no longer answers to her given name of Michael, has always felt like she is a woman.*

Transvestism:
a paraphilia in which a person is sexually aroused by wearing clothing of the other gender. *Example: Mitch gets an erection when he wears a bra and panties.*

Vaginismus:
a disorder in females characterized by involuntary contractions of the vaginal muscles making penetration painful or impossible. *Example: Every time Louisa tries to have sexual intercourse with her partner, her vagina seems to spasm such that penetration is not achieved.*

Voyeurism:
a paraphilia in which one is sexually aroused by observing unsuspecting strangers who are undressing or engaged in sexual activity. *Example: Troy frequently hides in a tree outside his neighbor's house and gets sexually aroused when he sees them undress or have sex.*

Fill-in Review of the Chapter

Can you fill in the missing terms for each section of the chapter? Items marked with an * encourage you to continue building the Big Picture of psychology by connecting the material in this chapter to material from previous chapters in the text.

The Big Picture: How Do We Develop a Gender and Sexual Identity?

1) _____ _____ is your personal experience of being male or female.

The way we experience and express ourselves as sexual beings is referred to as 2) _____.

Gender Identity and Gender Differences

The process of developing your sexual anatomy is called 3) _____ _____.

A baby born with both testicular and ovarian tissue is a(n) 4) _____.

Most children are able to label their gender and the gender of others by the time they are 5) _____ years old.

Gender identity is influenced by 6) _____ _____ and 7) _____ _____ influences.

Gender-schema theory is a combination of two psychological perspectives: 8*) _____ _____ and 9*) _____.

10) _____ _____, or the favoring of one gender over the other because of different views of male and female roles, exists in many places in society.

Sexual Behavior and Attitudes: And the Survey Says…

Alfred Kinsey used 11*) _____ research to detail the sexual attitudes and behaviors of U.S. adults.

A(n) 12) _____ _____ is a mental thought or image that is arousing to a person.

The notion that certain sexual acts are okay for a man but not for a woman is called a(n) 13) _____ _____.

Sexual Orientation

A man who is married to a woman and has never had sex with a man, but still is attracted only to men has a(n) 14) _____ sexual orientation.

Because homophobia is a negative attitude toward a group and its members, it would be of most interest to 15*) _____ psychologists.

Sexual Arousal and Response

16) _____ _____ is our motivation and interest in engaging in sexual activity.

Libido is affected by the part of the brain that controls our hormones, called the 17*) _____.

During the 18) _____ _____ of the sexual response cycle, men experience a full penile erection and the testes are fully elevated.

Sexual Disorders

Chronic erectile disorder is often caused by 19) _____ _____.

Painful sexual intercourse in either a man or a woman is called 20) _____.

Bill likes to wear his wife's clothes when she's not around. Although he would never admit it to her, he becomes sexually aroused by seeing himself dressed up in her finest wear. Bill seems to suffer from 21) _____.

Sexual Coercion

Inappropriate sexual contact between an adult and a child is called 22) _____ _____.

Sexually Transmitted Infections
Men and women between the ages of 23) _____and 24) _____ are most at risk for contracting a sexually transmitted infection.

Chlamydia, gonorrhea, and syphilis are 25) _____ infections.

Use It or Lose It!

Can you fill in the following table with the sexual disorder that is being described?

Sexual Disorder	Description
1.	Carmen has persistent difficulty in becoming sufficiently lubricated when she is sexually stimulated.
2.	Adam is sexually aroused by fantasies involving exposing his genitals to strangers.
3.	Tawnya has a persistent disgust toward sexual activity.
4.	Benja compulsively fantasizes about leather pants to get sexually aroused.
5.	Intercourse is almost always painful for Mindy.
6.	Griffin has repeated urges to observe strangers engaged in sexual activity.
7.	Rosalyn cannot achieve orgasm despite adequate stimulation.
8.	Oscar often wears his partner's lingerie to get sexually aroused.
9.	Clay has persistent difficulty in maintaining an erection.
10.	For over a year, Mandisa has had very little interest in sex or sexual activities.

Self-Check: Are You Getting the Big Picture?

After you have read and studied the chapter, see if you can answer the following quiz questions. Check your answers at the end of the chapter. If you miss a question, refer to your text and re-study the appropriate sections.

True or False Questions

Are these statements true or false?

1. A child's sexual differentiation is complete by the 5th week of pregnancy.
True
False

2. Studies show that boys begin to speak earlier in life than females.
True
False

3. Men are at higher risk for contracting an STI than women.
True
False

4. People who hold more traditional gender roles are more likely to be tolerant of rape and less tolerant of rape victims.
True
False

5. Studies indicate that males engage in sexual fantasy more often than females.
True
False

6. Mothers are much more likely to hold gender stereotypes and tend to be less accepting of cross-gender behaviors in their children.
True
False

7. In the U.S., the national average for frequency of sexual intercourse is about two times a week.
True
False

8. Modern data suggest that approximately 10% of males and 5% of females are homosexual.
True
False

9. For males, sperm can only be released during the orgasm phase of the sexual response cycle.
True
False

10. Hypoactive sexual desire disorder is more common in females than in males.
True
False

Multiple Choice Questions

Can you choose the best answer for these questions?

1. Last night, Rick's partner wanted to have sex, but he said he was tired and just wanted to sleep. This led to a brief argument after which Rick went to sleep without having sex. According to what you've learned, what is going on with Rick?
    A. He has hypoactive sexual desire disorder.
    B. He has male erectile disorder.
    C. He has sexual aversion disorder.
    D. He's normal, but tired.

2. Based on the available research, which of the following proposed gender differences seems to be the most clear-cut?
    A. Males are better at visual-spatial tasks.
    B. Females are more verbal.
    C. Males are better at math.
    D. None of these gender differences have much support.

3. Males tend to engage in more _____ aggression, whereas females tend to engage in more _____ aggression.
    A. relational; physical
    B. physical; relational
    C. verbal; relational
    D. relational; verbal

4. Which chemical is most responsible for prenatal sexual differentiation?
    A. testosterone
    B. estrogen
    C. H-Y antigen
    D. progesterone

5. At what age do children typically understand that their gender is stable and will not change?
    A. 2 years
    B. 3 years
    C. 4 years
    D. 6 years

6. Compared to males, females' sexual fantasies tend to be:
   A. more frequent.
   B. more violent.
   C. more prolonged.
   D. more romantic.

7. Which of the following statements is true?
   A. Oral sex is more common than anal sex in the U.S.
   B. Anal sex is more common than oral sex in the U.S.
   C. African Americans engage in more oral sex than Whites.
   D. Compared to more educated people, less educated people are more likely to engage in oral sex.

8. Which of the following statements is true concerning teenage sexuality?
   A. Hispanic American girls have more sex than European American girls.
   B. Hispanic American girls have less sex than European American girls.
   C. European American boys have more sex than African American boys.
   D. European American boys have more sex than Hispanic American boys.

9. Which of the following hormones governs libido or sex drive in both males and females?
   A. estrogen
   B. progesterone
   C. testosterone
   D. H-Y antigen

10. Stimulation of genitals, breasts, ears, mouth, and so on is sexually arousing for many people because these areas of the body are:
    A. sex organs.
    B. sensory zones.
    C. erogenous zones.
    D. primary sexual characteristics.

11. Fernando and Lupe are on a date. Fernando begins to kiss Lupe's ears and neck while touching her on the stomach. As he begins to do this, Lupe begins to feel excited. Her nipples become erect and she wants Fernando to continue what he's doing. Which stage of the sexual response cycle is Lupe at?
    A. excitement
    B. arousal
    C. plateau
    D. orgasm

12. _____ _____ guide children's decisions about how they and others should behave.
    A. Gender bias
    B. Gender reinforcement
    C. Gender schemas
    D. Sexual behaviors

13. Nancy and Jamal are having sex and Nancy just reached orgasm. How long will Nancy remain in the refractory period?
    A. Women do not go through a refractory period.
    B. 5 minutes
    C. 10 minutes
    D. 15 minutes
    E. 20 minutes

14. During a period of about 1 1/2 years, Will suffered erectile problems. As a result, he began to shy away from sexual activity with his partner because he was embarrassed. Now Will finds the idea of sex disgusting and he avoids situations and relationships that might lead to sexual activity. Currently, Will seems to be suffering from:
    A. hypoactive sexual desire disorder.
    B. sexual aversion disorder.
    C. male orgasmic disorder.
    D. dyspareunia.

15. Which of the following conditions could lead to diminished sexual desire in women?
    A. lowered hormone levels
    B. a history of sexual trauma
    C. certain prescription medications (e.g., antidepressants)
    D. all of the above

16. When having sex, Lamar tends to reach orgasm within a few seconds of beginning intercourse. Lamar is likely suffering from:
    A. performance anxiety.
    B. dyspareunia.
    C. premature ejaculation.
    D. an inability to judge his own degree of sexual arousal.

17. Which of the following is not a paraphilia?
    A. fetishism
    B. pedophilia
    C. sexual sadism
    D. homosexuality

18. Children of gay and lesbian parents:
    A. are less well-adjusted than children of other-sex parents.
    B. are better adjusted than children of other-sex parents.
    C. do not differ in adjustment compared to children of other-sex parents.
    D. start out with more adjustment problems in early childhood but end up better adjusted in adolescence compared to children of other-sex parents.

19. Since late adolescence, Lance has found that he becomes the most sexually aroused when watching others disrobe. This is especially true when the other people do not know that he is watching. Lately, he has begun spying on women as they undress in the changing rooms of the department store where he works. Lance appears to have which paraphilia?
    A. sadism
    B. exhibitionism
    C. voyeurism
    D. a fetish

20. Sue worked as a waitress in a truck stop for many years. While working there, she had to endure sexual comments, unwanted touches and kisses, and propositions from many of the male clients and some of her coworkers. Sue was experiencing:
    A. sexual harassment.
    B. sexual abuse.
    C. emotional rape.
    D. all of the above

21. Which of the following statements about child sexual abuse is incorrect?
    A. European American females report more sexual abuse in childhood than African American females do.
    B. Most children are abused by someone they know.
    C. Male and female children suffer child sexual abuse.
    D. The majority of child sexual abusers are heterosexual males.

22. Surveys suggest that what percentage of women will suffer a rape in their lifetime?
    A. 1-4%
    B. 5-15%
    C. 17-28%
    D. 35-46%

23. Holding which of the following attitudes tends to foster a climate in which rape is justified and victims are blamed?
    A. Real men should be sexually aggressive.
    B. Women who dress in provocative ways are just asking to be raped.
    C. All women fantasize about being raped.
    D. All of the above

24. Acquaintance rape is:
    A. less likely to be reported than stranger rape.
    B. less psychologically damaging than stranger rape.
    C. less common than stranger rape.
    D. none of the above

25. Which country has the highest rate of sexually transmitted infection in the industrialized world?
    A. Canada
    B. England
    C. France
    D. United States

Short-Answer Questions

Can you write a brief answer to these questions?

1. What is a paraphilia?

2. Explain how gender-role behavior develops in children.

3. What is sexual orientation?

4. Describe what we know about sexuality in youth and older adults.

5. What are the three classes of sexually transmitted infections? Give an example of each.

6. How have attitudes towards homosexuality changed over the years in the U.S.?

Developing a Bigger Picture: Making Connections Across Chapters

An important aspect of learning is learning to see the "Big Picture" of the subject you are studying. As you learn about psychology, you should try to understand how the material from different chapters fits together to help you form a broad-based understanding of what psychology is all about. To help facilitate the development of this "Big Picture" in your mind, try to answer these questions using the knowledge you have learned in this chapter, as well as the other chapters referenced in the questions.

1. Using what you've learned about operant conditioning in Chapter 5 and gender development in this chapter, give some examples of how you have seen parents use operant conditioning to foster gender development in their children.

2. Given what you learned in Chapter 8 and this chapter, what do eating behavior and sexuality have in common?

3. Some psychologists have applied the concept of a script (Chapter 6) to the area of human sexuality. A sexual script is a schema that you have for how sexual relationships are supposed to unfold between two people. Think about your particular scripts. What factors influenced you as you developed your scripts?

4. In the text, a study is reported that showed that scents, like pumpkin pie and licorice can elicit sexual arousal in people. Using everything you have learned about psychology at this point, generate a theory as to why this might be true.

Label the Diagram

Identify the processes of the sexual response cycle for males and females.

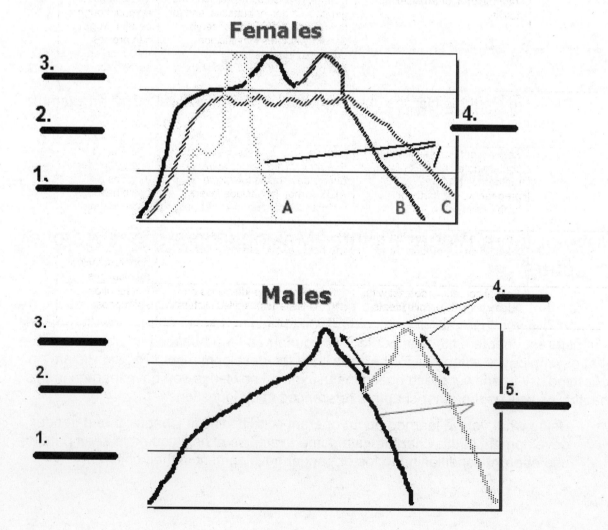

Big Picture Review

Identify each of the Sexually Transmitted Infections described in the table below.

STI	Transmission Modes	Symptoms	Treatments
1)	Vaginal, oral, or anal sexual activity, or from an infected mother to her newborn during a vaginal birth	In females: frequent and painful urination, lower abdominal pain, and vaginal discharge. In males: burning or painful urination, and slight penile discharge. However, many people show no symptoms	Antibiotics
2)	Vaginal, oral, or anal sexual activity, or from an infected mother to her newborn during a vaginal birth	In females: increased vaginal discharge, burning urination, or irregular menstrual bleeding (many women show no early symptoms). In males: yellowish, thick penile discharge, or burning urination.	Antibiotics
3)	Vaginal, oral, or anal sexual activity, or by touching an infected chancre or sore	A hard, round, painless chancre or sore appears at site of infection within 2 to 4 weeks	Penicillin or other antibiotics for penicillin-allergic patients
4)	Vaginal, oral, or anal sexual activity	Painful, reddish bumps around the genitals, thighs or buttocks, and for females on the vagina or cervix. Other symptoms may include burning urination, flu-like symptoms, or vaginal discharge in females	There is no cure, although certain drugs can provide relief and help sores heal
5)	Sexual contact or contact with infected towels or clothing	Painless warts appear in the genital area.	Cryotherapy (freezing), acid burning or surgical removal
6)	Sexual contact, infusion with contaminated blood, or from mother to child during pregnancy, childbirth, or breast-feeding	May develop mild flu-like symptoms that may disappear for many years before developing full-blown AIDS. AIDS symptoms include fever, weight loss, fatigue, diarrhea, and susceptibility to infection.	There is no cure; treatment includes a combination of antiviral drugs
7)	Sexual contact or contact with infested linens or toilet seats	Intense itching in hairy regions of the body, especially the pubic area.	Prescription shampoos or nonprescription medications
8)	Sexual contact or contact with infested linens or toilet seats	Intense itching, reddish lines on skin, welts, and pus-filled blisters in affected area.	Prescription shampoos

Solutions

Each solution is followed by its textbook page reference number and its corresponding chapter learning objective (LO) number. Items with a Big Picture LO help you build a Big Picture of psychology across the chapters you have studied so far.

Fill-in Review of the Chapter

1. Gender identity [p. 437; LO 3]
2. sexuality [p. 438; LO 1]
3. sexual differentiation [p. 440; LO 1]
4. hermaphrodite [p. 441; LO 1]
5. two [p. 442; LO 3]
6. genes (nature) [p. 445; LO 3]
7. environmental (nurture) [p. 445; LO 3]
8. social learning [p. 16-17; LO-Big Picture]
9. cognitive [p. 16-17; LO-Big Picture]
10. Gender bias [p. 444; LO 3]
11. survey [p. 31; LO-Big Picture]
12. sexual fantasy [p. 452; LO 5]
13. double standard [p. 453; LO 5]
14. homosexual [p. 457; LO 6]
15. social [p. 21; LO-Big Picture]
16. Sexual desire [p. 461; LO 7]
17. hypothalamus [p. 82; LO-Big Picture]
18. plateau phase [p. 464; LO 7]
19. physical problems [p. 467; LO 8]
20. dyspareunia [p. 468; LO 8]
21. transvestism [p. 469; LO 8]
22. child sexual abuse [p. 472; LO 9]
23. fifteen [p. 476; LO 10]
24. twenty-five [p. 476; LO 10]
25. bacterial [p. 477; LO 10]

Use It or Lose It! [p. 466-470; LO 8]

1. female sexual arousal disorder
2. exhibitionism
3. sexual aversion disorder
4. fetishism
5. dyspareunia
6. voyeurism
7. orgasmic disorder
8. transvestism

9. male erectile dysfunction
10. hypoactive sexual desire disorder

Self-Check: Are You Getting the Big Picture?

True or False Questions

1. F [p. 441; LO 1]
2. F [p. 447; LO 4]
3. F [p. 476; LO 10]
4. T [p. 474; LO 9]
5. T [p. 452; LO 5]

6. F [p. 444; LO 3]
7. F [p. 453; LO 5]
8. F [p. 458; LO 6]
9. F [p. 464; LO 7]
10. T [p. 466; LO 8]

Multiple Choice Questions

1. D [p. 466; LO 5]	10. C [p. 462; LO 7]	19. C [p. 469; LO 8]
2. A [p. 447; LO 4]	11. A [p. 464; LO 7]	20. A [p. 471; LO 9]
3. B [p. 449; LO 4]	12. C [p. 442; LO 2]	21. A [p. 472; LO 9]
4. C [p. 440; LO 1]	13. A [p. 465; LO 7]	22. C [p. 473; LO 9]
5. D [p. 442; LO 3]	14. B [p. 466; LO 8]	23. D [p. 474; LO 9]
6. D [p. 452; LO 5]	15. D [p. 466; LO 8]	24. A [p. 475; LO 9]
7. A [p. 454; LO 5]	16. C [p. 468; LO 8]	25. D [p. 476; LO 10]
8. B [p. 455-456; LO 5]	17. D [p. 469; LO 6 & 8]	
9. C [p. 462; LO 7]	18. C [p. 459; LO 6]	

Short-Answer Questions

Can you write a brief answer to these questions?

1. What is a paraphilia? [p. 469; LO 8]

   A paraphilia is a sexual disorder in which a person experiences sexual arousal in response to an unusual object, situation, or nonconsenting person. These include voyeurism, exhibitionism, fetishism, transvestism, pedophilia, sexual sadism, and sexual masochism.

2. Explain how gender-role behavior develops in children. [p. 442; LO 2 & 3]

   Gender role behavior develops through the interplay of genetic (nature) and environmental (nurture) influences. Hormones and genes exert a good deal of influence on some gender-related traits (e.g., aggressiveness). But environmental factors like parents, teachers, peers, and society and culture are also very important influences. According to gender-schema theory, young children are keen observers of the world around them, who develop gender through processes like social learning and operant conditioning. By watching what men and women behave like, children begin to model gender-appropriate behaviors. This learning is further enhanced when they are rewarded by others for behaving in gender-appropriate ways and punished for behaving in gender-inappropriate ways.

3. What is sexual orientation? [p. 457; LO 6]

Your sexual orientation is determined by whom you feel sexually attracted to. Heterosexuals are attracted to members of the other sex; homosexuals to members of their own sex; and bisexuals to members of both sexes. However, heterosexuality and homosexuality more often represent endpoints on a broad spectrum of behaviors identified as a continuum of sexual orientation. Moreover, sexual orientation may change over time, with women reporting greater change in orientation than men

4. Describe what we know about sexuality in youth and older adults. [p. 455-456; LO 5]

Even as infants, we have the capacity for sexual response, but the experience of sexual play in childhood is very different from the sexuality we later show as adults. At puberty, we undergo major physical changes that ready us for reproduction.

One of these changes is a heightened sex drive. As a result of this increased interest in sex, masturbation increases during adolescence—especially for males. By the time children are in high school, 50% of them report being sexually active, and those who are not are likely to be engaged in sexual experimentation like kissing and petting. By age 18, only 40% of teenagers are still virgins.

Sex is not just for the young, however. By the time people are senior citizens, interest in sex remains an important part of life. The overwhelming majority of people are still sexually active in their 60s and beyond. In fact, many report more sexual satisfaction than they did in their 40s. The biggest obstacle to senior sex appears to be a lack of partners and social stigma—such as nursing homes that segregate males and females and discourage sexual contact.

5. What are the three classes of sexually transmitted infections? Give an example of each. [p. 477-479; LO 10]

The three classes are bacterial (Chlamydia), viral (HIV), and parasitic (pubic lice).

6. How have attitudes towards homosexuality changed over the years in the U.S.? [p. 458; LO 6]

In the U.S., attitudes towards homosexuality have become somewhat more positive over the last several decades, but homophobia is still a serious problem. Most states refuse to recognize gay marriage and gay rights, and most homosexual youths report having experienced at least some form of harassment or discrimination. Interestingly, historical studies show that among Native

American Indian tribes, many freely accepted homosexuality as a variation of adult sexuality.

Developing a Bigger Picture: Making Connections Across Chapters

1. Using what you've learned about operant conditioning in Chapter 5 and gender development in this chapter, give some examples of how you have seen parents use operant conditioning to foster gender development in their children. [p. 211; 443; LO-Big Picture]

   There are many possible examples here. Correct answers will show how parents reward what they perceive to be gender-appropriate behaviors, as well as how they punish what they perceive to be gender-inappropriate behaviors. For example, a father may be visibly pleased when his daughter bakes her first batch of cookies. Or a mother may scold her son for crying after an argument with a peer.

2. Given what you learned in Chapter 8 and this chapter, what do eating behavior and sexuality have in common? [p. 342-346; 461-463; LO-Big Picture]

   Both are motivated behaviors or drives that are heavily influenced by both nature (biology) and the environment (nurture). On the biology side, both are influenced by the action of the hypothalamus and the secretion of hormones. On the environmental side, both are influenced by perception, thoughts, and the society in which we live.

3. Some psychologists have applied the concept of a script (Chapter 6) to the area of human sexuality. A sexual script is a schema that you have for how sexual relationships are supposed to unfold between two people. Think about your particular scripts. What factors influenced you as you developed your scripts? [p. 257; LO-Big Picture]

   The specific answers to this question will be very individual. However, in general our scripts are influenced by our culture, our firsthand experiences with sex, media influences, historical context, religious values, parental influences, peer influences, sexual orientation and other individual differences, and so on.

4. In the text, a study is reported that showed that scents, like pumpkin pie and licorice can elicit sexual arousal in people. Using everything you have learned about psychology at this point, generate a theory as to why this might be true. [p. 26; LO-Big Picture]

   There are many possible theories that can be generated to explain this, but a logical one would be that these smells have become classically conditioned stimuli that now have the power to elicit sexual arousal. For example, a male may associate the smell of pumpkin pie (NS/CS) with his former girlfriend (US) who had the power to sexually arouse him (UR) and who also used to bake pumpkin pie frequently. As a result, when he smells pumpkin pie (CS), he becomes sexually aroused (CR).

Label the Diagram [p. 463; LO 7]

Females:
1. Excitement phase
2. Plateau phase
3. Orgasm phase
4. Resolution phase

Males:
1. Excitement phase
2. Plateau phase
3. Orgasm phase
4. Refractory period
5. Resolution phase

Big Picture Review [p. 477-478; LO 10]

STI	
1.	Chlamydia
2.	Gonorrhea
3.	Syphilis
4.	Genital Herpes
5.	Genital Warts
6.	HIV/AIDS
7.	Pubic Lice
8.	Scabies

11

How Do We Understand and Interact with Others?

Learning Objectives

After studying each of the following sections of the chapter, you should be able to do these tasks:

Attitudes and Attitude Change

1. Describe attitudes, how they develop, and how they affect behavior.
2. Describe dissonance theory and explain the role of dissonance in attitude change.
3. Describe the major theories of persuasion and how the communicator, the message, and the audience affect persuasion.

How We Form Impressions of Others

4. Describe how we form impressions about ourselves and others and explain the attribution process.

Prejudice: How It Occurs, and How to Reduce It

5. Define and distinguish among prejudice, stereotypes, and discrimination, and explain how prejudice develops.

The Nature of Attraction

6. Discuss the factors affecting attraction: exposure, proximity, similarity, balance, and physical attractiveness.

Groups and Group Influence

7. Describe the factors that affect out tendency to conform to the norms of a group, and how this affects group decision making.

Requests and Demands: Compliance and Obedience

8. Describe the differences between obedience and compliance, and describe commonly used compliance techniques.

Aggression

9. Describe the factors that affect the tendency to behave aggressively.

Helping Behavior: Will You Or Won't You?

10. Describe helping behavior, and the factors that influence helping, including the bystander effect.

The Big Picture

The Big Picture: What Does It Mean To Be A Social Animal?

In this chapter you learned about social psychology or the study of how we understand and relate to others in our social world. The opening case of Luis Rodriguez highlighted the important influence that social groups can exert on our behavior. At times, Luis was influenced to engage in criminal behavior, but he was also influenced to engage in prosocial behavior by his teachers and his peers. We may not be influenced to engage in the same extremes of behavior as Luis, but we are influenced by others. Yet, we are often unaware of the effect that others have on both our behavior and our attitudes about the world.

Attitudes and Attitude Change

This section covers Learning Objectives 1-3. We acquire attitudes, or evaluative beliefs, about the world through the processes of classical conditioning, operant conditioning, and social learning. Once in place, these attitudes can direct our behavior towards the people and things we encounter in the world. For example, a dislike for a certain type of food may lead you to avoid eating that food. Or a liking for a certain person may motivate you to spend time with him or her. In general, specific attitudes tend to predict behavior better than general ones.

Throughout your lifetime, some of your attitudes will change. One of the processes that may drive such change is dissonance. The desire for cognitive consistency, or a match between your attitudes and your behavior and/or a match among your attitudes and beliefs, is at the heart of dissonance theory. When we discover that we have an inconsistency among our attitudes (or when our behavior is inconsistent with our attitudes), we feel dissonance — an unpleasant internal state that motivates us to remove the inconsistency.

Persuasion is another process that may lead you to change your attitudes. In persuasion, someone makes a concerted effort to change one or more of your attitudes by presenting you with persuasive messages. Such persuasive attempts may come from friends, the media, politicians, and so on. When you are processing persuasive messages, you may process them on the central route in a careful, systematic way. Or, you may process them on the peripheral route in a heuristic way. Whether you process arguments centrally or peripherally, there are a host of variables associated with the communicators, the message, or the audience that impact the likelihood that you will be persuaded.

How We Form Impressions of Others

This section covers Learning Objective 4. Attribution is a process that will affect the attitudes or impressions you form about other people. In attribution, you assign a cause to a behavior. For example, if you see someone trip, you must decide why he or she tripped. There are two types of attributions you can make: a trait attribution or a situational attribution. Because we often have to make attributions very quickly in the social world, we often use heuristics or shortcuts when doing so. These heuristics can lead to errors and biases in attribution. Some of the more important errors and biases include the fundamental attribution error, actor-observer bias, and self-serving bias.

Prejudice: How It Occurs, and How to Reduce It

This section covers Learning Objective 5. As we form impressions about people, we place this information in schemata. Schemata for groups of people are called stereotypes, and a prejudice is a negatively biased stereotype that is over-applied to individual people. A prejudiced person does not judge others based on their individual characteristics, but rather makes judgments about them based on their group membership. Prejudices are in part learned through the same processes as attitudes, but prejudices also result from in-group bias, the out-group homogeneity effect, and competition for scarce resources – known as the realistic-conflict theory of prejudice. The famous Robber's Cave experiment showed us just how easily prejudices can develop. It also showed us that co-operative contact, such as having superordinate goals, is better than mere contact in reducing prejudice.

The Nature of Attraction

This section covers Learning Objective 6. Prejudice, of course, shows the darker side of human nature. On the positive side, social psychologists also study the factors that attract us to both friends and lovers in the social world. Some of the factors that attract us to romantic partners are proximity (the mere exposure effect), similarity of attitudes and other characteristics (balance theory), and physical attractiveness (more important to males, but not unimportant to females as well).

Groups and Group Influence

This section covers Learning Objective 7. Much of our social lives are spent as members of groups. We join groups for many reasons such as: fulfilling social needs, security, social identity, to gain information, and to help us achieve goals. And once we are members of cohesive groups, they can influence us to conform to their norms or expectations for behavior. Solomon Asch's famous experiment showed us that most people are quite willing to conform at least part of the time, and Luis Rodriguez's story showed us that sometimes the cost of not conforming can be quite high.

There are several reasons why we conform. In normative conformity, we conform to avoid dissent in the group. In informational conformity, we conform because the group actually persuades us that it is the right thing to do. In either case, conformity often helps maintain social order, but it can also give rise to problematic behavior, such as that seen in the Stanford Prison Experiment.

Conformity is also one of the factors that lead to poor decision-making in groups. When groups operate under conditions of isolation, high cohesiveness, stress, and strong leadership, groupthink can occur. Groupthink leads to very poor decisions in part because individuals conform too easily and do not voice dissenting opinions during the decision making process.

Requests and Demands: Compliance and Obedience

This section covers Learning Objective 8. Compliance and obedience are two more ways that we can be influenced by others. In compliance, we are asked to give in to a simple request. Requests for compliance are daily occurrences, coming from friends, family, telemarketers, salespeople, and so on. Skilled manipulators know that techniques like foot-in-the-door and door-in-the-face increase their chances of getting you to comply.

Obedience is different from compliance in that in obedience, you are asked to yield to a demand. Under some circumstances, obedience can be destructive, as was the case in Nazis Germany. Researcher Stanley Milgram was inspired by the Holocaust to study more carefully the process of destructive obedience. In his famous study, Milgram showed that the average person would obey a demand to deliver a 450-volt shock to another human being. Some of the factors that make us more likely to obey are the presence of a perceived authority figure, the slippery slope (foot-in-the-door compliance), and psychological distance (not having to come to terms with how your actions are affecting others).

Aggression

This section covers Learning Objective 9. Milgram's experiment showed us that the average person will obey—even if it means hurting someone else. Unfortunately, aggression is part of the social world. Instrumental aggression is goal-directed aggression, whereas hostile aggression is motivated solely by the desire to hurt others. Individual differences in aggressiveness have been related to levels of testosterone and serotonin in the body. Childhood abuse, televised violence, and learning may also contribute to one's tendency to be aggressive in adulthood.

Helping Behavior: Will You Or Won't You?

This section covers Learning Objective 10. Despite the fact that humans do have the capacity to hurt others, we also have the capacity for altruism—or a willingness to help others without considering how it will benefit us. There are numerous examples of people who have risked their own well being to help complete strangers in need. When we do fail to help others, often it is not out of apathy or a lack of concern for others, but rather stems from cognitive processes like the bystander effect (diffusion of responsibility) and pluralistic ignorance.

Outlining the Big Picture

Chapter 11: How Do We Understand and Interact with Others?

The Big Picture: What Does It Mean To Be A Social Animal?
Luis J. Rodriguez's *Always Running: One man's life in L.A. Street Gangs*
Notes:

_____

_____

_____

_____

_____

Attitudes and Attitude Change (Learning Objectives 1-3)
Classical Conditioning of Attitudes
Operant Conditioning of Attitudes
Social Learning or Modeling of Attitudes
The Link Between Attitudes and Behavior
Cognitive Consistency and Attitude Change
Persuasion and Attitude Change
Notes:

_____

_____

_____

_____

_____

How We Form Impressions of Others (Learning Objective 4)
The Attribution Process
Heuristics and Biases in Attribution

The Fundamental Attribution Error
The Actor/Observer Bias
Self-Serving Bias
Notes:

_____

_____

_____

_____

_____

Prejudice: How It Occurs, and How to Reduce It (Learning Objective 5)

Prejudice and Stereotypes
  Spotlight on Diversity: Stereotype Threat: How Prejudice Affects Female and African American Performance
Social Transmission of Prejudice
Intergroup Dynamics and Prejudice
  In-Group Bias: Us vs. Them
  Intergroup Conflict and Prejudice: It's Their Fault
Does Social Contact Reduce Prejudice?
Notes:

_____

_____

_____

_____

_____

The Nature of Attraction (Learning Objective 6)

Proximity
Similarity
Physical Attractiveness

Notes:

_____

_____

_____

_____

_____

Groups and Group Influence (Learning Objective 7)
Social Forces within Groups: Norms and Cohesiveness
Conformity within a Group
    Resisting Conformity
    Explaining Conformity
    The Dark Side of Conformity: The Stanford Prison Experiment
Decision-Making in Groups
Notes:

_____

_____

_____

_____

_____

Requests and Demands: Compliance and Obedience (Learning Objective 8)
Compliance Techniques
    Foot-in-the-door Compliance
    Door-in-the-face Compliance
Obedience
Factors That Affect Obedience
Notes:

_____

_____

_____

_____

_____

_____

_____

Aggression (Learning Objective 9)
Biological Theories of Aggression: The Role of Sex Hormones,
    Neurotransmitters, and Brain Damage
    A Possible Role for Serotonin
    Childhood Abuse and Aggression
Learning Theories of Aggression
Violence and Television
Situations That Promote Aggressive Behavior
Notes:

_____

_____

_____

_____

_____

Helping Behavior: Will You Or Won't You? (Learning Objective 10)
The Murder of Kitty Genovese
The Bystander Effect
    Explaining the Bystander Effect
    A New Twist on the Bystander Effect: Taking Care of Our Own
When People Choose to Help
Notes:

_____

_____

_____

_____

Are You Getting the Big Picture?
Notes:

Seeing the Big Picture: A Mental Map of Chapter 11

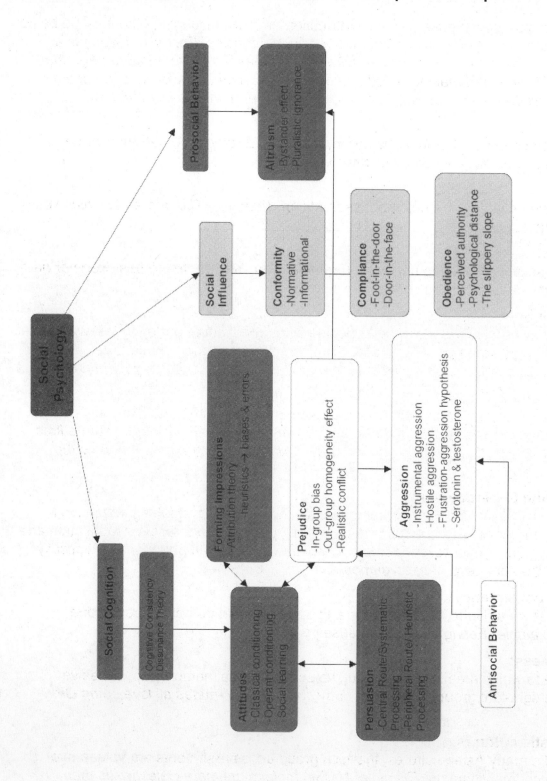

Key Points of the Big Picture

Actor-observer bias:
our tendency to make the fundamental attribution error when judging others, while being less likely to do so when making attributions about ourselves. *Example: If you fail an exam, you will examine the possible environmental reasons for your failure (e.g., the test was difficult) when making an attribution for your failure. However, if you see a classmate fail the exam, you will likely just assume that he/she is incompetent.*

Altruism:
helping another without being motivated by self-gain. *Example: A man runs into a burning building to save a complete stranger.*

Attitude:
an evaluative belief that we hold about something. *Example: The degree to which you like or dislike sushi.*

Attribution:
the act of assigning cause to behavior. *Example: You see your friend has dyed her hair orange—why did she do this?*

Balance theory:
a theory that when we are attracted to people who do not share our attitudes, we feel dissonance, which motivates us to change in some way so as to reduce this dissonance. *Example: Your significant other is likely to share many of your attitudes.*

Bystander effect:
the idea that the more witnesses there are to an emergency, the less likely any one of them is to offer help. *Example: If three people see you have an accident, you are less likely to get help from them than you would be if only one person saw you have the accident.*

Central route to persuasion:
a style of thinking in which the person carefully and critically evaluates persuasive arguments and generates counter arguments. The central route requires motivation and available cognitive resources. *Example: Carefully listening to a politician and critically evaluating the goodness of his arguments.*

Cognitive consistency:
the idea that we strive to have attitudes and behaviors that do not contradict one another. *Example: Eating spinach because you like it.*

Cohesiveness:
the degree to which members of a group value their group membership; cohesive groups are tight-knit groups. *Example: Judy and her troop-mates all love being Girl Scouts.*

Collectivistic cultures:
cultures, like many Asian cultures, in which group accomplishments are valued over individual accomplishments. *Example: Navajo Indians are more collectivistic than mainstream U.S. culture is.*

Compliance:
yielding to a simple request. *Example: Giving your friend a ride to school when she asks for one.*

Conformity:
behaving in accordance with group norms. *Example: Wearing stylish clothes to school.*

Contact hypothesis:
a theory that states that contact among groups is an effective means of reducing prejudice between them. *Example: Working with members of other groups may reduce your level of prejudice towards those groups of people.*

Debriefing:
.after an experiment, participants are fully informed of the nature of the study. *Example: After you participate in an experiment, the researcher tells you that the purpose of the experiment was to examine how well you know yourself and how this relates to your level of motivation to achieve academic success.*

Deindividuation:
a state in which a person's behavior becomes controlled more by external norms than by the person's own internal values and morals. *Example: While at a rock concert, you may jump up and down and scream with the crowd even if you are a shy, inhibited person by nature.*

Destructive obedience:
obedience to immoral, unethical demands that cause harm to others. *Example: A boy vandalizes a business because some older kids told him to do so.*

Diffusion of responsibility:
the idea that the responsibility for taking action is diffused across all people witnessing an event. *Example: If you are one of many people witnessing a fight, you are only partially responsible for doing something about it.*

Discrimination:
the behavioral expression of a prejudice. *Example: Wilma refuses to hire Mike to be a librarian because she thinks men do not make good librarians.*

Dissonance theory:
a theory that predicts that we will be motivated to change our attitudes and/or our behaviors to the extent that they cause us to feel dissonance. *Example: Toren's realization that his drinking behavior is inconsistent with his desire to be a successful man will produce dissonance that will hopefully motivate him to be more responsible about his drinking.*

Door-in-the-face:
increasing compliance by first asking the person to give in to a very larger request and after their refusal, asking them to give in to a smaller request. *Example: Asking your roommate to borrow her car for a week before asking her to loan you a dollar.*

Foot-in-the-door:
increasing compliance by first asking the person to give in to a smaller request that paves the way for further compliance. *Example: Asking your roommate to borrow her car for a week after she loaned you the car for an evening last month.*

Frustration-aggression hypothesis:
the idea that frustration causes aggressive behavior. *Example: After being frustrated by heavy traffic, you find yourself angry at the world.*

Fundamental attribution error:
our tendency to over use trait information when making attributions about others. *Example: Watching your favorite actor on TV, you assume that he has personality characteristics that are similar to that of the character he plays.*

Groupthink:
a situation in which a group fixates on one decision, and members blindly assume that it is the correct decision. *Example: A group of officials at a company meeting behind closed doors, cut off from outside feedback, may make a poorer decision than they would if they had some external input.*

Helping behavior:
another term for altruism. *Example: You help a lost tourist find the airport.*

Hostile aggression:
aggression that is meant to cause harm to others. *Example: Sandra hits another child just to see her cry.*

Impression Formation:
the way that we understand and make judgments about others. *Example: Jose wears his best suit to a job interview so as to make a good first impression on the interviewer.*

Individualistic cultures:
a culture, like many Western cultures, in which individual accomplishments are valued over group accomplishments. *Example: In the U.S., a car salesperson is promoted based on his or her own individual sales record.*

Informational conformity:
conformity that occurs when conformity pressures actually persuade group members to adopt new beliefs and/or attitudes. *Example: After hearing all of your friends rave about a movie you did not like, you begin to think that maybe they are correct—the movie was better than you originally thought.*

In-group bias:
our tendency to favor people who belong to the same groups that we do. *Example: A man assumes that men are a little bit superior to women.*

Instrumental aggression:
aggression used to facilitate the attainment of one's goals. *Example: A mugger hits another man in the face so that he can steal the man's wallet.*

Matching hypothesis:
the theory that we are attracted to people whose level of physical attractiveness is similar to our own. *Example: Your partner is likely to be about as physically attractive as you are.*

Norm:
an unwritten rule or expectations for how group members should behave. *Example: The expectation that you will sit facing forward in your desk during class.*

Normative conformity:
conformity that occurs when group members change their behavior to meet group norms, but are not persuaded to change their beliefs and attitudes. *Example: Saying that you like a new song on the radio that your friends are raving about, even though you really don't like the song.*

Obedience:
yielding to a demand. *Example: Stopping when a police officer tells you to do so.*

Out-group homogeneity bias:
our tendency to see out-group members as being pretty much all-alike. *Example: A woman thinking that all men behave as her boyfriend does.*

Peripheral route to persuasion:
a style of thinking in which the person does not carefully and critically evaluate persuasive arguments or generate counter arguments; the peripheral route ensues when one lacks motivation and/or available cognitive resources. *Example: When watching TV, you are not really paying much attention to the advertisements. As a result, you do not attempt to generate many counterarguments to the ads' claims.*

Persuasion:
a type of social influence in which someone tries to change our attitudes. *Example: A politician attempts to persuade you that her political policies are the best ones.*

Pluralistic ignorance:
the idea that we use the behavior of others to help us determine whether a situation is really an emergency requiring our help; if no one else is helping, we may conclude that help isn't needed. *Example: When the fire alarm goes off in the mall, everyone looks at each other to see how they are reacting. Seeing that no one is heading for the door, everyone assumes it is a false alarm.*

Prejudice:
a largely negative stereotype that is unfairly applied to all members of a group regardless of their individual characteristics. *Example: Joanna doesn't like people from France. When asked if she would like to meet a Jean, a new French exchange student, she declines because she assumes he will be aloof and boorish.*

Proximity:
geographical closeness. *Example: How close you sit to another person in the classroom.*

Psychological distance:
the degree to which one can disassociate oneself from the consequences of his/her actions. *Example: A teenager spreading vicious rumors about a classmate on MySpace may be able to avoid thinking about the pain they are causing the classmate with his/her actions.*

Realistic-Conflict Theory:
the theory that prejudice stems from competition for scarce resources. *Example: If unemployment rates skyrocket in your town, you could expect to see higher rates of prejudice among different groups of people in town as well.*

Reciprocity:
a strong norm that states that we should treat others as they treat us. *Example: Your friend helps you move into a new apartment. Later when he asks to borrow your car, you let him have the keys.*

Self-serving bias:
our tendency to make attributions that preserve our own self-esteem; for example, making trait attributions for our success and situational attributions for our failures. *Example: You attribute the overall success of your group project to your expert contribution, but you also attribute arguments with group members to their difficult personalities.*

Situational attribution:
an attribution that assigns the cause of the behavior to some characteristic of the situation or environment in which a behavior occurs. *Example: You attribute the fact that your friend is in a bad mood today to the fact that he is having a stressful day.*

Slippery slope:
the use of foot-in-the-door compliance in an obedience situation to get people to obey increasing demands. *Example: Your friends ask you to go out with them, and you do. They ask you to loan them some money for beer, and you do. They ask you to sneak into the movies without paying, and you do. And, so on.*

Social cognition:
the area of social psychology that deals with the ways in which we think about other people and ourselves. *Example: A social cognitive psychologist might study how people construct a schema that represents their own self-concept.*

Social influence:
pressures placed on us by others to change our behavior and/or our beliefs. *Example: You might agree to go eat pizza with your friends, even though you know you should stay home and study for your exams.*

Social psychology:
the branch of psychology that studies how we think and behave in social situations. *Example: A social psychologist might study how people work together in groups.*

Stereotype:
a schema for a particular group of people. *Example: Believing that nurses are compassionate, intelligent, assertive, and responsible.*

Superordinate goal:

a goal that is shared by different groups. *Example: All the students on campus may rally together to help plant flowers on campus.*

Trait attribution:

an attribution that assigns the cause of the behavior to the traits and characteristics of the person being judged. *Example: Deciding that you work in a restaurant because you like working with people.*

Fill-in Review of the Chapter

Can you fill-in the missing terms for each section of the chapter? Items marked with an * encourage you to continue building the Big Picture of psychology by connecting the material in this chapter to material from previous chapters in the text.

The Big Picture: What Does It Mean To Be A Social Animal?

The gang that Luis Rodriguez belonged to is an example of a(n) 1) _____.

Some people treated Luis differently because he is Latino. This is an example of 2) _____.

Attitudes and Attitude Change

A(n) 3) _____ is an evaluative, sometimes emotionally charged belief about people, places, or things.

The emotional and physiological aspects of attitudes most likely develop through 4*) _____ _____.

Humans tend to desire 5) _____ _____ among their attitudes, beliefs, and behaviors.

Noticing that you have just behaved in a manner that contradicts one of your attitudes is likely to produce feelings of 6) _____.

If a person critically evaluates the persuasive arguments she is hearing and generates counter-arguments, she is processing on the 7) _____ route.

When people are in a good mood, they tend to process persuasive arguments on the 8) _____ route.

How We Form Impressions of Others

In 9) _____ _____, we understand and make judgments about others.

If you attribute John's smiling to the fact that he is a happy person, you've made a(n) 10) _____ _____.

If you attribute John's smiling behavior to the fact that he just heard a funny joke, you've made a(n) 11) _____ _____.

Prejudice: How It Occurs, and How To Reduce It

Muzafer Sherif studied the formation of prejudice in young boys in the famous 12) _____ _____ study.

13) _____ is the behavioral expression of a prejudice.

When we exhibit more liking for people from our own group, this is referred to as the 14) _____bias.

We tend to think that out-group members are more alike than people in our in-group are. This is called the 15) _____ _____ bias.

16) _____ goals are very helpful for reducing prejudice.

17*) _____ allow us to assimilate in social situations, in that they allow us to quickly perceive others and make judgments about them.

The Nature of Attraction

The 18) _____ hypothesis predicts that we will end up with a romantic partner that is of about the same level of attractiveness as we are.

The geographic closeness or 19) _____ of another predicts our chance of entering into an interpersonal relationship with that person.

When choosing a mate, we tend to choose people who are 20) _____ to us.

Groups and Group Influence

When we change our behavior to meet the expectations of the group to which we belong, we are engaging in 21) _____.

22) _____ are the unwritten rules that guide behavior in a group.

Conformity that also results in persuasion is known as 23) _____ conformity.

Mike says that he loved the movie his friends are raving about, even though he didn't. Mike's behavior is an example of 24) _____ conformity.

Requests and Demands: Compliance and Obedience

Asking your roommate for a $100 loan (which he/she refuses) before asking for a $5 loan is an example of 25) _____ compliance.

You donated $50 last year to a charity. This year, they ask you to donate $100. It appears that they are trying to use 26) _____ compliance on you.

Stanley Milgram found that approximately 27) _____% of participants were willing to shock the learner at the maximum shock level of 28) _____ volts.

Aggression

Theodore hits his little sister so that he can take away the toy she has been playing with. Theodore is engaging in 29) _____ aggression.

Aggression that is aimed at hurting others is known as 30) _____ aggression.

Aggression is related to high levels of the hormone 31*) _____.

Aggression is related to low levels of the neurotransmitter 32*) _____.

Helping Behavior: Will You Or Won't You?

According to Darley and Latane, the first step to helping someone is that you must first 33) _____ that something is out of the ordinary.

Use It or Lose It!

Can you fill in the following table with the concepts that are demonstrated by these examples?

Concept	Example
1.	Jimena automatically assumes that her favorite musician must be a nice person because she saw a picture of him wearing a t-shirt advertising a charity organization.
2.	Han blames his low test score on his professor, without taking into consideration that he didn't study for the exam.
3.	Melissa is a shy person. Nonetheless, she found herself caught up in the excitement of the Mardi Gras crowd and ended up mooning the crowd.
4.	Cultures like those found in Japan and among the Navajo Indians.
5.	The idea that prejudice occurs when two groups of people compete for scarce resources like the Eagles and Rattlers did when they competed in sporting events.

6.	Kelly loves Rachel. Rachel loves hockey. Kelly hates hockey. Kelly feels dissonance and begins to love Rachel less.
7.	The Girl Scouts of Troop 774 all love being Girl Scouts and are very loyal to the troop.
8.	Dr. Lowe is careful to explain the true purpose of his experiment to his participants after their participation is ended.
9.	Even though he's late for work, Leon stops to help a stranded motorist change a tire.
10.	Foot-in-the-door compliance can be likened to this.

Self-Check: Are You Getting the Big Picture?

After you have read and studied the chapter, see if you can answer the following quiz questions. Check your answers at the end of the chapter. If you miss a question, refer to your text and re-study the appropriate sections.

True or False Questions

Are these statements true or false?

1. Knowing a person's attitudes allows you to know how he or she will behave.
   Choice T: True
   Choice F: False

2. In general, people with moderate self-esteem are easiest to persuade.
   Choice T: True
   Choice F: False

3. The actor-observer effect seems to occur in part because we as less able to examine the potential situational causes of our own behavior.
   Choice T: True
   Choice F: False

4. Discrimination is the behavioral expression of a prejudice.
   Choice T: True
   Choice F: False

5. Stereotype can be thought of as the emotional or affective component of an attitude.
   Choice T: True
   Choice F: False

6. Studies show that children's attitudes and values most closely match those of their parents when the parents hold prejudicial beliefs.
   Choice T: True
   Choice F: False

7. Physical attractiveness in a romantic partner is important to both men and women.
   Choice T: True
   Choice F: False

8. Group memberships can give us social identity, security, achievement of goals, fulfill social needs, and provide us with information.
   Choice T: True
   Choice F: False

9. Wearing blue jeans to class (as opposed to wearing a prom dress) is an example of conformity.
   Choice T: True
   Choice F: False

10. Increased cohesiveness within a group works to reduce conformity to the group's norms.
    Choice T: True
    Choice F: False

Multiple Choice Questions

Can you choose the best answer for these questions?

1. The other day at work, Renita was yelled at by a male customer who was wearing a football jersey. Now when Renita sees a man wearing a football jersey, she instantly feels a bit angry at him. Which of the following learning processes best explains why Renita would feel anger for a man she doesn't even know?
   A. operant conditioning
   B. classical conditioning
   C. social learning
   D. habituation

2. Janson ate linguini for the first time last week. Unfortunately, the linguini was spoiled and Janson became ill after eating it. As a result, Janson has vowed to avoid linguini in the future. Which of the following learning processes best explains Janson's behavior of avoiding linguini in the future?
   A. operant conditioning
   B. classical conditioning
   C. social learning
   D. habituation

3. Bobby was raised by parents who were lifelong Democrats. Although his parents never spoke to him about their political beliefs, Bobby grew up watching his parents vote for Democratic candidates and attend Democratic rallies. In preparing to vote for the first time, Bobby registers as a Democrat. Which of the following learning principles best explains why Bobby would hold positive attitudes toward the Democratic party?
    A. operant conditioning
    B. classical conditioning
    C. social learning
    D. habituation

4. Lynn really likes a certain politician because he supports environmental causes and Lynn believes in protecting the earth. However, she has just learned that this politician owns large amounts of stock in an oil company that has been accused of violating environmental protection laws while drilling in a national forest. How is this news likely to affect Lynn?
    A. She will begin to like the politician less.
    B. She will begin to like the politician more.
    C. She will become even more pro-environment.
    D. None of the above

5. Which of the following people is most likely to be processing on the central route to persuasion?
    A. Sally, who is watching a television commercial while doing her calculus homework at the same time.
    B. Herb, who is watching a television commercial about a product he has no interest in.
    C. Phyllis, who is not really paying attention to a television commercial.
    D. Walker, who is watching a television ad about a car he is thinking about buying.

6. Most television commercials are designed to work on people who are processing:
    A. on the central route.
    B. systematically.
    C. on the peripheral route.
    D. critically.

7. Which of the following variables would have its largest impact on people who are processing on the central route?
    A. the attractiveness of the communicator
    B. the length of the arguments
    C. the logic of the arguments
    D. whether or not the communicator looks like she knows what she is talking about

8. Who is most likely to be persuaded by complex, valid arguments?
   A. people low in IQ
   B. people moderate in IQ
   C. people high in IQ
   D. All of the above people would be equally likely to be persuaded.

9. The process of assigning a cause to behavior is called:
   E. attribution.
   F. impression management.
   G. persuasion.
   H. stereotyping.

9. While having lunch, you see a man yelling at his wife in the next booth. According to social cognitive theory, you are most likely to make which type of attribution?
   A. a situational attribution
   B. a trait attribution
   C. a correct attribution
   D. an incorrect attribution

10. Our tendency to over rely on trait information when making attributions is called the:
    A. self-serving bias.
    B. actor-observer bias.
    C. fundamental attribution error.
    D. personalism bias.

11. Which of the following people is least likely to jump to the conclusion that Jason tripped because he is clumsy?
    A. Kerry, who is from Canada
    B. Julie, who is from France
    C. Bridgett, who is from Denmark
    D. Li, who is from Korea

12. Heuristics have what benefit when we use them during the attribution process?
    A. They lead to quick attributions.
    B. They allow us time to carefully weigh our options before making an attribution.
    C. They are very accurate.
    D. They are less emotional.

13. Lana believes that all Italian men belong to the mafia. As such, she refuses to hire Italians to work in her restaurant. Lana is exhibiting:
    A. prejudice.
    B. discrimination.
    C. egalitarianism.
    D. A & B

14. Ramon, a Latino, is interviewing for a job at a local business where the interviewer is White. Because Ramon believes that the man is likely to hold negative views about Latinos, he is very nervous and makes several silly mistakes during the interview. Ramon is likely suffering from:
    A. reverse discrimination.
    B. prejudice.
    C. stereotype threat.
    D. tokenism.

15. Which of the following statements is false?
    A. We tend to favor people in our in-group over out-group members.
    B. Compared to our in-group members, we tend to see out-group members as being more similar to each other.
    C. Compared to out-group members, we tend to see more variability in our own in-group.
    D. Compared to out-group members, we tend to see less variability in our in-group.

16. According to realistic-conflict theory, what should happen during an economic recession?
    A. Prejudice should decrease.
    B. Prejudice should stay the same.
    C. Prejudice should increase.
    D. Prejudice should disappear.

17. We are most likely to be attracted to people with who we have a great deal of contact—a phenomenon known as the:
    A. mere exposure effect.
    B. familiarity effect.
    C. matching hypothesis.
    D. balance theory.

18. Judy loves to knit wool sweaters. Dave is allergic to wool and finds knitting boring. According to balance theory:
    A. Judy and Dave will likely fall in love.
    B. Judy will begin liking Dave less.
    C. Judy will find herself liking Dave more.
    D. Judy will force Dave to learn to knit.

19. Which of the following factors is likely to reduce conformity within a group?
    A. increased cohesiveness within the group
    B. an increase in majority group size
    C. anonymity within the group
    D. unanimity within the group

20. Saying you liked a particular movie that you did not enjoy, simply because all of your friends are raving about the movie, is an example of:
    A. informational conformity.
    B. normative conformity.
    C. compliance.
    D. obedience.

21. Which of the following is an example of compliance?
    A. wearing blue jeans to class
    B. giving a dollar to a person collecting for a charity
    C. stopping when a police officer pulls you over for a traffic violation
    D. deciding that a political candidate is the best choice for president after watching the presidential debates on TV

22. Stanley Milgram found that what percentage of his subjects were willing to give a 450 volt shock to the learner?
    A. 15%
    B. 35%
    C. 65%
    D. 90%

23. The slippery slope that increased obedience in Milgram's famous study is an example of:
    A. foot-in-the-door compliance.
    B. door-in-the-face compliance.
    C. reciprocity.
    D. perceptual contrast.

24. Which of the following have been shown to correlate with increased aggression?
    A. low serotonin levels
    B. brain damage
    C. watching violent TV
    D. all of the above

Short-Answer Questions

Can you write a brief answer to these questions?

1. How are prejudices different from stereotypes?

2. Why don't most television advertisements make a logical argument for the product they advertise?

3. Why did the witnesses fail to help Kitty Genovese the night she was murdered?

4. Give an example of a time where someone has used a compliance technique on you.

5. Describe a situation where groupthink is likely to occur.

Developing a Bigger Picture: Making Connections Across Chapters

An important aspect of learning is learning to see the "Big Picture" of the subject you are studying. As you learn about psychology, you should try to understand how the material from different chapters fits together to help you form a broad-based understanding of what psychology is all about. To help facilitate the development of this "Big Picture" in your mind, try to answer these questions using the knowledge you have learned in this chapter, as well as the other chapters referenced in the questions.

1. Based on what you learned about perception in Chapter 3 and memory in Chapter 6, how might prejudice affect a person's eyewitness memory for a robbery?

2. Use what you learned in Chapters 5, 9 and this chapter to explain why many people end up in romantic relationships with people who are similar in character to their opposite-sex parent.

3. Using what you learned about learning in Chapter 5, design a program to reduce aggression and increase altruism at a troubled high school.

Label the Diagram

Can you label the different social influence or social cognitive processes that match these descriptions?

Type of Social Influence or Social Cognitive Process	Description
1)	Giving in to a simple request or behavior
2)	Changing your attitudes after hearing arguments as to why you should change your mind
3)	Giving in to a demand for behavior

4)	Changing your behavior to meet the norms of a group.
5)	Changing your attitudes after realizing that your attitudes were in conflict with your behavior

Big Picture Review

Can you explain what type of an effect these variables have on conformity to group norms?

Factor	Effect on Conformity
Majority group size	1.
Unanimity of the group	2.
Anonymity	3.
Cohesiveness of the group	4.
Self-esteem	5.
Gender	6.
Knowledge/confidence about the issue at hand	7.
Tendency to feel anxious in social situations	8.

The need to be individuated, or individualistic and nonconforming	9.

Solutions

Each solution below is followed by its textbook page reference number and its corresponding chapter learning objective (LO) number. Items with a Big Picture LO help you build a Big Picture of psychology across the chapters you have studied so far.

Fill-in Review of The Chapter

1. group [p. 510; LO 7]
2. discrimination [p. 499; LO 5]
3. attitude [p. 487; LO 1]
4. classical conditioning [p. 200; LO 1, Big Picture]
5. cognitive consistency [p. 490; LO 2]
6. dissonance [p. 490; LO 2]
7. central [p. 492; LO 3]
8. peripheral [p. 492; LO 3]
9. impression formation [p. 494; LO 4]
10. trait attribution [p. 495; LO 4]
11. situational attribution [p. 495; LO 4]
12. Robber's Cave [p. 503; LO 5]
13. Discrimination [p. 499; LO 5]
14. in-group [p. 502; LO 5]
15. out-group homogeneity [p. 503; LO 5]
16. Superordinate [p. 504; LO 5]
17. Stereotypes [p. 498; LO 5, Big Picture]
18. matching [p. 508; LO 6]
19. proximity [p. 506; LO 6]
20. similar [p. 507; LO 6]
21. conformity [p. 512; LO 7]
22. Norms [p. 511; LO 7]
23. informational [p. 515; LO 7]
24. normative [p. 513; LO 7]
25. door-in-the-face [p. 519; LO 8]
26. foot-in-the-door [p. 518; LO 8]
27. 65 [p. 521; LO 8]
28. 450 [p. 521; LO 8]
29. instrumental [p. 525; LO 9]

30. hostile [p. 525; LO 9]
31. testosterone [p. 525; LO 9]
32. serotonin [p. 526; LO 9]
33. notice [p. 529; LO 10]

Use It or Lose It!

1. fundamental attribution error [p. 496; LO 4]
2. self-serving bias [p. 497; LO 4]
3. deindividuation [p. 515; LO 4]
4. collectivistic [p. 496; LO 4]
5. realistic-conflict theory [p. 503; LO 5]
6. balance theory [p. 508; LO 2, 6]
7. cohesiveness [p. 512; LO 7]
8. debriefing [p. 524; LO 8]
9. altruism [p. 528; LO 10]
10. slippery slope [p. 523; LO 8]

Self-Check: Are You Getting the Big Picture?

True or False Questions

1. F [p. 489; LO 1]	6. F [p. 502; LO 5]
2. T [p. 493; LO 3]	7. T [p. 508; LO 6]
3. F [p. 496; LO 4]	8. T [p. 510; LO 7]
4. T [p. 499; LO 5]	9. T [p. 512; LO 7]
5. F [p. 498; LO 5]	10. F [p. 512; LO 7]

Multiple Choice Questions

1. B [p. 498; LO 1, Big Picture]	10. B [p. 495; LO 4]	19. B [p. 508; LO 6]
2. A [p. 488; LO 1, Big Picture]	11. C [p. 496; LO 4]	20. C [p. 513; LO 7]
3. C [p. 489; LO 1, Big Picture]	12. D [p. 496; LO 4]	21. B [p. 513; LO 7]
4. A [p. 491; LO 2]	13. A [p. 495; LO 4]	22. B [p. 518; LO 8]
5. D [p. 492; LO 3]	14. D [p. 498; LO 5]	23. C [p. 521; LO 8]
6. C [p. 492; LO 3]	15. C [p. 500; LO 5]	24. A [p. 523; LO 8]
7. C [p. 492; LO 3]	16. D [p. 503; LO 5]	25. D [p. 525; LO 9]
8. C [p. 493; LO 3]	17. C [p. 503; LO 5]	
9. A [p. 494; LO 4]	18. A [p. 506; LO 6]	

Short-Answer Questions

1. How are prejudices different from stereotypes? [p. 498; LO 5]

   Stereotypes are schemas for groups of people. As such, they are no different from schemas that we have for any of the concepts in our world. On the other hand, prejudices are biased, negative stereotypes that we use to form judgments about others without taking into consideration their actual traits and characteristics.

2. Why don't most television advertisements make a logical argument for the product they advertise? [p. 492; LO 3]

   Because making a logical argument would be a waste of time at best, and might even be counter-productive. This is true because most people are processing on the peripheral/indirect route while watching television. As such, viewers are unlikely to carefully evaluate the logic of the arguments they hear in a TV ad. So, even if the ad makes a good case for the product, the average viewer will never come to appreciate it. In fact, a logical, but detailed argument may completely fail as the audience will turn away, unwilling to invest the energy needed to understand the argument. What will work better in this case is an argument that is shorter, catchy, funny, memorable, and at least superficially _seems_ to argue well for the product.

3. Why did the witnesses fail to help Kitty Genovese the night she was murdered? [pp. 529-530; LO 10]

   Contrary to popular public opinion at the time, Darley & Latane found that apathy was not the reason most of the witnesses failed to come to Kitty's aid that night. What these researchers found was that diffusion of responsibility and the bystander effect helped ensure that the witnesses believed that someone else would or had already called the police for help. They also found that pluralistic ignorance caused some of the witnesses to incorrectly perceive that Kitty was in mortal danger. And, others where afraid of the price they would have to pay for getting involved.

4. Give an example of a time where someone has used a compliance technique on you? [pp. 518-520; LO 8]

There are, of course, many possibilities here. A couple of examples would be: Having a telemarketer use foot-in-the-door on you by calling and asking if you have a moment to talk before they try to sell you a magazine subscription. By agreeing to talk, you've already complied one time and are therefore more likely to buy a subscription. Or, having a friend use door-in-the-face on you when she asks if you would be willing to babysit her children for the weekend. And when you refuse, she comes back with a request for you to babysit Friday evening only.

5. Describe a situation where groupthink is likely to occur? [pp. 516-517; LO 7]

Groupthink is most likely under conditions of group isolation, group cohesiveness, strong dictatorial leadership in the group, and high stress within the group. For example, imagine that a company has received word that they are about to be sued for millions of dollars by a consumer who claims the company sold her a defective product that lead to a terrible personal injury. The company cannot go public in advance with this news for fear of losing clients and stockholders. So, management gives a taskforce twenty-four hours to find a way to counteract this threat. Due to the seriousness of the situation, a leader is appointed to the group who is known for his strong leadership. Going into their first meeting, everyone on the taskforce knows that if they fail to counteract this threat, the company may go out of business.

Developing a Bigger Picture: Making Connections Across Chapters

1. Based on what you learned about perception in Chapter 3 and memory in Chapter 6, how might prejudice affect a person's eyewitness memory for a robbery? [pp. 126-127, 270-272, & 498-506; LO 5, Big Picture]

As you learned in Chapter 6, we do not store all the details of the events we witness. Rather, we use our schemas to guide us as we fill in these missing details with our expectations of what we likely saw. Therefore, a prejudiced person might use his or her prejudice to fill in personal details of the criminal. For example, if a witness believes that criminals are from lower economic classes, the witness might remember the perpetrator as being more shabbily dressed than he or she actually was.

Prejudice can also affect how we perceive the event in the first place through top-down-perceptual processing. For example, a person who believes that most minority members are criminally-minded might misperceive a shadowy figure running from a bank as being a minority member.

2. Use what you learned in Chapters 5, 9 and this chapter to explain why many people end up in romantic relationships with people who are similar in character to their opposite-sex parent. [pp. all of Chapter 5, 378-379, 394, 415, & 507-509; LO 6, Big Picture]

   We tend to be similar in many ways to our parents because of our shared genes, shared environment, and years spent modeling our parents' behavior. We also tend to be attracted to partners who are similar to us—therefore we may end up with a partner who is like our parent simply because we are also similar to our parent.

3. Using what you learned about learning in Chapter 5, design a program to reduce aggression and increase altruism at a troubled high school. [pp. all of Chapter 5 & 525-528; LO 9, Big Picture]

   There are many possible correct answers here, but all correct answers should contain some application of classical conditioning, operant conditioning, or social learning. For example, student leaders could be recruited to address the student body and role-play or model non-aggressive ways of dealing with typical student conflicts. Posters showing students engaging in altruistic behaviors could be placed around the school as models of ideal students. Or a token economy could be instituted to reward positive behaviors and punish aggressive ones.

Label the Diagram

Type of Social Influence or Social Cognitive Process
1. Compliance [p. 518; LO 8]
2. Persuasion [p. 492; LO 3]
3. Obedience [p. 518; LO 8]
4. Conformity [p. 512; LO 7]
5. Dissonance leading to consonance [p. 490; LO 2]

Big Picture Review

1. As majority group size increases to three members, conformity increases. [p. XXX; LO 7]
2. Unanimity increases conformity. One dissenter can dramatically reduce conformity. [p. XXX; LO 7]
3. When we are anonymous, we are much less likely to conform. [p. XXX; LO 7]
4. As cohesiveness increases, so does conformity. [p. XXX; LO 7]
5. Those high in self-esteem are less likely to conform. [p. XXX; LO 7]
6. Males and females conform at equal rates, but in different situations. It appears that gender-based knowledge differences account for this discrepancy. [p. XXX; LO 7]

7. The more expert we are about the issue or task at hand, the less likely we are to conform. [p. XXX; LO 7]

8. People who tend to feel anxious in social situations are more likely to conform. [p. XXX; LO 7]

9. Those who tend to feel the need to not conform are less likely to actually conform. [p. XXX; LO 7]

12

Health, Stress and Coping: How Can You Create a Healthy Life?

Learning Objectives

After studying each of the following sections of the chapter, you should be able to do these tasks:

What Is Stress? Stress and Stressors

1. Define stress, and identify stressors and conflict situations.

The Stress Response: Is This Stress? How Do I React?

2. Discuss the concept of appraisal in the stress response.
3. Explain how the body responds to stress and how that response influences immunity to disease.

How Can I Cope With Stress?

4. Distinguish between problem-focused and emotion-focused coping styles.
5. Indicate adaptive ways to manage stress.

Personality and Health

6. Discuss the relationship between personality and health.

Lifestyle and Health

7. Identify health-defeating and health-promoting behaviors.

The Big Picture

The Big Picture: What Can Psychology Tell Us About Health?

As the big picture story of Edward Pastorino illustrated, our health is a very important determinant of our quality of life. As such, it's worth protecting. How healthy you are is a function of several factors: genetics, personality traits, stress, coping skills, and your own behavior.

What Is Stress? Stress and Stressors

This section covers Learning Objective 1. Stress is your psychological and physiological reaction to stressors, situations and events that are perceived as threatening and tax your ability to cope. Many things function as stressors in our lives including major life events (e.g., death, marriage, or losing your job), catastrophes (e.g., natural disasters), daily hassles (e.g., traffic or taking exams), and conflict (e.g., having an argument with your significant other).

The Social Readjustment Rating Scale (SRSS) measures a person's stress level by examining how many life events he or she has experienced recently. Researchers Thomas Holmes and Richard Rahe found that the higher people scored on the SRSS, the more likely they were to experience illness. Life events that are involuntary, unscheduled, and perceived as undesirable are most likely to produce high levels of stress that could contribute to one becoming ill.

Catastrophes like natural disasters and unexpected attacks can produce overwhelming levels of stress. By nature, catastrophes are undesirable and unscheduled; they are also the type of events that few volunteer for—in short they are exactly the types of events that can produce enormous amounts of stress. Some catastrophes tend to occur more often in certain cultures.

Another stressor that occurs in some cultures is discrimination. A growing body of research shows that discrimination is a unique source of stress for many minority members. For example, minority members may be ridiculed, charged more for services, denied employment or housing—all of which are stressful and all of which are in addition to the daily hassles that we all face.

Daily hassles include little stressors like waiting in line, traffic, and job stress. By themselves, daily hassles are not too serious, but a bunch of little stressors taken together can add up to a major source of stress in your life. Your gender, race, age, and socioeconomic status may play a role in the type and amount of daily hassles you experience. For example, younger people tend to report more daily stress and African Americans report more economic stress than European Americans and Hispanic Americans.

Conflict or having to choose among two or more demands, desires, or needs is another type of stressor. In approach-approach conflicts both alternatives are appealing, but you can only choose one. This type of conflict is the easiest to resolve and the least likely to cause stress. Avoidance-avoidance conflicts involve choosing from alternatives that are all undesirable. These conflicts represent no-win situations and therefore cause more stress than approach-approach conflicts. Another type of conflict, approach-avoidance, involves being faced with a need that has both positive and negative qualities. These conflicts can be paralyzing and therefore produce high levels of stress. A final type of conflict is a multiple approach-avoidance conflict in which you must choose from among two or more options that each have positive and negative qualities. These conflicts can also lead to high levels of stress and may account for the common occurrence of buyer's remorse.

The Stress Response: Is This Stress? How Do I React?

This section covers Learning Objectives 2 and 3. One of the interesting things about stress is that whether or not a person feels stress is not just a function of the situation at hand. For example, one person may feel a great deal of stress while searching for a new job, while another feels no stress at all. Our initial interpretation or primary appraisal of a situation is one factor that determines how we will respond. We will only feel stress in situations that we perceive as being both stressful and relevant to us. If we appraise a situation as being threatening or harmful, it will likely cause us stress; but if we appraise the situation as being challenging, we are more likely to experience positive emotions.

Sometimes we experience stress over a prolonged period of time, such as we saw in the Big Picture story of Edward Pastorino. Prolonged stress can have a damaging effect on our health. Hans Selye described the long-term effects of stress in his general adaptation syndrome model (GAS). When we first experience an intense stressor, we experience an alarm reaction, during which our sympathetic nervous system and endocrine system engage and we experience the fight or flight response. If the stressor continues, we soon enter into the resistance stage, in which our sympathetic and endocrine systems remain on alert, but less intensely than they were during the alarm reaction. If we remain in a state of resistance for too long, we soon exhaust our physical resources and enter into the exhaustion stage. During exhaustion, we begin to experience physical wear and tear that can lead to cardiovascular problems and weakening of the immune system or immunosupression.

How Can I Cope With Stress?

This section covers Learning Objectives 4 and 5. One way to reduce the damaging effects of stress is to find ways of coping with it. In problem-based coping, you find a way to eliminate the stressor itself—for example, you might reduce your course load if you perceive that your workload is a stressor. In emotion-based coping, you attempt to manage your stress by controlling your emotional reaction to stressors. Cognitive reappraisal is one type of emotion-based coping in which you reduce stress by altering your perceptions of the stressor to see it in a less threatening manner. Ego defense mechanisms were first proposed by Sigmund Freud and are methods of reducing anxiety that can also reduce stress—at least temporarily.

Problem-based and emotion-based coping are cornerstones of stress management. In general, stress management techniques fall into four categories: physical (exercise, biofeedback, and relaxation techniques); emotional (social support, religion and spirituality); cognitive (guided imagery, meditation, and having an optimistic attitude); and behavioral (laughter and time management).

Personality and Health

This section covers Learning Objective 6. Personality is another factor that can affect our stress level and consequently our health. People with Type A personalities are hard driving, competitive, and aggressive, whereas Type B people are more relaxed and easy going. At one time, researchers thought that having a Type A personality was a risk factor for heart disease. Subsequent research has suggested that only the hostility component of the Type A personality increases one's chances of heart disease.

Another personality type, the hardy personality, seems to be related to less stress and less illness. People with hardy personalities tend to perceive that they have control over the events in their lives; they show a sense of personal commitment to the causes in their lives; and they tend to perceive life as a series of challenges.

Lifestyle and Health

This section covers Learning Objective 7. Lifestyle choices also impact our health. Health-defeating behaviors like alcohol abuse, unsafe sex, and smoking can leave us more vulnerable to illness. On the other hand, health promoting behaviors such as exercise, having a positive attitude, and avoiding stress can help protect our health and increase the quality of our lives.

Outlining the Big Picture

Chapter 12: Health, Stress, and Coping: How Can You Create a Healthy Life?

The Big Picture: What Can Psychology Tell Us about Health?
Notes:

_____

_____

_____

_____

_____

What is Stress? Stress and Stressors (Learning Objective 1)
Life Events: Change Is Stressful
Catastrophes: Natural Disasters and Wars
    Spotlight on Diversity: The Stress of Discrimination
Daily Hassles: Little Things Add Up!

Conflict: Approach and Avoidance
Notes:

_____

_____

_____

_____

_____

The Stress Response: Is This Stress? How Do I React? (Learning Objectives 2-3)
Appraisal: Assessing Stress
Selye's General Adaptation Syndrome
   Alarm Reaction
   Resistance Stage
   Exhaustion Stage
Stress and the Immune System: Resistance to Disease
Notes:

_____

_____

_____

_____

_____

How Can I Cope with Stress? (Learning Objectives 4-5)
Problem-Focused Coping: Change the Situation
Emotion-Focused Coping: Change Your Reaction
Managing Stress
   Physical Methods of Stress Management
   Emotional Methods of Stress Management
   Cognitive Methods of Stress Management
   Behavioral Methods of Stress Management
Notes:

_____

_____

_____

_____

_____

_____

Personality and Health (Learning Objective 6)
Type A Personality: Ambition, Drive, and Competitiveness
Learned Helplessness: I Can't Do It
The Hardy Personality: Control, Commitment, and Challenge
Notes:

_____

_____

_____

_____

_____

_____

Lifestyle and Health (Learning Objective 7)
Health-Defeating Behaviors
   Alcohol
   Smoking
   Unsafe Sex and the Risk of HIV
Health-Promoting Behaviors
Notes:

_____

_____

_____

_____

_____

_____

Are You Getting the Big Picture?
Notes:

_____

_____

_____

_____

_____

Seeing the Big Picture: A Mental Map of Chapter 12

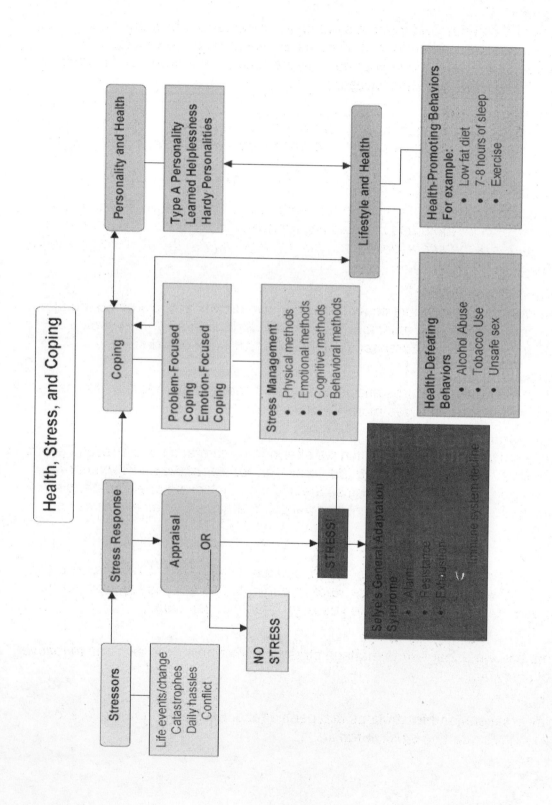

Key Points of the Big Picture

Alarm reaction:
the first phase of the general adaptation syndrome, characterized by immediate activation of the nervous and endocrine systems. *Example: You unexpectedly encounter a bear in the woods and your heart beats faster, you start breathing faster, adrenalin is released, and you start sweating.*

Approach-approach conflict:
a situation in which a person must choose between two likable events. *Example: You can't decide which dessert you would like to have; the chocolate cake or the fudge brownie sundae.*

Approach-avoidance conflict:
a situation in which a person is faced with a need that has both positive and negative aspects. *Example: Your tooth has been aching for two days. You don't want to go to the dentist because of the shots, drill, etc…, but if you get it fixed the pain will go away and you can enjoy eating again.*

Avoidance-avoidance conflict:
a situation in which a person must choose between two undesirable events. *Example: You dislike history courses but must take one to fulfill your graduation requirements. You have to choose between European History and Latin American History.*

Biofeedback:
an electronic device that measures and records bodily changes so that a person can monitor and control these changes more effectively.

Cognitive reappraisal:
an active and conscious process in which we alter our interpretation of a stressful event. *Example: Marty is nervous about riding the new roller coaster at the amusement park, fearing he may get hurt. Marty reappraises the situation by looking at all the people who are getting off the ride who are safe and happy. Marty's reappraisal reduces his anxiety and fear.*

Conflict:
having to choose between two or more needs, desires, or demands. *Example: You are running late for an appointment and are stuck in traffic, but have to use the bathroom. Stopping to use the bathroom will make you even later. Do you stop?*

Coping:
the behaviors that we engage in to manage stressors. *Example: You exercise to relieve the stress of studying.*

Daily hassles:
the every day irritations and frustrations that people face. *Examples: running late to class, burning dinner, getting stuck in traffic*

Defense mechanisms:
unconscious, emotional strategies that are engaged in to reduce anxiety and maintain a positive self-image. *Example: Nan often tells people she takes medication because of back pain. Nan's rationalization is a defense mechanism to reduce her anxiety over being addicted to the drugs.*

Emotion-focused coping:
behaviors aimed at controlling the internal emotional reactions to a stressor. *Example: Whenever anything upsets Ramona, she pushes it out of her mind and often forgets the details of the event.*

Exhaustion stage:
the third and final phase of the general adaptation syndrome, in which bodily resources are drained, and wear and tear on the body begins. *Example: After studying for final exams for a week, Prita comes down with a cold and is very tired.*

General adaptation syndrome (GAS):
the general physical responses we experience when faced with a stressor.

Hardy personality:
a personality high in the traits of commitment, control, and challenge, that appears to be associated with strong stress resistance. *Example: Even though Bertie has been in a high stress job as an air traffic controller for ten years, he is rarely sick and still has a positive attitude toward his work.*

Health-defeating behaviors:
behaviors that increase the chance of illness, disease, or death. *Examples: drinking too much alcohol, engaging in unprotected sex, smoking tobacco, using illegal drugs*

Health-promoting behaviors:
behaviors that decrease the chance of illness, disease, or death. *Examples: exercise, maintaining a nutritious diet, getting enough sleep, developing a social support network*

Health psychology:
the subfield of psychology that investigates the relationship between people's behaviors and their health. *Example: Dr. Lewis, a health psychologist, studies the influence of stress on health.*

Immunosuppression:
the reduction in activity of the immune system.

Learned helplessness:
a passive response to stressors based on exposure to previously uncontrolled, negative events. *Example: Because Mitch feels that he is uncoordinated, he doesn't even try to catch the ball when playing baseball during his physical education course.*

Life event:
a change in one's life, good or bad, that requires readjustment. *Examples: retirement; starting or ending a new relationship, graduating from college, starting your first job*

Meditation:
mental exercises in which people consciously focus their attention to heighten awareness and bring their mental processes under more control.

Multiple approach-avoidance conflict:
a situation that poses several alternatives that each have positive and negative features. *Example: Being offered several career positions and having to choose one.*

Primary appraisal:
our initial interpretation of an event as either irrelevant, positive, or stressful. *Example: Your initial reaction when you are told that have to give a class presentation is your primary appraisal.*

Problem-focused coping:
behaviors that aim to control or alter the environment that is causing stress. *Example: Marissa uses time management techniques to reduce the stress of her job.*

Progressive relaxation training:
a stress management technique in which a person learns how to systematically tense and relax muscle groups in the body.

Resistance stage:
the second phase of the general adaptation syndrome, in which the nervous and endocrine systems continue to be activated.

Social support:
having close and positive relationships with others. *Example: Carla and Samantha are best friends and confide in one another.*

Stress:
any event or environmental stimulus (stressor) that we respond to because we perceive it as challenging or threatening. *Example: Students who perceive taking 12 hours of college credits as a challenge will experience stress.*

Type A personality:
a personality that is aggressive, ambitious, and competitive. *Example: Stephanie is a driven person who is always on the go and who will not tolerate failure.*

Type B personality:
a personality characterized by patience, flexibility, and an easygoing manner. *Example: Terrence is a laid-back and mellow person.*

Fill-in Review of the Chapter

Can you fill-in the missing terms for each section of the chapter? Items marked with an * encourage you to continue building the Big Picture of psychology by connecting the material in this chapter to material from previous chapters in the text.

The Big Picture: What Can Psychology Tell Us about Health?

Edward Pastorino's personality would best be described as a(n) 1) _____.

Getting married and having five children are examples of 2) _____ _____ stressors for Edward Pastorino.

What is Stress? Stress and Stressors

Holmes and Rahe devised a scale to measure the amount of stress in a person's life by assessing the number and severity of major life events that a person is facing. This scale is called the 3) _____ _____ _____ _____.

Survivors of catastrophes may develop 4) _____ _____ _____.

Washington is trying to decide which new car to buy. On one hand, he likes the style of car X, but it doesn't get good gas mileage. On the other hand, he likes the gas mileage of car Y, but he doesn't really like its style. Washington appears to be experiencing a(n) 5) _____ _____ _____ conflict situation.

The Stress Response: Is This Stress? How Do I React?

The first step in assessing stress is called 6) _____ _____.

The nervous and endocrine systems continue to be activated during the 7) _____ stage of the general adaptation syndrome.

The branch of the nervous system that is at the heart of the stress response is the 8*)_____.

The master gland, or 9*) _____, activates the release of stress hormones.

The hormones released during times of stress actually work to dampen the effects of the immune system, a phenomenon known as 10) _____.

How Can I Cope with Stress?

If you are feeling stressed and take your frustration out on a loved one, you are engaging in 11) _____ _____ coping.

Envisioning yourself in a calm, tranquil place as a means of reducing stress is called 12) _____ _____.

Yoga is a form of 13) _____ that can be useful in reducing stress.

Cancer patients with a(n) 14) _____attitude do better than patients who lack this type of attitude.

The old saying that 15) "_____ is the best medicine," may not be far from the mark in that this activity promotes relaxation and reduces stress.

Personality and Health

In classical conditioning terms, the decrease in responding that occurs in learned helplessness is called 16*) _____.

Hardiness traits include 17) _____, 18) _____, and 19) _____.

Lifestyle and Health

Driving at excessive speeds is an example of a(n) 20) _____ _____ behavior.

Use It or Lose It!

Can you identify the defense mechanism being used in each situation?

Defense Mechanism	Situation
1)	Ignoring the signs that your friend is a drug addict.
2)	Stating that smoking pot helps you study better.
3)	Bumping into someone at the mall whom you dislike, but whom you approach and say warmly, "Hi. How have you been? You look great!"
4)	Throwing a tantrum when your friend has made other plans for the evening.
5)	After the break-up of a long-term relationship, you channel your emotions into writing several songs.
6)	Forgetting the details of a car accident that you were a witness to.
7)	Accusing another person of being suspicious and mistrustful of others when it is you who engages in this behavior.
8)	Hitting your sister after your parent yells at you.

Self-Check: Are You Getting the Big Picture?

After you have read and studied the chapter, see if you can answer the following quiz questions. Check your answers at the end of the chapter. If you miss a question, refer to your text and re-study the appropriate sections.

True or False Questions

Are these statements true or false?

1. Marriage, loss of your job, and winning the lottery are all life events that can cause stress.
True
False

2. Minority group members may feel stress due to prejudice and stereotyping from members of their own in-group, as well as from out-group members.
True
False

3. Having social support has been linked to living longer.
True
False

4. Challenge appraisals typically result in positive emotions such as excitement and are perceived as less stressful.
True
False

5. Being religious has been shown to prevent illnesses like cancer.
True
False

6. The HIV virus can be contracted through unprotected oral sex.
True
False

7. Being achievement-oriented is the key feature of Type A personality that makes people more likely to experience heart-related problems.
True
False

8. The largest number of new HIV cases each year is among women.
True
False

9. Finding a new job to replace the one that you hate is an example of emotion-focused coping.
True
False

10. During the resistance phase of the general adaptation syndrome, our defenses against stress are at their highest.
True
False

Multiple Choice Questions

Can you choose the best answer for these questions?

1. Research on the Social Readjustment Rating Scale (SRSS) has shown that which of the following factors affect(s) the impact that major life events have on our lives?
   A. the degree to which the change was voluntary
   B. whether you perceive the life change as positive or negative
   C. whether the life change was scheduled or unscheduled
   D. all of the above

2. Tom views his new job as a positive and challenging change. Sara views her new job as simply a way to earn more money. Henri is concerned about the additional responsibilities of his new job. All things being equal, who is most likely to feel job stress?
   A. Tom
   B. Sara
   C. Henri
   D. All three will feel stress.

3. Which of the following is classified as a catastrophe?
   A. divorce
   B. losing your job
   C. having your house flood
   D. having to move cross country because of a promotion at work

4. All other things being equal, which of the following events is likely to produce the most stress for the average person?
   A. losing your job after months of talk about the plant closing
   B. losing your job without any warning
   C. quitting your job to look for a different line of work
   D. keeping your job after others have lost their jobs due to downsizing

5. The adrenal gland secretes which two hormones during the stress response?
   A. adrenaline and corticosteroids
   B. adrenaline and GABA
   C. corticosteroids and insulin
   D. insulin and GABA

6. Which of the following most likely present the greatest source of stress and danger to our health?
   A. catastrophes
   B. conflicts
   C. daily hassles
   D. major life events

7. Whenever Dennis is angry and frustrated he bakes cookies. Dennis is most likely engaging in which defense mechanism?
   A. reaction formation
   B. regression
   C. projection
   D. sublimation

8. Carmen feels stressed from her full-time job and taking care of her two children. Carmen finds a more flexible job that allows her to spend more time with her children. Which style of coping does Carmen's behavior illustrate?
   A. emotion-focused
   B. problem-focused
   C. defensive
   D. both A and C

333

9. What percent of all deaths are in some way related to personal habits that damage our health?
   A. 15%
   B. 25%
   C. 45%
   D. 65%

10. Which one of the following behaviors promote health and well-being?
    A. perceiving events as controllable
    B. engaging in emotion-focused coping
    C. expecting failure
    D. All of the above promote health and well-being.

11. Danielle can't decide which of two dresses to buy with her birthday money. Danielle is experiencing a(n):
    A. approach-avoidance conflict.
    B. approach-approach conflict.
    C. avoidance-avoidance conflict.
    D. multiple approach-avoidance conflict.

12. When Celeste gets in an argument with her partner she covers her ears and walks away. Celeste is engaging in which of the following defense mechanisms?
    A. displacement
    B. repression
    C. regression
    D. reaction formation

13. Roberto wants to call up Marjorie and ask her out on a date, but he is afraid that she may reject him. He is anxiously pacing back and forth in front of the phone trying to decide what to do. Roberto is experiencing which type of conflict?
    A. approach-approach
    B. avoidance-avoidance
    C. approach-avoidance
    D. none of the above

14. Yasmine was sitting at the bus stop when she heard a person yelling angrily close by. Yasmine turned around to see who was yelling and she saw that a man was yelling at his girlfriend. So, Yasmine went back to reading her newspaper. In psychological terms, Yasmine just:
    A. made a primary appraisal.
    B. experienced stress.
    C. had an avoidance-avoidance conflict.
    D. all of the above

15. David is driving when a truck pulls out in front of him and almost causes a car accident. David's heart begins to pound and his blood pressure shoots up. David is likely in the _____ phase of the general adaptation syndrome.
    A. alarm
    B. resistance
    C. exhaustion
    D. final

16. A weakened immune system and vulnerability to disease is most likely to occur in which stage of the general adaptation syndrome?
    A. alarm
    B. resistance
    C. exhaustion
    D. People are equally vulnerable to disease in all three of these stages.

17. Fatima was initially very angry when she saw that her boyfriend was late for their lunch date. As she sat there fuming, Fatima began to consider the possibility that he had a good reason for being late, and she began to calm down. Fatima seems to have engaged in:
    A. problem-focused coping.
    B. emotion-focused coping.
    C. cognitive reappraisal.
    D. B & C

18. Which of the following is not a physical means of managing stress?
    A. exercise
    B. biofeedback training
    C. relaxation techniques
    D. talking to friends

19. Physical exercise increases which neurotransmitters in the brain?
    A. serotonin and GABA
    B. dopamine and glutamate
    C. serotonin and endorphins
    D. endorphins and acetylcholine

20. Steve is a workaholic. He never takes a vacation. He won't even speak to his children on the phone when they call him at his office. He is often angry and impatient with others. What type of personality does Steve appear to have?
    A. Type A
    B. Type B
    C. Type C
    D. A hardy personality

21. Which of the following components of the Type A personality is most closely related to heart disease?
   A. talking fast
   B. being competitive
   C. always being in a hurry
   D. being angry and hostile

22. In one study of people who had already had heart attacks, having which personality type was most associated with dying?
   A. Type A
   B. Type B
   C. Type C
   D. Type A and Type B persons had equal chance of dying.

23. Suzanne Kobasa found that executives who seemed to weather stress without experiencing health problems tended to:
   A. view set backs as failures.
   B. give up easily when their business strategies didn't seem to work.
   C. fear the future.
   D. remain committed to self, work, values, and family.

24. Alcohol abuse is related to:
   A. erectile dysfunction.
   B. cancer.
   C. heart disease.
   D. all of the above

25. Earl recently lost his high-paying job. While talking to a friend about his job loss, Earl told her that he was looking forward to finding a job in a new field. Earl appears to be exhibiting the hardy trait of:
   A. challenge.
   B. commitment.
   C. control.
   D. all of the above

Short-Answer Questions

Can you write a brief answer to these questions?

1. Describe the stages of Selye's General Adaptation Syndrome.

2. Using what you have learned about stress and health, explain why two people, who are both about to take exams react differently—one remains calm, while the other begins to panic.

3. Will is having troubles at school. He's taking a full load of courses and working part time. It appears that this workload is beginning to take its toll on him. Lately, he has been having headaches and he thinks he is developing an ulcer. Give an example of how Will could use problem-focused coping to reduce his stress level.

4. What are some health-defeating behaviors that people engage in during times of stress?

5. What is learned helplessness and what causes it?

Developing a Bigger Picture: Making Connections Across Chapters

An important aspect of learning is learning to see the "Big Picture" of the subject you are studying. As you learn about psychology, you should try to understand how the material from different chapters fits together to help you form a broad-based understanding of what psychology is all about. To help facilitate the development of this "Big Picture" in your mind, try to answer these questions using the knowledge you have learned in this chapter, as well as the other chapters referenced in the questions.

1. In Chapter 1, you learned about research methods. Using this knowledge, design a study to test the hypothesis that regular exercise reduces resting blood pressure.

2. Using what you learned in Chapter 5 about operant conditioning, design a program to increase a specific health promoting behavior.

3. Using what you learned about perception in Chapter 3, answer the following question. How do perception and appraisal relate to one another?

Label the Diagram

Can you label the missing parts of the stress response cycle?

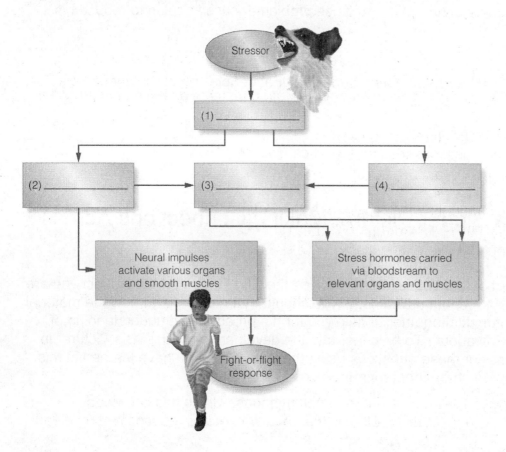

Big Picture Review

Identify what changes for each stress management technique and then list the methods that fall under each type of technique.

Physical: Change the body's 1) _____
- 2) _____
- 3) _____
- 4) _____

Emotional: Change the way you 5) _____
- 6) _____
- 7) _____

Cognitive: Change the way you 8) _____
- 9) _____
- 10) _____
- 11) _____

Behavioral: Change the way you 12) _____
  • 13) _____
  • 14) _____

Solutions

Each solution below is followed by its textbook page reference number and its corresponding chapter learning objective (LO) number. Items with a Big Picture LO help you build a Big Picture of psychology across the chapters you have studied so far.

Fill-in Review of the Chapter

1. Type A personality [p. 563; LO 6]
2. major life event [p. 542; LO 1]
3. Social Readjustment Rating Scale [p. 542; LO 1]
4. posttraumatic stress disorder [p. 546; LO 1]
5. multiple approach-avoidance [p. 549; LO 1]
6. primary appraisal [p. 550; LO 2]
7. resistance [p. 552; LO 3]
8. sympathetic nervous system [p. 552; LO-Big Picture]
9. pituitary gland [p. 82; LO-Big Picture]
10. immunosuppression [p. 553; LO 3]
11. emotion-focused [p. 555-556; LO 4]
12. guided imagery [p. 560; LO 5]
13. meditation [p. 560; LO 5]
14. optimistic [p. 561; LO 5]
15. laughter [p. 561; LO 5]
16. extinction [p. 207; LO-Big Picture]
17. commitment [p. 565; LO 6]
18. control [p. 565; LO 6]
19. challenge [p. 565; LO 6]
20. health-defeating [p. 567; LO 7]

Use It or Lose It! [p. 557; LO 4]

Defense Mechanism
1. Denial
2. Rationalization
3. Reaction formation
4. Regression
5. Sublimation
6. Repression
7. Projection
8. Displacement

Self-Check: Are You Getting the Big Picture?

True or False Questions

1. T [p. 542-543; LO 1]
2. T [p. 546-547; LO 1]
3. T [p. 559; LO 5]
4. T [p. 550; LO 2]
5. F [p. 560; LO 5]

6. T [p. 569; LO 7]
7. F [p. 564; LO 6]
8. F [p. 569; LO 7]
9. F [p. 555; LO 4]
10. T [p. 551; LO 3]

Multiple Choice Questions

1. D [p. 544; LO 1]	10. A [p. 570; LO 7]	19. C [p. 558; LO 5]
2. C [p. 544; LO 2]	11. B [p. 548; LO 1]	20. A [p. 563; LO 6]
3. C [p. 544; LO 1]	12. C [p. 557; LO 4]	21. D [p. 564; LO 6]
4. B [p. 544; LO 1]	13. C [p. 549; LO 1]	22. B [p. 564; LO 6]
5. A [p. 552; LO 3]	14. A [p. 550; LO 2]	23. D [p. 565; LO 6]
6. C [p. 547; LO 1]	15. A [p. 551; LO 3]	24. D [p. 567; LO 7]
7. D [p. 557; LO 4]	16. C [p. 552; LO 3]	25. D [p. 565; LO 6]
8. B [p. 555; LO 4]	17. D [p. 556; LO 5]	
9. C [p. 567; LO 7]	18. D [p. 558; LO 5]	

Short-Answer Questions

1. Describe the stages of Selye's General Adaptation Syndrome? [p. 551; LO 3]

   The stages of the GAS are alarm reaction, resistance, and exhaustion. In the alarm reaction, you have just been presented with a major stressor and your body tries to muster its defenses against this stress by calling into action the sympathetic nervous system. The sympathetic system will, in turn cause the endocrine system to release stress hormones into the blood stream. If the stressor does not abate, you will soon enter into the resistance phase, during which your body will seem to cope with the stress. The sympathetic nervous system and endocrine system continue to be activated, but less intensely than in the alarm reaction phase. If the stressor does not abate, your resources will soon dwindle and you will enter into the exhaustion stage. At this point, your body begins to falter and ill-health or possibly even death may ensue.

2. Using what you have learned about stress and health, explain why two people, who are both about to take exams react differently—one remains calm, while the other begins to panic. [p. 550; LO 2]

   For the most part, the reason these people react differently with different amounts of stress is due to how they appraise the situation. The person who panics probably appraises the situation as a threat, while the person who remains calm likely appraises the situation as a challenge or an opportunity to succeed.

3. Will is having troubles at school. He's taking a full load of courses and working part time. And, it appears that this workload is beginning to take its toll on him. Lately, he has been having headaches and he thinks he is developing an ulcer. Give an example of how Will could use problem-focused coping to reduce his stress level. [p. 555; LO 4]

   There are many possible answers to this question. Problem-focused coping seeks to eliminate or reduce stress by directly eliminating or reducing stressors. Here are some possible strategies Will could use to reduce his stress. He could lighten his course load. Reduce the number of hours that he works. He could also engage in some time management to use what free time he has more wisely.

4. What are some health-defeating behaviors that people engage in during times of stress? [p. 567-570; LO 7]

   People may self-medicate with alcohol or drugs during times of stress. They may smoke or eat poor diets when feeling stressed. They may also fail to exercise or get a proper night's sleep.

5. What is learned helplessness and what causes it? [p. 564-565; LO 6]

   Learned helplessness is a psychological state of feeling as if you have no control over what happens to you. In this state, you feel as if you cannot fix your own problems and you tend to see challenges as threats that cause much stress. This state can result from experiencing punishment that one perceives as being unpredictable and uncontrollable. It can also result from being taught (e.g., by your parents) that you have no control over the events in the world.

Developing a Bigger Picture: Making Connections Across Chapters

1. In Chapter 1, you learned about research methods. Using this knowledge, design a study to test the hypothesis that regular exercise reduces resting blood pressure. [p. 32-33; LO-Big Picture]

   There are many possible ways to do this. Here is one. Select a random sample of 100 people and measure and record their resting blood pressure. Then randomly assign the people to either a condition where they are placed on a program of one hour a day of aerobic exercise or a condition where they watch a health-related program for one hour a day. After six months, retest their resting blood pressure. If your hypothesis has merit, the average decline in resting blood pressure should be significantly larger in the aerobic exercise group.

2. Using what you learned in Chapter 5 about operant conditioning, design a program to increase your health promoting behavior. [p. 211; LO-Big Picture]

   Health promoting behaviors include: committing yourself to a value and belief system; viewing stressors as challenges rather than as threats; perceiving events as controllable; not relying exclusively on one or two defense mechanisms for coping; engaging in problem-focused coping; cultivating an optimistic, positive attitude; developing a social support network; not expecting failure; being patient and flexible; laughing; managing your time wisely; engaging in relaxing activities; getting regular physical exercise; avoiding being hostile, bitter, and resentful; avoiding the use of cigarettes; using alcohol in moderation; and engaging in safe sex.

   You can develop a program of self-modification in which you reward yourself for engaging in these behaviors. For example, for every week that you engage in a health-promoting behavior each day, you get to treat yourself to a movie that weekend.

3. Using what you learned about perception in Chapter 3, answer the following question. How do perception and appraisal relate to one another? [p. 126-127; LO-Big Picture]

   The concept of top-down-perceptual processing is closely related to the concept of appraisal. In top-down perceptual processing, you use your knowledge and expectations about the world to interpret a situation or stimulus. When appraising a stressor, you also use your knowledge and expectations about the world to help you appraise the situation. For example, if you encounter a snake while hiking, you must use your knowledge about snakes to perceive what type of snake it is and whether or not it is poisonous. If you perceive that it is poisonous, this will influence your appraisal of the situation; and it will impact the level of stress you experience in this situation.

Label the Diagram [p. 551; LO 3]

1. hypothalamus
2. sympathetic nervous system
3. adrenal gland
4. pituitary gland

Big Picture Review [p. 562; LO 5]

1. response
2. physical exercise
3. biofeedback training

4. relaxation techniques
5. feel
6. social support
7. religion and spirituality
8. think
9. guided imagery
10. meditation
11. optimistic attitude
12. act
13. laughter
14. time management

13

What Is Personality, and How Do We Measure It?

Learning Objectives

After studying each of the following sections of the chapter, you should be able to do these tasks:

The Psychoanalytic Approach: Sigmund Freud and the Neo-Freudians

1. Discuss Freud's perspective on personality, detailing how the levels of consciousness, resolution of psychosexual stages, and component parts of the personality interact to generate behavior.
2. Detail neo-Freudian perspectives on personality, indicating their differences from and similarities to Freud's theory.

The Trait Approach: Describing Personality

3. Define traits and compare the various trait approaches to understanding personality (Allport, Cattell, Eysenck, the "big five" theory).
4. Discuss genetic contributions to personality, and address whether personality is consistent and stable over time.

The Social Cognitive Approach: The Environment and Patterns of Thoughts

5. Describe social cognitive approaches to personality, such as Bandura's reciprocal determinism and Rotter's locus of control.

The Humanistic Approach: Free Will and Self-Actualization

6. Define self-actualization, and describe how the humanistic views of Maslow and Rogers propose that it can be achieved.
7. Compare and contrast the four perspectives on personality, indicating the strengths and weaknesses of each approach.

Measuring Personality

8. Detail the various methods psychologists use to measure personality and the theoretical perspective that gave rise to each method. Compare the advantages and disadvantages of each measure.

The Big Picture

The Big Picture: How Can We Understand Personality?

Personality is the unique set of attitudes, emotions, thoughts, impulses, and behaviors that define how a person typically behaves across situations. As the story of James McBride shows us in the Big Picture, personality is complex and the personality traits you possess can affect the way you lead your life.

The Psychoanalytic Approach: Sigmund Freud and the Neo-Freudians

This section covers Learning Objectives 1 and 2. Sigmund Freud was one of the earliest psychologists to study the development of personality. His psychoanalytic perspective on personality emphasizes the influence of unconscious forces on our thoughts and behavior. Freud proposed that the human personality operates on three different levels of consciousness. The conscious level contains the thoughts and feelings that we are currently aware of. The preconscious level contains memories, information, and urges that you are not currently aware of, but could become aware of in the future. And, the unconscious level contains thoughts, impulses, memories, and urges that you are not consciously aware of now and cannot become consciously aware of in the future. Although information in the unconscious is cutoff from consciousness, it can still affect your behavior. According to Freud, you sometimes behave in particular ways without awareness of your own motives.

According to Freud, personality is composed of three structures that operate in interdependent ways. The id, the irrational, impulsive part of personality operates at the unconscious level. The id is responsible for your unconscious urges and desires, and it operates on the pleasure principle. The ego operates in a partly conscious fashion and its job is to mediate between the unconscious desires of the id and the moral dictates of the third part of personality, the superego.

Because the ego mediates the conflicts between the id and the superego, the ego often experiences internal conflicts that lead to anxiety. When you experience such anxiety, coping strategies called ego defense mechanisms may be used.

According to Freud, these components of personality develop as you pass though certain stages of psychosexual development. From birth through adolescence, you experience a series of conflicts as you try to balance your desire for sexual pleasure or stimulation of the erogenous zones on your body with the parental and societal restrictions and rules. These stages, named for the dominant erogenous zone that characterizes the stage, are the oral, anal, phallic, latency, and genital stages.

Freud believed that healthy personality development requires that you resolve these conflicts and receive an optimal level of gratification of your sexual needs at each of the stages. Too much or too little gratification of your sexual needs at any particular psychosexual stage can lead to what Freud called a fixation. Fixation means that you get stuck at a particular stage of personality development and end up with immature personality traits.

Freud's work has always been controversial within the fields of medicine and psychology. Many subsequent theorists have been influenced by Freud's ideas and have incorporated some of Freud's concepts into their own theories. Collectively, these theorists are referred to as the neo-Freudians. Influential neo-Freudians include Carl Jung, Alfred Adler, and Karen Horney.

Carl Jung, rejected much of Freud's emphasis on sexuality, but he retained the idea that the personality was a function of the interplay between conscious and unconscious forces. Jung expanded the idea of the personal unconscious to also include the idea of a collective unconscious, a universal unconscious shared by all humans that contains archetypes or mental representations and symbols for concepts commonly found in human cultures (e.g., man and woman).

Alfred Adler also rejected Freud's emphasis on sex as a driving force behind personality. For Alder, a child's desire to overcome his or her feelings of helplessness and master the environment is what drives personality. According to Adler, moderate feelings of inferiority can be motivating, but deep feelings of inferiority can impede growth and development, resulting in an inferiority complex.

Unlike Freud, Karen Horney emphasized environmental influences on personality development. According to Horney, early problems in the family or other disturbances can lead a child to develop basic anxiety, persistent feelings of helplessness. To cope with this anxiety, a child may be driven to pursue love, power, prestige, or detachment.

The Trait Approach: Describing Personality

This section covers Learning Objectives 3 and 4. Another approach to personality is the trait approach. In this approach, psychologists attempt to define the internal dispositions or traits that influence our behavior. According to Gordon Allport, personality traits can be classified as being central traits (core aspects of your personality that guide your behavior in most situations), secondary traits (traits that are less consistent and more situation-specific), and cardinal traits (traits that describe how you behave in all situations).

Raymond Cattell took a different approach to examining our traits. Cattell used a statistical method, called factor analysis to see what the important dimensions of personality are. Cattell ultimately identified 16 basic human traits called source traits, the somewhat universal broad dimensions that form the core of our personalities.

Building on Cattell's work, Hans Eysenck found two dimensions of personality that he felt formed the foundation of people's personality: introversion/extraversion and emotional stability and instability. According to Eysenck, introversion/extraversion is linked to our baseline physiological level of arousal, but the research on this has been mixed. Eysenck later added a third dimension called psychoticism to the model. Psychoticism includes tendencies toward recklessness, disregard for common sense and cultural norms, and hostility. Eysenck's three factor model of personality is referred to as the PEN (Psychoticism, Extraversion, Neuroticism) model. Currently, the most

347

widely accepted trait theory is Paul Costa and Robert McCrae's Five Factor theory. According to this theory, the basic dimensions of personality are: extraversion, neuroticism, openness, agreeableness, and conscientiousness.

The trait approach to personality assumes that we have stable personality traits that influence our behavior across many different situations. As such, some have wondered whether personality traits may be inherited characteristics. Research on adopted children has shown that adopted children often have traits that are more similar to their biological parents than to their adoptive parents, indicating a genetic basis for personality. Likewise twin studies and familial studies also suggest some genetic influence on personality. Furthermore, gene marker studies suggest that genes, which influence levels of serotonin in the brain, may be one mechanism through which genes influence personality.

Given that genetics may influence personality, it is reasonable to expect that personality traits remain stable over time. Research on the stability of personality traits across the lifespan suggests that at least some personality traits are stable from childhood to adulthood. However, not all studies suggest such stability. Other studies suggest that personality can change dramatically within adulthood—for example, many people become more androgynous as they age.

Situational context can also impact our behavioral expression of our personality traits. For example, your shyness may be in evidence when you are in public, whereas you may be out-going when with your close friends. The fact that our behavior is a product of both our traits and the situation is referred to as the person-situation interaction.

The Social Cognitive Approach: The Environment and Patterns of Thoughts

This section covers Learning Objective 5. The social cognitive approach to understanding personality assumes that your thoughts and situational influences work together to influence your behavior. Two examples of this approach are Albert Bandura's reciprocal determinism and Julian Rotter's locus of control theory.

Reciprocal determinism proposes that your environment influences your thoughts and behavior, while at the same time your thoughts and behavior influence your environment. For example, an outgoing person may seek out exciting social environments that in turn bring out their outgoing personality. Self-efficacy is a critical cognitive element in this interplay of personality and environmental influences. People high in self-efficacy have confidence in their ability to be successful in a particular situation and are therefore more likely to actually be successful. Then when they do succeed, it further increases their self-efficacy.

In Julian Rotter's locus of control theory, the degree to which you perceive that you can control the outcomes of the events in your life affects how you approach these events. People with an internal locus of control tend to believe that they can control how the situations in their lives turn out. On the other hand, people with an external locus of control tend to perceive that their fate is in the hands of some external force such as others, God, or fate. According to Rotter, your locus of control can affect both your personality and your behavior.

The Humanistic Approach: Free Will and Self-Actualization

This section covers Learning Objectives 6 and 7. The humanistic approach to personality emphasizes the human desire to reach one's full potential, a concept known as self-actualization. According to Abraham Maslow, before we can strive for self-actualization, we first must meet our physiological needs, safety needs, and psychological needs. Because Maslow's theory predicts which needs we will strive to meet first, it is also a theory of motivation (Chapter 8).

Fellow humanist, Carl Rogers, shared Maslow's belief that people strive for self-actualization. According to Rogers, our journey toward self-actualization begins when we start to form a self-concept in childhood. Underlying the process of self-actualization is the organismic valuing process through which we come to prefer situations and things that validate or value us as a person. As others validate or fail to validate us as a person, we begin to see ourselves as others see us. One important determinant of how our personality develops is the degree to which we receive unconditional positive regard from others—especially our parents. Unconditional positive regard in childhood allows a child to develop into an adult whose self-concept is based on their own internal values and beliefs rather than on how other perceive them.

Each personality perspective has its strengths and weaknesses. The psychoanalytic perspective emphasizes the unconscious and the importance of early development, yet has difficulty in being tested experimentally. The trait perspective does a good job of *describing* people's personalities, yet it does not *explain* why we behave in a particular way. The social cognitive approach details the influence of cognitive processes such as thinking, expectations, and other mental events on behavior, but does not address the biological and emotional factors that influence personality. The humanistic approach has encouraged many people to become more aware of themselves and their interactions with others. However, it assumes that all people are motivated toward good in attaining self-actualization, perhaps underestimating the capacity for evil in some people. Humanistic concepts are also difficult to test experimentally. The four personality perspectives are complementary and when taken together, provide a much more complex and richer view of the forces that make us unique than any single perspective could.

Measuring Personality

This section covers Learning Objective 8. In addition to describing personality and its development, psychologists are also interested in measuring personality. Two important considerations involved in measuring personality are the reliability and validity of the measurement tools. Reliability refers to the consistency of the measurement tool. Validity refers to the ability of the measurement tool to actually measure what it is designed to measure. Personality tests that lack reliability or validity are of little use.

Several different types of personality assessments exist—personality inventories, projective tests, direct observations and rating scales, and clinical interviews. Personality inventories are questionnaires like the Minnesota Multiphasic Personality Inventory (MMPI). One of the main drawbacks to personality inventories is the possibility that the test taker may lie. To get around this problem, many inventories like the MMPI contain validity scales that are designed to detect when someone is lying.

On the other hand, projective tests like the Rorschach Inkblot Test and the Thematic Apperception Test (TAT) are less prone to problems with lying. These tests involve showing the participant an ambiguous stimulus and asking him or her to interpret it. The rationale for projective tests is that participants will project some of their unconscious wishes and desires into their interpretation of the stimulus. Due to the subjectivity inherent in these tests, coding systems have been devised to decrease varying clinical interpretations.

In direct observation and rating scales the person may be directly observed or his behavior may be rated on a rating scale. When ratings are made, they are often conducted by someone other than the participant to avoid problems with lying and self-distortion.

In clinical interviews, the person being evaluated is interviewed by a trained clinician who evaluates certain aspects of the client's personality. The types of questions and evaluations made in a clinical interview will vary from clinician to clinician.

Outlining the Big Picture

Chapter 13: What Is Personality, and How Do We Measure It?

The Big Picture: How Can We Understand Personality?
Notes:

_____

_____

_____

_____

_____

The Psychoanalytic Approach: Sigmund Freud and the Neo-Freudians (Learning Objectives 1-2)
The Levels of Awareness
The Structure of Personality
Psychosexual Development
Neo-Freudians: Alfred Adler, Karen Horney, and Carl Jung
   Carl Jung and the Collective Unconscious
   Alfred Adler and the Inferiority Complex
   Karen Horney and Basic Anxiety
Contributions and Criticisms of the Psychoanalytic Approach

Notes:

_____

_____

_____

_____

_____

The Trait Approach: Describing Personality (Learning Objectives 3-4)

Gordon Allport's Trait Theory

Raymond Cattell's Factor Analytic Trait Theory

Hans Eysenck Narrows Down the Traits

The Five-Factor Trait Theory: The "Big Five"

Genetic Contributions to Personality

Stability and Change in Personality

 Spotlight on Diversity: How Age, Culture, and Gender Influence Personality

Contributions and Criticisms of the Trait Approach

Notes:

_____

_____

_____

_____

_____

The Social Cognitive Approach: The Environment and Patterns of Thoughts (Learning Objective 5)

Reciprocal Determinism: Albert Bandura's Interacting Forces

Julian Rotter's Locus of Control: Internal and External Expectations

Contributions and Criticisms of the Social Cognitive Approach

Notes:

_____

_____

_____

_____

_____

_____

_____

The Humanistic Approach: Free Will and Self-Actualization (Learning Objective 6)
Abraham Maslow and the Hierarchy of Needs Theory
Carl Rogers and Self Theory
Contributions and Criticisms of the Humanistic Approach
Notes:

_____

_____

_____

_____

_____

Measuring Personality (Learning Objective 8)
Personality Inventories: Mark Which One Best Describes You
Projective Tests: Tell Me What You See
Rating Scales and Direct Observation
Clinical Interviews
Notes:

_____

_____

_____

_____

_____

Are You Getting the Big Picture?
Notes:

_____

_____

_____

_____

_____

_____

Seeing the Big Picture: A Mental Map of Chapter 13

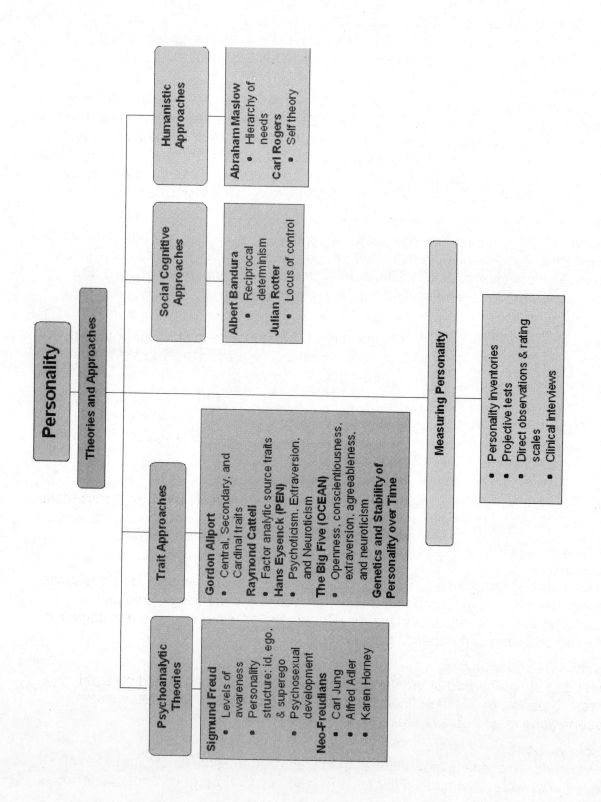

Personality

Theories and Approaches

Psychoanalytic Theories

Sigmund Freud
- Levels of awareness
- Personality structure: id, ego, & superego
- Psychosexual development

Neo-Freudians
- Carl Jung
- Alfred Adler
- Karen Horney

Trait Approaches

Gordon Allport
- Central, Secondary, and Cardinal traits

Raymond Cattell
- Factor analytic source traits

Hans Eysenck (PEN)
- Psychoticism, Extraversion, and Neuroticism

The Big Five (OCEAN)
- Openness, conscientiousness, extraversion, agreeableness, and neuroticism

Genetics and Stability of Personality over Time

Social Cognitive Approaches

Albert Bandura
- Reciprocal determinism

Julian Rotter
- Locus of control

Humanistic Approaches

Abraham Maslow
- Hierarchy of needs

Carl Rogers
- Self theory

Measuring Personality
- Personality inventories
- Projective tests
- Direct observations & rating scales
- Clinical interviews

Key Points of the Big Picture

Actualizing tendency:
the natural drive in humans to strive for fulfillment and enhancement, according to Rogers. *Example: A baby naturally strives to keep warm and fed.*

Anal stage:
Freud's second psychosexual stage, which occurs from approximately 18 months to three years, in which the parents' regulation of the child's biological urge to expel or retain feces affects personality development. *Example: A mother may ask her toilet-training toddler if she has to use the potty. The child may not want to stop playing to go potty so she ignores the mother's request. How the mother handles this situation over the course of potty-training influences the child's personality development.*

Archetypes:
according to Jung, mental representations or symbols of themes and predispositions to respond to the world in a certain way that are contained in the collective unconscious. *Example: Movies and videos often have a "villain" character that is a symbol of the shadow archetype or negative qualities of a person.*

Basic anxiety:
according to Horney, the feeling of helplessness that develops in children from early relationships. *Example: A young child feels helpless at not being able to make his own lunch so he gives his parent a kiss to reduce his anxiety.*

Cardinal traits:
according to Allport, those dominant elements of our personalities that drive all of our behaviors. *Example: Tyra is always nice and friendly and has never been rude. Being nice and friendly are cardinal traits for Tyra.*

Central traits:
according to Allport, those tendencies we have to behave in a certain way across most situations. *Example: Mitchell is typically outgoing, but there are a few occasions when he has wanted to be by himself. Being outgoing is a central trait for Mitchell.*

Clinical interview:
the initial meeting between a client and a clinician in which the clinician asks questions to identify the difficulty in functioning that the person is experiencing. *Example: Annabelle goes to a therapist who meets with her and asks her why she has come for counseling and what she hopes to gain through counseling.*

Collective unconscious:
according to Jung, the part of the unconscious that contains images and material universal to people of all time periods and cultures. *Example: All cultures have representations of appropriate male and female behavior.*

Conscious level:
the level of consciousness that holds all the thoughts, perceptions, and impulses of which we are aware. *Example: What you are currently thinking of is in your conscious level.*

Defense mechanism:
a process used to protect the ego by reducing the anxiety it feels when faced with the conflicting demands of the id and the superego. *Examples: repression, sublimation, rationalization, denial etc...*

Ego:
the conscious part of the personality that attempts to meet the demands of the id in a socially appropriate way. *Example: Although you are really hungry, your ego would tell you to offer part of your pizza to your friends when they stop by for a visit.*

Electra complex:
in the female, an unconscious sexual urge for the father that develops during the phallic psychosexual stage. *Example: Young girls may profess that they are going to marry their daddy when they grow up during this stage.*

Extraversion:
personality traits that involve energy directed outward. *Example: Bettina has a lively and excitable personality.*

Genital stage:
Freud's final psychosexual stage of development, which occurs during puberty, in which sexual energy is transferred toward peers of the other sex (heterosexual orientation) or same sex (homosexual orientation). *Example: Young teens in middle school often start dating or hanging out with people they are attracted to during this stage.*

Humanistic approach:
a personality perspective that emphasizes the individual, personal choice, and free will in shaping personality; assumes that humans have a built-in drive toward fulfilling their own natural potential. *Examples: Maslow's hierarchy of needs theory and Roger's self-theory*

Id:
the unconscious part of the personality that seeks pleasure and gratification. *Example: Stealing a CD from a music store because you don't have the money to buy it and want it now would be fulfilling an id impulse.*

Introversion:
personality traits that involve energy directed inward. *Example: Caterina has a calm and peaceful personality.*

Latency stage:
Freud's fourth psychosexual stage of development, which occurs from around age 6 to puberty, in which the child's sexuality is suppressed due to widening social contacts with school, peers, and family. *Example: Boys and girls in elementary school may go through a "cootie" stage in which they do not want to affiliate with members of the other sex because of suppressed sexuality.*

Locus of control:
the expectation of control we have over the outcome of an event; an internal locus expects some degree of personal control whereas an external locus expects little personal control. *Example: Believing that luck will get you a good job is an external*

locus of control whereas believing that hard work will land you opportunities is an internal locus of control.

Minnesota Multiphasic Personality Inventory (MMPI-2):
a personality inventory that is designed to identify problem areas of functioning in a person's personality.

Neuroticism:
the degree to which one is emotionally unstable. *Example: Doug seems to fly off the handle at the smallest inconvenience and is often anxious. Doug would be described as neurotic.*

Oedipus complex:
in the male, an unconscious sexual urge for the mother that develops during the phallic psychosexual stage. *Example: Young boys may want to sleep with their mommies during this phase.*

Oral stage:
Freud's first psychosexual stage of development, which occurs during the first year of life, in which the handling of the child's feeding experiences affects personality development. *Example: Baby care books often suggest weaning a baby from the breast or bottle in a gradual manner rather than abruptly because it maintains a sense of trust and comfort that foster personality development.*

Personality:
the unique collection of attitudes, emotions, thoughts, habits, impulses, and behaviors that define how a person typically behaves across situations.

Personality inventory:
objective paper-and-pencil self-report form that measures personality on several dimensions. *Examples: The MMPI-2 measures psychological adjustment; the Myers-Briggs measures the degree to which one is introverted or extraverted.*

Personal unconscious:
according to Jung, the part of the unconscious that consists of forgotten memories and repressed experiences from one's past. *Example: Personal memories and events of which you are unaware of, like your birth.*

Person-situation interaction:
the influence of the situation on the stability of traits; when in the same situation, we display similar behavior, but when the situation is different, behavior may change. *Example: Nate is quiet in the classroom, but loud and boisterous with his friends.*

Phallic stage:
Freud's third psychosexual stage of development, which occurs between three and six years of age, in which little boys experience the Oedipus complex and little girls the Electra complex. *Example: Preschoolers often explore their bodies and are curious about other people's bodies during this stage.*

Pleasure principle:
the basis on which the id operates; to feel good and maximize gratification.

Preconscious level:

the level of consciousness that holds thoughts, perceptions, and impulses of which we could potentially be aware. *Example: Memories that you easily remember like the name of your 4th grade teacher or what rides you went on at the amusement park are stored in your preconscious.*

Projective test:

an unstructured and subjective personality test in which an individual is shown an ambiguous stimulus and is asked to describe what he or she sees. *Examples: the Rorschach Inkblot Test and the Thematic Apperception Test*

Psychoanalytic perspective:

a personality approach developed by Sigmund Freud that sees personality as the product of driving forces within a person that are often conflicting and sometimes unconscious.

Psychoticism:

the degree to which one is hostile, nonconforming, impulsive, and aggressive. *Example: Earl often breaks the rules and makes snide remarks about others. Earl has a high level of psychoticism in his personality.*

Reality principle:

the basis on which the ego operates; finding socially appropriate means to fulfill id demands.

Reciprocal determinism:

according to Bandura, the constant interaction among one's behavior, thoughts, and environment determines personality. *Example: Ophelia sees her older sister and mother put lipstick on in the morning. Ophelia believes women should wear lipstick. Ophelia does not go anywhere without wearing lipstick.*

Reliability:

the consistency of a test's measurements over time. *Example: If an intelligence test is reliable it should produce similar results when you take it on two different occasions.*

Rorschach Inkblot test:

a projective personality test consisting of ten ambiguous inkblots in which a person is asked to describe what he or she sees; the person's responses are then coded for consistent themes and issues.

Secondary traits:

according to Allport, the tendencies we have that are less consistent and describe how we behave in certain situations. *Example: Frieda is typically meek and submissive, so it was quite a surprise to see her stand up for herself at the committee meeting.*

Self-actualization:

the fulfillment of one's natural potential. *Example: Quentin is a gifted athlete and fulfills this potential by playing several sports through high school and college.*

Self-concept:

one's perception or image of his/her abilities and uniqueness. *Example: Glenn sees himself as an astute business person and loyal friend. This is Glenn's self-concept.*

Self-efficacy:
the expectation that one has for success in a given situation. *Example: Irene knows that her language skills are good and is looking forward to traveling abroad. Irene's language self-efficacy is high.*

Social cognitive approach:
a personality perspective that emphasizes the influence of one's thoughts and social experiences in formulating personality. *Examples: Rotter's locus of control theory and Bandura's reciprocal determinism*

Source traits:
universal tendencies that underlie and are at the core of surface traits, according to Cattell. *Examples: the degree to which one is shy or bold; the degree to which one is dominant or submissive*

Superego:
the part of the personality that represents your moral conscience. *Example: Lenny was babysitting his siblings when his parents were out of town. His friends wanted him to have a party but Lenny said no, as his superego reasoned his parents would not like it.*

Surface traits:
basic traits that describe people's personalities, according to Cattell.

Thematic Apperception Test (TAT):
a projective personality test consisting of a series of pictures in which the respondent is asked to tell a story about each scene; the responses are then coded for consistent themes and issues.

Trait approach:
a personality perspective that attempts to describe personality by emphasizing internal, biological aspects of personality called traits. *Examples: Cattell's trait theory, Eysenck's PEN model, Costa and McCrae's Five Factor theory*

Trait:
tendency we have across most situations to behave in a certain way. *Example: Vanessa is typically generous. Generosity is a trait for Vanessa.*

Unconditional positive regard:
acceptance and love of another's thoughts and feelings without expecting anything in return. *Example: Romeo accepts and loves Juliet, and would do anything for her.*

Unconscious level:
the level of awareness that contains all the thoughts, perceptions, and impulses of which we are unaware. *Example: Suri hit her younger brother when he took her toy. When asked why she hit him, Suri said she didn't know why, she just did. Suri's impulse to hit came from her unconscious level.*

Validity:
the ability of a test to measure what it says it is measuring. *Example: An intelligence test is valid if it measures qualities that have to do with intelligence.*

Fill-in Review of the Chapter

Can you fill-in the missing terms for each section of the chapter? Items marked with an *
encourage you to continue building the Big Picture of psychology by connecting the
material in this chapter to material from previous chapters in the text.

The Big Picture: How Can We Understand Personality?

James McBride describes himself as shy, passive and quiet. A trait theorist would
describe James' personality as 1) _____ whereas Freud would see James'
2) _____ as the predominant component part of his personality.

The Psychoanalytic Approach: Sigmund Freud and the Neo-Freudians

Your memories of your high school graduation or first date reside at the 3) _____
level of consciousness.

Lucinda meant to tell Jack that she couldn't "live" with his behavior. But, instead she
said that she couldn't "love" with his behavior. According to the psychoanalytic view of
personality, Lucinda just made a(n) 4) _____ _____.

Ego defense mechanisms seek to protect the ego by reducing conscious 5) _____.

Freud's superego reflects the development of our thoughts about right and wrong
referred to as 6*) _____ _____.

Karen Horney suggests that disturbances in early relationships lead to 7) _____
_____ in children.

The Trait Approach: Describing Personality

A(n) 8) _____ is a tendency that we have to behave in a certain way across a
variety of situations.

The trait approach emphasizes the 9*) _____ perspective.

Isabel is always the life of the party. She speaks loudly, loves to dance, and generally
likes to draw attention to herself. According to Eysenck, Isabel is a(n) 10) _____.

The fact that our behavior may change from one situation to the next is known as the
11) _____ interaction.

The Social Cognitive Approach: The Environment and Patterns of Thoughts

According to the principle of 12) _____ _____, we influence our environment and our
environment influences us.

Learned helplessness reflects more of a(n) 13*) _____ locus of control.

Your expectation for success in a given situation is called 14) _____ _____.

The Humanistic Approach: Free Will and Self-Actualization

Attaining one's full potential is referred to as 15) _____ _____.

Rogers believed that human beings naturally strive for fulfillment and enhancement, a basic motive that he referred to as the 16) _____ _____.

One weakness of the humanistic and psychoanalytic approaches is its reliance on the 17) _____ ____ research method.

Measuring Personality

A test is 18) _____ if it measures what it is designed to measure. A personality test is 19) _____ if it yields consistent scores.

Personality tests are more often administered by 20*) _____ psychologists.

Use It or Lose It!

Identify the psychosexual stage for each of the following examples.

Psychosexual Stage	Behavior
1.	Samuel asks a young woman out on a date who unconsciously reminds him of his mother.
2.	Tia has no interest in boys and prefers to spend her time with her best friends and school interests.
3.	Chuck puts every toy in his mouth before playing with it.
4.	Karianne often prevents her parents from hugging each other by inserting herself in the middle.
5.	Tyrone refuses to go to the bathroom before he goes to bed.

Self-Check: Are You Getting the Big Picture?

After you have read and studied the chapter, see if you can answer the following quiz questions. Check your answers at the end of the chapter. If you miss a question, refer to your text and re-study the appropriate sections.

True or False Questions

Are these statements true or false?

1. The superego operates on the reality principle.
True
False

2. Research on Hans Eysenck's idea that introverts have higher levels of physiological arousal than extraverts has generally been supported.
True
False

3. Alfred Adler divided the unconscious into the personal unconscious and the collective unconscious.
True
False

4. Personality traits seem to arise from a combination of genetic and environmental influences.
True
False

5. As people age, they tend to become more androgynous.
True
False

6. One strength of Freud's theory is his emphasis on explaining the developmental nature of personality.
True
False

7. Generally speaking, it is healthier to have an external locus of control.
True
False

8. According to Abraham Maslow, few people ever reach a state of self-actualization.
True
False

9. Carl Rogers believed that humans are motivated by an actualizing tendency.
True
False

10. A major problem associated with personality inventories is the fact that test takers may choose to lie when taking the inventory.
True
False

Multiple Choice Questions

Can you choose the best answer for these questions?

1. Which of the following is not one of the universal traits suggested by the five factor theory?
   A. conscientiousness
   B. neuroticism
   C. agreeableness
   D. aggressiveness

2. Which personality perspective emphasizes the role of unconscious motives and desires?
   A. the psychoanalytic approach
   B. the trait approach
   C. the social cognitive approach
   D. the humanistic approach

3. Ted is hungry and he feels like eating a candy bar. According to Sigmund Freud, in which part of Ted's personality does this desire originate?
   A. id
   B. ego
   C. superego
   D. the conscience

4. After thinking of stealing a candy bar, Ted is appalled at himself. He feels bad and he vows never to steal. According to Sigmund Freud, from which part of Ted's personality are these moral thoughts coming?
   A. id
   B. ego
   C. superego
   D. none of the above

5. The superego develops during the _____ stage of psychosexual development.
   A. oral
   B. anal
   C. phallic
   D. genital

6. According to Freud, fixation occurs if a child receives:
   A. too much satisfaction during a particular psychosexual stage.
   B. too little satisfaction during a particular psychosexual stage.
   C. just the right amount of satisfaction during a particular psychosexual stage.
   D. A & B

7. Carl Jung added the idea of the _____ to Freud's conceptualization of the mind.
   A. personal unconscious
   B. collective unconscious
   C. unconscious
   D. preconscious

8. Neo-Freudian, Alfred Adler, emphasized _____ as motivators of personality development.
   A. fears
   B. sexual urges
   C. feelings of inferiority
   D. aggressive impulses

9. Neo-Freudian, Karen Horney, emphasized the role of _____ as a motivator of personality development.
   A. sexual desire
   B. instinctual conflict
   C. inferiority
   D. basic anxiety

10. Which of the following is not a criticism that has been made about Freud's approach to personality?
    A. It is too simplistic.
    B. It overemphasizes sexuality.
    C. It underemphasizes the influence of the environment.
    D. For the most part, it cannot be scientifically tested.

11. According to Gordon Allport, a _____ trait describes how a person behaves in all situations.
    A. central
    B. secondary
    C. cardinal
    D. self-actualized

12. Ultimately, Raymond Cattell proposed the existence of _____ source traits.
    A. 5
    B. 12
    C. 13
    D. 16

13. Research on the stability of personality traits over the lifespan shows that in general after age _____ changes in one's personality traits are small.
    A. 12
    B. 25
    C. 30
    D. 45

14. The trait approach to personality has been criticized for:
    A. describing people's personalities.
    B. for not explaining the causes of our behavior.
    C. for being non-scientific.
    D. for being too complicated.

15. Umberto has a lot of confidence in his ability as a student. According to Albert Bandura, Umberto is high in:
    A. self-efficacy.
    B. arrogance.
    C. self-determinism.
    D. none of the above

16. Xavier believes that his fate is in the hands of God. According to Julian Rotter, Xavier has a:
    A. internal locus of control.
    B. external locus of control.
    C. learned helplessness orientation.
    D. mastery orientation.

17. The current trend in the United States is that young people are adopting an increasingly:
    A. internal locus of control.
    B. external locus of control.
    C. helpless orientation.
    D. none of the above

18. According to Carl Rogers, underlying the human actualizing tendency is:
    A. sexual desire.
    B. an organismic valuing process.
    C. an inferiority complex.
    D. none of the above

19. Ivan yells at his daughter for getting a "C" on a test in school. In doing so, Ivan tells her that she needs to make better grades. According to Carl Rogers, Ivan is showing his daughter:
    A. unconditional positive regard.
    B. conditional positive regard.
    C. hatred.
    D. tough love.

20. Which of the following is a projective personality test?
    A. the MMPI-2
    B. the Myers-Briggs Personality Inventory
    C. the Thematic Apperception Test
    D. none of the above

21. To help identify dishonest test takers, some personality inventories like the MMPI-2 include:
    A. validity scales.
    B. trick questions.
    C. ambiguous questions.
    D. simplistic questions.

22. During Luis' first meeting with his therapist, the therapist asks him a lot of questions about his attitudes and behaviors. Luis' therapist is likely conducting a:
    A. projective personality test.
    B. personality inventory.
    C. clinical interview.
    D. rating scale.

23. Differences in anxiety levels from person to person are associated with which neurotransmitter?
    A. dopamine
    B. norepinephrine
    C. serotonin
    D. endorphins

24. Yanna is very emotionally unstable. Yanna would most likely score high on which of the Big Five personality traits?
    A. openness
    B. conscientiousness
    C. extraversion
    D. neuroticism

25. Tamika takes an IQ test and scores above average on it. Six months later, she takes the test again and this time, she scores far below average on it. The IQ test Tamika took appears to be:
    A. invalid.
    B. valid.
    C. unreliable.
    D. reliable.

Short-Answer Questions

Can you write a brief answer to these questions?

1. What is reciprocal determinism?

2. Of Freud's three components of personality (i.e., the id, ego, and superego), which one is likely to experience the greatest stress and strain on a daily basis? Why?

3. What is the logic behind a projective personality test?

4. What are the Big Five personality traits?

5. Is personality inherited through our genes?

Developing a Bigger Picture: Making Connections Across Chapters

An important aspect of learning is learning to see the "Big Picture" of the subject you are studying. As you learn about psychology, you should try to understand how the material from different chapters fits together to help you form a broad-based understanding of what psychology is all about. To help facilitate the development of this "Big Picture" in your mind, try to answer these questions using the knowledge you have learned in this chapter, as well as the other chapters referenced in the questions.

1. Given what you learned about motivation in Chapter 8 and personality in this chapter, why does Abraham Maslow appear in both chapters?

2. Given what you learned about health and stress in Chapter 12 and locus of control in this chapter, answer this question: Do you think it is healthier to have an internal or an external locus of control? Why?

3. Using what you learned about memory in Chapter 6, relate Freud's levels of consciousness to the three stages model of memory.

Label the Diagram

Can you label these different personality concepts with the theorist who developed them?

1.	Psychoanalytic theory
2.	Collective unconscious
3.	Reciprocal Determinism
4.	Hierarchy of needs theory
5.	Locus of Control
6.	Self-theory
7.	Basic anxiety

Big Picture Review

Identify the traits that are suggested by each of the following trait theories.

Gordon Allport	1. 2. 3.
Raymond Cattell	4. 5.
Hans Eysenck	6. 7. 8.
Five Factor theory	9. 10. 11. 12. 13.

Solutions

Each solution below is followed by its textbook page reference number and its corresponding chapter learning objective (LO) number. Items with a Big Picture LO help you build a Big Picture of psychology across the chapters you have studied so far.

Fill-in Review of the Chapter

1. introverted [p. 591; LO 3]
2. superego [p. 582; LO 1]
3. preconscious [p. 581; LO 1]
4. Freudian slip [p. 583; LO 1]
5. anxiety [p. 583; LO 1]
6. moral reasoning [p. 395; LO-Big Picture]
7. basic anxiety [p. 587; LO 2]
8. trait [p. 589; LO 3]
9. biological [p. 15; LO-Big Picture]
10. extravert [p. 591; LO 3]
11. person-situation [p. 596; LO 4]
12. reciprocal determinism [p. 598; LO 5]
13. external [p. 564; LO-Big Picture]
14. self-efficacy [p. 599; LO 5]
15. self-actualization [p. 601; LO 6]
16. actualizing tendency [p. 602; LO 6]
17. case study [p. 588; 604; LO 7]
18. valid [p. 605; LO 8]
19. reliable [p. 605; LO 8]
20. clinical [p. 23; LO-Big Picture]

Use It or Lose It! [p. 584-585; LO 1]

1. genital
2. latency
3. oral
4. phallic
5. anal

Self-Check: Are You Getting the Big Picture?

True or False Questions

1. F [p. 582; LO 1]
2. T [p. 591-592; LO 3]
3. F [p. 586-587; LO 2]
4. T [p. 595; LO 4]
5. T [p. 596; LO 4]

6. T [p. 588; LO 7]
7. F [p. 600; LO 5]
8. T [p. 602; LO 6]
9. T [p. 602; LO 6]
10. T [p. 606; LO 8]

Multiple Choice Questions

1. D [p. 593; LO 3]	10. A [p. 588; LO 7]	19. B [p. 603; LO 6]
2. A [p. 580; LO 1]	11. C [p. 590; LO 3]	20. C [p. 607; LO 8]
3. A [p. 581; LO 1]	12. D [p. 590; LO 3]	21. A [p. 606; LO 8]
4. C [p. 582; LO 1]	13. C [p. 595; LO 4]	22. C [p. 609; LO 8]
5. C [p. 582; LO 1]	14. B [p. 597; LO 7]	23. C [p. 595; LO 4]
6. D [p. 585; LO 1]	15. A [p. 599; LO 5]	24. D [p. 593; LO 3]
7. B [p. 586; LO 2]	16. B [p. 599; LO 5]	25. C [p. 605; LO 8]
8. C [p. 587; LO 2]	17. B [p. 600; LO 5]	
9. D [p. 587; LO 2]	18. B [p. 603; LO 6]	

Short-Answer Questions

Can you write a brief answer to these questions?

1. What is reciprocal determinism? [p. 598-599; LO 5]

   Reciprocal determinism is Albert Bandura's idea that our thoughts, behaviors and environment all interact and affect each other. Our environment affects how we think and how we behave, but our thoughts and behaviors also affect our environment. For example, a happy-go-lucky person may put others at ease, thereby creating calm, happy social environments. These calm, happy social environments, in turn, make it easier for the person to remain happy-go-lucky!

2. Of Freud's three components of personality (i.e., the id, ego, and superego), which one is likely to experience the greatest stress and strain on a daily basis? Why? [p. 582-583; LO 1]

The ego is most likely to suffer stress and strain because it must attempt to meet the demands of both the id and the superego. Given that the id and superego have very different motives, sometimes the ego has a hard time finding a solution to everyday problems. For example, if you forgot to study for an exam and your id wants to pass, how can you find a morally acceptable solution (your superego has to approve) to this problem? The ego may be unable to find a solution in this situation.

3. What is the logic behind a projective personality test? [p. 606-607; LO 8]

    In a projective test, the participant is shown an ambiguous stimulus of some sort (e.g., an inkblot or ambiguous picture) and asked to interpret it in some fashion. The idea is that because the stimulus is ambiguous, the participant will have to "project" some of his or her personality traits into his/her interpretation of the stimulus.

    In doing so, the participant leaves clues as to his/her personality in the interpretation, and a skilled examiner can use these clues to assess the participant's personality.

4. What are the Big Five personality traits? [p. 593; LO 3]

    The Big Five can be represented with the acronym, OCEAN— openness (the degree to which one is thoughtful and rational in considering new ideas), conscientiousness (the degree to which one is aware of and attentive to other people and/or the specifics of a task), extraversion (the degree to which energy is directed outward), agreeableness (the degree to which one gets along with others), and neuroticism (the degree to which one is emotionally unstable).

5. Is personality inherited through our genes? [p. 593-595; LO 4]

    Personality does seem to be at least partially inherited. For one thing, genetic temperament tends to remain fairly stable across long periods of time. Twin and adoption studies also indicate that some specific traits may have a genetic basis. And, gene marker studies have suggested that levels of certain neurotransmitters, like serotonin, may be genetically determined and may influence aspects of personality. For example, aggressiveness may be related to having low levels of serotonin.

Developing a Bigger Picture: Making Connections Across Chapters

1. Given what you learned about motivation in Chapter 8 and personality in this chapter, why does Abraham Maslow appear in both chapters? [p. 339; LO-Big Picture]

    Maslow appears in both chapters because his theory describes both what motivates our behavior at specific points in time and it conceptualizes the development of personality as we strive for self-actualization in life.

2. Given what you learned about health and stress in Chapter 13 and locus of control in this chapter, answer this question: Do you think it is healthier to have an internal or an external locus of control? Why? [p. 565; LO-Big Picture]

Having an internal locus of control is generally associated with being psychologically healthy. People with an internal locus of control tend to perceive that they have more control over what happens to them. As you may recall, having a sense of control is one of the factors involved in being a hardy person that can withstand stress without becoming ill.

3. Using what you learned about memory in Chapter 6, relate Freud's levels of consciousness to the three stages model of memory. [p. 242; LO-Big Picture]

The conscious level is analogous to the contents of short-term memory at any point in time—it's the information you are currently using.

The preconscious level is analogous to accessible long-term memory. It contains information you are not currently using, but could access and bring to consciousness should you choose to do so.

The unconscious level is most analogous to inaccessible long-term memory. It contains information that is available, but not accessible in long-term memory. Due to its inaccessibility, this information cannot be brought to consciousness.

Label the Diagram

1. Sigmund Freud [p. 580; LO 1]
2. Carl Jung [p. 586; LO 2]
3. Albert Bandura [p. 598; LO 5]
4. Abraham Maslow [p. 601; LO 6]
5. Julian Rotter [p. 599; LO 5]
6. Carl Rogers [p. 602; LO 6]
7. Karen Horney [p. 587; LO 2]

Big Picture Review [p. 593; LO 3]

Gordon Allport	1. cardinal traits 2. central traits 3. secondary traits
Raymond Cattell	4. surface traits 5. source traits
Hans Eysenck	6. psychoticism 7. extraversion 8. neuroticism
Five Factor theory	9. openness 10. conscientiousness 11. extraversion 12. agreeableness 13. neuroticism

14

What Are Psychological Disorders, And How Can We Understand Them?

Learning Objectives

After studying each of the following sections of the chapter, you should be able to do these tasks:

What Makes Behavior Abnormal, and How Prevalent Is Abnormal Behavior?

1. Identify the criteria that psychologists use for determining abnormal behavior.

Explaining Abnormal Behavior: Perspectives Revisited

2. Compare and contrast the varying perspectives on explaining abnormal behavior, and formulate an integrated perspective to explain a particular behavior.

The *DSM* Model for Classifying Abnormal Behavior

3. Describe the nature of the *DSM* model, and identify its strengths and weaknesses.

Anxiety Disorders: It's Not Just "Nerves"

4. Distinguish among the symptoms of the five anxiety disorders, and discuss our current understanding of the causes of anxiety disorders.

Mood Disorders: Beyond the Blues

5. Distinguish between the symptoms of unipolar and bipolar depressive disorders, and discuss our current understanding of the causes of mood disorders.

6. Detail common misconceptions that people hold about suicide.

Schizophrenic Disorders: Disintegration

7. Identify and describe the symptoms of schizophrenia, discriminate between the types of schizophrenia, and discuss our current understanding of the causes of schizophrenia.

Dissociative and Somatoform Disorders: Personalities and Illnesses

8. Describe the nature of dissociative and somatoform disorders.

Personality Disorders: Maladaptive Patterns of Behavior

9. Describe the nature of personality disorders.

The Big Picture

The Big Picture: How Does a Beautiful Mind Go Awry?

In this chapter, you learned about the study of mental illness or abnormal behavior. As the opening stories of John Nash, Amy Tan, and Howard Hughes illustrate, psychological disorders can make life very difficult for those who suffer from them.

What Makes Behavior Abnormal, and How Prevalent is Abnormal Behavior?

This section covers Learning Objective 1. Abnormal behavior is characterized by its statistical infrequency or unusualness. Violating social norms is another indication of mental illness. People with mental illnesses often behave in ways that many of us would consider to be different or odd. However, behaving unusually or in violation of norms is not enough by itself to warrant a diagnosis of mental illness. Differing cultural norms, eccentricity, situational pressures, or possessing rare, but normal abilities could all account for why a healthy person may behave in an unusual manner.

Another criterion for judging abnormality is behavior that causes the person distress. Many times, people with mental illness find that their behavior causes them so much suffering that they seek therapy to ease their distress. However, this criterion alone is not enough to label a person as abnormal. Unhappiness can come from normal levels of behavior; whereas in other cases, abnormal behavior may fail to cause personal distress at all.

Psychologists often combine these criteria and define abnormal behavior as behavior that interferes with a person's ability to function and/or causes distress to oneself or others.

Forty-six percent of individuals will meet the criteria for a mental health disorder at some time in their lives with males and females showing differences in the types of psychological disorders they are more likely to experience. Mental disorders are the leading cause of disability in the United States and Canada for people between the ages of 15 and 44. So it is likely that you or someone close to you will at some time experience a mental health disorder.

Explaining Abnormal Behavior: Perspectives Revisited

This section covers Learning Objective 2. Why do people behave abnormally? For centuries, people have asked this question. Western cultures predominantly lean toward three main models for understanding abnormal behavior: biological or natural theories, psychological theories, and social or cultural theories.

The idea that mental illnesses result from biological dysfunction can be traced back to the ancient cultures of China, Egypt, and Greece. These cultures' ideas on mental illness laid the foundation for what today is called the medical model, the idea that abnormal behavior is an illness.

Psychological theories of abnormal behavior attribute it to internal and external stressors facing the individual. Psychological perspectives on mental illness include the psychoanalytic approach, social learning approach, cognitive approach, and humanistic approach. The psychoanalytic approach emphasizes the role that unconscious psychological conflicts play in causing abnormal behavior. The social learning approach proposes that abnormal behavior is learned through classical conditioning, operant conditioning, and social learning. The cognitive approach states that maladaptive thought processes underlie abnormal behavior. And the humanistic approach suggests that mental illness results from having a distorted sense of self and reality.

Mental illness can also be viewed from a sociocultural approach—the notion that social and cultural factors play a role in the development of psychological disorders. For example, the ultra-thin standard of female beauty found in the U.S., Europe and Asia may account for increasing levels of eating disorders in those cultures.

Most psychological disorders result from a combination of biological, psychological, and socio-cultural factors; they do not have just one cause. Psychologists often integrate the perspectives to achieve a more comprehensive picture of abnormality.

The *DSM* Model for Classifying Abnormal Behavior

This section covers Learning Objective 3. Another consideration in dealing with abnormal behavior is classifying which mental illness or disorder a person has. Since 1952, psychologists have used the Diagnostic and Statistical Manual of Mental Disorders (DSM) to determine which psychological disorder a person suffers. The current version of the DSM is the DSM-IV-TR, which lists the specific and concrete criteria for diagnosing nearly four hundred different disorders. The DSM is a multi-dimensional instrument that involves making five different judgments about a person. Axis I indicates the conditions that impair a person's ability to function; Axis II, the lifelong conditions that impair functioning; Axis III, the medical problems from which the person suffers; Axis IV, an assessment of the stressors in the person's life; and Axis V, the person's global level of functioning rated on a scale of 1-100.

Evaluation of the DSM shows that Axis I is very high in reliability and validity but Axis II is not, suggesting that valid diagnosis of lifelong disorders like personality disorders is difficult to achieve. Subsequent versions of the DSM will have to address this issue. Other problems with the DSM include the possibility that a clinician may still make an incorrect diagnosis and the possible stereotyping and prejudice that a person may face after being labeled with a DSM diagnosis.

Anxiety Disorders: It's No Just "Nerves"

This section covers Learning Objective 4. Anxiety disorders are Axis I diagnoses in which a person suffers from abnormal levels of physical, cognitive, emotional, and behavioral anxiety. This category includes panic disorder (panic attacks), specific phobias (phobias for specific things), social phobias (phobias for social situations), obsessive-compulsive disorder (persistent unwanted thoughts and compelled ritualized behaviors), post-traumatic stress disorder (maladaptive behavior in the aftermath of a life-threatening trauma), and generalized anxiety disorder (persistent, maladaptive worry and anxiety without specific focus).

Biological explanations suggest that the neurotransmitters serotonin, norepinephrine, and GABA may play a role in some anxiety disorders. Furthermore, genetics and specific brains areas like the amygdala and striatum have been implicated. Psychological factors may also play a role. For example, phobias can be classically conditioned and according to Freud, anxiety stems from unconscious tension among the id, ego, and superego. Cognitive processes may also be involved, for example how a person interprets his or her bodily symptoms may impact his or her tendency to have panic attacks. And finally, cultural and gender factors may also play a role in anxiety disorders. Being female, experiencing war or rapid social change, and having been abused in childhood are all risk factors for developing anxiety disorders.

Mood Disorders: Beyond the Blues

This section covers Learning Objectives 5 and 6. Mood disorders are Axis I disorders that all involve significant disturbances in one's mood state. Mood disorders include unipolar depression (major levels of dysphoria and/or apathy), dysthymia (a milder form of depression), bipolar disorder (alternating major depression and mania), and cyclothymia (a milder from of manic-depressive symptoms). Suicide may accompany these disorders, but it may also occur outside of a mood disorder.

Biological factors involved in mood disorders are genes (especially for bipolar disorder), problems with the neurotransmitters serotonin and norepinephrine, and high levels of stress hormones. Psychological factors may also play a role in the development of mood disorders. According to psychoanalytic theory, childhood abandonment, rejection, and loss may predispose one to depression. Learned helplessness or coming to believe that you have no control over what happens to you, has also been suggested as a cause of depression. Cognitive factors such as a ruminative coping style, distorted cognitions or thoughts about the world, and making pessimistic attributions about yourself and others have all been associated with depression. Being female is also associated with having a higher risk of depression.

Schizophrenic Disorders: Disintegration

This section covers Learning Objective 7. Although not as common as the anxiety and mood disorders, schizophrenia is a very serious, disabling disorder that affects 1-2% of the general population. Schizophrenia usually develops during adolescence or young adulthood and may include thought disorder, delusions, hallucinations, disordered emotion, and/or disordered behavior. Positive symptoms of schizophrenia are symptoms that represent unusual perceptions, thoughts, or behaviors. Negative symptoms include losses of normal abilities such as flat affect, social withdrawal, or catatonic stupor. Some people may have only positive or negative symptoms, whereas others may exhibit both. People who suffer only the positive symptoms of schizophrenia usually have a better prognosis and respond better to medication.

There appears to be a strong genetic basis involved in schizophrenia. A longstanding assumption is that dopamine plays a role in schizophrenia—particularly the positive symptoms. However, recently the relationship between dopamine and schizophrenic symptoms has proven to be complex. Other neurotransmitters like serotonin and glutamate may also play a role. Abnormalities in the structure of the brain may also be involved—especially in the negative symptoms. People with schizophrenia often tend to have enlarged ventricles and smaller or inactive frontal lobes. Lifestyle and family factors do not appear to cause schizophrenia per se, but they may interact with biological predispositions to the disease and affect the course of the disorder for those at risk.

Dissociative and Somatoform Disorders: Personalities and Illnesses

This section covers Learning Objective 8. Dissociative and somatoform disorders are extremely rare in the general population. Dissociative disorders are associated with abnormal levels of dissociation or splitting of one's consciousness. Dissociative Identity Disorder (DID), formerly called multiple personality disorder, is characterized by having more than one identity and frequent bouts of blacking-out or amnesia as one switches among these identities. Somatoform disorders involve physical complaints that have no physical basis. One such disorder is hypochondriasis, in which a person experiences excessive worry about his or her health and believes that he or she is ill despite medical evidence to the contrary.

Personality Disorders: Maladaptive Patterns of Behavior

This section covers Learning Objective 9. Personality disorders are lifelong disorders in which one's personality develops maladaptive characteristics. Antisocial personality disorder is characterized by a disarming sense of charm coupled with a disturbing lack of conscience. People with antisocial personality disorder or psychopaths are likely to manipulate others, lie, cheat, and fail to maintain social relationships. Low levels of serotonin, a genetic predisposition, brain dysfunction, and low levels of nervous system arousal have all been suggested as causes of antisocial personality disorder. However, psychological and social factors are also involved.

377

Borderline personality disorder (BPD) is a personality disorder characterized by instability in moods, relationships, self-image, and behavior. BPD is often seen in conjunction with other disorders like substance abuse, depression, and anxiety. Self-injury and suicide attempts are commonly seen in people with BPD. The cause of BPD is not known at this time, but low levels of serotonin, abnormal brain functioning, and childhood abuse, neglect, or separation have been suggested.

Outlining the Big Picture

Chapter 14: What Are Psychological Disorders, and How Can We Understand Them?

The Big Picture: How Does A Beautiful Mind Go Awry?
Notes:

_____

_____

_____

_____

_____

What Makes Behavior Abnormal and How Prevalent is Abnormal Behavior? (Learning Objective 1)
Prevalence of Abnormal Behaviors
Notes:

_____

_____

_____

_____

_____

Explaining Abnormal Behavior: Perspectives Revisited (Learning Objective 2)
Biological Theories: The Medical Model
Psychological Theories: Humane Treatment and Psychological Processes

Sociocultural Theories: The Individual in Context
Integrating Perspectives: Putting the Puzzle Together
Notes:

_____

_____

_____

_____

The *DSM* Model for Classifying Abnormal Behavior (Learning Objective 3)
A Mulitdimensional Evaluation
How Good Is the *DSM* Model?
Notes:

_____

_____

_____

_____

_____

Anxiety Disorders: It's Not Just "Nerves" (Learning Objective 4)
Components of the Anxiety Disorders
   Physical Anxiety: Fight or Flight
   Cognitive and Emotional Anxiety
   Behavioral Anxiety
Types of Anxiety Disorders
   Generalized Anxiety Disorder
   Panic Disorder
   Phobic Disorders
   Obsessive-Compulsive Disorder (OCD)
   Post-Traumatic Stress Disorder (PTSD)
Explaining Anxiety Disorders
   Biology and the Brain
   Psychological Factors

Sociocultural Factors
Notes:

_____

_____

_____

_____

_____

_____

Mood Disorders: Beyond the Blues (Learning Objective 5-6)
Unipolar Depressive Disorders: A Change to Sadness
Bipolar Depressive Disorders: The Presence of Mania
Suicide Facts and Misconceptions
Explaining Mood Disorders
   Biological Factors: Genes, Neurotransmitters, and Stress Hormones
   *Psychological Factors: Abandonment, Learned Helplessness, and Negative
      Thinking*
   Sociocultural Factors
   Spotlight on Diversity World: Women and Depression
Notes:

_____

_____

_____

_____

_____

_____

Schizophrenic Disorders: Disintegration (Learning Objective 7)
Onset, Gender, Ethnicity, and Prognosis
Symptoms of Schizophrenia
   Disordered Thoughts: Loose Associations and Delusions
   Disordered Perceptions: Hallucinations
   Disordered Affect, or Emotion: Laughing at All the Wrong Things
   Disordered Motor Behavior: Agitation and Stupor
Types of Schizophrenia: Positive and Negative Symptoms

Explaining Schizophrenia: Genetics, the Brain, and the Environment
  A Strong Genetic Factor
  The Brain: Neurotransmitters and Structural Abnormalities
  Prenatal and Developmental Factors
  The Role of Family and Environment
Notes:

_____

_____

_____

_____

Dissociative and Somatoform Disorders: Personalities and Illnesses (Learning Objective 8)

Dissociative Identity Disorder: Multiple Personalities
Hypochondriasis, or Doctor, I'm Sure I'm Sick
Notes:

_____

_____

_____

_____

Personality Disorders: Maladaptive Patterns of Behavior (Learning Objective 9)

Antisocial Personality Disorder: Charming and Dangerous
Borderline Personality Disorder: Living on Your Fault Line
Notes:

_____

_____

_____

_____

_____

_____

_____

Are You Getting the Big Picture?
Notes:

_____

_____

_____

_____

_____

_____

Seeing the Big Picture: A Mental Map of Chapter 14

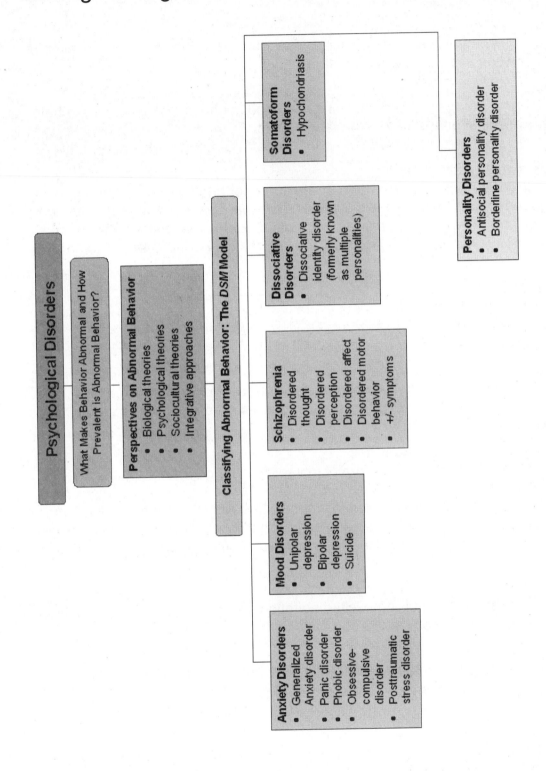

Key Points of the Big Picture

Affect:
one's expressed emotion toward an action at a given time. *Example: Lila was excited or had lively affect when she was given a present.*

Agoraphobia:
an excessive fear of being in places from which escape might be difficult or where help might not be available if one were to experience panic. *Example: Gabriella will not go to the mall because she fears she will have a panic attack. Gabriella has agoraphobia.*

Antisocial personality disorder:
a personality disorder marked by a pattern of disregard for and violation of the rights of others with no remorse or guilt for one's actions. *Example: Ted works in a nursing home where he frequently steals items from the older adults. He blames the stealing on a coworker and justifies his actions with a laugh saying the old people are just going to die anyways.*

Anxiety disorder:
a disorder marked by excessive apprehension that seriously interferes with a person's ability to function. *Examples: panic disorder, OCD, generalized anxiety disorder, PTSD, and phobic disorder*

Bipolar disorder:
a mood disorder characterized by both depression and mania. *Example: Melvin alternates between bouts of severe depression and an excited mood, constant talking, and a decreased need for sleep.*

Borderline personality disorder (BPD):
a personality disorder marked by a pattern of instability in mood, relationships, self-image, and behavior. *Example: Vicki has been married three times and despises her ex-partners, blaming all of them for her misfortunes. She flits from job to job and from career to career, and has never been able to establish close personal relationships with other women. At times she is enraged and angry while at other times she is depressed and suicidal.*

Catatonic excitement:
a disorder in motor behavior involving excited agitation. *Example: Felix is a person with schizophrenia who cannot sit still and is constantly moving with catatonic excitement.*

Catatonic stupor:
a disorder in motor behavior involving immobility. *Example: Ty had to be hospitalized in a mental health facility when he would not move and appeared frozen in the same position for several hours. Ty was later diagnosed with catatonic schizophrenia.*

Cognitive distortion:
thought that tends to be pessimistic and negative. *Example: Dinah believes she will never have a relationship because she thinks she is fat, ugly, and stupid.*

Compulsion:
repetitive behavior that a person feels a strong urge to perform. *Example: Brigette makes and remakes her bed until the stripes in the bedspread line up perfectly.*

Cyclothymic disorder:
a mood disorder that is a less severe but more chronic form of bipolar disorder. *Example: Cooper's mood swings make it difficult for him to cope. Sometimes he seems blue and sad while at other times he is energetic and hyper.*

Delusion:
a thought or belief that a person believes to be true but in reality is not. *Example: Petra believes that her apartment has been bugged by extra-terrestrial beings who are planning to abduct her in the near future.*

Diagnostic and Statistical Manual of Mental Disorders (DSM):
a book published by the APA that lists the criteria for close to 400 mental health disorders.

Dissociative disorder:
a disorder marked by a loss of awareness of some part of one's self or one's surroundings that seriously interferes with the person's ability to function. *Examples: dissociative fugue, dissociative amnesia, dissociative identity disorder*

Dissociative identity disorder (DID):
a disorder in which two or more personalities coexist within the same individual; formerly called multiple personality disorder. *Example: After seven years, Eve's therapist suspects she has three alter personalities; one is a seventy-two year old woman who is dependent and cautious, one is a forty-year-old man who is aggressive and ambitious, and the third is an eight-year old child who constantly sucks her thumb and talks in a sing-song voice.*

Dysphoria:
an extreme state of sadness. *Example: Kristin cries and sobs all day long; she is very dysphoric.*

Dysthmic disorder:
a mood disorder that is a less severe but more chronic form of major depression. *Example: Darius always seems to be down in the dumps and shows little energy or emotional expression.*

Generalized anxiety disorder (GAD):
an anxiety disorder characterized by chronic, constant worry in almost all situations. *Example: Melba constantly worries over her job, her children, and her relationships, fearing that something will go wrong or someone will get hurt.*

Hallucination:
perceiving something that does not exist in reality. *Example: Dominic hears voices that comment on his actions and tell him what will happen.*

Hypochondriasis:

a somatoform disorder in which the person believes he or she has a disease, without any evident physical basis. *Example: Helena believes she has breast cancer even though a mammogram, CAT scan, and blood work appear normal.*

Learned helplessness:

the belief that one cannot control the outcome of events. *Example: Ian believes he will always do bad on his science tests so he rarely studies or even tries to comprehend the material.*

Major depression:

a mood disorder involving dysphoria, feelings of worthlessness, loss of interest in one's usual activities, and changes in bodily activities such as sleep and appetite that persists for at least 2 weeks. *Example: For the past three weeks, Trudy has had several crying fits, has difficulty concentrating, can't sleep, feels worthless, and has had no appetite.*

Mania:

a period of abnormally excessive energy and elation. *Example: Emmanuel seems to be in constant motion. He doesn't sleep. He talks really fast and believes he can accomplish anything.*

Medical model:

perspective that views psychological disorders as similar to physical diseases; they result from biological disturbances and can be diagnosed, treated, and cured like other physical illnesses. *Example: Dr. Huang is a psychiatrist who believes that depression is caused by abnormal levels of serotonin. He prescribes his patients who are depressed, antidepressant medication to restore normal serotonin levels.*

Mood disorder:

a disorder marked by a significant change in one's emotional state that seriously interferes with one's ability to function. *Examples: major depression, bipolar depression, cyclothymic disorder, dysthymic disorder*

Obsession:

a recurrent thought or image that intrudes on a person's awareness. *Example: After leaving for work in the morning, Neva can't stop thinking about whether she locked the door to her house. She keeps on imaging getting home from work and seeing that all her possessions have been stolen because she forgot to lock the door.*

Obsessive-compulsive disorder (OCD):

an anxiety disorder involving a pattern of unwanted intrusive thoughts and the urge to engage in repetitive actions. *Example: Benson believes if he steps on a crack, his mother will get ill. He feels compelled to avoid all the cracks on the sidewalk when he goes to school. If he makes a mistake, he quickly starts over to prevent anything bad from happening to his mother. Some days it takes him two to three hours to get to school.*

Panic disorder:

an anxiety disorder characterized by intense fear and anxiety in the absence of danger that is accompanied by strong physical symptoms. *Example: During the last month, every time Kyra gets on the highway she has a panic attack in which her heart starts beating faster, she has difficulty breathing, and she starts sweating. Kyra has no idea why this is happening as she has never been in a car accident or even seen one on this highway.*

Personality disorder:
a disorder marked by maladaptive behavior that has been stable across a long period of time and across many situations. *Examples: antisocial personality disorder, borderline personality disorder, narcissistic personality disorder*

Phobic disorder:
an anxiety disorder characterized by an intense fear of a specific object or situation. *Example: Jared can't stand the sight of spiders. If he sees one in his yard or even on television, he gets extremely agitated, anxious, and upset.*

Posttraumatic Stress Disorder (PTSD):
an anxiety disorder, characterized by distressing memories, emotional numbness, and hypervigilance, that develops after exposure to a traumatic event. *Example: After witnessing a robbery, Ada has had difficulty sleeping, often having nightmares of the event. As she goes to work she is constantly looking over her shoulder and seems to have lost her usual exuberance and passion for life.*

Ruminative coping style:
the tendency to persistently focus on how one feels without attempting to do anything about one's feelings. *Example: Gabby constantly complains to her mother about how her partner treats her, but does nothing to change the situation.*

Schizophrenia:
a severe disorder characterized by disturbances in thought, perceptions, emotions, and behavior. *Example: Heath giggles all the time and talks in a word salad. He frequently flaps his fingers and seems to be in an agitated state.*

Social phobia:
an irrational, persistent fear of being negatively evaluated by others in a social situation. *Example: Nicole will not eat in front of others. She is afraid she may get food stuck in her teeth and people will laugh at her, so she eats all her meals by herself.*

Somatoform disorder:
a disorder marked by physical complaints that has no apparent physical cause. *Examples: conversion disorder, somatization disorder, hypochondriasis*

Specific phobia:
a persistent fear and avoidance of a specific object or situation. *Example: Lasalle fears any large body of water. He does not go to the beach or lake, or even stay at a hotel with a pool. Even the thought of swimming in a lake, pool, or ocean makes him sweat and his heart beat faster.*

Thought disorder:
a symptom of schizophrenia that involves a lack of associations between one's ideas and the events that one is experiencing. *Example: Rita, a person with schizophrenia, states that the moon appears in the sky as the morning garbage is lifted from the bin. She goes on to state that bins are for carrying large seashells and all crabs have shells. Rita's statements are an example of thought disorder.*

Fill-in Review of the Chapter

Can you fill-in the missing terms for each section of the chapter? Items marked with an * encourage you to continue building the Big Picture of psychology by connecting the material in this chapter to material from previous chapters in the text.

The Big Picture: How Does a Beautiful Mind Go Awry?

Howard Hughes likely suffered from an anxiety disorder called 1) _____ _____.

The three case studies in the Big Picture illustrate the goal of psychology called 2*) _____.

What Makes Behavior Abnormal, and How Prevalent is Abnormal Behavior?

Approximately 3) _____ of people meet the criteria for a mental health disorder at some time in their lives.

Andrea can't help feeling anxious most of the time. It upsets her that she can't calm down and seem "normal". Andrea's behavior most fits the criterion of abnormality called 4) _____.

Explaining Abnormal Behavior: Perspectives Revisited

The idea that abnormal behavior is the result of mental illnesses that are similar to physical illnesses is also known as the 5) _____ _____.

Dr. Frick believes that mental illness is the result of unresolved, unconscious conflicts. Dr. Frick views mental illness from the 6)_____ perspective.

The effect of daily hassles and stress on mental health is emphasized in the 7*)_____ perspective.

The *DSM* Model for Classifying Abnormal Behavior

The *DSM* evaluates patients along 8) _____ _____ or dimensions.
The reliability of *DSM* 9) _____ is low calling into question their validity.

Anxiety Disorders: It's Not Just "Nerves"

Increased heart rate and blood pressure are examples of 10) _____ anxiety symptoms.

Anxiety disorders are most closely linked to the neurotransmitters 11) _____ and 12) _____.

Mood Disorders: Beyond the Blues

13) _____ is a milder form of bipolar disorder.

The two neurotransmitters that are most clearly linked to mood disorders are 14) _____ and 15) _____.

People with are diagnosed with depression tend to have a 16) _____ coping style.

Schizophrenic Disorders: Disintegration

Symptoms of schizophrenia usually develop during 17) _____ or 18) _____.

In signal detection terms, delusions would represent a 19*) _____ _____.

20) _____ schizophrenia is marked by delusions and hallucinations which represent 21) _____ symptoms of schizophrenia.

Dissociative and Somatoform Disorders: Personalities and Illnesses

By their definition, somatoform disorders would not be explained from a 22*) _____ perspective.

Some clinicians believe that dissociative identity disorder may represent an extreme form of the anxiety disorder called 23) _____.

Personality Disorders: Maladaptive Patterns of Behavior

People who have 24)_____ personality disorder are malicious, blame others for their problems, and typically are charming and sociable in order to manipulate others into doing what they want.

People with borderline personality disorder have difficulty establishing what Erikson calls a(n) 25*)_____, the main crisis of adolescence.

Use It or Lose It!

Can you fill in the table with the psychological disorder described by the examples?

Psychological Disorder	Symptoms
1.	Oscar has had alternating periods of sadness and mania for two months.
2.	Clarissa believes she has the blood disorder, lupus, although no physical evidence can be found to explain her symptoms.
3.	James believes that Martians are trying to control his mind by beaming radio waves onto his head. He believes they are doing this to get him to give up important state secrets that have been entrusted to him by the CIA.
4.	Nate has stage fright and can't speak in front of large groups.
5.	For the last month, Paula has been dysphoric, has felt worthless, has been losing weight, can't concentrate, and constantly feels tired.

6.	Colby is charming and bright but seems to have a sinister side in which he hurts others and shows no remorse for his actions.
7.	Pamela is obsessed with the shape of her nose. She has had 5 plastic surgery procedures on it, yet still feels that her nose is the ugliest nose in the world. She is so ashamed of her nose that she rarely goes out into public.
8.	Terry either hates you or loves you. She seems to cling to people and adopt their attitudes and interests as if she doesn't really know who she is.

Self-Check: Are You Getting the Big Picture?

After you have read and studied the chapter, see if you can answer the following quiz questions. Check your answers at the end of the chapter. If you miss a question, refer to your text and re-study the appropriate sections.

True or False Questions

Are these statements true or false?

1. Violation of social norms is the main criterion of abnormal behavior.
True
False

2. To say that Howard Hughes learned to be reclusive and avoid others because it relieved the anxiety he felt about germs and disease is a statement that is consistent with the social learning perspective on mental illness.
True
False

3. The reliability of Axis-II diagnoses on the DSM is considered to be good.
True
False

4. Research into the cognitive bases of PTSD has shown that the shattering of certain basic assumptions about life may bring on PTSD.
True
False

5. Men are more likely than women to suffer from depression.
True
False

6. People who talk about suicide should not be taken seriously as they are only doing it for attention.
True
False

7. Currently, there is more evidence to suggest a genetic basis for bipolar depression than there is for unipolar depression.
True
False

8. People with schizophrenia often have more than one personality.
True
False

9. Dissociative disorders are more common than anxiety disorders.
True
False

10. People with personality disorders can be diagnosed with clinical disorders such as anxiety and depression.
True
False

Multiple Choice Questions

Can you choose the best answer for these questions?

1. Jared was shopping at the local supermarket when all of a sudden his chest felt tight, he couldn't catch his breath, his heart began to pound, and he felt shaky and dizzy. Jared thought he was having a heart attack. Since that day, Jared has had several more episodes like this. They always strike without warning and in different types of situations. Based on these facts, what is Jared likely suffering from?
    A. a phobia
    B. panic disorder
    C. post-traumatic shock disorder
    D. generalized anxiety disorder

2. Belinda is afraid of flying. Her fear is so great that she turned down a dream job because it would have required flying. Belinda's behavior meets which criteria of abnormality?
    A. personal distress
    B. inability to function
    C. violation of social norms
    D. A & B

3. Rick is a veteran of the Vietnam War. After returning from Vietnam, Rick found it impossible to fit back into his former life. He and his wife divorced, and Rick went to live in a cabin in the mountains. He continues to suffer from nightmares and flashbacks of Vietnam. What is Rick likely suffering from?
    A. depression
    B. generalized anxiety disorder
    C. posttraumatic stress disorder
    D. A & B

4. Anxiety disorders may be linked to which part(s) of the brain?
   A. amygdala
   B. striatum
   C. corpus callosum
   D. A & B

5. Which of the following is not a symptom of unipolar depression?
   A. dysphoria
   B. changes in sleep patterns
   C. excessive thirst
   D. difficulty making decisions

6. How is dysthymia different from unipolar depression?
   A. It doesn't last as long.
   B. It's symptoms are milder.
   C. It doesn't impair the person's functioning.
   D. It doesn't involve sleep disturbances.

7. Dr. Hernandez believes that mental illness is related to poverty, discrimination, and other societal ills. Dr. Hernandez is endorsing which theoretical perspective on explaining abnormal behavior?
   A. psychoanalytic
   B. social-learning
   C. cognitive
   D. sociocultural

8. Todd was arrested for running around on top of a gazebo in a public park and yelling obscenities at passersby. When arrested, Todd did not seem to understand why what he did was either dangerous or inconsiderate of others. Todd's behavior may be considered abnormal according to which criterion?
   A. personal distress
   B. violation of social norms
   C. inability to function
   D. all of the above

9. When people who commit suicide are found to have suffered from a mental illness, more often than not the mental illness is:
   A. a depressive disorder.
   B. a substance abuse disorder.
   C. an anxiety disorder.
   D. A & B

10. The idea that depression is linked to unresolved childhood issues of abandonment and rejection is consistent with which perspective on mental illness?
   A. cognitive
   B. sociocultural
   C. psychoanalytic
   D. social learning

11. According to Aaron Beck, what underlies a person's depression?
    A. fear
    B. cognitive distortions
    C. illogical thinking
    D. a chemical imbalance

12. Major depression is more likely in:
    A. women.
    B. men.
    C. young adults.
    D. A & C

13. John Nash went through a period where he believed that he was the Emperor of Antarctica. During this period, Nash seemed to be suffering from:
    A. grandiose delusions.
    B. delusions of reference.
    C. delusions of thought control.
    D. persecutory delusions.

14. Which of the following represent a positive symptom of schizophrenia?
    A. hallucinations
    B. a lack of motivation
    C. not talking
    D. social withdrawal

15. Which of the following people with schizophrenia will likely have the best prognosis?
    A. Marvin, who has negative symptoms of schizophrenia
    B. Sally, a person with catatonic schizophrenia
    C. Lamont, a person with paranoid schizophrenia
    D. Wilma, a person with disorganized schizophrenia

16. Jovan does not like being around people. It's not that they make him nervous he just prefers to be by himself. He doesn't really have any close relationships. What personality disorder does Jovan likely have?
    A. schizotypal
    B. antisocial
    C. schizoid
    D. histrionic

17. Which neurotransmitter is most likely involved in schizophrenia?
    A. acetylcholine
    B. GABA
    C. endorphin
    D. dopamine

18. Which of the following has not been proposed as a potential cause of schizophrenia?
    A. defective genes
    B. over pruning of synapses in the brain
    C. growing up in a family with many siblings
    D. prenatal exposure to a virus

19. Which disorders involve a splitting off of one's consciousness?
    A. anxiety disorders
    B. mood disorders
    C. dissociative disorders
    D. somatoform disorders

20. Multiple personality disorder is now called:
    A. dissociative identity disorder.
    B. body dysmorphic disorder.
    C. dissociative amnesia.
    D. schizophrenia.

21. Gunther has always been extremely suspicious and mistrustful of others. Gunther most likely has which personality disorder?
    A. obsessive-compulsive
    B. paranoid
    C. narcissistic
    D. borderline

22. Suggesting that anxiety disorders result from an unrealistic self-image endorses which psychological perspective?
    A. cognitive
    B. sociocultural
    C. psychoanalytic
    D. humanistic

23. Yolanda complained to her doctor for years that she is having extreme headaches. Her doctor ordered every test she can and none of them have revealed any physical basis for Yolanda's headaches. Which mental disorder does Yolanda seem to be suffering from?
    A. hypochondriasis
    B. pain disorder
    C. somatization disorder
    D. body dysmorphic disorder

24. Hannah is always worried. She worries that her kids will get sick. She worries that her husband will lose his job. She worries that her house will be destroyed by a tornado. Sometimes she is worried without even knowing why she is worried. Which disorder does Hannah seem to be suffering from?
    A. schizophrenia
    B. generalized anxiety disorder
    C. multiple phobias
    D. panic disorder

25. Clinical disorders such as mood disorders and anxiety disorders are on which *DSM* axis?
    A. Axis I
    B. Axis II
    C. Axis III
    D. Axis IV

Short-Answer Questions

Can you write a brief answer to these questions?

1. What is a personality disorder?

2. Compare and contrast phobic disorder and panic disorder.

3. What are some of the myths about suicide?

4. What are the axes of the *DSM*?

5. What are the criteria for judging whether or not a behavior is abnormal?

Developing a Bigger Picture: Making Connections Across Chapters

An important aspect of learning is learning to see the "Big Picture" of the subject you are studying. As you learn about psychology, you should try to understand how the material from different chapters fits together to help you form a broad-based understanding of what psychology is all about. To help facilitate the development of this "Big Picture" in your mind, try to answer these questions using the knowledge you have learned in this chapter, as well as the other chapters referenced in the questions.

1. How are learned helplessness (Chapter 12) and depression related?

2. Take the Big Picture case study of Michael Watson from Chapter 3 and using what you've learned about abnormality in this chapter decide whether Michael Watson meets the criteria for abnormality.

3. How does the general adaptation syndrome (GAS) discussed in Chapter 12 relate to the topic of mental illness?

Label the Diagram

Can you label the different personality disorders?

Disorder	Major Feature
1.	Excessive suspicion and mistrust of others.
2.	Intense need for attention. Always wants to be the center of attention. Excessively dramatic behavior. Rapidly changing moods.
3.	Lack of desire to form close relationships with others. Emotional detachment and coldness toward others.
4.	Preoccupation with own sense of importance and view of self as above others. Typically ignores the needs and wants of others.
5.	Considered a mild version of schizophrenia. The person shows inappropriate social and emotional behavior, and unusual thoughts and speech.
6.	Intense and chronic anxiety over being negatively evaluated by others, so avoids social interactions.
7.	Chronic pattern of impulsive behavior. Violates rights of others and does not show remorse or guilt for actions.
8.	Excessive need to be cared for by others. Denies own thoughts and feelings and clings to others.
9.	Instability in mood, self-concept, and interpersonal relationships.
10.	Pattern of rigid and perfectionist behavior. High self-control and emotionally restricted. Maintains an orderly routine and experiences anxiety when routine is disrupted.

Big Picture Review

Identify the anxiety disorder from the symptoms given.

Disorder	Symptoms
1.	Abrupt experiences of unexpected intense fear accompanied by physical symptoms such as heart palpitations, shortness of breath, or dizziness that interfere with a person's functioning.
2.	Persistent fear of a specific object or social situation that is excessive and unreasonable, and interferes with a person's functioning.
3.	Exposure to a traumatic event during which one feels helplessness or fear followed by recurrent and intrusive memories or nightmares of the event, avoidance of stimuli associated with the event, numbing of emotions, and increased arousal that impair the person's functioning.
4.	A pattern of recurrent, persistent, intrusive thoughts or images that are followed by repetitive behaviors or mental acts that a person feels driven to perform to reduce stress or to prevent some event from happening. The thoughts or behaviors are time-consuming and interfere with the person's functioning.
5.	Excessive worry for at least 6 months about a number of events accompanied by physical symptoms such as muscle tension, mental agitation, and irritability that impair a person's functioning.

Solutions

Each solution below is followed by its textbook page reference number and its corresponding chapter learning objective (LO) number. Items with a Big Picture LO help you build a Big Picture of Psychology across the chapters you have studied so far.

Fill-in Review of the Chapter

1. obsessive-compulsive disorder [p. 631; LO 4]
2. description [p. 30; LO-Big Picture]
3. 46% [p. 620; LO 1]
4. personal distress [p. 620; LO 1]
5. medical model [p. 622; LO 2]

6. psychoanalytic perspective [p. 622; LO 2]
7. sociocultural [p. 623; LO-Big Picture]
8. five axes [p. 625; LO 3]
9. personality disorders [p. 627; LO 3]
10. physical [p. 629; LO 4]
11. GABA [p. 633-634; LO 4]
12. serotonin [p. 633-634; LO 4]
13. Cyclothymia [p. 639; LO 5]
14. serotonin [p. 642; LO 5]
15. norepinephrine [p. 642; LO 5]
16. ruminative [p. 644; LO 5]
17. adolescence [p. 647; LO 7]
18. young adulthood [p. 647; LO 7]
19. false alarm [p. 97; LO-Big Picture]
20. Paranoid [p. 649; LO 7]
21. positive [p. 650; LO 7]
22. biological [p. 654; LO-Big Picture]
23. posttraumatic stress disorder [p. 654; LO 8]
24. antisocial [p. 656; LO 9]
25. identity [p. 415; LO-Big Picture]

Use It or Lose It!

1. Bipolar disorder [p. 639; LO 5]
2. Hypochondriasis [p. 654; LO 8]
3. Schizophrenia [p. 648-649; LO 7]
4. Social phobia [p. 631; LO 4]
5. Major depression [p. 638; LO 5]
6. Antisocial personality disorder [p. 656; LO 9]
7. Body dysmorphic disorder [p. 655; LO 8]
8. Borderline personality disorder [p. 657-658; LO 9]

Self-Check: Are You Getting the Big Picture?

True or False Questions

1. F [p. 620; LO 1]
2. T [p. 622; LO 2]
3. F [p. 629; LO 3]
4. T [p. 636; LO 4]
5. F [p. 639; LO 5]
6. F [p. 640; LO 6]
7. T [p. 641; LO 5]
8. F [p. 647; LO 7]
9. F [p. 653; LO 8]
10. T [p. 656; LO 9]

Multiple Choice Questions

1. B [p. 630; LO 4]	10. C [p. 622; LO 2 & 5]	19. C [p. 653; LO 8]
2. D [p. 620; LO 1]	11. B [p. 644; LO 5]	20. A [p. 653; LO 8]
3. C [p. 632; LO 4]	12. D [p. 639; LO 5]	21. B [p. 657; LO 9]
4. D [p. 634; LO 4]	13. A [p. 648; LO 7]	22. D [p. 623; LO 2 & 4]
5. C [p. 638; LO 5]	14. A [p. 650; LO 7]	23. B [p. 655; LO 8]
6. B [p. 639; LO 5]	15. C [p. 650; LO 7]	24. B [p. 629-630; LO 4]
7. D [p. 623; LO 2]	16. C [p. 657; LO 9]	25. A [p. 625; LO 3]
8. B [p. 620; LO 1]	17. D [p. 651; LO 7]	
9. D [p. 640; LO 6]	18. C [p. 652; LO 7]	

Short-Answer Questions

1. What is a personality disorder? [p. 656; LO 9]

    A personality disorder is typically a lifelong disorder in which one has developed patterns of personality traits that are maladaptive. Because personality disorders are long-standing disorders, the person suffering from a personality disorder often does not perceive that he or she has a problem. Two of the better-known personality disorders are anti-social personality disorder and borderline personality disorder.

2. Compare and contrast phobic disorder and panic disorder. [p. 630-631; LO 4]

    These disorders are similar in that they both involve intense, relatively short-lived attacks of fear and anxiety. They are different, in that, in phobic disorder the fear and anxiety is set off by a specific stimulus; but in panic disorder, the fear and anxiety occur out of the clear blue with no specific trigger.

3. What are some of the myths about suicide? [p. 640-641; LO 6]

    a. People who talk about suicide will not actually do it. Untrue, people who commit suicide often spoke of it prior to taking their own life. b. Asking someone who is depressed whether they have ideas of suicide will plant the idea of suicide in their head. Untrue, people who are depressed may have already thought about suicide. Asking them to talk about suicidal feelings may open the door for them to get the help that they need prior to an actual suicide attempt. c. People who have failed at a suicide attempt will not try it again. Untrue, many successfully commit suicide after past failed attempts at it. d. A better mood means the risk of suicide has passed. Untrue, in fact a depressed person may be more at risk for suicide when they feel better. A lift in mood and energy levels may enable the person to make and carry out suicide plans. e. Only depressed people attempt suicide. Untrue, people may commit suicide for reasons other than being depressed and unhappy (e.g., because they are terminally ill).

4. What are the axes of the *DSM*? [p. 625-626; LO 3]

    The *DSM* has 5 axes. Axis I is a diagnosis of the major condition that is impairing the person's ability to function. Axis II is a diagnosis of lifelong disorders like personality disorders and mental retardation that inhibit the person's ability to function. Axis III is a diagnosis of any medical conditions that the person has. Axis IV is a diagnosis of recent stressors in the person's life. And, Axis V is a global assessment of functioning.

5. What are the criteria for judging whether or not a behavior is abnormal? [p. 619-620; LO 1]

There are several clues we can use to judge whether a person's behavior is abnormal. They are: statistical infrequency of the behavior, behavior that violates social norms, behavior that causes personal distress, and behavior that interferes with the person's ability to function. Of these, the last two are probably the most important criteria. If a behavior interferes with a person's ability to function and it causes distress in them or others, then there is a good chance that the behavior in question is abnormal.

Developing a Bigger Picture: Making Connections Across Chapters

1. How are learned helplessness (Chapter 12) and depression related? [p. 643; LO-Big Picture]

People who have developed learned helplessness feel as if there is nothing they can do to change their situation. Therefore, when bad things happen, they will not attempt to make things better because they perceive that there is nothing that they can do. For example, if a person with learned helplessness loses his job, he may feel as if he is incapable of finding another one. As a result, he may give up and stay in bed all day, hiding from the situation. Some researchers believe that depression is the result of such learned helplessness because even when presented with solutions to their problems, depressed people often fail to implement these solutions. They are more likely to ruminate about their problems then consider solutions to their problems. Therefore, their lives do not improve and they remain depressed.

2. Take the Big Picture case study of Michael Watson from Chapter 3 and using what you've learned about abnormality in this chapter decide whether Michael Watson meets the criteria for abnormality. [p. 94-95; 619-620; LO-Big Picture]

Watson meets some of the criteria, but not others. His behavior is statistically rare, but it does not really violate social norms. It caused him some minor distress in that he felt different and silly, yet it did not make him less able to function in his life. All in all, Watson's behavior does not warrant a diagnosis of abnormality. His distress was mild and he was able to function very well. He would not require treatment for his behavior.

3. How does the general adaptation syndrome (GAS) discussed in Chapter 12 relate to the topic of mental illness? [p. 551; LO-Big Picture]

According to the GAS, in the exhaustion phase our bodies begin to breakdown after having battled prolonged stressors. Once we reach exhaustion, we become more vulnerable to physical illnesses and death. Perhaps it is possible that we also become more vulnerable to mental illnesses as well when we are severely stressed. For example, depression has been linked to high levels of stress hormones and schizophrenic relapses have been shown to correlate with living in a stressful environment.

Label the Diagram [p. 657; LO 9]

TYPES OF PERSONALITY DISORDERS	
1.	Paranoid personality disorder
2.	Histrionic personality disorder
3.	Schizoid personality disorder
4.	Narcissistic personality disorder
5.	Schizotypal personality disorder
6.	Avoidant personality disorder
7.	Antisocial personality disorder
8.	Dependent personality disorder
9.	Borderline personality disorder
10.	Obsessive-compulsive personality disorder

Big Picture Review [p. 634; LO 4]

1. Panic disorder
2. Phobic disorder
3. Posttraumatic stress disorder
4. Obsessive-compulsive disorder
5. Generalized anxiety disorder

15

What Therapies Are Used to Treat Psychological Problems?

Learning Objectives

After studying each of the following sections of the chapter, you should be able to do these tasks.

Providing Psychological Assistance

1. Identify when a person should consider seeking therapy, who is qualified to give therapy, and the ethical standards that psychotherapists must follow.

Psychoanalytic Therapies: Uncovering Reasons for Psychological Problems

2. Describe the aim of psychoanalytic therapies, and distinguish between traditional and modern psychoanalysis.

Humanistic Therapy: Empathizing to Empower

3. Describe humanistic therapy approaches.

Behavior Therapies: Learning Healthier Behaviors

4. Describe the aim of behavior therapy approaches, and explain how they operate through classical or operant conditioning processes.

Cognitive Therapies: Thinking Through Problems

5. Describe the aim of cognitive therapy approaches, and distinguish between rational-emotive therapy and Beck's cognitive therapy.

Group Therapy Approaches: Strength in Numbers

6. Describe the advantages and disadvantages of group therapy approaches.

Effective Psychotherapy: What Treatments Work?

7. Examine the effectiveness of psychotherapy, detailing those factors that contribute to effective therapy.

Biological and Medical Therapies: Changing the Chemistry

8. Describe the aim of biological therapies, and distinguish among the varying drug therapies.

The Big Picture

The Big Picture: The Ups and Downs of Life

This chapter details the ways in which psychologists use therapy to treat people with mental illnesses. As the Big Picture story of Emily Fox Gordon illustrates, therapists may take different approaches to treating psychological problems. Some of these approaches may be more successful than others.

Providing Psychological Assistance

This section covers Learning Objective 1. Psychotherapy should be administered only by trained professionals such as clinical psychologists, psychoanalysts, licensed counselors, social workers, psychiatrists, and marital or family therapists. At minimum, therapists will hold master's degrees, and in many cases, a doctorate degree is required. Usually, biological therapies are administered by psychiatrists or medical doctors who hold medical degrees.

All persons involved in the delivery of psychotherapy must abide by the ethical guidelines laid down by the American Psychological Association. Clients are entitled to competent treatment, confidentiality, appropriate interactions with the therapist, and informed consent to any treatment they receive.

People seek psychotherapy for a variety of reasons. They may be suffering from mental disorders, experiencing maladaptive behavior, be legally mandated to receive treatment by the courts, or simply wish to finds ways of coping with the challenges in their lives.

Psychoanalytic Therapies: Uncovering Reasons for Psychological Problems

This section covers Learning Objective 2. Psychoanalytic therapies are based on Sigmund Freud's theory of personality. Because Freud theorized that psychological problems are caused by unconscious conflicts, psychoanalytic therapy techniques aim to bring unconscious conflicts to consciousness where they can be resolved. Freud called this approach psychoanalysis.

Freud's traditional psychoanalysis involved the techniques of free association and dream analysis in which the therapist interprets the hidden meaning of the client's behavior. For example, a therapist will record the free associations of a client and then interpret what unconscious conflicts these ramblings indicate. Similarly, a therapist may interpret the unconscious symbolism of a client's dreams to help the client resolve unconscious conflicts.

In interpreting the meaning or symbolism of a client's behavior, the therapist pays careful attention to resistances or topics the client does not wish to discuss. Reluctance to pursue a topic may indicate that the topic is related to an underlying unconscious conflict. Another factor that a therapist pays careful attention to is transference where a client will unconsciously project his or her feelings for others onto the therapist. For example, unconscious resentment toward one's parent may be expressed as conscious anger toward one's therapist.

Modern psychodynamic therapy utilizes some of Freud's original techniques, but the time frame for therapy is often much shorter than in traditional psychoanalysis. Psychodynamic therapy tends to focus less on the client's past than traditional psychoanalysis does. Current problems and the nature of interpersonal relationships are seen as more important in improving the client's behavior. The therapist also plays a more direct role, rapidly interviewing and questioning the client to uncover unconscious issues and themes in a shorter time. Then the therapist and client agree to focus on a limited set of problems that are seen as causing the client the most trouble.

Humanistic Therapy: Empathizing to Empower

This section covers Learning Objective 3. Humanistic psychologists assume that all humans strive to reach their potential and that psychological problems result when our journey toward self-fulfillment is thwarted or blocked. Therefore, the role of the humanistic therapist is to create a safe, supportive environment in which the client can pursue self-fulfillment.

One of the best-known humanistic therapies is client-centered or person-centered therapy. In this therapy, the focus or direction of the therapy comes from the client. The therapist exudes empathy, genuineness, and unconditional positive regard for the client. The therapist listens to the client's problems and reflects the client's statements back to the client without judgment or direction. The idea is that by respecting and valuing clients, they will gain the self-confidence necessary to effect positive changes in their own lives.

Behavior Therapies: Learning Healthier Behaviors

This section covers Learning Objective 4. Behavior therapies focus on changing the client's current behavior by utilizing the principles of classical conditioning, operant conditioning, and social learning that you learned about in Chapter 5.

Systematic desensitization utilizes classical conditioning to replace an anxiety response with an incompatible response of relaxation and calm. The first step is to teach the client how to relax by using a technique such as progressive muscle relaxation. The second step is to have the client create an anxiety hierarchy or images of the feared stimulus that cause increasing levels of anxiety. The third step is to combine these images systematically with the relaxation. Beginning at the lowest level of the hierarchy, the client learns to remain calm while encountering the object they fear.

In aversion therapy, the client is classically conditioned to have a negative response to some stimulus that they wish to avoid. For example, an alcoholic may be given the drug Antabuse, which when combined with alcohol produces intense nausea. After pairing the experience of drinking alcohol with nausea, a conditioned taste aversion ensues, causing the client to feel ill when he or she encounters alcohol. Another form of aversion therapy, covert sensitization therapy, works on the same basic principle only in this case the stimulus one wishes to avoid is paired with aversive thoughts and mental images. For example, a smoker may pair the image of a diseased lung with the stimulus of a cigarette.

Operant conditioning behavior therapies use reinforcement and punishment to increase adaptive behavior and decrease maladaptive behavior. Non-reinforcement or extinction therapies work to reduce undesired behaviors by removing the reward that maintains the behavior. Shaping involves rewarding successive approximations of a final, desired response to build a new behavior in a client. Token economies are systems of secondary reinforcement in which points or tokens are awarded for certain behaviors. After a specified period of time, these tokens can be cashed in for primary reinforcers (e.g., food, toys, etc.). Token economies are especially useful when modifying the behavior of groups of people, such as in mental hospitals and classrooms.

Cognitive Therapies: Thinking Through Problems

This section covers Learning Objective 5. Cognitive therapies seek to help people by modifying the maladaptive thoughts and beliefs that play a role in mental health disorders such as depression and anxiety. Based on the idea that depression is caused by irrational and maladaptive beliefs about the world, Albert Ellis' rational-emotive therapy (RET) works to get clients to interpret the events in their lives in a more rational manner. In RET the therapist is direct and confrontational in attacking the irrational beliefs of the client. For example, a client may state that she feels that she lost her one chance at love when she was dumped by her boyfriend. To this statement, the therapist might demand to know what proof the client has of this assertion. By slowly exposing the lack of logic underlying the client's maladaptive beliefs, the therapist hopes the client will abandon these illogical beliefs in favor of more logical, adaptive ones. Similarly, in Aaron Beck's cognitive therapy the client and therapist work together to identify and discredit the cognitive distortions and negative automatic thoughts underlying the client's depression or anxiety.

Group Therapy Approaches: Strength in Numbers

This section covers Learning Objective 6. In group therapy, people with similar problems come together to work on their problems. Any one of the four approaches previously described can be used for treating groups of people. Unique forms of group therapy include family therapy and couples therapy. Group therapy may be led by a therapist, or it may be self-directed as in self-help groups (e.g., Alcoholics Anonymous).

Effective Psychotherapy: What Treatments Work?

This section covers Learning Objective 7. In general, psychotherapy seems to improve clients more than a placebo treatment. However, studies that compare the effectiveness of different forms of psychotherapy show mixed results. Some studies indicate they are comparable, whereas others show that some therapies are better at treating particular types of disorders.

Whether therapy works for a person depends in part on the therapeutic alliance that forms between the client and the therapist. Mutual respect and trust in the client-therapist relationship seems to help foster success. Characteristics of the therapist also impact the effectiveness of therapy. The most successful therapists are those who are empathetic, encourage their clients to confront painful emotions, offer explanations for the client's behavior, and are sensitive to cultural differences between themselves and their clients.

These days, the Internet has opened many new possibilities for psychotherapy. Some of these include real-time online therapy, email therapy, mental health sites, and chat room group therapy. These opportunities may help make therapy more accessible, but they also pose ethical concerns, such as confidentiality issues and the quality of therapists delivering therapy in cyberspace.

Biological and Medical Therapies: Changing the Chemistry

This section covers Learning Objective 8. Biological therapies for treating mental disorders include medications, electroconvulsive therapy, and psychosurgery. Biological therapies are administered by a physician or a psychiatrist. As with any medical procedure, side effects can occur and must be considered in any treatment plan.

The most common biological therapy used to treat mental health problems is medications. Antianxiety drugs (e.g., Xanax, Valium, and BuSpar) reduce anxiety by acting on GABA, serotonin, and norepinephrine. Antipsychotic drugs (e.g., Thorazine, Haldol) reduce psychotic symptoms of schizophrenia by blocking dopamine in the brain. Atypical antipsychotic drugs (e.g., clozapine, risperadone, and aripiprazole) reduce both the positive and negative symptoms of schizophrenia by influencing serotonin and dopamine in the brain.

There are three types of antidepressant medications to reduce depression: selective serotonin reuptake inhibitors (e.g., Prozac) that block the reuptake of serotonin in the brain; tricyclic antidepressants (e.g., Elavil) that affect serotonin and norepinephrine in the brain; and monoamine oxidase (MAO) inhibitors that increase the levels of monoamine neurotransmitters in the brain by paralyzing the enzyme that breaks down these neurotransmitters. MAO inhibitors are less frequently prescribed than the other antidepressants because of their serious side effects and numerous food and drug interactions.

Antimanic drugs reduce the mania seen in bipolar disorder. Lithium is a common antimanic that appears to affect glutamate, serotonin, and dopamine in the brain. It is often prescribed in conjunction with antidepressants in treating bipolar disorder.

Anticonvulsant drugs like Tegretol and Depakote are also sometimes prescribed to treat mania because they have fewer side effects than lithium.

Electroconvulsive therapy (ECT) is used to treat severe cases of depression in which psychosis is present, a suicide attempt is imminent, or medication and other therapies have failed. In ECT, a seizure is deliberately induced with electricity. Although no one completely understands why ECT works, it is quick and effective in many cases. Side effects may include memory loss and learning problems.

Psychosurgery is the most drastic form of biological therapy for mental disorders. In one type of psychosurgery, brain structures that are thought to be at the root of some psychological disorders are deliberately destroyed. One example of such a surgery is used in treating obsessive-compulsive disorder. Another type of psychosurgery can be seen in modern treatments for Parkinson's disease. Here, instead of destroying brain tissue, stimulators are implanted in the brain to stimulate it and reduce the symptoms of the disease. As we learn more about the brain and its role in mental illness, it is likely that new psychosurgical procedures will be developed.

Outlining the Big Picture

Chapter 15: What Therapies Are Used to Treat Psychological Problems?

The Big Picture: The Ups and Downs of Life
Notes:

_____

_____

_____

_____

_____

Providing Psychological Assistance (Learning Objective 1)
Who Is Qualified to Give Therapy?
Ethical Standards for Psychotherapists
  Competent Treatment and Informed Consent
  Confidentiality
  Appropriate Interactions
When Does One Need to Consider Psychotherapy?

Notes:

_____

_____

_____

_____

_____

_____

Psychoanalytic Therapies: Uncovering Reasons for Psychological Problems (Learning Objective 2)

Traditional Psychoanalysis
Modern Psychoanalysis
Notes:

_____

_____

_____

_____

_____

Humanistic Therapy: Empathizing to Empower (Learning Objective 3)

Client-centered Therapy
   Empathy: Understanding the Client
   Genuineness: Sharing Thoughts, Feelings, and Experiences
   Unconditional Positive Regard: Valuing the Client
Notes:

_____

_____

_____

_____

_____

_____

_____

Behavior Therapies: Learning Healthier Behaviors (Learning Objective 4)

Classical Conditioning Techniques

Systematic Desensitization: Relax and Have No Fear

Aversion Therapy: We Don't Do Something If We Dislike It

Operant Conditioning Techniques

Notes:

_____

_____

_____

_____

_____

_____

Cognitive Therapies: Thinking Through Problems (Learning Objective 5)

Ellis's Rational-Emotive Therapy

Beck's Cognitive Therapy

Notes:

_____

_____

_____

_____

_____

Group Therapy Approaches: Strength in Numbers (Learning Objective 6)

The Benefits of Group Therapy

The Nature and Types of Group Therapy

Family Therapy: The Whole System

Couples Therapy: Improving Communication

Self-Help Groups: Helping Each Other Cope

Notes:

_____

_____

_____

_____

Effective Psychotherapy: What Treatments Works? (Learning Objective 7)
Which Type of Psychotherapy Is Best?
Factors That Contribute to Effective Psychotherapy
   Spotlight on Diversity: Culture and Therapy
Modern Delivery Methods of Therapy: Computer Technology and Cybertherapy
Notes:

_____

_____

_____

_____

_____

Biological and Medical Therapies: Changing the Chemistry (Learning Objective 8)
Drug Therapies
   Antianxiety Drugs
   Antipsychotic Drugs
   Antidepressants
   Antimanics
Electroconvulsive Therapy (ECT)
Psychosurgery
Notes:

_____

_____

_____

_____

_____

_____

_____

Are You Getting the Big Picture?
Notes:

_____

_____

_____

_____

_____

_____

Seeing the Big Picture: A Mental Map of Chapter 15

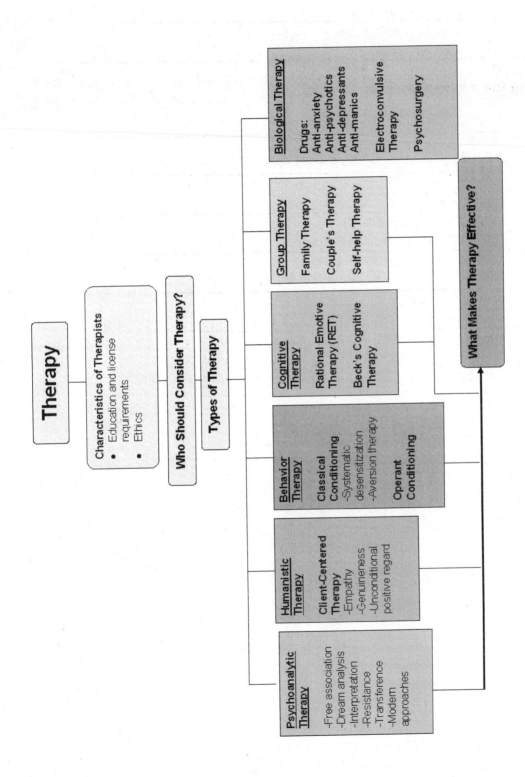

Therapy

Characteristics of Therapists
- Education and license requirements
- Ethics

Who Should Consider Therapy?

Types of Therapy

Psychoanalytic Therapy
-Free association
-Dream analysis
-Interpretation
-Resistance
-Transference
-Modern approaches

Humanistic Therapy

Client-Centered Therapy
-Empathy
-Genuineness
-Unconditional positive regard

Behavior Therapy

Classical Conditioning
-Systematic desensitization
-Aversion therapy

Operant Conditioning

Cognitive Therapy

Rational Emotive Therapy (RET)

Beck's Cognitive Therapy

Group Therapy

Family Therapy

Couple's Therapy

Self-help Therapy

Biological Therapy

Drugs:
Anti-anxiety
Anti-psychotics
Anti-depressants
Anti-manics

Electroconvulsive Therapy

Psychosurgery

What Makes Therapy Effective?

Chapter 15

Key Points of the Big Picture

Antianxiety medication:
minor tranquilizers that are prescribed to reduce tension and anxiety. *Example: Edie was prescribed Xanax to reduce her anxiety.*

Antidepressant:
medication prescribed to alleviate the symptoms of depression, eating disorders, and some anxiety disorders. *Example: Mel was prescribed Prozac after he was diagnosed with major depression.*

Antimanic medication:
drugs that are prescribed to alleviate manic symptoms of bipolar disorder. *Example: Calista was prescribed lithium after her manic episode.*

Antipsychotic medication:
major tranquilizers that are prescribed to relieve psychotic symptoms such as delusions and hallucinations. *Example: Fernando was hospitalized after a psychotic break in which he was hearing voices and believing he was being followed by foreign agents. The psychiatrist in the hospital prescribed Haldol to reduce his symptoms.*

Anxiety hierarchy:
outlines, according to the degree of fear, the threatening images elicited by a feared object or situation; the outline starts with the least frightening images and progresses to the most distressing. *Example: An anxiety hierarchy for fear of dogs may start with seeing a picture or movie of a dog and progress to being confronted with a barking dog and then having to pet a dog.*

Aversion therapy:
a behavior therapy technique in which a specific behavior is paired with an unpleasant stimulus in order to reduce its occurrence. *Example: Every time Melinda attempts to smoke, her cigarette lighter delivers a small unpleasant shock.*

Behavior therapy:
therapy that applies the principles of classical and operant conditioning to help people change maladaptive behaviors. *Examples: Systematic desensitization, aversion therapy, token economies.*

Biological therapy:
the use of medications or other medical interventions to treat mental health disorders.

Client-centered therapy:
a humanistic psychotherapy approach formulated by Rogers that emphasizes the use of empathy, genuineness, and unconditional positive regard to help the client reach his/her potential. *Example: Imelda's therapist does not judge her behaviors or decisions, but accepts her for who she is and often discloses similar situations that she has experienced.*

Cognitive distortion:
distorted thinking patterns that according to Beck lead to depression, anxiety, and low self-esteem. *Examples: all-or-none thinking, selective abstraction, overgeneralization*

414

Cognitive therapy:
a therapy created by Aaron Beck that focuses on uncovering negative automatic thought patterns that impede healthy psychological functioning. *Example: Rosa's therapist has her identify when she mentally labels herself negatively and then has her replace the negative thought with one that is more positive.*

Couple therapy:
therapy that focuses on improving communication and intimacy between two people in a committed relationship.

Covert sensitization therapy:
a milder form of aversion therapy in which graphic imagery is used to create unpleasant associations with specific stimuli. *Example: Ted is asked to imagine a diseased liver and decaying brain every time he wants a drink of alcohol.*

Dream analysis:
a technique in psychoanalysis in which the therapist examines the hidden symbols in a client's dreams. *Example: Connie tells her therapist that she had a dream that she was drowning in the ocean. Her therapist suggests that the dream reflects Connie's feelings of being overwhelmed in her relationships.*

Eclectic approach:
therapy that incorporates an integrated and diverse use of methods. *Example: Trent's therapist uses systematic desensitization and cognitive therapy to reduce his anxiety.*

Electroconvulsive therapy (ECT):
a series of treatments in which electrical current is passed through the brain, causing a seizure; used to alleviate severe depression.

Empathy:
the ability of a therapist to understand a client's feelings and thoughts without being judgmental. *Example: Saundra's therapist really seems to listen to her when she speaks. He nods when she speaks and maintains eye contact and then repeats the thoughts and feelings that he hears Saundra express.*

Family therapy:
therapy that focuses on creating balance and restoring harmony to improve the functioning of the family as a whole system.

Free association:
a technique in psychoanalysis in which the client says whatever comes to mind. *Example: Deidre's therapist asks her to talk about her relationship with her mother and say anything that comes to mind.*

Genuineness:
the ability of a therapist to openly share his/her thoughts and feelings with a client. *Example: After talking about how he was teased by his classmates, Aaron's therapist disclosed that he too was teased when he was in school.*

Group therapy:
therapy that is administered to more than one person at a time.

415

Interpretation:

the psychoanalyst's view on the themes and issues that may be influencing the client's behavior. *Example: Jack, a psychoanalyst, believes his client's dreams and free associations reflect feelings of rejection. He shares this analysis with his client.*

Lithium:

a naturally occurring mineral salt prescribed to control manic symptoms in people with bipolar disorder; it influences several neurotransmitters in the brain, including glutamate, serotonin, and dopamine.

Psychoanalysis:

a method of therapy formulated by Freud that focuses on uncovering unconscious conflicts that drive maladaptive behavior. *Example: Marlene's therapist has her freely associate her thoughts and feelings about her childhood so that she can gain insight into her issues and problems.*

Psychodynamic therapy:

modern psychoanalysis delivered in a shorter time that focuses less on the client's past and more on current problems and the nature of interpersonal relationships. *Example: Conner's therapist has him freely associate about his current relationships so that he can gain insight into his issues and problems.*

Psychosurgery:

a biological treatment approach involving neurosurgery to alleviate symptoms in someone with a mental health disorder. *Example: Roman's obsessive-compulsive symptoms are not responding to drug therapy or psychotherapy. His symptoms are so severe that a neurosurgeon is going to lesion a small part of his brain to reduce his symptoms.*

Psychotherapy:

the use of psychological principles and techniques to treat mental health disorders. *Examples: psychoanalysis, behavior therapy, client-centered therapy, cognitive therapy*

Rational Emotive therapy:

a cognitive therapy approach created by Albert Ellis that focuses on changing the irrational beliefs that people hold and that are believed to impede healthy psychological functioning. *Example: Lauren goes to a therapist for extreme anxiety. The therapist uncovers Lauren's irrational belief that she must be perfect at work and home or she won't be loved. Her therapist challenges this belief in a series of exercises to reduce Lauren's anxiety.*

Resistance:

a process in psychoanalysis whereby the client behaves in such a way as to deny or avoid sensitive issues. *Example: Ralph seems to make a joke every time his therapist brings up his divorce.*

Selective serotonin reuptake inhibitor (SSRI):

a type of antidepressant drug that inhibits the reuptake of the neurotransmitter serotonin, thereby improving mood. *Examples: Prozac, Paxil, Zoloft*

Self-help group:
group comprised of people who share the same problem who meet to help one another. *Examples: Alcoholics Anonymous, AL-Anon, Narcotics Anonymous*

Systematic desensitization:
a behavior therapy technique in which a client is desensitized to a fear in a gradual, step-by-step process. *Example: Clive's therapist teaches him progressive muscle relaxation and creates an anxiety hierarchy for his fear of public speaking. Clive is then asked to imagine the lowest item on the hierarchy while remaining relaxed. Over several weeks, the therapist progresses further and further up the hierarchy until Clive can imagine he is giving a speech in an auditorium while remaining totally relaxed.*

Tardive dyskinesia:
a side effect of antipsychotic medications involving involuntary motor movements of the mouth, tongue, and face.

Therapeutic alliance:
the interactive and collaborative relationship between the client and the therapist.

Therapy:
techniques that are used to help people with psychological or interpersonal problems.

Token economy:
a behavioral therapy technique in which people are rewarded with tokens for desired behavior; the tokens can then be exchanged for what is reinforcing to them. *Example: While in a drug rehabilitation center, Lindsay receives five points for every task that she is assigned. Lindsay can exchange her points to make telephone calls or watch television programs.*

Transference:
a process in psychoanalysis in which the client unconsciously reacts to the therapist as if the therapist were a parent, friend, sibling, or lover. *Example: Libby has fallen in love with her therapist.*

Unconditional positive regard:
the ability of a therapist to accept and value a client for who he or she is, regardless of his/her faults or problems. *Example: Although Sam states that he has done some pretty horrible things to his family, his therapist communicates caring and respect for him.*

Fill-in Review of the Chapter

Can you fill-in the missing terms for each section of the chapter? Items marked with an * encourage you to continue building the Big Picture of psychology by connecting the material in this chapter to material from previous chapters in the text.

The Big Picture: The Ups and Downs of Life

1) _____ consists of techniques that are used to help people with psychological or interpersonal problems.

Dr. Farber used a variety of methods and techniques in his treatment of Emily. Dr. Farber adopted a(n) 2) _____ approach to Emily's treatment.

Providing Psychological Assistance

In general, people who give psychotherapy must have at least a(n) 3) _____ degree and in most states hold an appropriate license or certificate.

According to the ethical guidelines set forth by the American Psychological Association, therapists must obtain 4) _____ _____ from their clients prior to beginning psychotherapy.

Many people seek therapy because they meet the criterion of abnormal behavior referred to as 5*) _____.

Psychoanalytic Therapies: Uncovering Reasons for Psychological Problems

Fred's therapist asks him to lie down on a couch and say out loud whatever thoughts enter into his mind. The psychoanalytic technique that Fred's therapist is using is called 6) _____ _____.

Modern psychoanalysis is referred to as 7) _____.

Humanistic Therapy: Empathizing to Empower

The three key therapist behaviors of client-centered therapy include 8) _____, 9) _____, and 10)_____.

Behavior Therapies: Learning Healthier Behaviors

Systematic desensitization is based on the learning principles of 11*) _____.

Sally is undergoing psychotherapy to deal with her weight problem. Sally's therapist asks her to think of a plate full of garbage every time she has the urge to eat pizza, her favorite food. Sally appears to be participating in a therapy known as 12) _____ _____.

Manuel is trying to quit smoking. For every day that he goes without smoking, Manuel's wife gives him a big kiss and tells him that she is proud of him. Manuel's wife is using 13) _____ as a therapy to help Manuel stop smoking.

Susanna is using an incentive program to encourage her first graders to read more. She has each child create a paper Native American headband out of construction paper. For every book that the children read, they receive a paper feather to add to their headdress. At the end of the week, students can then cash in their feathers for prizes. Susanna is using a(n) 14) _____ _____ in her class.

Cognitive Therapies: Thinking Through Problems

Negative thinking patterns are most evident in the psychological disorders of 15*) _____ and 16*) _____.

Ellis's therapy focuses on the role of 17) _____ in psychological distress whereas Beck's therapy highlights the role of 18) _____.

Group Therapy Approaches: Strength in Numbers

The goal of family therapy is to 19) _____.

20) _____ are comprised of people who share the same problem who meet to help one another.

Effective Psychotherapy: What Treatments Work?

The interactive and collaborative relationship between the client and the therapist is termed the 21) _____.

Because it is difficult to find people who all have the same problem to the same degree, research on therapy effectiveness is often hampered by 22*) _____ problems.

Biological and Medical Therapies: Changing the Chemistry

Prozac is an example of a(n) 23) _____ medication.

Lithium is often prescribed for the 24) _____ symptoms of 25) _____.

Use It or Lose It!

Identify which type of therapy is indicated by the following terms and techniques.

Type of therapy	Term/Technique
1.	Empathy
2.	Systematic desensitization
3.	Free association
4.	Prescribing medications
5.	Irrational beliefs
6.	Token economies
7.	Genuineness
8.	Transference
9.	Self-help
10.	Cognitive distortions

Self-Check: Are You Getting the Big Picture?

After you have read and studied the chapter, see if you can answer the following quiz questions. Check your answers at the end of the chapter. If you miss a question, refer to your text and re-study the appropriate sections.

True or False Questions

Are these statements true or false?

1. Under some conditions, the American Psychological Association allows therapists to date their clients.
True
False

2. Dream analysis is a common behavioral therapy for treating addictions.
True
False

3. The need for a therapist to be genuine in dealing with clients is an idea that is emphasized in humanistic therapy.
True
False

4. Gerald is undergoing psychoanalysis. Lately, he has begun to have romantic feelings towards his female therapist, who reminds him of his beloved mother. According to psychoanalytic theory, Gerald is experiencing transference.
True
False

5. Electroconvulsive therapy has been shown to be particularly effective for the treatment of anxiety.
True
False

6. Systematic desensitization has been shown to be a particularly effective treatment for phobias.
True
False

7. The concept of an "identified patient" is most applicable to rational emotive therapy.
True
False

8. Most studies have shown that psychotherapy is more effective than placebo treatments.
True
False

9. One advantage of group therapy is the increased one-on-one time with the therapist.
True
False

10. Studies indicate that a person's cultural background is an important determinant of how therapeutic a particular therapist-client relationship will be for that person.
True
False

Multiple Choice Questions

Can you choose the best answer for these questions?

1. Which of the following is least likely to be emphasized by a psychoanalyst?
    A. free association
    B. dream analysis
    C. systematic desensitization
    D. interpretation

2. Which of the following is not an ethical standard that has been set forth for therapists by the American Psychological Association?
    A. maintaining client confidentiality
    B. getting informed consent from clients
    C. giving appropriate treatment to clients
    D. giving low-cost treatment to all clients

3. Which of the following people is most likely to administer drugs to clients suffering with mental disorders?
    A. a psychiatrist
    B. a social worker
    C. a pastoral counselor
    D. a psychotherapist

4. Which of the following is not a reason why psychoanalysis has become less popular in recent decades?
    A. the increased availability of drug therapies
    B. questions about the effectiveness of psychoanalysis
    C. other less time consuming and less expensive therapies were developed
    D. psychoanalysis was proven ineffective

5. Which of the following questions would be of least interest to a behavioral psychotherapist treating a client for alcoholism?
    A. how often the client drinks alcohol
    B. the settings in which the client drinks alcohol
    C. the childhood traumas that motivate the client to drink
    D. what reinforces the client for his or her drinking

6. Psychodynamic therapy is most closely related to:
    A. cognitive therapy.
    B. behavior therapy.
    C. psychoanalysis.
    D. rational emotive therapy.

7. Which of the following therapists would be most likely to agree with the statement, "All people hold within themselves the keys to their own recovery"?
    A. a psychoanalyst
    B. a behavioral therapist
    C. a cognitive therapist
    D. a humanistic therapist

8. Which of the following is a humanistic therapy?
   A. client-centered therapy
   B. systematic desensitization
   C. shaping
   D. rational emotive therapy

9. Will told his therapist that he stole a canoe while at summer camp. Afterwards, his therapist said, "I still believe that you are a person of value and worth." In saying this, Will's therapist was showing the quality (or qualities) of:
   A. genuineness.
   B. unconditional positive regard.
   C. empathy.
   D. all of the above

10. Darren is suffering from a serious phobia of flying. Which of the following therapies would be most likely to help Darren with is problem?
    A. client-centered therapy
    B. systematic desensitization
    C. psychoanalysis
    D. a token economy

11. Having clients smoke as many cigarettes as they can, as fast as they can is an example of what type of therapy?
    A. systematic desensitization
    B. covert sensitization
    C. token economy
    D. aversion therapy

12. Which of the following therapies involves pairing disturbing mental images with a stimulus the client wishes to avoid?
    A. shaping
    B. covert sensitization
    C. relaxation therapy
    D. rational-emotive therapy

13. Juanita's therapist teaches her how to recognize and keep track of her negative automatic thoughts. Juanita's therapist is using what type of psychotherapy?
    A. behavior therapy
    B. cognitive therapy
    C. psychoanalysis
    D. client-centered therapy

14. Wilbur's mother has taken Wilbur to a psychologist because of his frequent, and prolonged temper tantrums. The therapist suggests that Wilbur's mother ignore him when he acts up because she believes that his tantrums are reinforced by the mother's attention when he is bad. Which therapy is the therapist using?
    A. extinction
    B. reinforcement
    C. shaping
    D. punishment

15. Elisa has slipped into a deep depression after being dumped by her boyfriend. In therapy, Elisa tells her therapist that she fears she will be alone for the rest of her life now that she has been dumped by her "soul mate". In response, Elisa's therapist asks, "how could he have been your soul mate, when he dumped you? Is that logical?" Elisa's therapist appears to be using what type of therapy to treat Elisa's depression?
    A. psychoanalysis
    B. behavioral therapy
    C. rational-emotive therapy
    D. client-centered therapy

16. Alcoholic Anonymous is an example of _____ therapy.
    A. family
    B. self-help
    C. behavioral
    D. humanistic

17. Which of the following is not a benefit of group therapy over individual therapy?
    A. Group therapy gives the client more individualized treatment.
    B. Group therapy is cheaper.
    C. Group therapy provides a safe environment to try out new social behaviors.
    D. In group therapy, the therapist can witness the client's social behavior first hand.

18. Which of the following is not a characteristic of clients who most benefit from psychotherapy?
    A. social support
    B. a previous history of psychological disorders
    C. the ability to express one's thoughts and feelings
    D. optimistic attitude toward therapy

19. Which of the following therapy approaches best attempts to match an individual with a therapy that is suited to his or her particular situation and problem?
    A. cognitive
    B. behavioral
    C. group
    D. eclectic

20. Which of the following qualities are important qualities in a psychotherapist?
    A. genuineness
    B. empathy
    C. cultural awareness and sensitivity
    D. all of the above

21. Which of the following technologies are now being used in psychotherapy?
    A. personal digital assistants (PDAs)
    B. the Internet
    C. computer programs
    D. all of the above

22. Which of the following drugs would be most likely to be used to treat a person with generalized anxiety disorder?
    A. Xanax
    B. Haldol
    C. Lithium
    D. an MAO inhibitor

23. Prozac blocks the reuptake of which neurotransmitter?
    A. dopamine
    B. GABA
    C. acetylcholine
    D. serotonin

24. Which class of drugs is most likely to block the action of dopamine in the brain?
    A. antianxiety drugs
    B. antidepressants
    C. antipsychotic drugs
    D. antimanic drugs

25. Which of the following types of drugs is most likely to cause the side effect of tardive dyskinesia?
    A. antidepressants
    B. antimanic drugs
    C. antipsychotic drugs
    D. antianxiety drugs

Short-Answer Questions

Can you write a brief answer to these questions?

1. In what type of situation would electroconvulsive therapy be warranted?

2. What are the different types of antidepressants and how do they change brain chemistry?

3. Cognitive therapy appears to be particularly effective in treating which types of disorders?

4. Assume that you are working in a mental hospital where you are in charge of 25 patients who have been diagnosed with schizophrenia. Design a behavioral therapy to help ensure that these patients engage in the basic life skills, such as getting up in the morning, making their beds, participating in group therapy, and refraining from self-injurious behaviors each day.

5. Write an example dialogue between a therapist and client to illustrate the psychoanalytic concept of resistance.

Developing a Bigger Picture: Making Connections Across Chapters

An important aspect of learning is learning to see the "Big Picture" of the subject you are studying. As you learn about psychology, you should try to understand how the material from different chapters fits together to help you form a broad-based understanding of what psychology is all about. To help facilitate the development of this "Big Picture" in your mind, try to answer these questions using the knowledge you have learned in this chapter, as well as the other chapters referenced in the questions.

1. Using your knowledge of experimental design from Chapter 1, design an experiment to test whether or not rational-emotive therapy is as effective as Prozac in treating depression.

2. Using what you learned about operant conditioning in Chapter 5, what considerations would you have to take into account when designing a system of positive reinforcement to help a client get over her shyness?

3. Given what you learned about the brain in Chapter 2, why would ECT typically be administered to the right hemisphere of the brain and not the left?

Label the Diagram

Can you label these examples of common cognitive distortions that may lead one to develop symptoms of depression or anxiety?

Cognitive Error	Description	Example
1.	Seeing each event as completely good or bad, right or wrong, a success or a failure	"If I don't get this job, I am a failure."
2.	Concluding that something negative will happen or is happening even though there is no evidence to support it	"My neighbor did not say hello to me. She must be mad at me."
3.	Rejecting positive experiences	"Anyone can paint. It's no big deal."

4.	Assuming that negative emotions are accurate without questioning them	"I feel fat, so I must be fat."
5.	Placing a negative, global label on a person or situation	"I can't do anything right, so why should I try?"
6. & 7.	Overestimating the importance of negative events and underestimating the impact of positive events	"In my job evaluation, my boss said I need to work on my time management skills. She only said I was a productive worker and good team manager to be nice."
8.	Applying a negative conclusion of one event to other unrelated events and areas of one's life	"I messed up on my math test, so I won't do well in history or Spanish. I should drop out of school."
9.	Attributing negative events to oneself without reason	"My parents are in a bad mood because they have an idiot for a son."
10.	Focusing on a single, irrelevant, negative aspect of a situation, while ignoring the more relevant and important aspects of the situation	"It doesn't matter that I got a raise and promotion. I have to go to work an hour earlier."

Big Picture Review

Identify the goal of each of the main types of psychotherapies.

Approach	Goal
Psychoanalytic	1.
Humanistic	2.
Behavioral/Learning	3.
Cognitive	4.

Solutions

Each solution below is followed by its textbook page reference number and its corresponding chapter learning objective (LO) number. Items with a Big Picture LO help you to build a Big Picture of psychology across the chapters you have studied.

Fill-in Review of the Chapter

1. Therapy [p. 665; LO 1]
2. eclectic [p. 690; LO 7]
3. master's [p. 668; LO 1]
4. informed consent [p. 669; LO 1]
5. inability to function [p. 667; LO-Big Picture]
6. free association [p. 671; LO 2]
7. psychodynamic therapy [p. 672; LO 2]
8. empathy [p. 674; LO 3]
9. genuineness [p. 675; LO 3]
10. unconditional positive regard [p. 675; LO 3]
11. classical conditioning [p. 676; LO-Big Picture]
12. covert sensitization [p. 679; LO 4]
13. positive reinforcement [p. 680; LO 4]
14. token economy [p. 680; LO 4]
15. depression [p. 681; LO-Big Picture]
16. anxiety [p. 681; LO-Big Picture]
17. irrational beliefs [p. 682; LO 5]
18. cognitive distortions [p. 682; LO 5]
19. restore family harmony and improve family functioning [p. 686; LO 6]
20. Self-help groups [p. 687; LO 6]
21. therapeutic alliance [p. 690; LO 7]
22. sampling [p. 689; LO-Big Picture]
23. antidepressant [p. 697; LO 8]
24. manic [p. 698; LO 8]
25. bipolar disorder [p. 698; LO 8]

Use It or Lose It!

1. Client-centered therapy [p. 674; LO 3]
2. Behavior therapy [p. 677; LO 4]
3. Psychoanalysis [p. 671; LO 2]
4. Drug therapy [p. 693; LO 8]
5. Rational-emotive therapy [p. 682; LO 5]
6. Behavior therapy [p. 680; LO 4]
7. Client-centered therapy [p. 675; LO 3]
8. Psychoanalysis [p. 672; LO 2]
9. Group therapy [p. 687; LO 6]
10. Cognitive therapy [p. 682; LO 5]

Self-Check: Are You Getting the Big Picture?

True or False Questions

1. F [p. 669; LO 1]	6. T [p. 677; LO 4]
2. F [p. 672; LO 2 & 4]	7. F [p. 686; LO 5 & 6]
3. T [p. 675; LO 3]	8. T [p. 688; LO 7]
4. T [p. 672; LO 2]	9. F [p. 685; LO 6]
5. F [p. 699; LO 8]	10. T [p. 690-691; LO 7]

Multiple Choice Questions

1. C [p. 671-672; LO 2]	10. B [p. 677; LO 4]	19. D [p. 690; LO 7]
2. D [p. 669; LO 1]	11. D [p. 679; LO 4]	20. D [p. 690-691; LO 7]
3. A [p. 693; LO 1]	12. B [p. 679; LO 4]	21. D [p. 692; LO 7]
4. D [p. 672; LO 2]	13. B [p. 681; LO 5]	22. A [p. 693; LO 8]
5. C [p. 673; LO 4]	14. A [p. 680; LO 4]	23. D [p. 697; LO 8]
6. C [p. 672; LO 2]	15. C [p. 682; LO 5]	24. C [p. 694; LO 8]
7. D [p. 673; LO 3]	16. B [p. 687; LO 6]	25. C [p. 695; LO 8]
8. A [p. 674; LO 3]	17. A [p. 685; LO 6]	
9. B [p. 675; LO 3]	18. B [p. 691; LO 7]	

Short-Answer Questions

Can you write a brief answer to these questions?

1. In what type of situation would electroconvulsive therapy be warranted? [p. 699; LO 8]

   ECT is used to treat cases of severe depression that have not responded to other drug therapies or psychotherapies. Often the patients are suicidal or psychotic. ECT is administered in conjunction with anesthesia and muscle relaxants to reduce the possibility of injuries to the patient.

2. What are the different types of antidepressants and how do they change brain chemistry? [p. 696-697; LO 8]

   MAO inhibitors block the breakdown of monoamine neurotransmitters in the brain. SSRIs selectively block the reuptake of serotonin in the brain. And, tricyclic antidepressants affect the action of norepinephrine and serotonin in the brain.

3. Cognitive therapy appears to be particularly effective in treating which types of disorders? [p. 684; LO 5]

Cognitive therapies, like rational-emotive therapy or Beck's cognitive therapy, have been shown to treat anxiety disorders, depression, eating disorders, and substance abuse disorders very effectively, especially when they are combined with the behavioral therapies.

4. Assume that you are working in a mental hospital where you are in charge of 25 patients who have been diagnosed with schizophrenia. Design a behavioral therapy to help ensure that these patients engage in the basic life skills, such as getting up in the morning, making their beds, participating in group therapy, and refraining from self-injurious behaviors each day. [p. 680; LO 4]

There are several possible answers to this question, but a logical approach would be to design a token economy in which the clients would receive tokens or points for engaging in adaptive behaviors and lose points for engaging in maladaptive behaviors. At the end of each week, the clients would be permitted to cash in their tokens for primary reinforcers (e.g., food, cigarettes, coffee, etc) or other hospital privileges such as using the phone or watching a movie.

5. Write an example dialogue between a therapist and client to illustrate the psychoanalytic concept of resistance. [p. 672; LO 2]

There are many possibilities here, but the dialogue should include an example of a client failing to engage in a behavior that is related to his or her unconscious conflicts. For example:

Therapist: You were about to tell me about the dream you had last night about your mother.

Male Client: Oh, it's not important. Did you have a good weekend?

Therapist: I did. What about the dream? Where did it take place?

Male Client: You know, I can't remember. Do you think it will rain today?

In this dialogue, the client keeps shifting the conversation away from the topic of his mother. To a psychoanalyst, this resistance to talking about his mother may indicate that he harbors some form of unconscious conflict that involves her.

Developing a Bigger Picture: Making Connections Across Chapters

1. Using your knowledge of experimental design from Chapter 1, design an experiment to test whether or not rational-emotive therapy is as effective as Prozac in treating depression. [p. 32-34; LO-Big Picture]

There are several ways to do this. Here is one example:

Obtain a sample of 100 people seeking therapy for depression at an outpatient facility and obtain informed consent from them. Using a standardized pers~ questionnaire for depression, measure the depression level of all of th~ participants. Next, randomly assign half of the participants to a condit they are prescribed a standard dosage of Prozac. Assign the other half of the participants to a condition where they receive rational-emotive therapy once a week from a skilled cognitive therapist. After eight weeks, reevaluate the participants and assess their level of depression using the same personality questionnaire used at the outset of the study. Compare the groups to see if either group has experienced more improvement in its depression scores.

2. Using what you learned about operant conditioning in Chapter 5, what considerations would you have to take into account when designing a system of positive reinforcement to help a client get over her shyness? [p. 220; LO-Big Picture]

You would have to think about the following things before proceeding:

What reinforcer will you use with the client? Will it be a primary or secondary reinforcer?

Is the reinforcer really reinforcing for your client?

What schedule of reinforcement will you use with the client (i.e., continuous, FR, FI, VR, or VI)?

How will you avoid extinction of your client's new, socially out-going behaviors after therapy ends?

What specific behaviors will you reward in your client (e.g., going to social functions)?

3. Given what you learned about the brain in Chapter 2, why would ECT typically be administered to the right hemisphere of the brain and not the left? [p. 73; LO-Big Picture]

For most people the left hemisphere of the brain controls language functions and the movement of the dominant (right) side of the body. By inducing an ECT seizure in the right hemisphere, disruptions to these processes are minimized.

Label the Diagram [p. 683; LO 5]

COGNITIVE ERROR
1. All-or-nothing thinking
2. Arbitrary inference
3. Disqualifying the positive
4. Emotional reasoning
5. Labeling
6. Magnification &
7. Minimization
8. Overgeneralization
9. Personalization
10. Selective abstraction

Big Picture Review [p. 684]

1. Insights and resolution regarding unconscious conflicts [LO 2]
2. Acceptance of genuine self and personal growth [LO 3]
3. Eliminate maladaptive behaviors and acquire adaptive behaviors [LO 4]
4. Reduce negative thinking and irrational beliefs, and develop more realistic thinking [LO 5]